D0758412

LITTLE GIRL BLUE

Chris Tassin
2009

LITTLE GIRL BLUE

The Life of
KAREN CARPENTER

RANDY L. SCHMIDT

Foreword by Dionne Warwick

An A Cappella Book

Library of Congress Cataloging-in-Publication Data

Schmidt, Randy (Randy L.)

　　Little girl blue : the life of Karen Carpenter / Randy L. Schmidt ; foreword by Dionne Warwick. — 1st ed.

　　　　p. cm.

　　Includes bibliographical references and index.

　　ISBN 978-1-55652-976-4 (hardcover)

　　1. Carpenter, Karen, 1950-1983.　2. Singers—United States—Biography. I. Title.

ML420.C2564S36 2010

782.42164092—dc22

[B]

2009049044

INTERIOR DESIGN: Monica Baziuk

INTERIOR ILLUSTRATION: © 2010 by Chris Tassin

First edition

Published by Chicago Review Press, Incorporated

814 North Franklin Street

Chicago, Illinois 60610

ISBN 978-1-55652-976-4

Printed in the United States of America

5　4　3　2　1

For Camryn and Kaylee

In loving memory
Lindeigh Scotte (1956–2001)
&
Cynthia G. Ward (1975–2005)

Never lose an opportunity of seeing anything that is beautiful;

for beauty is God's handwriting—a wayside sacrament.

Welcome it in every fair face, in every fair sky, in every fair flower

and thank God for it as a cup of blessing.

—RALPH WALDO EMERSON

CONTENTS

FOREWORD

K AREN CARPENTER was and still is the voice that I listen to with a smile on my face. Her clarity, her approach to the lyric being sung, and the smile I could hear in her voice just fascinated me.

We all are familiar with the hits and the performances, but I was privy to the person. She was a sweet, innocent young lady who had a so much to give—and she wanted to give. She and her brother gave us *music*—music that reached the innermost parts of our being; and that music is truly missed.

When I first heard her sing a song that I had recorded some years ago ("Knowing When to Leave" from the Broadway show *Promises, Promises*), I felt quite surprised that anyone would attempt this song, simply because of the complex time signature and range required to sing it. She seemed to have no trouble riding the notes as they were supposed to be ridden, and I was impressed!

I felt a need to get to know this young lady, and fortunately it appeared she desired to meet me. I first met her at A&M just after their recording of "Close to You." Years later I happened to be staying in the same hotel as Karen in New York when I ran into her; she was there going through therapy for anorexia nervosa. Since I had not seen her in quite a while, I must say it was shocking to see how very thin she was.

I invited her to my suite the following day for lunch, not knowing that eating was the last thing on her mind, but she graciously accepted the invitation and showed up not really ready to eat but to talk. Little did I know that I succeeded in doing something no one else had been able to do. I was able to get her to eat a cup of soup with a few saltine crackers. We spent the afternoon talking about many things, and she finally told me why she was in New York. It was apparent that anorexia was something she was at odds with and trying to combat, and I felt compelled to let her know I was in her corner and gave her as much encouragement as I could for her to continue her fight. We exchanged phone numbers and promised to keep in touch.

The last time I saw her was at a Grammy photo shoot in January 1983. It was a joyous reunion, and the first thing out of her mouth when she saw me was, "Look at me, I've got an ass!" We laughed so hard and loud that the rest of the group took great notice, to say the least. We both agreed that she had a lot of living to do.

To hear of her untimely transition hurt me as if I had lost a family member. She had so much to live for. Being at her funeral was as difficult for me as it was for her immediate family and host of friends. Yes, I will always remember the day we met and that day in New York, and I cherish the continuing friendship I have with her brother, Richard.

—Dionne Warwick

AUTHOR'S NOTE

"**W**E START out with the answers, and we end up with the questions." Karen Carpenter treasured this quotation, which fellow singer Petula Clark first shared with her, and recited it to close friends in difficult times. Indeed, no matter how many ways Karen's story has been told, the "answers" always seem to prompt more questions.

On New Year's Day 1989, I sat spellbound as *The Karen Carpenter Story* unfolded. The CBS biopic, which opened with the disturbing reenactment of the events of February 4, 1983, the day of Karen's death, made an immediate and enduring impression on this teenage viewer. In the weeks following the airing, Karen Carpenter haunted me. There was something about the way that film presented the pathos of her story atop the soundtrack of her sometimes optimistic but often mournful voice that drew me in. Perhaps it had to do with the movie's slightly sensationalistic nature. More likely it was the depth and density of Karen's voice. Whatever the reason, I could not get her out of my mind. The filmmakers had provided many answers, but I still had questions—about Karen's life, about her death, and certainly about her music. I wanted to know more. And I have spent many years searching for those answers.

I look upon *Little Girl Blue* as a continuation of similar efforts. Barry Morrow's struggles to write a screenplay for *The Karen Carpenter Story* that would offend no one are detailed in this book's prologue. The baton was then passed to Ray Coleman, who had the arduous task of writing the family's authorized biography. It is my understanding that both men became frustrated (and even furious at times) with the unavoidable confines of their respective assignments. Both were strongly cautioned by several inside the Carpenters camp against taking on the assignments in the first place. According to Karen "Itchie" Ramone, wife of legendary record producer Phil Ramone, "Ray Coleman *really* had a rough time in terms of editing. And Barry Morrow, *forget it!* I felt so bad for him. After a while, Ray threw his arms up. As for Barry, he just had his arms tied."

In the face of these admonitions I approached Richard Carpenter with some trepidation. I first met Richard and his wife, Mary, at their Downey home in August 1996 and since that time have been fortunate to visit with him on a number of occasions. Although he has always been genial and accommodating, Richard has rarely lent support to outside ventures without insisting upon editorial control. As expected, he declined to be interviewed for this project. David Alley (his manager at the time) explained that Richard has "said all he wishes to say" in regard to Karen's personal life. But Alley wished me the best with the project and even declared that he and Richard would not discourage others from contributing, which is as close to an endorsement as anyone could hope for.

I believe the lack of collaboration with the Carpenter family, however, has proved to open rather than close important avenues of information. In conducting interviews for this book, it became obvious to me that many details of Karen's life story had never been allowed to see the light of day. In fact, a number of those I interviewed expressed their frustration with the heavy-handed editing that has kept her story concealed this long. I have made every effort to keep this book, unlike the previous, authorized accounts, free of an agenda and the Carpenter family's editorial control. This lack of censorship has permitted me to dig deeper, explore the story beneath the surface, and give people outside the family who were close to Karen ample opportunity to express themselves.

Terry Ellis, Karen's boyfriend and the cofounder of Chrysalis Records, had previously spoken only with biographer Ray Coleman, refusing all other requests to talk about his relationship with Karen. "I could never see the point in helping somebody do a book or a film or a TV show about Karen," Ellis told me. "I always say to myself, 'It's not going to do *her* any good.' That's all I care about. Her." He agreed to speak with me but questioned me at length prior to our interview: "What story do you think you're going to tell?" he asked. How would I address the relationship between her and Richard? How did I plan to deal with her illness? Or her relationship with her mother? It was only after I answered these questions—with honesty and sincerity—that we were able to proceed.

Further important aspects of Karen's life—the ones that traditional means of research could never divulge—were revealed to me during an afternoon I spent in the Beverly Hills home of Frenda Franklin, Karen's longtime best friend and closest confidant. "I want you to know and understand the many layers of Karen," Franklin told me. "She was such an *unusual* human being. . . . You were better for having known her. I don't know one person who knew her who doesn't feel that way. . . . She changed your life."

Franklin, more than anyone, was vocal about wanting someone to finally do justice to her best friend's life story, and as our interview drew to a close, she gave me a quick hug and kiss, patted me on the back, and whispered, "Do good for Karen." Needless to say, this was a very special commandment coming from someone who knew Karen so intimately and loved her so deeply. I hope that I have succeeded.

LITTLE GIRL BLUE

RAINY DAYS AND *RAIN MAN*

"**I WANT YOU** to know I did not kill my daughter."

Agnes Carpenter's first words to Barry Morrow were piercing. Set to interview the Carpenter family matriarch, he was thunderstruck as the woman suddenly jumped in front of the family's housekeeper, who had answered his knock at the door. This startling and awkward occurrence interrupted Morrow's introduction. "Yes, ma'am," he replied with caution. "May I come in?"

THE YEAR was 1984. Hollywood producer Jerry Weintraub had called a meeting with Barry Morrow, a screenwriter whose resume included two recent popular television movies starring Mickey Rooney and Dennis Quaid: the Emmy award winner *Bill* (1981) and *Bill: On His Own* (1983). Both were based on the writer's real-life friendship with Bill Sackter, a mentally challenged man he befriended and saved from the institution where Sackter spent forty-four years of his life.

On Thursday, October 18, Weintraub asked Morrow to write the screenplay for an upcoming television movie with the working title *A Song for You: The Karen Carpenter Story*. "You know, I am just not a fan of the Carpenters," Morrow told Weintraub, who had managed the duo's career since 1976.

Morrow knew of the Carpenters' music and recalled news reports of Karen's untimely death the previous year, but he didn't particularly like their music. "It was considered elevator music," he recalls. "I was listening to acid rock, Dylan, and Crosby, Stills and Nash."

Determined, Weintraub began to cajole Morrow. "All right, listen," he said. "Here's what you have to do. I am going to give you three or four albums and a great bottle of wine. I want you to go to a room, turn off the lights, drink this wine and listen to these albums."

Morrow, who admits he had never enjoyed a good bottle of wine at that point in his life, much less a great one, followed Weintraub's orders. "I had never heard her before; I had never stopped to listen," he says. "I had never heard the sadness and the sorrow and the pain in her voice. I thought when she sang 'I'm on the top of the world' she was serious. I never heard the undertones to it, the layers. When I heard the guitar solo in the middle of 'Goodbye to Love,' I thought, wait a second, I never even knew the Carpenters!"

Finishing the bottle of wine, Morrow phoned Weintraub. "I'm in," he said, "if you still want me."

BARRY MORROW knew very little of the story he was hired to write. Naturally, one of his first interviews was with Karen's brother, Richard Carpenter, who was ambivalent about lending his name to a film about his sister. He saw the potential for pain in such a production, not only for himself but for his elderly, still-grieving parents, devastated by the loss of their daughter. Morrow found Richard to be extremely guarded during their first meetings. More than anything, he saw the surviving Carpenter as highly protective, not only of his sister's but also his own image and, even more so, that of his family. The interviews were frustrating and at times proved futile. This confused Morrow because he knew the Carpenter circle had initiated and endorsed the project. Even so, he was determined to ask tough and direct questions like "Why did Karen die?"

With little to go on, Morrow relied on hopes that others would offer more information. He prepared to interview Karen's parents, who still lived in the house where their daughter collapsed. Immediately sensing the dynamics of the Carpenter family, Morrow knew he would have to take things slowly and cautiously. "I want you to know I did not kill my daughter" was the last thing he expected to hear from Agnes Carpenter. "I felt sorry for her that she would have to say something so shockingly direct and have it be the first thing out of her mouth. I realized this' woman was very defensive and may have good reason to be. Agnes was still in denial. These were very commonplace stages that families go through or hide from. They didn't invent that level of dysfunction, but it was certainly there." After an hour spent interviewing Agnes in the living room that day, they were joined by Harold Carpenter, Karen's father, who had little to add.

Morrow began to realize he might never get the story of Karen Carpenter from the Carpenter family themselves. Maybe there was something to what longtime friend and business associate of the Carpenters Ed Leffler had said when he warned him against writing the screenplay for this highly anticipated TV movie of the week. "You have no idea what you're getting into," Leffler said. "*Good luck!*"

It was Leffler's ex-wife, Frenda Franklin, who became Morrow's primary source for reconstructing the events of Karen's life for the screenplay. After their initial meetings, the two spoke often by phone, sometimes for hours at a time. Richard was not pleased to learn this. For years Frenda had been viewed as a threat to Karen's reliance on her family. "Richard started having really strong feelings about what he knew I was going to write," Morrow says.

Morrow submitted the initial draft of the screenplay for review in the spring of 1986. "The first draft just hung this on my mother," Richard said in 1988. "I said, 'I will not have this. I won't, because it's not true.' My mom, she is possessive. A lot of moms are, but she was never what this first draft implied. Forget it."

Carpenter and Morrow met again to look over the second draft. In exchange for modifications to the script, which included the omission of some scenes in their entirety, Richard negotiated with Morrow. He offered to tell more of his personal story, including an addiction to quaaludes and a brief stay in Topeka's Menninger Clinic in 1979. In return, Morrow was to soften some of Agnes's "sharp edges."

By July 1987, CBS gave the green light to Morrow's third draft of the screenplay, which meant a picture commitment was in order. *A Song for You: The Karen Carpenter Story* entered the pre-production stage, and Weintraub hired Emmy winner Joseph Sargent as director. Richard Carpenter, by then named the film's executive producer, was still unhappy with the script. "It put his family under a microscope," Barry Morrow believes. "But that was inevitable." Yet another revision, dated September 30, 1987, did little to soothe Richard's concerns. Harsh and hurtful words from Agnes were still present. "You don't know the first thing about drums," the character tells her daughter. "Karen, sweetheart, Richard is a musician . . . a serious musician. Don't you see the difference?"

Morrow was adamant that the screenplay's scenes were built on solid facts revealed during the interviews he had conducted, all of which the Weintraub Entertainment Group approved and coordinated. "People in the touring group called Agnes the 'dragon lady,'" he says, so he was disinclined to further water down her character.

By December 1988, four drafts of the screenplay existed. When a fifth was requested, Morrow refused, and within a matter of days network executives informed him that writer Cynthia Cherbak had been hired to overhaul his script. Morrow was indifferent. "I was busy and happy to do other things," he says. "Those were heady times for me!" (The screenwriter had also penned *Rain Man*, starring Tom Cruise and Dustin Hoffman, for which he won the Oscar for Best Original Screenplay at the Sixty-first Academy Awards in 1989.)

Even Cherbak's changes could do little to alter Agnes Carpenter's hard-edged character once the director cast Academy Award winner Louise Fletcher in the role. Known for her 1975 role in *One Flew Over the Cuckoo's Nest*, Fletcher brought a passive-aggressive slant to every line of dialogue. "I had nothing to do with the casting," Morrow explains. "Sargent comes in and casts 'Nurse Ratched!' Louise Fletcher could say a nursery rhyme and give you the creeps."

Additionally Joseph Sargent fought to convince the network that a virtual unknown, twenty-seven-year-old Mitchell Anderson, was their "Richard." The choice for "Karen" was twenty-four-year-old Cynthia

Gibb, an attractive character actress who had appeared for three seasons in the original *Fame* TV series. The actress came into the project knowing very little about the story, aside from general facts. "I knew she and her brother were a music team, that they were enormously successful around the world, and I knew their hit singles," she says. "I also knew she had an eating disorder and that she died of it. Beyond that I knew nothing."

When filming began in February 1988, Gibb was dismayed by the number of script revisions occurring on the set each day. "On a daily basis we would go to work prepared to do certain scenes," she says. "We would always have cuts or rewrites. Anything that was controversial at all was either diluted or removed. Because the family was so attached to the project, there was some whitewashing that went on in the telling of the story."

Working so closely with Richard, filming in the parents' home, wearing the Carpenters' clothing, and driving their cars, the cast and crew quickly came to their own conclusions about Karen's story. "If you looked from the outside in, you saw exactly what happened to that family," Mitchell Anderson says. "But from Richard's perspective and his mother's perspective, it was completely different."

Gibb agrees the family's intricate involvement made it even more difficult to portray the complex characters they were attempting to channel. "There were some aspects of Karen's upbringing that I felt had contributed to her illness," she says, "however, the family never felt that she had an emotional disorder. The family did not believe that anorexia was an emotional disorder that becomes a physiological disorder. Therefore, they didn't believe that Karen had anything other than a weight problem. It was difficult to portray certain emotional challenges that Karen had, because the family did not agree that they existed."

Richard has always held firm in his belief that the stress of showbiz and an overprotective family had nothing to do with Karen's anorexia. "What would possess a woman like her to starve herself?" he asked in his 1988 essay for *TV Guide*. "Some people blame it on career pressures or a need to take more control over her life. I don't think so. I think she would have suffered from the same problem even if she had been a homemaker." Richard felt anorexia nervosa was something "genetic, the same way talent is," as he explained to Susan Littwin in a piece for the same publication. "I have no answers. People have been trying to get that out of me. If I had it, I'd give it."

The filming of a watered-down version of one of Barry Morrow's original scenes, set in 1982 in the New York office of Karen Carpenter's therapist Steven Levenkron, remains vivid in the minds of the cast and crew, even today. "Have you told her that you love her?" the therapist asks the family.

The father starts to respond, but his nervous voice is overpowered by the mother's. "We don't do things that way. You show a person, you don't tell them all the time. . . . I don't think you understand our family."

This pivotal scene, Gibb feels, sheds light on the family's level of denial and unwillingness to fully support Karen's mission to get well. "She was making progress, and her family came to see her," she observes. "There was no support for the work that she was doing what-soever. The family was more old-fashioned in their beliefs that 'normal' families don't need therapy, only 'crazy' people do."

"Mrs. Carpenter, go ahead," the therapist says, prompting Agnes to voice her love for her daughter.

"For heaven's sake," she exclaims. "This is ridiculous! We came three thousand miles for this nonsense?" Gibb's head drops slowly to the side, her character seemingly ashamed, having burdened the parents with her personal problems. Missing the point, the mother retorts, "We don't need to prove anything to Karen. She knows we love her."

Heartbroken and horrified by the scene's content, the cast was forced to remain neutral, not voicing their opinions or reacting to their emotions. So many revisions had taken place prior to shooting that Richard was unaware of the reactions on the set and seemed pleased with the outcome. "The response from the family and from Richard himself was as if he were in the *Twilight Zone*," recalls Mitchell Anderson. "When we were doing that scene we were like, 'Oh my god, Agnes was such an asshole!' But after we finished shooting, Richard was so proud of it because he thought the doctor looked like an asshole."

No matter the amount of dilution, Morrow's screenplay spoke between the lines and was ultimately as close to the actual series of events in Karen Carpenter's life as anyone could ask of a biopic. "If there's an arch-villain of the story, it's probably Agnes Carpenter," wrote Ron Miller in a review for the *San Jose Mercury News*. He illustrated her character as "an imposing woman who found it almost impossible to show her love to her troubled daughter, even after her illness had been diagnosed and the threat to her life was clear."

In the final scene of *The Karen Carpenter Story*, however, Agnes Carpenter's character does soften. She almost repents. For a moment the viewer might forgive and forget her sins of the previous ninety minutes. Louise Fletcher's "Agnes" gazes affectionately up the staircase at her grown-up little girl for the last time.

"And Karen," she says with a tender hesitation, "I love you."

"I love you, too, Mom," Karen replies. "Goodnight."

Sadly, the mother's "I love you" on the eve of her daughter's untimely death was a fabrication—creative license justified by CBS Standards and Practices for the purpose of dramatic effect.

1

CALIFORNIA DREAMIN´

<hr />

HAROLD BERTRAM Carpenter had a rather peripatetic childhood and even more itinerant adolescence. The eldest son of missionaries George and Nellie Carpenter, he was born November 8, 1908, in Wuzhou, a city in southern China where the Gui and Xi rivers meet. Siblings Esther and Richard were born several years later. The Carpenter parents were both fine pianists and often played and sang for guests at their frequent formal dinner parties. Although he greatly enjoyed their performances, Harold was not as interested in making music. Against his will he took piano lessons for a while but loathed practicing. More an appreciator of good music than a musician himself, Harold began listening to records on the family's beautiful Victrola. He especially loved the classics.

Harold's mother was greatly concerned about the limited education her children received in China, where they had no formal education, only tutors. In 1917 Nellie took the children and headed for England where the children were enrolled in boarding schools. Their father joined them four years later when granted a leave of absence. Harold's younger sisters Geraldine and Guinevere were born shortly before their mother moved with the children to the United States. There they stayed on Ellis Island for several months before settling with relatives in Wellsville, New York.

Waking each morning at 5:00 A.M., Harold delivered newspapers before going to Wellsville High School. After two years he was forced to drop out and go to work when his mother became ill with a lung ailment. His uncle Frank Stoddard, a night superintendent at a paper box company in Middletown, Ohio, offered him a job, and he moved in with his uncle and aunt Gertrude. Harold moved several times with the Stoddards, finally settling in Catonsville, Maryland, a small community just west of Baltimore, where the men found work in a printing firm. Harold's mother and father separated shortly before Nellie succumbed to pleurisy in 1927 at the age of forty-four.

AGNES REUWER Tatum's childhood was somewhat less eventful than that of Harold Carpenter, or perhaps only less documented. She was born on March 5, 1915, in Baltimore, where she spent her youth. Her father, George Arthur Tatum, was part owner in Tatum, Fritz, and Goldsmith, a wholesale undergarment business. He and his wife, Annie May, were the parents of four girls: Jenny, Agnes, Audrey, and Bernice.

Agnes was athletic and played several sports, notably basketball, during her years at Baltimore's Western High School, the nation's oldest public all-girls school. She enjoyed sewing and became a fine seamstress. She made many of the Tatum girls' dresses and coats, in addition to the heavy, pleated, velour drapes that hung in the windows of the family home at 1317 Mulberry Street in Baltimore.

In 1932 George and Annie moved to nearby Catonsville, seeking a quieter existence for their daughters. Agnes's older sister Jenny was no longer living at home, but the other three girls were present when a neighbor introduced them to twenty-three-year-old Harold Carpenter. Agnes was smitten upon meeting the handsome young man and was surprised to see him again just a few days later driving up the street in his shiny Chevrolet. Noticing Agnes and Audrey waiting for a bus, Harold stopped to say hello and offered them a ride.

Agnes and Harold soon began dating, and a four-year courtship ensued. The two were married at Catonsville Methodist Church on

April 9, 1935. Times were tough, and there was little pomp and circumstance. There was no wedding cake, and Agnes sewed her own wedding gown. The only gift was a General Electric iron from the bride's aunt Myrtle and uncle Arthur, who happened to work for GE. Instead of a honeymoon, the newlyweds went for a night out at the movies.

For the next three weeks the couple lived with Agnes's parents in the Tatum home. Following Harold's uncle Frank to yet another box printing company, the couple relocated to Richmond, Virginia, where their first home together was a five-dollar-a-week furnished efficiency apartment. After a year they moved into a larger furnished apartment on Fendall Avenue in Richmond's Highland Park area.

When Agnes's older sister Jenny separated from husband George Tyrell, she felt her sister and brother-in-law would offer a more stable future for the Tyrells' eighteen-month-old baby girl, Joanie. Agnes and Harold became surrogate parents and soon moved to Mechanicsville on the northeast side of Richmond, securing a larger home for the growing family. The Carpenters were Richmond residents for five years before returning to Baltimore for a few months and in 1940 finally settling in an apartment on Sidney Street in New Haven, Connecticut. Jenny reunited with her daughter and moved in with Agnes and Harold, where she remained until 1943.

Working for the New Haven Pulp and Board Company, Harold became skilled at running the company's color printing equipment. Agnes began working, too. She worked eight-hour shifts either six or seven days a week, operating a thread mill machine for Mettler Brothers, a subcontractor of Pratt-Whitney Motor Mounts. Agnes stayed with Mettler's until World War II came to an end in 1945.

AFTER MORE than ten years of marriage, Agnes Carpenter became pregnant. With their first child on the way, she and Harold began house hunting and settled on a new construction going up on Hall Street in New Haven's conservative, suburban East Shore Annex neighborhood. Hall Street was cozy and inviting, an almost fairy-tale lane for young families looking to build homes after World War II. Its string of modest, colonial-style homes was just a few miles from Lighthouse Point, a popular beach and amusement park across New Haven Harbor.

The Carpenters and their live-in niece, by then ten years old, moved into the new $8,900 home at 55 Hall Street on August 27, 1946. In less than two months they welcomed a son, born October 15 at Grace-New Haven Hospital. He was named Richard Lynn for Harold's only brother.

As he grew, Richard became interested in his father's extensive record collection. The selections were varied and eclectic to say the least, encompassing everything from Rachmaninoff, Tchaikovsky, and Bourdin to Lannie McEntire, Red Nichols, and Spike Jones and his City Slickers. Even before he could read, young Richard would go through the records and listen for hours. He was able to distinguish the records by feeling the edges and grooves of each 78. At the age of three Richard asked for his own record of "Mule Train," a popular novelty cowboy song. His first 45 was Theresa Brewer's Dixieland-tinged "Music, Music, Music," and shortly after that he asked for "How Much Is That Doggy in the Window?" by Patti Page.

At 11:45 A.M. on Thursday, March 2, 1950, just three days shy of her thirty-fifth birthday, Agnes gave birth to a little girl, Karen Anne. Her first words were "bye-bye" and "stop it," the latter a natural response to the antics of an older brother.

Numbering five, the family shared the tidy little 1,500-square-foot, two-story home and its three bedrooms and two bathrooms. "They had nice furniture, everything was neat, everything matched, and everything was clean and shiny," recalls neighbor Debbie Cuticello, daughter of Carl and Teresa Vaiuso. "It had a finished basement, a garage, a beautiful front yard and backyard we all played in. They had a screen porch in the back and neatly manicured lawns and landscaping. Everybody took pride in their neighborhood. There were always shiny cars in the front yards."

In a tradition that continues to the present day, the houses on Hall Street came to be identified by the names of the families that lived there in the 1950s and 1960s. Number 55 is the Carpenter house, across the street is the Catalde house, and so on. "The LeVasseurs were on one side, and they're still there," Cuticello explains. "The Catanias were across the street, and they're still there. The Jones family was next door. The Shanahans were a couple of doors down. It was just a wonderful 1950s neighborhood."

According to Frank Bonito, whose parents bought 83 Hall Street in 1960, "It was a middle-class neighborhood with a lot of working folks. My father was a butcher and owned a grocery store. The Vaiusos, Debbie's parents, owned a farm. He was a wholesale farmer in Branford, which is one town over. I was at 83. Debbie lived at 77. On the other side were the DeMayos. Mr. DeMayo had worked in the post office. Across the street was a family whose father was a professor at Yale. Millstone was their name. Next to them were the DeVitas. They were an older couple with no children, and the husband was a dentist."

The New Haven area was settled by a number of Italian immigrants, providing residents with some remarkable pizza parlors in the area. Nearby Fort Nathan Hale Park was the site of many family picnics and play dates. There the children could swim, fish, and fly kites. In winter the fun turned to sledding and snowballing.

The Bonito, Vaiuso, and Carpenter children spent a great deal of time in one another's homes. Debbie and her brother thought of Agnes and Harold more as aunt and uncle figures, an extended family of sorts. "My brother Joey played with Rich, and I played with Karen," she says. "Our parents shared the same values and seemed to enjoy the hardworking American ethics. As children, we watched very little television and were outside as long as we could stay . . . playing basketball, baseball, roller-skating, hula-hooping, and playing in the yards. Everybody got along. . . . We didn't have a lot of money, and they didn't have a lot of money."

For extra income, Agnes and Harold started their own car washing business, and the two took great pride in their work. Their pickup and delivery service became popular among the neighborhood families and proved to be a success for the frugal couple, who wanted to give their children a comfortable existence. It was the perfect job for Agnes. She was known to be so persnickety in regard to keeping a clean house that she was often seen standing in the front windows scrubbing the locks with a toothbrush. "Mom was known for having the cleanest garage in Connecticut," Karen recalled in 1971. "My God, if you mopped, the mop didn't get dirty!"

According to Frank Bonito, Agnes was "compulsively clean, almost to the point of having some kind of psychiatric issues. . . . The woman made sure everything was immaculate. I can remember her going next door one time and cleaning the next-door neighbors' windows on her side of the house because they upset her. She was a very nice woman but very uptight. She seemed to be very stressed all the time."

Harold Carpenter hung swings from the rafters in the basement of the Carpenters' home, a favorite hang-out spot for neighborhood kids when it was too cold to play outside. It was a music haven for Richard, who even designated the area with a sign that read RICHIE'S MUSIC CORNER, his version of the family's favorite local record shop. The children would swing in the basement and listen to the music Richard selected from his library, which was categorized, alphabetized, and documented. "Richard had a beautiful sound system," Bonito recalls. "In those days they were called hi-fi's. He would have music on, and Karen and I would be swinging and doing our homework."

As she would do for much of her life, Karen took on Richard's interests. Music became their shared passion, and the two would swing to the music for hours. "I did everything that Richard did," she said in a 1981 interview. "If he listened to music, I listened to music. It was unconscious, but because I idolized him so much . . . every record that we've ever listened to is embedded in my mind." They enjoyed the sounds of Nat "King" Cole, Guy Mitchell, and Perry Como, and both sat spellbound listening to the overdubbed sounds of Les Paul and Mary Ford, particularly on the duo's masterpiece "How High the Moon." According to Richard, Karen could sing every Les Paul solo. The first record she asked for was "I Need You Now" by Eddie Fisher on RCA-Victor. The two also enjoyed listening to the radio, notably WMGM and Alan Freed's Top 40 show on WINS, "1010 on Your Dial," out of New York.

Karen liked to dance and by the age of four was enrolled in ballet and tap classes. Prior to recitals she could be found singing and dancing on the sidewalk in front of the house in a full costume of sequins, satin, tap shoes, and a huge bonnet. Karen was a short, stocky little girl with her dark blond hair cut in a Dutch-boy style. Debbie Cuticello admits to having looked up to Karen, who was two years her senior: "She was my best buddy. I tried to do everything that she did, basically. She was older than I was, and the two years made a big difference back then. Richard was older. You looked up to him, not necessarily a ringleader but the oldest of the group. He and Karen loved each other. . . . There was sibling rivalry—maybe a little pinching here and there—but it was typical; nothing unusual, nothing different."

While Debbie and Joey Vaiuso attended St. Bernadette School, a Catholic school in the area, Karen was a student at Nathan Hale School, just around the corner from Hall Street on Townsend Avenue. "Karen was a year younger than us," says Frank Bonito. "She was the youngest in the class and one of the best students in the class. We were very close through sixth, seventh, and eighth grades, and we always studied together." Karen and Frank walked to school each morning and returned home at lunchtime. "It was an era when women didn't work outside the house, so we'd come home," Bonito says. "There was no cafeteria or anything, so all the kids just went home for lunch. On the way back I'd stop and pick Karen up, and then we'd walk to school together, picking up other friends as we went along."

Like most little girls who grew up in the 1950s, Karen had the Ideal Toy Company's Betsy Wetsy doll, but she preferred playing with her dog, Snoopy, or her favorite toy machine gun or participating in various sports. A favorite was Wiffleball, a variation on baseball that used a perforated plastic ball invented just thirty miles away by a man in Fairfield, Connecticut. Karen pitched and sometimes played first base. "I was a tremendous baseball fan," she later said. "I memorized all the batting averages long before I knew the first word to a song. The Yankees were my favorites." She also delivered the *New Haven Register* on her paper route each day, sometimes adding weekend routes for extra money.

Teenage Richard was tall, thin, and gangly, somewhat uncoordinated, and not as physically active as Karen. He spent most of his free time indoors with his music. "It was slightly embarrassing," he recalled.

"Karen was a better ballplayer than I was, and when choosing sides for sandlot games, she'd be picked first." The school bullies sometimes teased and picked on him. This left him temperamental, and he could be upset quite easily. Richard's rants were short and usually ended with him storming off and back into the house where he remained the rest of the day. Agnes encouraged him to fight back, but she also relied on Karen to watch over her older brother. "She can take care of herself and Richard," Agnes explained in 1972. "When they were little kids, she always defended him. She'd take on all the roughnecks and make them leave Richard alone."

THE CARPENTERS' dining room was home to the family's piano and therefore one of the highest-traffic areas in the house. The piano was purchased by cousin Joan, by then a teenager, when Richard was eight years old. He grew disinterested after a frustrating year under the direction of the rigid Ms. Florence June, and in a mutual agreement both teacher and parent decided the talent and interest were lacking and the lessons should cease.

Three years later Richard taught himself to play by ear, excelling at flourishes and arpeggios. His parents decided to give it another chance, and he began studying with Henry "Will" Wilczynski, a student from Hartford. This time Richard's interest was sparked and his talent emerged. "During the summer when all the windows were open you would hear Richard play the exercises you have to play," Debbie Cuticello says. "There was always lots of music coming from that house."

Neighbor Bill Catalde saw the Carpenter kids in the same light as any others on Hall Street. "In our world we never thought of them as anything but the wonderful kids that they were. We were just children. With the possible exception of Richard, we never really projected ourselves into the future."

Karen looked up to Richard, his musical talents and intuition, so when he began accordion lessons with Henry Will, she wanted to take lessons as well. Will became a regular around the Carpenter house and soon began courting Joan. Although Karen enjoyed her lessons, she was more interested in exploring her other hobbies, most notably her fascination with drawing. She won a poster contest while attending Nathan Hale and expressed interest in becoming either an artist or perhaps a nurse.

Seeing their son's natural ability and marked progress, Agnes and Harold invested in a new piano, a black Baldwin Acrosonic. By the age of fourteen, Richard was sure his life would be centered on music in some way. His progress reached a point where Henry Will, who by 1959 had received his music degree from the University of Hartford, felt he could no longer challenge the young pianist. He recommended Richard audition at nearby Yale Music School, where he soon began lessons under the direction of professor Seymour Fink.

HAROLD CARPENTER spent years loathing the cold New England winters, which meant shoveling snow and placing chains on car tires before braving the icy roads. He watched the annually televised Tournament of Roses Parade and longed to be in sunny Southern California with its palm trees and mild climate. As early as 1955, he made tentative plans to relocate after a friend of the family who had previously made the move out West himself offered him a job at the Container Corporation of America in California. Instead, the money he saved for the move went to pay for a much-needed mastoid operation.

By 1960 the family's savings allowed Harold, Agnes, and Richard to vacation in Los Angeles, and they used this opportunity to scout out possible sites for relocation. Karen stayed with her aunt Bernice, uncle Paul, and their children to avoid the lengthy car trip. In addition to their quest for a milder climate, the Carpenter parents saw California—and especially Hollywood—as a place where Richard's dreams of becoming a famous pianist would have a better chance of coming true. Anticipating the expense of the pending relocation, Agnes went back to work in 1962. She became one of the top machine operators at Edal Industries, a New Haven rectifier manufacturer.

By early 1963 it was official. Harold sat the family down one evening and announced they would be leaving Hall Street and New Haven altogether. Richard was ecstatic after having visited Southern California with his parents three years earlier, but Karen was not happy. "She didn't want to leave her friends," says Frank Bonito. "She had even received scholarships to go to one of the local private schools." Before leaving New Haven, Karen graduated with the eighth grade class of Nathan Hale School. "Even though it was just a grammar school graduation, they made a big deal about it," Bonito says. "We had a little dance, and Karen and I made dance cards." In a class prophecy for the year 2000, Frank was predicted to be the mayor of a city on the moon and Karen to be his wife. "I guess they were wrong," he says.

In June 1963 the Carpenters filled their car to the brim with only a sampling of their belongings and said good-bye to their cherished friends and neighbors, leaving behind cousin Joan, who married Henry Will that year. "I remember the day that they left in their shiny car," Debbie Cuticello says. "I remember that day because I was very disappointed. It was a sad day for me. I was very upset. I was losing my best friend, and she was going so far away that I couldn't visit. California was way over on the other side of the world from me. I walked over to say good-bye and brought her a dish filled with macaroni."

Bill Catalde was also there to watch the Carpenters drive away that summer morning. "I remember a secret pact between Karen and I that we would someday marry," he says. "I doubt that Karen would have remembered that vow from long ago, but in retrospect we would have probably fared a lot better than what destiny had in store for the two of us."

2

CHOPSTICKS ON BARSTOOLS

U PON MOVING to Downey, California, Harold Carpenter
started his job as a lithograph printer in the nearby city of
Vernon at the Container Corporation of America, where he
worked double shifts to earn extra money for his family. Although
Karen was upset to leave her friends in New Haven, the Carpenters
never regretted their decision to relocate. California was a land of
opportunity in many ways, and just as they had hoped, Richard was
busy within two weeks of their arrival. Downey also allowed the Carpenter family to maintain a quiet, middle class, suburban way of life,
not unlike their New Haven beginnings.

"Head down the Santa Ana Freeway, turn off on San Gabriel, make
a couple of rights, and you're in Downey, a right-wing, unpretentious suburb of the sprawling conurbation that makes up Los Angeles."
According to British journalist Chris Charlesworth, "It's where the
homes are neat and tidy, where the kids graduate from high school, go
to college and [play] football so that bruises will stand them in good
stead later in life. It's where the moms and dads go to each other's
cocktail parties once a week and where they eat TV dinners during the
Million Dollar Movie on Channel 9. It's safe and sound."

Waiting for their New Haven house to sell, the Carpenter family struggled to maintain mortgage payments on the East Coast while
renting an apartment in the West. "They were all just struggling like

the rest of us and trying to get by," says Veta Dixon, who managed the forty-three-unit Shoji complex, located at 12020 Downey Avenue. "The Carpenters were just wonderful, wonderful people. We loved them immediately, and the kids, too. They lived upstairs on the right in #22."

The family soon moved across the breezeway to #23 when a larger apartment vacated. There they lived directly above a police officer for the City of Downey. When the musical vibrations penetrated the floor, he soon complained to the managers about the sounds coming from upstairs. "Do I have to listen to that piano day and night?" he asked.

"Yes," Dixon claims to have replied, "and if you don't like it you can move out! One of these days you'll be paying big money to see them and hear their music."

Driving around Downey one sunny afternoon, Harold pulled the family car into Furman Park on Rives Avenue to ask for directions. A park groundskeeper by the name of Nip noticed the Connecticut plates and asked if they were new to Downey. Agnes began to tell of her prodigy son and how his talents led them to Southern California. Karen and Richard, embarrassed by their mother's boasting, slumped deep into the backseat of the family car. Nip told the Carpenters that Furman Park's gazebo was the site of a weekly talent show held every Sunday afternoon. At first opportunity, Richard entered the talent show performing "Theme of *Exodus*," Ernest Gold's Grammy for Song of the Year in 1961, and a 1923 Zez Confrey piece called "Dizzy Fingers." He also accompanied Karen singing "The End of the World," a hit for Skeeter Davis in the spring of 1963. Singing with a light, pure, head tone, Karen had an airy quality to her voice, much like other girls her age. There were no signs of the rich, smoky alto register to come.

As he left the stage that day, Richard was approached by Vance Hayes, the choir director at Downey Methodist Church. In need of an interim organist, Hayes felt the young pianist would be well qualified based on the performance he had just witnessed. Having little experience on the organ, Richard was hesitant to accept the offer, but Hayes would not take no for an answer. He began the following Saturday playing for two weddings at fifteen dollars each. Playing for the weekly church services, Richard was responsible for preludes, offertories, and postludes. He often improvised, disguising melodies from his favorite Beatles tunes, even up-tempo numbers, like "From Me to You" or "All My Loving." In his words, he would "church them up." Karen was never far from her brother in those days. She would be in the back of the church or singing in the choir and notice melodies from the Beach Boys, the Beatles, and Burt Bacharach.

A reporter with the local *Downey Live Wire* newspaper heard of the new young organist at Downey Methodist and felt the story would make for a pleasant human interest feature. Along with a photographer, the reporter came to the family's apartment and took Richard's picture next to the family's black Baldwin Acrosonic, one of the few large items they had been sure to move across the country that past summer.

In the fall of 1963, thirteen-year-old Karen entered Downey's South Junior High as Richard, just shy of his seventeenth birthday, began his senior year at Downey High School and enrolled in the school band. "What can you play?" asked Bruce Gifford, the band director.

"Piano," Richard replied.

"Baby or grand?"

The two shared a laugh as Gifford explained he had no need for a pianist in his marching band. Richard went home and unpacked a trumpet he had purchased years earlier for four dollars at an auction. He attempted to play the instrument but to no avail. Luckily, the band director did not require an audition after Richard distracted him with a few impressive piano arpeggios. Outside of his teaching career, Gifford also led a nightclub band with his brother Rex. Richard was recruited and became the group's pianist for a short time, playing at dances, clubs, and weddings. He felt the group's sound was reminiscent of Louis Prima with Sam Butera and the Witnesses.

The Carpenter family's New Haven home finally sold in November 1964. Having tolerated cramped apartment living for a little more than a year, the family packed up and moved to a storybook house located at 13024 Fidler Avenue in Downey. To help offset the purchase of the new home and the higher cost of living in Southern California, Agnes Carpenter took a job running several mimeograph machines in the stockroom at North American Rockwell Corporation. The aircraft assembly plant, Downey's number-one employer, was responsible for manufacturing systems designed for the Apollo spacecraft program.

In the living room of their new home on Fidler, Richard finally had space for a larger piano. With money earned teaching piano lessons and playing the organ at church, in addition to the help of his parents, he traded in the spinet for a Baldwin Model L, a six-foot three-inch parlor grand. For a short period of time he studied piano at the University of Southern California.

ENTERING DOWNEY High School in the fall of 1964, Karen was just fourteen years old, an entire year younger than most of her classmates. Although Karen enjoyed playing sports, she did not like to exercise and detested the idea of running around a track every morning. So she paid a visit to band director Bruce Gifford, by then a family friend, who confirmed her participation in marching band would count toward a physical education credit. Karen also succeeded in opting out of geometry class in favor of joining the school choir.

Gifford presented Karen with a glockenspiel and a set of mallets and put her right to work in his marching band, where she marched in the percussion section alongside the drums. Karen quickly found the glockenspiel cumbersome. Additionally, the tone of the instrument began to bother her. She detected that it played a quarter-step sharp in relation to the rest of the band.

Rehearsing with the percussion section, Karen became increasingly intrigued by what classmate Frankie Chavez and the other drummers were doing. As in the Carpenter home, in the Chavez residence music was part of daily life. "He'd been playing the drums since he was three," Karen said, calling him "a Buddy Rich freak. He even ate the same food as Buddy Rich!" But Chavez denies this allegation. "No," he says, "I didn't eat the same foods as Buddy," but he admits that Buddy Rich certainly influenced his playing.

Karen marched with the glockenspiel for about two months, by which time it became evident to her that Chavez was the only drummer in the band who had a real passion for his music. "I used to march down the street playing these stupid bells, watching Frankie play his tail off on the drums," she later said. "It hit me that I could play drums as good as nine-tenths of those boys in the drum line, outside of Frankie."

Meeting with band director Gifford, Karen informed him of her desire to switch instruments. She wanted to join the drum line. "I finally had to talk him into it," she recalled. "At that time, no girl any-where was in the drum line of a marching band in any school." This was met with a tepid response from Gifford, to say the least. "Girls don't play drums," he told her. "That's not really normal."

"All I ever heard was 'girls don't play drums,'" Karen later recalled. "That is such an overused line, but I started anyway. I picked up a pair of sticks, and it was the most natural-feeling thing I've ever done."

Karen saw Gifford's cynicism as a challenge. "Well, let me try," she told Gifford.

Although the director was doubtful, he agreed to let Karen transition to the drums. First he assigned her to play a pair of cymbals, which was not her goal but did bring her closer to Frankie and the other drummers. Chavez was in charge of writing and developing drum cadences for the group, and his goal was to have fun and encourage listeners to move or dance. "They were funky and syncopated and kind of infectious," he says. "We were having such a great time that Karen wanted to play the cadences with the drum line, so she left the cymbals and started playing tenor drum." Never one to settle short of her goal, Karen aspired to play the snare drum during parades and the halftime shows at football games. According to Chavez, "the most interesting parts were assigned to the snare drums, so that's where she ultimately ended up. That was the conduit to playing drums."

Immediately at ease with the snare drum, Karen spent countless hours rehearsing before and after school. At home she assembled the kitchen barstools and even a few pots and pans to simulate a drum kit. Her father's chopsticks served as drumsticks. Karen began playing along to LPs like the Dave Brubeck Quartet's *Time Out* and *Time Further Out*, which were filled with difficult time signatures like 9/8 and 5/4. "They liked to play jazz," Chavez recalls. "Richard was a huge Dave Brubeck fan, and Karen and I both loved Joe Morello. They liked everything from Brubeck to Beatles. I remember being at their house and the Beatles' *Rubber Soul* had just come out. I remember sitting around listening to 'Norwegian Wood,' and we were all saying what a great production the album was and how great the songs were. Karen and Richard were good students of the art form."

Karen also sought the guidance of Frankie, with whom she may have been smitten. "There wasn't a romantic interest on my part," Chavez says, "but I always felt there may have been on hers. I had a girlfriend at the time, so Karen and I just became very good friends." Karen's only steady boyfriend during her high school years was a clarinet player by the name of Jerry Vance. Although the two dated for several years, most recall the relationship to have been nothing serious and more of a "buddy" situation than a romance.

As for Karen and Frankie, they too remained "just good buddies," he says. "She had that little tomboy streak to her and used to talk like a beatnik. I loved that she would talk like a jazz player. What developed was a very good friendship and a mutual interest in drums and music. She'd come over after school and we'd talk drums. She always had a ton of questions about playing so we used to talk about the most effective ways to hold the stick, traditional grip versus matched grip, stick control, playing technique, drum styles. We'd talk about different drummers and listen to jazz records and big bands. Karen took to drumming quickly, and it was very natural to her. She showed great ability, had good timing, and kept getting better and better. She ended up being one of the better snare drum players in the drum line in no time."

Given Karen's track record with musical instruments, her parents were skeptical. They were quite sure it was just another passing fancy. Additionally, Agnes and Harold were already struggling to pay for Richard's new Baldwin. But thanks to his urging, their parents agreed to invest in a basic drum kit for Karen. Karen loved the sound of Ludwigs and wanted them because two of her favorite drummers, Joe Morello and Ringo Starr, played Ludwigs exclusively. Agnes wanted Richard's input, and he felt Ludwig drums would be a good investment since they were known to have a higher resale value than most other lines.

On a Sunday afternoon the family drove to the San Fernando Valley with Frankie Chavez in tow to the home of a music teacher who dealt instruments on the side. They settled on an entry-level set that was dark green with a yellow stripe around the center of each piece. Karen contributed some of her own savings to assist with the three-hundred-dollar purchase. "Ludwig makes a great product," Chavez says. "It was a good move." And with that purchase Frankie became Karen's first drum teacher. Although the rudiments of drumming, time signatures, cadences, and fills came naturally to her, she wanted to know more. "A lot of what she picked up early on was influenced by what she heard on recordings," Chavez explains. "As her interest in certain portions of the art of playing came up, I would try to teach her the concepts and answer her questions."

Karen soon began studying drum technique under the tutelage of Bill Douglass at Drum City on Santa Monica Boulevard in Hollywood. Douglass was a well-known jazzer who played with the likes of Benny Goodman and Art Tatum. "Bill was well respected and a great teacher," says Chavez, who also studied with Douglass for eight years. "We used to play on practice pads reading concert music. Bill had Karen reading very complex material and thought she had become quite a reader." The lessons continued for the next year and a half.

After only two months of playing, Karen was convinced she had outgrown her first drum kit and by Christmas persuaded her parents to trade in the entry-level set toward the purchase of a show set identical to one belonging to Joe Morello—a 1965 Ludwig Super Classic in silver sparkle with double floor toms. She also asked for the all-chrome, top-of-the-line Super Sensitive Snare. At first her parents opted for the more economical Supra-phonic 400 but later gave in and purchased the Super Sensitive Snare, too. Bragging to friends about her son's piano talents, Agnes secured him the job of pianist for a local production of the Frank Loesser musical *Guys and Dolls*. Karen packed up her new set of drums and joined Richard for their first instrumental performance together, an unlikely piano-drum duo accompanying the production.

Karen soon became the drummer for Two Plus Two, an all-girl band comprising Downey High School students including Linda Stewart and Eileen Matthews. "We wanted only girls because an all-girl band in those days was very rare," Stewart explains. She and Matthews carried their guitars and amps to school, where they would catch the bus to the Carpenter home for rehearsal each week. Karen recommended friend

Nancy Roubal join to play bass. "Nancy came on board but did not have a bass guitar," Stewart says. "She did what she could on the bass strings of a six-string guitar. It didn't sound as good as we wanted, but we worked through that. The other problem we had was our amps were so small that Karen had to play softly. We were kind of a surf band, but one of Karen's favorite songs to play was 'Ticket to Ride' by the Beatles. None of us sang at that time, so I never heard Karen sing, but I never heard such a good drummer in my young life at that time." After only a few rehearsals Karen approached Linda and the other girls suggesting that Richard join the group. "I said no," Stewart recalls, "because I wanted an all-girl band. Boys were out." The girls were finally booked to play for a local pool party, but when Eileen's mother refused to let her attend, Linda became discouraged. "I was so upset I just broke up the band."

HAVING GRADUATED from high school in the spring of 1964, Richard enrolled at nearby California State University at Long Beach. In June of the following year he met Wes Jacobs, a tuba major from Palmdale, California, who was also a skillful upright bassist. "We met in theory class," Jacobs recalled in a 2009 interview. "It was obvious to me that he was a genius. Right from day one he could take all the dictation that the teacher could dish out; he would just write it out. . . . He wanted to do something jazzy. . . . We played, and it just clicked right away. Since I had considerable keyboard experience, I could look at his hands and read what he was doing. I could almost play along with him as if I were reading music. We really locked in stylistically. Within a short time, it was apparent that we had to do something musically, but we didn't know what. At one point he said, 'I'll tell my sister to learn how to play drums, and we'll have a trio.' Within three weeks she could play drums better than anybody that I heard at the college."

In actuality Karen had been playing a number of months by the time she teamed with Richard and Wes to form what became the Richard Carpenter Trio, an instrumental jazz group with the classic combo of piano, bass, and drums. Richard did all the arrangements, and by the end of the summer they were rehearsing on a daily basis, sometimes playing well into the night.

Financing a piano and drum kit, in addition to paying for music lessons, Agnes and Harold were barely making ends meet. Now the newly formed trio wanted amplifiers and microphones. Plus Richard felt a new electric piano would make their act more portable. Even so, a tape recorder took precedence, as this would allow the group to make demos. For several months Richard saved to make a down payment on a Sony TC-200 Stereo Tapecorder. The first recordings of the trio were made during the summer of 1965 in the Carpenters' living room at the house on Fidler.

Richard met trumpet major Dan Friberg, a junior college transfer, in choir during the fall of 1965. The two had several other classes together including music history and counterpoint, and Richard began to call upon Friberg when he needed a trumpet player for the trio's weekend gigs. "Karen was the drummer and didn't sing at all yet," Friberg recalls. "She was listening to Louie Bellson and Buddy Rich. Those were some of her idols. I remember going into her room at their house, and she had pictures on the wall of all these great drummers. Her goal was to be as good as they were. She was great then, by all I could tell, but not good enough for her." Friberg became a recurring soloist with the Richard Carpenter Trio. "We had a girl vocalist named Margaret Shanor," he recalls. "With Karen strictly drumming at this point, Margaret fronted the group."

IT WAS not until 1966 that Karen came into her full voice. Although she had always sung in tune, her voice had lacked vibrato and any real depth or presence. It was mostly a light falsetto with a noticeable break between her lower and higher registers. "I can't really remember why I started to sing," Karen said in 1975. "It just kind of happened. But I never really discovered the voice that you know now—the low one—until later, when I was sixteen. I used to sing in this upper voice, and I didn't like it. I was uncomfortable, so I think I would tend to shy away from it because I didn't think I was that good. And I wasn't."

Karen deplored the sound of her tape-recorded voice at first but continued to experiment with her abilities as a singer. "It's kind of corny to listen back," she recalled. "We had an original recording of one of Richard's songs that I'd sung, and the range was too big. I'd be going from the low voice to the high voice, and even though it was all in tune, the top part was feeble and it was different. You wouldn't know it was me. Then suddenly one day out popped this voice, and it was natural."

Richard soon introduced Karen to his college choir director, Frank Pooler, with whom she began taking voice lessons every Saturday morning. This would be the only formal vocal training she would ever receive. "We'd have a half-hour or forty-five-minute voice lesson," Pooler says. "She always had her drums with her in the car. From there Richard would take her over to study with Bill Douglass in Hollywood." The lessons with Pooler focused on both classical voice study and pop music. The first half was devoted to art songs by Beethoven, Schumann, and other composers. During the last half Karen would sing the new songs Richard had written. "Karen was a born pop singer," Pooler says. "She wasn't particularly interested in that other stuff, but she had to do it to get into school."

Unlike Richard, who practiced endlessly, Karen rarely, if ever, rehearsed between her lessons with Pooler. Concerned that their money might be better spent somewhere else, the Carpenter parents met with her teacher to inquire about Karen's progress. "The folks were very supportive of both of them, but they weren't rich. I was getting paid five bucks an hour for those lessons, and they finally came up to see if Karen was getting her money's worth!"

Pooler told Karen her voice was "arty" and "natural" and discouraged the idea of subjecting it to any sort of intense vocal training. "He heard this voice and he wouldn't touch it," Karen said in 1975. "He said I should not train it . . . and the only thing I did work with him on was developing my upper register so I would have a full three-octave range. . . . Something else you don't think about is being able to sing in tune. Thank God I was born with it! It's something I never thought about. When I sing, I don't think about putting a pitch in a certain place, I just sing it."

Becoming more confident in Karen's vocals, Richard began to feature her with their act and called less upon Margaret Shanor. The group's set strayed from jazz to Richard's pop-influenced originals and tried-and-true standards like "Ebb Tide," "The Sweetheart Tree," "The Twelfth of Never," and "Yesterday." No matter how much singing she was asked to do, Karen also seemed to consider herself first and foremost a drummer who just happened to sing.

Around this time Agnes Carpenter met Evelyn Wallace, a fellow employee at North American Aviation. The women became close friends when Agnes came to Evelyn in tears following a heated disagreement with another coworker. After Wallace was promoted to the division of laboratory and tests for the Apollo program, Agnes took over her old job. "Why don't you stop in and hear the kids?" Agnes would often ask Evelyn. "They practice after school every day."

But Evelyn always seemed to find some excuse. "I thought she was talking about *little* kids," she recalls. "Then I thought it might be that acid rock, and I couldn't stand to listen to that. Finally I couldn't keep saying no. I had to say yes." Reluctantly Evelyn agreed to join the Carpenters in their home for dinner one evening and to hear Karen and Richard rehearse. Proud to finally find a captive audience, Agnes called out to her daughter seated behind the drums. "Sing it, Karen," she said. "*Sing out!*"

Wallace sat spellbound. "I had never heard a voice like that in all my life," she says. "What a beautiful, beautiful voice she had, and I told her when she finished, 'That was beautiful, Karen.' She thought I was just being nice."

LIKE MANY college music majors, trumpeter Dan Friberg directed a church choir on the weekends for extra income. At a church in Hawthorne he met Don Zacklin, a member of the congregation. "I was doing lead sheets for him," Friberg recalls. "He would bring me tapes of different artists that he had recorded on Sunday, and I'd write out lead sheets. He would send them in for copyright purposes." Zacklin encouraged Friberg to share some of his original compositions and recordings with his friend Joe Osborn, a business partner in a small record label called Magic Lamp Records.

Joe Osborn was one of the most prominent and sought-after studio bassists on the West Coast pop music scene in the 1960s. He frequently played in tandem with drummer Hal Blaine and keyboardist Larry Knechtel, an association known as the Wrecking Crew. The three were featured on numerous hits by the Beach Boys, the Mamas and the Papas, and many other popular artists of the late 1960s. "We were a bunch of guys in Levis and T-shirts," says Blaine, who first worked with Joe Osborn on the live *Johnny Rivers at the Whiskey a Go Go* album. "The older, established musicians in three-piece suits and blue blazers who had been in Hollywood all their life started saying, 'These kids are going to *wreck* the business,' so I just started calling us the Wrecking Crew."

As the spring semester of 1966 drew to a close, Friberg saw Richard on campus and told him of his upcoming audition with Osborn. "I've got a guy that wants to hear some songs that I wrote, but I need somebody to play piano for me," he said.

Richard agreed to accompany Friberg on the informal try-out. "It all goes back to that fateful night at Joe Osborn's in his garage with egg cartons on the wall," he says. It was April 1966. Both Karen and Richard traveled with Friberg and his young wife to Osborn's house, located at 7935 Ethel Avenue in the San Fernando Valley. The audition and recording session were slated for 1:00 A.M. since Osborn was usually in sessions each night until midnight.

Unbeknownst to Karen and Richard, Don Zacklin had asked Friberg to recommend other talented kids from the college to audition for Magic Lamp. So when Karen and Richard showed up, Zacklin and Osborn assumed they'd come along to audition, too. The brother and sister were befuddled but cooperative. "Karen ended up singing that night," Friberg says. "She sang and that was the end of me! To me, her voice was just like nothing else I'd ever heard before or since. It was just so distinctive. To think of all the times I saw her sitting behind the drums, never knowing that she could even sing. It's really weird the way things worked out because that night was what started the whole thing for them. If Richard had said, 'I'm busy,' I probably would have gotten somebody else, and they never would have met Joe."

Captivated by Karen's raw, husky voice, Osborn asked musician friend and drummer Mickey Jones to travel with him to Downey to see this "chubby little girl" perform. "We went to a small dinner house where we heard Karen sing," Jones recalls. "I was shocked. I had never heard a more pure voice in my life." Hearing Karen again, Osborn was won over. He told Mickey Jones he planned to contact the girl's parents. He wanted to record her. This was surely good news, but it did not sit well with Agnes Carpenter. She was set on the idea of her son becoming the family's famous musician. After all, they'd moved across the country in hopes of Richard getting into the music business, and now he was being disregarded in favor of his kid sister, a musical novice. "I know that Agnes was really, really mad about that," recalls Evelyn Wallace. "There are many piano players that are very, very good. But let's face it, all pianos more or less sound alike. All voices do not."

On May 9, 1966, Osborn signed sixteen-year-old Karen Carpenter to Magic Lamp Records' small roster of artists, which included Johnny Burnette, James Burton, Mickey Jones, Dean Torrence (of Jan and Dean), and Vince Edwards, best known as television's Dr. Ben Casey. Since Karen was not of legal age, Agnes and Harold signed on her behalf. Two days later, Magic Lamp's publishing division, Lightup Music, signed Richard as a songwriter in an effort to help reconcile Agnes's displeasure with Osborn having initially overlooked her son's talents. "Joe thought that Richard was a pain in the ass," Mickey Jones recalls. "Richard not only wanted to play the piano but to run everything. Joe did not want him around when he was working with Karen, so he made Richard wait outside the studio."

Any resentment between the two soon gave way to new friendships as Karen, Richard, and Wes Jacobs began spending hours on end at Osborn's studio. That summer Karen recorded several of Richard's original compositions including "The Parting of Our Ways," "Don't Tell Me," "Looking for Love," and "I'll Be Yours." She also played drums on the recordings, which featured Osborn on electric bass and sometimes Wes Jacobs on upright bass. Richard was on piano and the Chamberlin Music Master, a version of the Mellotron, both of which were popular analog synthesizers that provided taped string and woodwind sounds. Osborn used a Scully 4-track recorder and Neumann U87 condenser microphones to tape the sessions. Playback was done through Altec 604 studio monitors. When four tracks were complete, they were bounced or "ping-ponged" to his Scully 2-track machine, which condensed multiple tracks to two or sometimes even one. This process freed additional tracks for overdubbing and layering voices or instruments.

"Looking for Love / I'll Be Yours" (ML 704) was the first and only single by Karen Carpenter for Magic Lamp Records. Five hundred copies were pressed, and most extras were given to family and friends. "There was no distribution that I am aware of," Mickey Jones says. "It was mainly a tax shelter." Like most small labels, Magic Lamp did not have the means to promote their singles, and by late 1967 the company folded.

THE SUMMER of 1966 brought several milestones in the lives of Karen and Richard Carpenter. Shortly after having joined forces with Magic Lamp Records, the Richard Carpenter Trio made it to the finals of the Seventh Annual Battle of the Bands, a prestigious talent competition held at the Hollywood Bowl. The event was sponsored by the County of Los Angeles Department of Parks and Recreation and dubbed "a musical showdown under the stars." Open to nonprofessionals under the age of twenty-one, the contest began with hundreds of groups competing in five preliminary contests held around Los Angeles County. Acts were quickly narrowed to just three entries in each of the following categories: dance band, school band, combos, vocal soloists, and vocal groups.

On Friday night, June 24, the trio performed Richard's multi-time signature arrangement of Antonio Carlos Jobim's "The Girl from Ipanema" and an original whole-tone-inspired jazz waltz entitled "Iced Tea," an ode to their favorite beverage, featuring Wes Jacobs on tuba. From their introduction by master of ceremonies Jerry Dexter, the trio gained full audience attention before even playing a note. The sight of Karen sitting behind a drum kit with her hair piled high was definitely a novelty. "I remember when we walked into the Bowl there were twenty acts on the show, and I was still new to the drums," Karen later explained to Ray Coleman. "It took me a while to set them up. We'd only been together for like six months, and what was even funnier, I couldn't lift them. I couldn't move them, so I had to have everybody carrying my drums, and then I put them together. All the guy drum-mers were hysterical."

A lengthy drum solo in the middle of "Iced Tea" gave Karen an opportunity to demonstrate her technique. The enthusiastic audience responded with a roar of applause, cheers, and whistles, which even drowned out the music at one point on a recording of the evening's performance. "By then she had gone from having a good rhythmical sense and steady time—the foundation you want—to being a very good player," Frankie Chavez recalls. "She could make some male drummers stand up and take notice, and she actually could outplay some of them, too. She was that good. I thought she made very good progress for the very short time she'd been playing, and it's a credit to her musicality."

Despite having to play on a dreadful upright piano the night of the contest, Richard won outstanding instrumentalist. In addition to win-ning best combo, the trio took home the sweepstakes trophy for the highest overall score in the competition, beating out Gentlemen and Trombones, Inc. "They won!" Agnes Carpenter proudly exclaimed to Frank Pooler, phoning him the day after the Battle of the Bands. "It's the biggest trophy I've ever seen in my life. My God, they've *got* to be good!"

Gerald Wilson, Calvin Jackson, Jerry Goldsmith, and Bill Holman joined Leonard Feather, chief jazz critic for the *Los Angeles Times*, as the official judges for the event. "The musical surprise of the evening was the Trio of Richard Carpenter," wrote Feather, describing the group's leader as a "remarkably original soloist who won awards as the best instrumen-talist and leader of the best combo. Flanking his piano were Karen Car-penter, his talented sixteen-year-old sister at the drums, and bassist Wes Jacobs who doubled amusingly and confidently on tuba." The competi-tion was later broadcast in color on KNBC Channel 4 in Los Angeles.

"The Hollywood Bowl performance was a great place to get expo-sure," Chavez says. "People that went there were oftentimes movers and shakers who could make things happen with a career. It was a good move." On the way to their car following the win at the Bowl, Richard was approached by a man who congratulated the trio and asked if they would be interested in cutting some records. Richard told the man they already had a contract but took his business card anyway. Once Richard realized it was Neely Plumb, prominent West Coast A & R (artists and repertoire) man for RCA-Victor Records, he quickly explained the contract was only a solo singing contract for Karen with Magic Lamp. Plumb (whose daughter Eve would go on to star as Jan in the classic TV series *The Brady Bunch*) thought the idea of rock tuba might be the wave of the immediate future and wanted to spotlight Wes Jacobs.

The trio signed to RCA-Victor in September 1966 and soon cut eleven tracks, including instrumentals of the standard "Strangers in the Night" and the Beatles' "Every Little Thing." They also recorded "I've Never Been in Love Before" from the musical *Guys and Dolls* and a Richard original, "Flat Baroque." Although he was excited to see the trio signed to a major record label, Richard shared with Plumb his concerns over the rock tuba approach, which he knew had little potential, and even the powers at RCA agreed. Richard told them of Karen's voice and how she had been signed to a vocal contract earlier that year, but after agreeing to listen, the response was: "Just another folk-rock group. No thank you." RCA decided against releasing the trio's music, and the three soon left the label with a few hundred dollars and no record. They considered themselves to have been an artistic success but a commercial failure. "It was really great playing, but we didn't really have that focus," Wes Jacobs recalled. "Karen wasn't singing, and the tuba wasn't going to sell records. There was a lot of talent, but we didn't have direction."

Back on the campus at Cal State Long Beach, Richard spent many hours in the music department practice rooms, where he was able to focus on his own music. As he did on occasion, Richard consulted Frank Pooler for inspiration, in this case in planning their holiday music set. "We're sure sick of 'White Christmas,' 'Silent Night,' and doing the same songs every night," he told Pooler, asking for suggestions.

"I don't know any *new* Christmas songs," he replied, "but I wrote one a long time ago."

Pooler had written "Merry Christmas, Darling" as a young man. In fact, he composed his original version in 1946, the year Richard was born. Twenty years later, in December 1966, Pooler shared "Merry

Christmas, Darling" with Richard Carpenter. "[Richard] was writing tunes at that time," says Pooler, "and I knew that whatever tune he could write would be better than the one I had already written, so I didn't give him the tune. I just gave him the words." Richard said he would work on a new melody, and about fifteen minutes later he was finished. "Merry Christmas, Darling" was written by two teenagers a generation apart. It was among the earliest songs Karen sang with the trio and would provide them with many successes in the years to come.

UPON GRADUATION from Downey High School in the spring of 1967, Karen was presented with the John Philip Sousa Band Award, the highest achievement for high school band students, recognizing superior musicianship and outstanding dedication. "She didn't strike me as musically talented at first," band director Gifford later recalled, "but I've learned to give people time before judging their talent."

In a farewell message inscribed in mentor Frankie Chavez's yearbook, Karen praised his abilities as a drummer and thanked him for inspiring and guiding her talents.

Frankie,

Listen man, it's hard to believe it, but we made it. Anyway, it's been a gas in every sense of the word. I can honestly say that it wouldn't have been near as crazy without ya. I want to thank you for getting me interested in drums. I learned a great deal from you and I'll always owe it to ya. . . . Oh well, it's time to split so keep in touch in between gigs.

Love ya,

Karen '67

3

STAND IN LINE, TRY TO CLIMB

A STRUGGLING POLITICAL science student from San Pedro who often slept on campus in his station wagon overnight, John Bettis had given up on his mother's dream for him to become an international attorney. Entering Cal State Long Beach, the long-haired folk singer was known for his sense of humor and creativity. He knew very little about music theory but ended up joining Frank Pooler's college choir as an elective. Still, he had a remarkable talent for writing lyrics.

"John used to slip me little notes," Pooler recalls. "They were little pieces of poetry; his observations of rehearsals and observations he had about me. I thought they were really kind of beautiful and very unusual."

Bettis began to compile his observations for what became "A Cappella Music," a composition that according to Pooler was not even considered a song. "It was a cantata!" he exclaims. John was quite sure he would be kicked out of the choir once they heard the finished product, which introduced the various sections of the choir and proceeded to poke fun at each with a tongue-in-cheek approach. The choir listened as Bettis struggled to premiere "A Cappella Music" with only a sparse guitar accompaniment. "Buddy, you need a pianist!" Richard blurted out before coming to Bettis's rescue. Pooler had a feeling the young men's talents might complement one another. "I thought they were a perfect pair so I said, 'You guys should work together.'"

Richard and John Bettis shared a love of music, cars, and girls and became close friends. Agnes Carpenter was not as quick to welcome new faces into the Carpenter circle, especially someone with the gypsy existence of Bettis. She was infuriated to learn Richard was splitting performance fees equally with Bettis once they began playing various gigs together. She reminded Richard that he carried the musical load, and he was the only musically literate one of the two. In her opinion Bettis did not do enough or have the experience to warrant half of the profits.

Through mutual friend Doug Strawn, Richard and John learned of an opening for a ragtime piano-banjo act at Coke Corner on Disneyland's Main Street U.S.A. The two were hired for the summer season of 1967 and worked eighteen-hour shifts. The musicians' union salary of $180 per week was a fortune to two college students, but they wisely invested their earnings in musical instruments and sound equipment.

Disneyland's entertainment supervisor, Vic Guder, made frequent stops throughout the park, walkie-talkie in hand, overseeing the park's wide range of talent. He made certain all acts were in proper costume and performing in accordance with the park's policies. Stopping by Coke Corner, Guder expected to hear turn-of-the-century ditties, like "A Bicycle Built for Two" and Scott Joplin's "Maple Leaf Rag" and "The Entertainer." Instead he discovered the duo granting requests from thirsty patrons wanting to hear modern tunes like "Light My Fire" and "Yesterday." After months of gentle redirection by Guder, their time with Disneyland came to an end. "They had very strict regimens as to what one could and could not do in the park," Bettis recalled. "Richard and I were fired for combing our hair in the park. Now, I grant you we did a lot of other things that did not please them before that time, but that actually caused us to be fired."

According to Guder, the duo was never fired, the season merely came to an end. "Heck no, they weren't fired," he says. "Richard was hired for the summertime. He went back to school in the fall and didn't plan to work full time. Coke Corner is a spot that is a part-time summer job. They'd come back when we'd use the Coke Corner pianist at night for private parties. It's not a full-time gig."

Seeking musical revenge, so to speak, the two set out to write a song about the incident immediately upon termination. "We got all the way to the bridge and didn't finish it because I wasn't at all sure that it was something that we ought to be doing," Bettis said. "Richard really felt so strongly about it and liked the music well enough that he actually wrote the bridge to that, lyrically, and finished it." Like many of their early musical collaborations, "Mr. Guder" was set aside and would resurface several years later.

FOLLOWING HER brother's lead, Karen enrolled at Cal State Long Beach as a music major in the fall of 1967. Despite the beauty of her newly discovered chest voice, she was expected to use her head voice as it was better suited to the classical art song repertoire required of private voice students. She was also required to sing before a panel of professors called a jury for evaluation at the end of each semester. Such a critical review proved stressful for even the most accomplished musicians. With Larry Peterson, head of the music department, and several other members of the voice faculty present, Karen performed selections from her repertoire before Pooler interrupted. "Look, this is all so serious," he told his colleagues. "This girl's really versatile. Do you guys want a laugh?" Pooler urged Karen to do one of many impersonations he had witnessed in their lessons. In particular he requested the "spastic, hare-lipped singer."

"They'll kick me out of school," Karen objected.

She was surprised and embarrassed by her teacher's request, especially before such an esteemed gathering. "The thing that really endeared me to Karen," Pooler recalls, "was the sense of humor she had about everything and how she could imitate people. She could do anything with her voice."

Pooler was a bit of a maverick in the choral music world, displaying an eccentric approach to his style and work. He was never predictable— at least not musically. Opening the floor to members of the A Cappella

Choir, Pooler would allow students to suggest music literature and styles. The subject of black spirituals surfaced. "I don't want to do a piece that's foreign to me," Pooler told the choir. Though he was experienced in music sung in foreign languages, spirituals and gospel music were unfamiliar territory.

"Well, if you can't show them, *I'll* show them," a voice said, and out stepped Wanda Freeman, one of the few African Americans in the choir. She faced the choir and began to sing.

"I had never done spirituals or black music," Pooler says. "I just didn't feel it, but she did. She was sensational. She was the start of a whole host of first-class gospel musicians that came out of that choir."

Unlike other college choirs in the area that specialized in one style or another, Pooler's groups tackled a wide range of choral genres. "Frank was very innovative," Freeman recalls. "We were doing avant-garde stuff and things that other choirs had never done before; songs with just sounds and things. He was very open to trying gospel."

Made popular by Blood, Sweat and Tears, "And When I Die" was one of several contemporary hits the choir performed. The gospel-style arrangement called for a duet, and Pooler chose the unlikely pairing of Wanda Freeman and Karen Carpenter. "Karen had a nice alto voice," Freeman recalls. "I never really thought anything of it, but it was a very clear voice. When we did 'And When I Die' she really opened up. She really wanted to do that song."

Pooler often praised Karen's versatility as a singer and even used her as a model for other choir students. "Her range was spectacular," he recalls. "She could sing higher than anybody else but also lower than anybody else. At that time her voice was like most adolescent voices. It was not completely unified from the top to the bottom, but she knew how to do it."

WITH THE departure of bassist Wes Jacobs, who in 1967 left the Richard Carpenter Trio and Los Angeles to study classical tuba at Juilliard, Richard was open to exploring new musical opportunities. He had long been fond of vocal ensembles like the Hi-Lo's, the Four Freshmen, and the Beach Boys. He had also enjoyed the close harmony sounds of overdubbing pioneers Les Paul and Mary Ford since childhood. But it was Frank Pooler's choral influence that left a lasting impression on both him and Karen. His philosophy stressed vocal blend, vowel shaping, and precise attack and release. These fundamentals were the basis for what would ultimately become the trademark Carpenters sound.

Richard's first attempt at forming a vocal group produced a quintet assembled during Karen's senior year of high school. They called themselves Summerchimes but soon renamed the group Spectrum. Their first recruit was John Bettis, who sang and played rhythm guitar. Over a period of several months, he, Karen, and Richard conducted informal auditions to complete the group. Gary Sims lived in Downey and, like Karen, was still attending high school when the group originated. "He used to perform with an acoustic guitar, like a folk singer," recalled Bettis, who went with Richard to catch Sims's act. "He had this great baritone voice and joined the group as a guitar player." The final recruit was Dan Woodhams, a tenor vocalist enlisted to sing and play bass guitar, although he "didn't have a clue how to play the bass," according to Bettis. "He played violin, so Richard actually taught him how to play the bass. Danny was the final member. That was the original Spectrum."

The addition of Leslie "Toots" Johnston in the fall of 1967 made the group a sextet. "Johnny Bettis and Gary Sims were friends of mine," Johnston recalls. "Gary was the Carpenters' neighbor, and they were looking for another girl to add to the group. They listened to me, and I had a good pop voice style. Richard was looking for someone who could blend with Karen, which I did very well." A member of the college choir, Johnston sat next to Karen in the alto section during the daily afternoon rehearsals. "We threw jokes back and forth and got along really well," she says. "Karen was such a great musician but didn't read music as well as I did, so she listened to me for the part. We struck up a friendship. She had a dry sense of humor and was funny. She thought I was funny, too. She didn't have a lot of girlfriends, so I think Karen enjoyed having another female around."

Spectrum rehearsed in the garage at the house on Fidler, where there was never a shortage of Agnes Carpenter's famous iced tea—the perfect blend of Lipton instant tea and frozen lemonade. "There had to be a jug of that on the table for every rehearsal," Johnston recalls. "That was *the drink!*"

KAREN BECAME increasingly mindful of her appearance during her first year of college. She had been chubby as a kid. In fact, Richard often called her Fatso (to which she would reply, "Four eyes!"). It was the type of teasing characteristic of most sibling relationships. But as a seventeen-year-old young woman, Karen was five feet four inches tall and weighed 145 pounds. Her classic hourglass figure was a common trait among family members, including her mother and aunt Bernice. "I was heavier," Karen said in a 1973 interview. "About twenty pounds heavier, to tell you the truth. I was just tired of being fat so I went on a diet. . . . I found this sweater I used to wear in high school. Good Lord, I think I could get into it three times today. I don't know how I ever got through a door."

Frankie Chavez recalls Karen as only slightly overweight in high school, but if she had body image issues at the time, he never noticed. There were no warning signs during the period they were close. "She never gave any indication that it bothered her that she carried a little extra weight," he says. "She always seemed very self-confident, and I don't think she ever even contemplated dieting when I knew her. Karen was a perfectionist as far as her performances were concerned, and she set the bar very high for herself, but there was no indication that she had any problems at all."

During the summer of 1967 Agnes took her to see their family doctor, who recommended the popular Stillman water diet that was introduced that year by Dr. Irwin Maxwell Stillman. The plan promised quick weight loss through limiting intake of carbohydrates and fatty foods while increasing daily water intake to eight glasses. Karen hated water, but after only six weeks she shed twenty-five pounds and was determined to maintain her new figure. When Spectrum's late-night rehearsals ended, everyone in the band was hungry and went for dinner, which was frustrating for Karen. "All the guys would want to go to eat at Coco's," she said, "and I would sit there with my hamburger patty and cottage cheese while the guys ordered forty-seven-layer cheeseburgers and giant sundaes." From the summer of 1967 until early 1973, Karen remained at or around the comfortable weight of 115 to 120 pounds.

IN EARLY 1967 Richard had received a call from a local singer named Ed Sulzer, whom he had accompanied during a gig back in 1963. Sulzer heard Spectrum was recording in Joe Osborn's garage and offered to shop their demo to various record labels around Los Angeles. He quickly became acting manager of the group. With rare exceptions, Sulzer's enthusiasm for Spectrum's distinctive sound was not shared by the record labels and venues he approached. "People hear what we accomplished, and it sounds like such a natural now," John Bettis explained. "Back then, what we were recording and what we were writing went completely against the grain of what anyone else was doing. And they told us so."

Leslie Johnston describes Spectrum's sound as rich, thick, tight harmony, but she feels the group's creativity was out of sync with most of their audiences. "Here's this middle-of-the-road group with this great sound," she says. "We were such an in-between kind of group. Back then it was either hard psychedelic rock or it was elevator music. We had this pretty sound; it was nice to listen to us, but we weren't a dance group. Agents that would come to the Troubadour just kept telling our manager, 'They're *terrific*, but where do we put them?' Radio stations were afraid to play us because we were too mild for some and yet we weren't the old style either. We were having a tough time, and we were getting discouraged. We really were and should have been a recording group exclusively."

Sulzer secured Spectrum a block of studio time at United Audio Recording Studio in Santa Ana. The group cut several demos of original songs, including "All I Can Do," "All of My Life," "Another Song," "What's the Use," and "Candy." The latter would later become "One

Love" on the 1971 *Carpenters* album. Positioning microphones in the studio, Glen Pace, United Audio's owner and engineer during the Spectrum sessions, noticed a young girl unpacking a set of Ludwigs. "Gee, your boyfriend has you trained really well," he called out to her across the room.

"What do you mean?" Karen asked.

"He has you trained really well for you to come and set up his drums for him."

With a sheepish grin she replied, "*I'm* the drummer."

"This was the first girl drummer I'd ever come across," Pace explains.

Unable to afford more studio time, Spectrum moved their recording sessions back to the Carpenters' living room. Using Richard's Sony Tapecorder, the group began making recordings at home and employing the bathroom as an echo chamber. A string of live performances arranged by Ed Sulzer found Spectrum at the legendary Troubadour in West Hollywood where every Monday night was Hoot Night. Dozens of acts lined up in the alley in hopes of securing a performance time slot. "You had to wait in this huge line to play," Karen explained to the *Los Angeles Times* in 1972. "I often stood there talking with kids, along with people like Jackson Browne and Brewer and Shipley."

Richard purchased a Wurlitzer 140-B electronic piano from Jeff Hanna of the Nitty Gritty Dirt Band and in keeping with his fascination with automobiles personalized the instrument with a 426 HEMI engine decal. Spectrum members routinely unloaded the station wagon and lugged the new Wurlitzer, drums, and various instruments and amplifiers down the alley and through the crowds to perform for fifteen or twenty minutes. Then they turned around and hauled everything back through the crowds to the car. "You should have seen us with our crew-cuts and blue velvet jackets," says Leslie Johnston.

Randy Sparks, who led a group called the New Christy Minstrels, heard Spectrum at the Troubadour and offered the group a week's engagement at Ledbetter's, his club on Westwood Boulevard. This was one of their first major paid engagements. "They were a bit more like a lounge act than a folk group," Sparks says, "which was my niche in the business of music. But Karen was a wonderful singer, and they had a pleasing—if not exciting—sound. They were much appreciated by my crowd." Sparks believed Karen and Richard each displayed unmistakable talent, far beyond that of the group's other members. "The other folks in their band were essentially invisible, in my estimation." As Spectrum spent several weeks on the stage at Ledbetter's, Sparks witnessed their growth with each successive performance. "That's what my operation was all about. Ledbetter's was a place to perform, to experiment, to rehearse, and to develop skills in dealing with audiences."

Next, Sulzer booked Spectrum at the Whisky a Go-Go, where the group opened for Evergreen Blue Shoes, a band whose bass player, Skip Battin, would later join the Byrds. The Whisky (often misspelled "Whiskey") was a popular nightclub on the Sunset Strip and inspiration for the Loggins and Messina song "Whisky." Its lyric instructs:

Don't do anything mellow at the Whisky . . .
Don't sing anything pretty at the Whisky . . .
'Cause if you do, your musical insurance better be paid up

For the most part Spectrum was mellow and their music indisputably pretty. They did not stand a chance. "The customers sat and listened to us," Karen said of the engagement. "That wasn't what the club wanted. If you sit, you don't dance. If you don't dance, you don't get thirsty. In that case you don't spend, so we were kicked out."

Karen also recalled opening for Steppenwolf at the Blue Law, a large warehouse-turned-club. "At first, the audience was so restive," she said. "We thought we were going to get killed, but we kept going, and they shut up and listened." Again, not what club management preferred.

"Steppenwolf? Oh my God, I was so embarrassed to be there," says Leslie Johnston. "We're in the dressing room with Steppenwolf, and they couldn't have been any more hard rock. In fact, I liked them, but we were so mad at Eddie for that booking. I think we were there maybe two nights. I was just dying because the people were waiting for some hard rock to dance to. They didn't *boo* us, but they looked at us like we were nuts. We had this great, full sound, but Steppenwolf was probably in the dressing room laughing."

As Sulzer struggled to secure live performance opportunities in venues appropriate for Spectrum, the group's sights were set on securing a recording contract. When two major recording companies, Uni and White Whale, presented contracts on the same night at the Troubadour, the group was encouraged, but Richard declined the offers once he realized the labels were demanding too big a cut. Spectrum's members became disheartened and soon began to scatter. Leslie Johnston was asked to go on the road with another group as lead vocalist. "I agreed," she says, "because nothing else was happening!"

CONTINUING TO record in Joe Osborn's studio, gratis, Karen and Richard worked toward the creation of a new demo tape. They usually recorded on weekends or after midnight when Osborn's other sessions ended. According to Karen, "Since Richard did all the arranging and chose the material, and we did our own playing and singing, Richard said, 'We might as well do it ourselves, just overdub it.' . . . All of a sudden that sound was born." She marveled over the quality of sound they were able to achieve in Joe's studio. "That garage studio had a sound that I don't think we ever matched. It was big and fat."

For an a cappella arrangement called "Invocation" they began with two-part harmonies, then built to four-part, and finally eight. Their eight-part harmonies were tripled, totaling twenty-four voices in all. "Wow, we couldn't believe the results," Karen later recalled. "All of a sudden this ten-ton thing was born. This *couldn't* miss!" Their demo tape also featured Richard's original "Don't Be Afraid" and another he penned with John Bettis called "Your Wonderful Parade." Although the arrangements were identical to those of Spectrum, there was something special about the familial sound that resulted from the layering of Karen's voice with Richard's. Now officially a duo, Karen and Richard chose the name Carpenters, sans prefix. They thought it was simple but hip, like Buffalo Springfield or Jefferson Airplane.

As recording demanded more and more of their time and energy, Karen and Richard saw their obligations at Cal State Long Beach as less of a priority. They often carried copies of *Billboard* and *Cashbox* with them to class and would read them behind their textbooks, so it is no wonder Karen flunked out of a psychology course twice. And she loathed biology: "What good is biology going to do me?" she asked rhetorically in a 1970 interview. "On the stage it's of no use, right? A biology major doesn't have to take a music course." Frank Pooler went to bat for Karen several times in attempts to justify her continued absences from several classes. "She wasn't showing up for some boring class," he says. "I remember going to talk to the president of the university about her. I said, 'Hey, some people need special consideration. Besides, I wouldn't take the class myself.'"

In the summer of 1968 Richard heard about a new national television program called *Your All-American College Show*. Produced by radio legend Wendell Niles and sponsored by the Colgate-Palmolive Corporation, the program gathered top musical talent from college campuses across the country. Along with new recruit Bill Sissoyev on bass, their act was well received during auditions, and they ultimately advanced to the televised portion of the competition. Wearing showy white go-go boots and a wide white headband, Karen tore through their Mamas and the Papas–inspired "Dancing in the Street" with much energy and gusto. Her drumming was intense and her singing strong and deliberate. They appeared as a trio several times during that year, and the group won $3,500.

The publicity alone was enough to keep the trio excited about *Your All-American College Show*, but Wendell Niles and his organization also expressed interest in representing them. Everyone was surprised when celebrity judge John Wayne wanted Karen to audition for the role of young frontier girl Mattie Ross in his upcoming film *True Grit*. The part ultimately went to actress Kim Darby, and Karen continued to explore various musical opportunities. With Richard's blessing, she auditioned for the girl singer spot in Kenny Rogers's group the First Edition. The position had been vacated after vocalist Thelma Camacho was fired for missing too many rehearsals and performances. Surprisingly, Karen was overlooked, most likely due to the fact that it was not a recording audition, and much of Karen's appeal was facilitated by a microphone. The spot was filled by Camacho's roommate Mary

Arnold, an Iowa-born singer who later married Roger "King of the Road" Miller.

With the ongoing assistance of Ed Sulzer, Karen and Richard continued their mission to get their demo tape around to each and every record label in Hollywood. But Columbia Records had hits with Gary Puckett and the Union Gap's "Young Girl" and Bobbie Gentry's "Ode to Billie Joe" and were looking for soundalike acts. Similarly, Warner Brothers Records asked the Carpenters if they could sound like Harper's Bizarre, but they had no interest in emulating others. Richard was convinced that their overdubbed sound and Karen's vocals were commercially viable and that it would only be a matter of time before they would be recognized. Karen felt strongly that A&M Records, a label known for its attention to artistry, would give their music a fair listen, but even the guard at the gate turned them away. Not to worry, Ed Sulzer assured them. He had a friend who knew a trumpet player named Jack Daugherty who might possibly deliver their demo to A&M's cofounder Herb Alpert. It seemed like a circuitous route, but Karen and Richard gave their approval.

In the meantime, a call came in from brothers John and Tom Bähler, well-known jingle singers in Los Angeles. The Bählers had caught one of the Carpenters' appearances on *Your All-American College Show* and invited the duo to audition for a campaign called "The Going Thing," which was in development by the J. Walter Thompson advertising agency for the Ford Motor Company. The brothers auditioned approximately two hundred acts in New York and another two hundred at Sunset Sound in Hollywood, where Karen and Richard were ultimately selected. Visiting the agency, they signed individual contracts and were informed the group would assist in premiering the new 1970 Ford Maverick. It was not a recording contract as they desired, but the contracts came with the promise of fifty thousand dollars each and a new Ford automobile of their choice.

4

SPRINKLED MOONDUST

A&M RECORDS was unlike any other record label on the West Coast. Capitol, Warner Brothers, and others had undergone numerous reorganizations and were starting to be seen as enormous, impersonal conglomerates. A&M was a "family" label, founded precariously in 1962 by trumpet player Herb Alpert and Jerry Moss, his partner in production and promotion. Each contributed one hundred dollars to start what was first called Carnival Records, but after learning the name belonged to an existing label the two renamed the company with the initials of their surnames. A&M Records' first single was Alpert's "The Lonely Bull" recorded with the Tijuana Brass. Records by the Brass, the Baja Marimba Band, and Sergio Mendes and Brasil '66 helped keep A&M afloat throughout the late 1960s. Other artists signed to the label included Leon Russell, Joe Cocker, and Burt Bacharach. The Bacharach-penned "This Guy's in Love with You" became a #1 hit single for Herb Alpert in 1968, A&M's first chart topper.

The A&M Records lot itself was as unique as the label. The studio opened in November 1966 with a skeleton crew of thirty-two employees. Located at 1416 North La Brea Avenue in Hollywood, just south of Sunset Boulevard, the site once housed Charlie Chaplin's movie studio. Says songwriter Paul Williams, who came to the young and vibrant company in 1967, "There was such a sense of history just because of the location. It was charming in its look, and it reeked of Hollywood history. I showed up in a stolen car. I was an out-of-work actor and stumbled into the songwriting career. They were looking for a lyricist for Roger Nichols, and I wound up with a career. It was one of those great accidents. One door slammed shut, and another one opened."

Roger Nichols remembers A&M as an artist-friendly company and attributes most of the label's early success to the recordings of Herb Alpert and the Tijuana Brass. "Thanks to them, A&M really had money," he says. "They didn't have money to burn but money to do things right. They treated people nicely. It was like the crème de la crème of the record companies at that time and a great place to be. There was a great creative energy to the lot, and the premise of the company was that you could pretty much do whatever you wanted to. When I was asked to record for A&M they said, 'Make whatever kind of record you want to.' That was unique. I don't know where you'd go to find that today. There wasn't so much control of the product."

Nichols and others around A&M were acquainted with Jack Daugherty, a Cincinnati-born musician who worked at North American Aviation in Downey, where he made presentations detailing the company's work with the Apollo program. Daugherty worked part time as a music copyist and in his spare time wrote counterpoint exercises and chorales. It was while working at North American that he received a copy of the Carpenters' demo. "I had it for about two months," he recalled in a feature for *High Fidelity*, "and every once in a while I'd listen again. That's a pretty good test."

Daugherty visited A&M's publishing office almost every week to drop off lead sheets he had prepared for Chuck Kaye, head of Almo/Irving Music, A&M's publishing arm. "You have to hear this group," Daugherty told Roger Nichols. "They're a brother and sister. Call themselves Carpenters." But it was Daugherty's friend, Tijuana Brass guitarist John Pisano, who ultimately handed the Carpenters' demo tape to Herb Alpert. "I put on the tape, and I was really knocked out with the sound of Karen's voice to start with," Alpert said in 1994. "It touched me. It had nothing to do with what was happening in the market at that moment, but that's what touched me even more. I felt like it was time."

Manager Ed Sulzer contacted Richard and let him know that Alpert had heard their demo, loved their sound, and wanted Carpenters on the A&M Records roster. The standard recording contract outlined a 7 percent royalty on all record sales and an advance of ten thousand dollars. Karen and Richard were thrilled, but timing posed a problem. Only days earlier they signed with the J. Walter Thompson agency's "Going Thing" campaign for Ford. Though they were grateful for the opportunity and honor, the two asked for release from the contract, each surrendering the fifty thousand dollars and new car. A recording contract with a major label like A&M had the potential for longevity. John and Tom Bähler understood the dilemma and convinced J. Walter Thompson to let Karen and Richard out of their contracts.

Herb Alpert and Jerry Moss took great pride in their artists, "encouraging them to reach their creative potential," as they wrote years later in *From Brass to Gold*, an exhaustive A&M Records discography. "We looked for artists who had a strong sense of themselves musically and surrounded them with an environment and people who could help them express their unique talents." For Alpert, musical honesty and sincerity took priority over potential sales when considering a new artist. "It doesn't matter if they're a jazz musician, a classical musician, or rap or pop," he explained. "I think the real measure is if you are really doing it from your heart. The music that the Carpenters made was straight from their hearts. Richard was and is a real student of the record business. He knows a good song, he knows where to record it, he knows the musicians. Karen had this extraordinary voice, and they put the right combination together, and it was touching."

It was Jerry Moss who officially signed the Carpenters to A&M, just before noon on Tuesday, April 22, 1969. "You think we could meet Herb?" Ed Sulzer asked. Alpert entered, greeted his new acquisitions, and said, "Let's hope we have some hits!"

———— ∞ ————

A&M DID not micromanage their artists, even the newest and youngest on the roster. They held their artists in such high regard that they would often turn them loose to explore and create. Even so, Alpert suggested

Jack Daugherty be signed to serve as producer for the Carpenters. This meant Daugherty would leave his twenty-thousand-dollar-a-year job at North American Aviation and go to work for A&M in hopes the Carpenters' successes would warrant his stay. According to Ollie Mitchell, who played trumpet in Daugherty's band, "Jack was lucky to be in a position to work with Richard, who seemed to do most of the real producing on the recording dates."

Most agree it was Richard who arranged and artistically produced the Carpenters' albums. Daugherty was more of an A & R person for Karen and Richard. "Jack was very user-friendly as far as Roger Nichols and I were concerned," remembers Paul Williams. "He's the one who introduced all of us to the Carpenters. He was a very detailed man, not shy but very reserved. There was something almost 'country gentleman' about him at times. I liked him."

The Carpenters were immediately given run of the entire studio and its amenities. Recording began just a week after having signed with the label. At the time, eight-track recording equipment was standard, and for the first time Richard had a sophisticated recording studio at his disposal. For their first recording sessions, Richard chose to record a ballad version of Lennon and McCartney's "Ticket to Ride," from the 1965 Beatles' album *Help!* Foreshadowing "Ticket" had been a demo of the Beatles' "Nowhere Man" recorded by Karen in 1967. That recording took the up-tempo song and reworked it as a plaintive piano-accompanied ballad with a lead vocal full of melancholia. "Ticket to Ride" also employed this woeful approach, set atop a series of straightforward, arpeggiated chords from the piano.

Rather than seeking out or writing new material, the Carpenters chose to record much of their existing repertoire, most of which was written during the Spectrum years. The album was finished in Richard's mind long before they ever signed with A&M. Several songs were even lifted from the demos cut in Joe Osborn's studio. "Your Wonderful Parade" was given a new lead vocal and the addition of strings, while "All I Can Do" was the original demo as previously recorded. "Don't Be Afraid," one of the songs Alpert had listened to on their demo, was re-recorded entirely. Osborn was recruited to play his trademark sliding bass on the album as he would continue to do on all future Carpenters albums. It was under his guidance that Karen was able to play bass guitar on two recordings, "All of My Life" and "Eve." (Although Karen's bass work may be heard on the original album mix, recent compilations feature Richard's latest remixes, which have substituted Osborn's more sophisticated bass lines.)

Several elements of what would become the Carpenters' trademark style were already in place on this debut. For instance, "Someday," a collaboration with John Bettis, was one of Richard's finest sweeping melodies. It was also the perfect vehicle for Karen's mournful delivery. Richard sang lead on about half of the songs on the debut album, but his solo vocals became less prominent with each successive release until they disappeared entirely.

Recording sessions for the debut album came to a close in the summer of 1969. An August release was slated but delayed when additional mixing was required. Jim McCrary, A&M staff photographer, took the photo for the record jacket, driving Karen and Richard up Highland Avenue and posing them by the roadside. Richard was never happy with the photo, which depicts the blank-faced duo holding a bundle of sunflowers. But when Herb Alpert picked out the cover photo, they were not about to argue.

Offering was finally released on October 9, 1969. Frank Pooler recalls the night the album became available. "White Front Stores, a series of discount stores, were one of the first in the area that was selling it in their record department," he says. "They played the whole thing that night starting at midnight over some local station, so we all stayed up. We had to hear this whole album being played." *The Southeast News*, Downey's newspaper, reported that the local White Front Store "couldn't keep enough albums on the shelves.... A spot check of other local dealers revealed that the album has been moving well throughout the area."

According to music journalist Tom Nolan, "*Offering* tends toward being the sort of album many rock critics were encouraging at the time: a post-folk, soft-psychedelic, Southern Californian mini-oratorio." The debut album did spark enough interest to be featured as a "Billboard Pick" in *Billboard* magazine, citing "fresh and original concepts... With radio programming support, Carpenters should have a big hit on their hands."

The release of the debut single, "Ticket to Ride / Your Wonderful Parade," followed on November 5, nearly a month after the LP, and became a moderate hit. Covering a previous hit song and changing it up a bit was a way many artists achieved midchart hits. This proved to be true for Karen and Richard as well, and even a minor hit was a huge feat for a new artist. It stayed on the charts for six months, finally peaking at #54 by April 1970.

With the bill for *Offering* coming in around fifty thousand dollars, A&M lost money on the Carpenters' first release. That was not a cheap album to make, and initial sales of only 18,000 units left Karen and Richard somewhat nervous about their future with the label. A&M was going through a rough period in 1969, perhaps the worst year in their history, but despite the urging of others, Alpert was convinced the Carpenters had potential. He had no plans of cutting them from the roster. He felt their audience would "catch up to them" and admired the fact that they were so unique and driven.

Instead of setting forth to record another album, Alpert suggested that the Carpenters record several tracks to be considered for single release. "The first album did exactly what I thought it was going to do," he later recalled. "It takes a while for people to get onto a new artist and the frequency and the message that they are trying to send out. It didn't surprise me that the public didn't take to it. It was just a matter of time before they found the right song at the right moment and things turned around. With 'Ticket to Ride,' the idea that we were accustomed to that melody, and that they presented it in another format, was attractive to people. It wasn't their breakthrough record but it certainly got them a little bit of attention."

The duo next laid down several tracks for possible singles: "Love Is Surrender," a contemporary Christian tune with an altered secular lyric; "I'll Never Fall in Love Again," recorded by Dionne Warwick but not yet released as a single; and a cover of the Beatles' "Help!"

"THE THREE B's." Karen and Richard often cited the Beach Boys, the Beatles, and Burt Bacharach as their major pop music influences. The winding path to what ultimately became their second single began in December 1969 when the group played a benefit concert following the Hollywood premiere of the film *Hello, Dolly!* Opening the show with Burt Bacharach's "I'll Never Fall in Love Again," the group was unaware the esteemed composer was in attendance. As Karen and Richard exited the stage, Bacharach was waiting with congratulations and an invitation for them to join him as his opening act for an upcoming Reiss-Davis Clinic benefit to be held at the Century Plaza Hotel on February 27, 1970. The invitation was extended to include various concert dates at which time Bacharach requested that Richard select, arrange, and perform a medley of Bacharach-David songs.

As the Carpenters rehearsed furiously on A&M's soundstage and the medley began to take shape, Herb Alpert came through with a lead sheet for a lesser-known Bacharach-David song entitled "They Long to Be Close to You," first recorded by Richard "Dr. Kildare" Chamberlain in 1963. The song was also arranged by Bacharach for *Make Way for Dionne Warwick* the following year. Alpert had been given the tune several years earlier as a possible follow up to "This Guy's in Love with You" but disliked the "sprinkled moondust" lyric and set it aside. Richard considered Alpert to be a great A & R man but felt the song would not fit in his plan for the medley, which was ultimately narrowed to include "Any Day Now," "Baby It's You," "Knowing When to Leave," "Make It Easy On Yourself," "There's Always Something There to Remind Me," "I'll Never Fall in Love Again," "Walk On By," and "Do You Know the Way to San Jose."

The lead sheet for "They Long to Be Close to You" remained on Richard's Wurlitzer for several weeks. Though it was not suited for the medley, Richard saw its potential as a stand-alone song and with Alpert's urging began to construct his own arrangement. Alpert owned a copy of Warwick's recording but would not let Richard hear it. Aside from two piano quintuplets at the end of the bridge, he wanted nothing to influence Richard's concept.

Three very distinct arrangements of "They Long to Be Close to You" were put to tape, the first with Karen singing in a style similar to that of Harry Nilsson. The result sounded too contrived and was forcibly accenting the word "you." For the second attempt Alpert suggested Jack Daugherty bring in pianist Larry Knechtel and drummer Hal Blaine. "I was Herb's drummer with the Tijuana Brass," Blaine explains. "He had a lot of faith in me." Alpert felt Karen's drumming lacked the muscle of competitive Top 40 records and knew Blaine would add the desired power for this recording. Agnes Carpenter did not agree. Karen, barely twenty, and Richard, soon to be twenty-four, still lived under her roof, where she kept close tabs on all their activities, both personal and professional. When she got word that Karen had been replaced by Blaine, she let him know of her displeasure. "I've seen so many drummers on television," Agnes told him, "and Karen's as good as any of them."

"Karen is a wonderful drummer," he explained. "The problem is she doesn't have the studio experience that some of us have."

This did little to appease Agnes, who was quick to praise her daughter when put on the defensive, but Blaine was not concerned with the parents. He was confident knowing Karen was happy having him in the studio, and that was all that mattered to him. "She had a lot of respect for me," Blaine says. "We had an instant professional love affair because she knew everything I'd done, and she loved what I was doing on their records."

Although Blaine went on to drum on this and numerous Carpenters records, Knechtel's piano performance proved too forceful for the mood of the song. Richard returned to the keys for a third and final approach. "Hold it, Richard," Blaine interjected during his first Carpenters session. "Where are you going with this tempo?" This stunned Richard, who was accustomed to calling all the shots in the studio.

"What do you mean?" he asked.

"Well, are we going to play the beginning tempo or the middle tempo or the ending tempo? You're kind of running away with it after the intro."

After several attempts with the same result, Jack Daugherty cut in, asking, "Well, what do we do about this?"

Blaine suggested using a click track, which is essentially a metronome marking time in the musicians' headphone mix. Like many artists, the Carpenters considered click tracks to be stifling, often resulting in robotic music. They finally gave in after Blaine explained it to be a reference tempo that need not be followed at every moment of a song. "After that," Blaine says, "they wanted all their songs done with click track."

Herb Alpert was pleased with the third version of "They Long to Be Close to You," and as the recording began to take shape, excitement over the new creation spread throughout A&M. Breaking studio protocol, A&M staffers interrupted sessions and pushed open the doors to studio C to ask, "What is that?" When engineer Ray Gerhardt cranked studio monitors to what he often referred to as "excitement level," the reaction was overwhelming for all involved. "Thank God it didn't fit in the medley," Karen recalled of the song. "That was an instant thing from the minute it hit tape. It was really wild."

Despite the fuss, there was talk of releasing "I Kept on Loving You," a recording with Richard's lead vocal, as the A-side. Sharing both recordings with Frank Pooler's choir, Karen and Richard conducted an informal poll of their college friends. "They played both sides of it for them to see which one they liked best," Pooler says. While "I Kept on Loving You" was radio friendly and consistent with other hit songs of the day, "Close to You" refused to conform to Top 40 trends. As a result, Pooler explains, "The choir applauded more for 'Kept on Loving You.'"

Nichols-Williams compositions like "I Kept on Loving You" were frequently appearing as album cuts and B-sides around this time, but the songwriting duo had been hopeful to get an A-side with this second Carpenters single. "It was almost a joke that we'd die in anonymity and never having a hit single," Williams says. "All I wanted was for 'I Kept on Loving You' to be the single until I heard 'Close to You.' They put ours on the B-side, and it was one of the greatest free rides of all time. They were both really fine records, but 'Close to You' just proved to be magical."

IN EARLY 1970, advertising agent Hal Riney hired Beach Boys' lyricist Tony Asher to write a jingle for the Crocker Bank of California.

After Asher broke his arm in a skiing accident he recommended Roger Nichols and Paul Williams for the job. "It actually turned out to be something very different," Williams recalls. "Almost all commercials up to that point had pitch. They had copy, like 'come to our bank' or whatever. For this one they just wanted to show a little short movie of a young couple getting married and riding off into the sunset. They asked Roger and me to write a one-minute song that would accompany that movie." With a budget of three hundred dollars and less than two weeks to write and record the song, Riney provided the songwriters with a bit of inspiration—his own slogan for the soft-sell campaign: "You've got a long way to go. We'd like to help you get there. The Crocker Bank."

Nichols and Williams were busy with other projects and put this one aside until just before the deadline. "I came in that morning and was working on the tune," Nichols says. "Paul came in a little after that, and within ten minutes he had written the first verse." Williams grabbed an envelope and scribbled on the back:

We've only just begun to live
White lace and promises
A kiss for luck and we're on our way

Within a half hour they had written two one-minute jingles. After the original commercials aired, Crocker Bank executives wished to give copies of the song to their employees and asked the songwriters to make it a complete song. "We finished the complete song as an afterthought," Williams says. "When we put all the copy together and added a bridge we had the song. You can see some imperfection in the rhyme scheme in the third verse. It doesn't rhyme like it's supposed to. 'Grow' and 'begun' don't rhyme like they should because that was actually the first verse of the second commercial."

It was after a late-night recording session that Richard Carpenter caught the Crocker Bank commercial on television. Recognizing Paul Williams's lead vocal he figured it had to be a Nichols-Williams tune. "We got two phone calls right away," Williams says. "The first was from Mark Lindsay and the second from Richard."

Richard immediately went to the publishing offices on the A&M lot and picked up a reference disc of the demo. Playing it in their road manager's office, he was ecstatic to hear the bridge and third verse. He took the lead sheet to their next rehearsal where the group put together their arrangement. "It was about borrowing money, but for Pete's sake it was a great thought," Karen remarked in a 1970 interview. "I compliment the bank for having that much awareness of what's going on."

So taken with "We've Only Just Begun" were the Carpenters that they considered holding back the slated single release of "Close to You." Something about "Begun" stood up and proclaimed itself a hit song, whereas "Close to You" seemed more of a risk. But since "Begun" was still in its embryonic stages and not even put to tape, the single release of "(They Long to Be) Close to You" went as planned for May 1970. Richard felt the title was too wordy and opted for this parenthetical variant. "What do you think it's going to do?" Alpert asked Richard as the two sat on the steps outside A&M Studios.

"As far as I'm concerned," Richard said, "it's either going to be #1 or a monumental stiff. No in-between."

5

YOU PUT US ON THE ROAD

"(THEY LONG to Be) Close to You" entered the Hot 100 at #56, the highest debut of the week ending June 20, 1970. As the record moved up the charts, making stops at #37, #14, #7, and #3, the Carpenters set out to form a permanent "in person" band to travel with and support their live shows. Having recently been appointed principal tuba player with the Detroit Symphony Orchestra, Wes Jacobs weighed two significant opportunities. He could play pop music with the Carpenters or continue pursuing his own dream of playing tuba in a major orchestra. "[Richard] called me, and he basically offered me a lot of money...," Jacobs recalled, "but I realized that I would play the same concert two hundred times a year while touring with the Carpenters instead of two hundred different concerts per year in a symphony. I chose the symphony."

Karen and Richard returned to members of Spectrum in hopes of reassembling the original group to cover additional vocal harmonies. "We can't sing six parts," they explained. "Would you like to come back?"

"No, thanks," said Leslie Johnston, who was still singing lead for another group. "I knew that with the Carpenters I'd just be a backup," she explains. "So they became famous and I didn't!"

Former Spectrum bassist Dan Woodhams did accept the invitation to join the group, as did guitarist Gary Sims following his return from a stint in the Army Reserve. High-spirited college friend Doug Strawn was recruited to play multiple reed instruments. He also sang and had a great musical ear after years of experience fine-tuning chords in various barbershop quartets like the Dapper Dans, who had appeared on *Your All-American College Show* in 1968. Bob Messenger, the introverted and eldest member of the group, was equally adroit on bass guitar, saxophone, and flute. The group assembled was one of multiple talents with a common thread of determination to please Karen and Richard. Each would later learn that was not easy to accomplish, but they remained steadfast in their efforts nonetheless.

John Bettis was managing a club called the Babylon in San Francisco when a patron gave him a copy of *Cashbox* showing "Close to You" at #3 with a bullet. He immediately returned to Los Angeles but did not wish to sing with the group. Instead he signed on as a writer with Almo Publishing for a salary of seventy-five dollars a week. For years he would spend six days a week, fifty-two weeks a year, on the A&M lot. He likened it to Metro-Goldwyn-Mayer in its heyday, only smaller.

The new group spent months rehearsing daily on the A&M soundstage, where they tweaked every nuance and worked to accomplish the optimal mix between microphones and instruments. For the singers, pure, tall, and unified vowel sounds and shapes were of prime importance for the desired blend. Each chord was isolated and tuned. Passages were rehearsed a cappella with each singer trying a different vocal part until the finest balance was achieved. For the earliest gigs, most of which were one-nighters, rented cars and a Ryder truck were the standard means of transportation. Karen, Richard, and the guys in the band would unload, set up, perform, tear down, and reload for each appearance. Family friend Evelyn Wallace was asked to set up a bookkeeping system to keep track of the group's earnings and expenses and began working from the Carpenters' home in order to set up forms, pay bills, and distribute any remaining money between Karen, Richard, and the band.

The Carpenters continued as the opening act in a series of shows for Burt Bacharach, including a run at Westbury Music Fair in New York and a week-long stay at the Greek Theater in Los Angeles. "The five-member group is at its best on whisper-like vocals on their hit and the Beatles' 'Ticket to Ride,'" wrote *Los Angeles Times* music critic Robert Hilburn. "They were far less effective on up-tempo efforts like 'Can't Buy Me Love.' The group received only fair response."

Receiving far more than "fair response" was "Close to You," which was climbing the charts and gaining widespread recognition. As a result the Carpenters were booked to make numerous television appearances as guests of David Frost, Ed Sullivan, and Johnny Carson. Seeing Karen and Richard at the premiere taping of *The Don Knotts Show* during the summer of 1970, college friend Dan Friberg came to understand the magnitude of the duo's newfound stardom. "That was when I knew they were hot stuff," he says. "If I didn't realize it before, I sure did at that point." Following the taping, Friberg went backstage, where Karen called out to him in the hallway, and the two exchanged hugs. "We just found out it went to #1!" she exclaimed.

In just two months the "Close to You" single secured the top spot on the Hot 100, where it stayed for four weeks and quickly sold two million copies. "Everything seems to be going the way we wanted it to be," Karen said in a 1970 interview. "The records are selling like mad, and we're just flipped. It's out of sight, you know. I'm happy.... I think the greatest thing that's happened so far is having the #1 record in the country, having it go over two million records, and having it be the biggest single that A&M Records ever had. I think that's the greatest feeling in the world.... I really don't know what we're going to be doing in five years, but I hope it's the same thing."

SELECTING THE right follow-up single to "Close to You" was of utmost importance. It occurred to Karen and Richard that "Close to You" might be their one and only hit, but they believed strongly in their recording of "We've Only Just Begun," which by then had been completed and was ready for release. An ecstatic Jack Daugherty came to Roger Nichols one afternoon at A&M. "Roger, you've got to hear this song," he said. "I think it's a smash."

Nichols remembers being surprised by his enthusiasm. It was merely a bank commercial. He and Williams certainly never figured it would become a monster hit. "When I heard it I thought I was going to faint," he says. "I still think to this day it's one of the greatest records ever made. I'm not just talking about the song, I'm talking about the record. That record is something else. I just freaked out when I heard it. It was unbelievable."

"Begun" displayed all the great qualities of the Carpenters sound and their capabilities as artists. At only twenty years old, Karen was already showing skill as an instinctive vocalist and a master at phrasing. In one breath she sang, "We've only just begun to live," something most other singers of this song never knew or cared to do. Her delivery was compelling, her interpretation convincing. "The thing about Karen's voice is that it's a strange combination of innocence and sensuality," Williams explains. "She had the sound of a bride when she sang that, so it's innocent and sensual at the same time."

"We've Only Just Begun" was released alongside the *Close to You* album in August 1970 and within eight weeks was at #2 on the Hot 100. The song lingered for four weeks, unable to push the Jackson Five's "I'll Be There" or the Partridge Family's "I Think I Love You" from the top spot. Whether it was #1 or #2 made little difference in the grand scheme of things. "Begun" assured the Carpenters were not one-hit wonders, and it went on to become the wedding song for an entire generation of newlyweds in the 1970s.

Mark Lindsay's recording of "Begun" had been put to tape before the Carpenters', but his remained an album cut. "Mark's was a lovely record," says Paul Williams, "but when people heard Karen sing it, that song belonged to her. It's *her* song."

As the *Close to You* album gained momentum and the group's popularity grew, word of the song "Mr. Guder," written some three years earlier about the Disneyland supervisor of the same name, reached the ears of its inspiration. Victor Guder returned from a hiking trip in the High Sierra to stacks of mail. Picking up a copy of a trade paper he read a review for *Close to You* that mentioned "Mr. Guder" by name. He immediately called his secretary and asked, "Do you guys know anything about this?"

"No, we were waiting for you to read it," she said.

"Well, I'd like to hear the record!"

Obtaining a copy of the LP, Guder shut the door to his office and placed the needle to the vinyl.

Mr. Guder, say, Mr. Guder
Someday soon you may realize
You've blown your life just playing a game
Where no one wins but everyone stays the same

"We were kind of shocked at first," Guder says, "but that's just part of the game we play. When you're working for Disney or working for a public company... you're vulnerable to all that stuff. But you know, it didn't faze us as negative at all. It was done when everybody was kind of anti-establishment, and it was a gimmick they used. They were reflecting the Disney image, 'coat and tie,' 'shine your shoes.' That's what Disney stands for. It was very cleverly written."

Richard later admitted "Mr. Guder" was written out of anger. "Looking back, it's a bit harsh, really...," he explained. "We were a little rebellious and we were finally fired. We wrote this song. But now that the years have gone by and I'm looking back at this, it really wasn't a very nice thing to do because the man was just doing his job."

"Mr. Guder, party of two," a waitress in a Newport Beach restaurant called as Victor Guder and his wife awaited seating. As if on cue, the house band began playing the tune. "We sat there and enjoyed it very much," Guder recalls, "and then had our dinner."

HERB ALPERT was mindful of the Carpenters' inexperience with the music industry and made numerous efforts to surround them with his most trusted friends and associates, many of whom he had known and respected since the beginning of his own success. He showed care and concern for all artists on the roster but seemed especially protective of Karen and Richard. He viewed A&M Records as a family label, as perceived by radio host Dick Biondi, who called it the "White Motown" during a 1970 interview with Karen and Richard. "Every direction we could have gone, we didn't go unless Herbie checked it," explained Karen several years later. "All I can say is thank heavens for Herb Alpert, because he protected us in every way. There aren't a lot of people in this world who would do that."

Shortly after the Carpenters' arrival at A&M in 1969, Alpert had forwarded a copy of their *Offering* album to his manager, Sherwin Bash of BNB Management, and suggested he listen and consider representing the act. "The vocal harmonies, the construction, the thoughts, and the songs were all very good," Bash recalled, "but there was one thing that I thought was very, very special. It was a girl's voice that I'd never heard anything like before and I don't think I've ever heard anything like since. There are so many people in the world today who are good.... Good is not good enough in our business anymore. This was an exceptional voice that was totally identifiable. Listening to that voice for the first time, I knew that radio could never submerge it, camouflage it, or confuse [it for] anybody. That voice coming out of that radio would be immediately identified for the ages."

Karen and Richard met with Sherwin, and it was agreed BNB would represent their professional careers. Ed Leffler drew the contract on the Carpenters and was assigned to supervise the act. This especially pleased Karen, who had developed a bit of a crush on the handsome gentleman. Leffler was equally charmed but by Karen's talents. "I hadn't seen him this excited in a long, long time," says Frenda Franklin, Leffler's wife at the time. "Eddie came home and said, 'Oh my God, there's something you've just got to hear. You're just not going to believe this!'"

When the Lefflers drove to Santa Monica one evening to see the Carpenters perform in a small club, Frenda was equally entranced by Karen's vocal abilities. "They got up on this little stage," she recalls, "and all of a sudden this sound came out. I was just dumbfounded. It was unbelievable. She had something that just pulled you in."

But after meeting Karen, Frenda was not as impressed with her personality. "I didn't like her much," she says. "I thought she acted like a spoiled brat. She wasn't particularly friendly to me either, but I was used to that. If you're around show business a lot it is like that. Karen was the only girl in the band, and I remember thinking, 'My God, she's so rough around the edges!' She was very much a tomboy. Actually, 'tomboy' would be putting it mildly. She always had this façade so nobody could get through."

BY THE fall of 1970 the Carpenters were the hottest young act in the recording industry, with two hit singles and a hit album on its way up the charts. Capitalizing on the duo's newfound popularity, A&M Records reissued the Carpenters' debut album, *Offering*, with a new cover and title, *Ticket to Ride*. Sales of that record quickly soared to over 250,000 copies. Between December 1969 and December 1970, the Carpenters' personal appearance fee jumped from two figures to five figures. Additionally, the first royalty check from A&M Records arrived in the amount of fifty thousand dollars. "I'd never seen anything like that check in my life," Karen said. "We stared at it all through dinner. That is when you start noticing a change. You feel the same inside. You're the same person, but when you've been through the sort of financial situation we grew up with, you realize you have an awful lot of money."

Although the Carpenters had three gold records—the "Close to You" single, *Close to You* album, and "We've Only Just Begun"—they still lived on Fidler Street in Downey in a $27,000 house. In search of a new home, Agnes, Evelyn Wallace, and real estate agent Beverly Nogawski spent several days driving around the residential neighborhoods on Downey's northeast side. The only orders from Karen and Richard were that the new house must be big and have a swimming pool. The ladies were especially taken with a newly constructed home situated on a cul-de-sac near the San Gabriel River. With no FOR SALE sign in the yard or anything suggesting the sprawling split-level ranch-style home was on the market, Nogawski knocked on the door and brazenly asked the owners to sell their house. "I've got people interested," she told them. The owner, who happened to be the home's builder, was in the process of separating from his wife, and their divorce was imminent. After much discussion they agreed to sell.

On Thanksgiving Day 1970 Harold, Agnes, Richard, and Karen left their house in south Downey and settled into their new $300,000 real estate investment located at 9828 Newville Avenue. The five-bedroom house was huge compared to their previous residence but still quite modest in relation to the fame that awaited them. Reporting on their investment, *Forbes* magazine called it the duo's "suburban dream home," and the details of "chez Carpenter" were published in a 1971 A&M Records press release.

> The home—which they themselves designed and decorated, with the help of an interior decorator—was made for comfort, relaxation and precisely those leisure-time activities they prefer. The living room is a bastion of tranquil elegance. It's decorated in cool colors— white, blue, green—and lavished with velvet, crystal and glass. The dining room is ideal for California meals: it features a glass-top table elegantly supported by a carved wood base. The Spanish-style den is stunningly fabric'd in black and red and ocelot, and features a pool table over which Richard and Karen spend many hours poking cues. To facilitate another favorite sport of the Carpenters, there's a big swimming pool, and there are plans for the building of a fish pond. For an ace cook like Karen, the kitchen of the new house is a dream come true: there's everything in the way of household conveniences from a trash-masher down to "a refrigerator that shoots ice cubes."

Karen selected one of four upstairs bedrooms but was appalled by the gaudy wallpaper and proceeded to redecorate in shades of yellow and black. The king-sized bed and its black fur bedspread became home to her overflowing collection of stuffed animals. "They all have names," she told *Teen* magazine a year later. "That's Gru-pig and there's Marsh-field," she said, pointing to a checkered pig and oversized pink dog.

Richard claimed the large master bedroom downstairs, but Agnes objected. "No, you bought this for us," she said. "You told us you were going to buy us a house, so it's ours. We get this bedroom." He settled for two of the rooms across the hall from Karen's and tore out a wall to create one large space.

Many of the duo's music industry associates wondered why two budding superstars would choose to stay in Downey and live at home with their parents when they could be on their own enjoying the fruits of their labor somewhere nearer to Hollywood. "We can live a normal life here," Karen explained in 1972. "Roam around, do whatever we like. Everyone knows who we are everywhere we go, but here they don't bother us. Sometimes cars pass slowly by the house and people look in, but we expect that. Our friends are here from school—the kids Rich went to college with and my high school friends."

Karen and Richard justified the decision saying they were on the road so much it would make no sense to leave a house sitting empty. In truth it was easier to stay, and neither wanted to rock the boat. Both felt a great obligation to their parents for their support during their formative years. Agnes had been laid off from North American Aviation several years earlier, and Harold was still working his printing job. He retired only when it became obvious his children's success was enduring. YOU PUT US ON THE ROAD was Karen's needlepoint inscription to her parents in a design that illustrated a yellow brick road leading to an emerald dollar sign.

To keep their new residence tidy, Agnes was encouraged to hire a housekeeper. Beverly Nogawski suggested her own employee, Florine Elie, who lived in nearby Compton. Florine's cleanliness and work ethic won even Agnes's approval, and for the next quarter century Elie spent five days a week working for the family. Even so, she admits she was never a real fan of their music: "I'm a Pentecostal person. I just listened to gospel music."

MANAGERS SHERWIN Bash and Ed Leffler soon discovered numerous red flags within the Carpenters' accounting records. They found that Agnes Carpenter had taken charge of her children's finances and essentially put Karen and Richard on an allowance. According to Bash, "Even though they were making hundreds of thousands of dollars, they were treated by their parents—especially their mother—as if they were still children at home and on an allowance. The allowance part didn't bother me, but not having someone who was sophisticated in the handling of monies, tax consequences, and contracts did. It was an area I knew would become a serious problem for the two of them."

Going through what Sherwin called a "library full of bank books" they realized Agnes had opened numerous savings accounts in banks all over Downey and throughout the surrounding area. She had been careful to see that the accounts never exceeded the maximum amount insured by the government. When one account reached its limit she would move on to another bank and open a new account. Evelyn Wallace was juggling as many as five different checkbooks at a time and all the while trying to reserve adequate funds for taxes, but there was no formula in use. She would simply set aside extra funds in hopes it would suffice at tax time. The job quickly became too much for her to handle, and she asked the Carpenters to hire a professional accountant. But Agnes was paranoid. She had heard too many stories of managers and accountants running off with their stars' money and was confident her children's finances would be safe if left in her control.

Management finally called a meeting with Karen, Richard, and their parents, during which Sherwin and Ed explained the desperate need for sophisticated and scrupulous supervision as far as their finances were concerned. "When you start earning millions of dollars you need professional guidance," they were told.

Enter attorney and financial advisor Werner Wolfen of the Law Offices of Irell and Manella. Wolfen had been in charge of Herb Alpert's investments for years and came highly recommended. "He made himself known as the boss," recalls Wallace. "He assured everyone he was going to make the kids rich, and the rest of us were told to do whatever we were told to do to make it happen." Agnes left the table during that first meeting with Wolfen. She refused to talk to him and communicated through handwritten notes. "It took some doing," Bash recalled, "because Agnes felt it was a personal attack and didn't realize it was for everybody's good. Eventually she allowed professional attorneys and accountants to prevail."

The accounting firm of Gelfand, Rennert, and Feldman had the arduous task of cleaning up the financial mess they inherited. Luckily Evelyn had documented everything in her well-intentioned but amateur bookkeeping practices. She was relieved of her accounting duties but continued to work for the Carpenter family in the capacity of secretary, assisting Harold Carpenter in sifting through and replying to what quickly became a barrage of fan mail. By the end of 1971, the Carpenters Fan Club consisted of more than ten thousand members.

Werner Wolfen went on to make other financial recommendations and helped the Carpenters manage their newfound wealth by investing in real estate. Newville Realty Company, a joint partnership for Karen and Richard, was formed, and with the help of Beverly Nogawski they set out to purchase two apartment houses located at 8353 and 8356 East Fifth Street in Downey, site of the old Downey Hospital. Tex McAlister, the owner and builder, named the apartments the Geneva in honor of his mother, Geneva, who'd died in the hospital some time earlier. "The Carpenters asked if I would mind if they changed the name to 'Close to You' and 'Only Just Begun,'" he recalls. "I said 'No, not at all. They're yours. You can do what you want with them now.'" Tex and his wife, Charlene, became close friends of the Carpenter family after this first business transaction. Shortly thereafter, the McAlisters built their own house on Newville Avenue across from the Carpenter home.

IN NOVEMBER 1970, the search was on for what would become the Carpenters' next single. In Toronto, where the Carpenters were set to open three weeks of shows for Engelbert Humperdinck, Sherwin Bash suggested that the group go out and enjoy their last free evening. "Why don't you just get your minds off your business?" he said. "Go see this movie I saw called *Lovers and Other Strangers*."

While watching the film, a melody in the underscore caught Richard's attention. The song was "For All We Know," written for the movie's wedding scene. Richard immediately called the office at A&M and asked that a lead sheet be waiting for him upon his return to Los Angeles. Although credited to Fred Karlin, Robb Wilson, and Arthur James, Wilson and James were actually pen names for Robb Royer and James Griffen, members of the pop group Bread.

The Carpenters were also offered "(Where Do I Begin) Love Story" from *Love Story* but were hesitant to record two successive movie themes. They passed on "Love Story" and chose to record and release "For All We Know," which went on to win the Oscar for Best Original Song that year. Though the chart performance of the Carpenters' single was responsible for most of the song's popularity, Academy rules prevented the Carpenters from performing on the telecast since they had never appeared in a film, and the song was assigned to Petula Clark.

The offer of yet another movie theme came in March 1971 during a recording session at A&M when engineer Ray Gerhardt pressed the talkback button and said, "Richard, Stanley Kramer's on the phone for you."

"*Sure!*" Richard looked at Karen with a sarcastic expression. He went into the booth, picked up the phone, and realized it truly was the legendary filmmaker (*Judgment at Nuremburg, Guess Who's Coming to Dinner*) calling to offer the Carpenters the opportunity to record the title song on the soundtrack of his upcoming film *Bless the Beasts and Children*. Kramer agreed to meet Karen and Richard in Las Vegas where they were set to open for comedian Don Adams at the Sands in what became their final stint as an opening act. Richard dreaded the idea of meeting with Stanley Kramer because chances were slim the song would be a fit with the Carpenters and their style. Pleasantly surprised by the work of the film's composers, Barry De Vorzon and Perry Botkin Jr., he and Karen accepted the offer and recorded "Bless the Beasts and Children" in a matter of days to meet Kramer's deadline.

The Carpenters' first major recognition within the music industry came on the evening of March 16, 1971, at the Thirteenth Annual Grammy Awards. Filmed at the Hollywood Palladium, the show was the first Grammy ceremony to be broadcast live via television. Karen and Richard won for Best New Artist and were especially thrilled to take home a second Grammy for Best Contemporary Performance by a Duo, Group, or Chorus, a category in which they were nominated alongside the Jackson Five, Simon and Garfunkel, Chicago, and the Beatles.

THE SEARCH for hit songs continued in early 1971 as Richard sat down with a stack of demos from A&M's publishing houses, Almo and Irving.

His attention was captured by another Roger Nichols–Paul Williams tune. In spite of the demo's sparse instrumentation, Richard was taken with the song's lyrical hook.

Hangin' around
Nothin' to do but frown
Rainy days and Mondays always get me down

By second listen Richard was certain it was a perfect song for Karen, especially with its melancholy and plaintive melody. The opening line—"Talking to myself and feeling old"—was inspired by Williams's mother. "She used to talk to herself," he says. "She was a sweet little old lady who smoked cigarettes and had a little drink every night. She used to walk through the room mumbling and would swear under her breath. I would ask, 'What the hell's wrong, Mom?' She'd say, 'Oh, you wouldn't understand. You're too young. I'm just old. I'm feeling old.' That's how far away from the Carpenters that the lyric began. It was something from out of my own past."

Along with Roger Nichols, Williams went into the studio as the Carpenters' recording of "Rainy Days and Mondays" was taking shape. There they listened as Bob Messenger tracked his saxophone solo. "I think my face just fell off my skull," Williams says. "That's the greatest record I've heard of one of my songs. From the harmonica intro to the last notes it just made me crazy. When Karen sang it you heard the sadness and the loneliness. For me, listening to her sing that song is almost like a bridge from what was contemporary to the roots of the emotion, back to a Billie Holiday kind of thing. It's just a classic."

As good as "Rainy Days and Mondays" was, Nichols says Karen preferred another of his and Paul's songs she had recorded. She wanted "Let Me Be the One" to be the next Carpenters single. After hearing their arrangement of "Rainy Days," Nichols pleaded, "'Rainy Days and Mondays,' *please!*" He hoped they would hold off on "Let Me Be the One," at least temporarily.

In the summer of 1971 Paul Williams treated his mother to a European vacation. He remembers she was not impressed with the desolation she saw in Germany and was pleasantly surprised to see beautiful flowers in all the window boxes as they crossed into France. Just then, "Rainy Days and Mondays" played over the car radio. "It was the first time we'd ever heard it on the radio, and my mother started crying," he says. "I was hearing Karen singing 'talking to myself and feeling old,' and the woman who gave me the line—the woman who raised me—was sitting behind me, and she didn't even know. Once I told her she laughed and said, 'Oh, I don't talk to myself. You're crazy!'"

"Rainy Days and Mondays" was held out of the #1 spot by Carole King's double A-side single featuring "It's Too Late" and "I Feel the Earth Move." Perhaps a double A-side featuring both "Rainy Days" and "Let Me Be the One" would have pushed the Carpenters to the top of the chart. Instead, the latter never saw release as a single. According to Williams, "Let Me Be the One" has never been a hit, despite its popularity. "It's one of those songs that everybody's recorded, but it's never been a single. It was used very briefly by ABC-TV in 1976. 'Let us be the one you turn to / Let us be the one you turn to / When you need someone to turn to / Let us be the one.' It evolved through the years to a whole ad campaign."

In hopes of getting another potential hit song recorded by the Carpenters, Williams set out on his own to write a song specifically for Karen and Richard. What resulted was a Top 10 hit, not for the Carpenters but for Three Dog Night. "I wrote 'Old Fashioned Love Song' for the Carpenters," he says. "I'd heard that one of my songs had gotten on the charts again and just went gold, so I said to this girl I was dating, 'The kid did it again with another old-fashioned love song.' I sat down at her piano and in about twenty minutes wrote 'Old Fashioned Love Song.' It's real simple. I ran in and did a demo of it and sent it over to Richard, and I don't think he even listened to it all the way through at the time. They didn't love it as I had figured they would so I sent it to Three Dog Night." Later rethinking their dismissal of the song, Karen and Richard performed it in a medley with Carol Burnett on her television series in 1972.

⎯⎯⎯⎯⎯ ∞∞∞ ⎯⎯⎯⎯⎯

Arriving home relatively early after a recording session at A&M Records, Karen went to bed while Richard sat down to watch *The Tonight Show* with Johnny Carson. The musical guest was newcomer Bette Midler, performing a song about a groupie who longs for one more tryst with her rock star. Originally titled "Groupie," its roots go back to Rita Coolidge, who gave songwriter Leon Russell the basic idea for its theme. Coolidge joined Russell and the song's cowriter, Bonnie Bramlett (of Delaney and Bonnie), on Joe Cocker's *Mad Dogs and Englishmen* tour where she performed it. By tour's end it had been renamed with the simple yet dramatic one-word title: "Superstar."

Although Karen had heard "Superstar" on a promo copy of the *Mad Dogs and Englishmen* live album, Midler's performance was Richard's first exposure, and he immediately heard its potential. It was understated and backed only by piano, a contemporary twist to the classic torch song style. He was especially taken with the song's hook, perhaps even catchier than that of "Rainy Days and Mondays."

Don't you remember you told me you loved me baby
You said you'd be coming back this way again baby
Baby, baby, baby, baby, oh, baby
I love you, I really do

As Midler's "Superstar" came to an end, Richard ran through the house and bounded up the stairs. "I've found *the tune*," he told Karen.

"That's nice," she said after hearing the song.

"*Nice?*"

This was one of only a few times Karen was known to have objected to a song selected for her by Richard. But even in this case, she eventually agreed to record "Superstar," although she did so begrudgingly. It was only after hearing the finished product that she heard what Richard had in mind all along. According to Frank Pooler, "Richard was the brains behind the Carpenters. Karen did what she was told."

Karen's vocal track on "Superstar" was her work lead, the first "take" to familiarize the other musicians with the song. Not only that, she read the words from a paper napkin on which Richard had scribbled the lyric as the session began. Knowing the song would never find a place on Top 40 radio stations with the lyric "I can hardly wait to *sleep* with you again," the Carpenters opted for the more radio friendly "*be* with you again." The song's publishers were delighted with the word change and told Richard how that singular line had kept numerous artists from recording the song.

The intensity and emotion in Karen's voice led many to assume she was an "old soul" and wise beyond her years. In a 1972 interview she explained how she delivered such a convincing performance on a song like "Superstar" though it dealt with subject matter she had never experienced. "I've seen enough groupies hanging around to sense their loneliness, even though they usually don't show it," she explained. "I can't really understand them, but I just tried to feel empathy, and I guess that's what came across in the song."

According to Frank Pooler, "When Karen sang, it sounded like she had experienced all this stuff. She couldn't possibly have experienced all that; she was too young. There's a difference between being a singer and having a fine voice. Good singers can have average voices, but there's something about the word communication. That she had. You felt like she was singing it for the first time and only for you."

It was Rod Stewart's "Maggie May / Reason to Believe" single that held "Superstar" a spot shy of #1 this time. It remained at #2 for two weeks, a frustrating location for Karen and Richard and one they had grown accustomed to. The flip side, "Bless the Beasts and Children," also charted at a respectable #67 and was nominated for a Best Original Song Oscar at the Academy Awards.

It seemed as though Bette Midler might have been miffed by the Carpenters' success with "Superstar," the song she introduced to the duo, as she began to poke fun at Karen's goody-two-shoes image during her live act. "She's so white she's invisible!" she would say, but Karen took it all in stride, claiming that it was a tribute. Besides, as she pointed out, the gold record for "Superstar" was on the Carpenters' wall, not Bette's.

Midler curtsied sarcastically to Karen when the Carpenters presented her with a Grammy for Best New Artist in 1974. "Me and Miss

Karen!" she exclaimed. "What a hoot. I'm surprised she didn't hit me over the head with it!"

The two visited with each other at a Grammy after-party. "We got along fine," Karen recalled in an interview later that year. "Bette said, 'I don't know what I'm gonna do now that we're friends.' She's funny as heck.... She likes to pick on me, but I think that's just a good showbiz bit for her."

Returning to the Grammys as presenter the following year, Bette recalled the event in her monologue. "It was only a year ago that Karen Carpenter crowned me the Best New Artist of the year," she told the audience. "If that ain't the kiss of death, honey, I don't know what is."

THE DAYS of the Carpenters performing as an opening act were over. On May 14, 1971, they headlined a sold-out concert at New York City's legendary Carnegie Hall, where Karen and the group performed an already impressive set of their hits in succession. "Rainy Days and Mondays" and "For All We Know" received immediate and enthusiastic response from the audience, who knew their songs word-for-word. "Karen Carpenter has one of those magical voices," wrote Nancy Erlich for *Billboard* in her review from Carnegie Hall. "There are maybe three of them among all the ladies in pop music that create a direct line of communication with their very tone. Words and music are secondary; there is always that quality that comes through."

The concert was a homecoming of sorts, with family and friends from nearby New Haven in attendance. For most, this was their first reunion with the duo in eight years. Karen and Richard were honored with a party thrown at the home of their cousin Joanie and her husband, Hank Will. Though the guest list was small, the gathering became more of an event as word spread that the Carpenters were in town. Festivities were moved outdoors to accommodate a crowd of more than a hundred attendees. "I never really saw Karen as a celebrity," says Frank Bonito, who visited with her that day. "Even when I attended her concerts, I enjoyed them, but it was the time backstage before the concert or at a party afterwards that I enjoyed most. We would just sit and talk and catch up on each other's lives. Karen never flaunted her wealth and position. She actually downplayed it and was always sincerely interested in what was happening in my life. She wanted to know about old school friends and teachers, and she maintained a wonderful childlike quality about herself."

The Carpenters' eponymous album, often referred to as the *Tan Album* (perhaps a nod to the Beatles' *White Album*), was released the same day as the Carnegie Hall concert. It was the first of a string of Carpenters albums to "ship gold," which at the time indicated presales of more than a million copies. But just as Carole King held "Rainy Days and Mondays" out of the #1 spot on *Billboard*'s Hot 100, her epic *Tapestry* LP shut out *Carpenters* on the album charts, too, where it peaked at #2.

Upon returning to Los Angeles, Karen and Richard began taping a summer replacement series for NBC Television the last week of May 1971. "Make Your Own Kind of Music" was a popular recording by Mama Cass and became the theme for this television variety hour that aired Tuesday nights in the eight o'clock time slot usually occupied by *The Don Knotts Show*. "Karen was a mic singer," recalls Allyn Ferguson, who served as a musical supervisor on the series. He remembers her to be quite shy and says she sang very close to the microphone with a "tiny" voice. "She would have never been OK on a musical stage," he says. "You would not be able to hear her at all if you were thirty or forty feet away because she didn't project at all. She understood how to sing on a microphone, and that brought a sort of intimacy to everything she did."

Ferguson was impressed with the duo's unpretentious demeanor. "You work with a lot of people, like Mama Cass. She was really tough to work with. The Carpenters were very nice to work with. There were no big problems, no egos involved or anything. They just liked to do what they did and were very closely connected in their work." In addition to working with regulars Al Hirt, Patchett and Tarses, Mark Lindsay, and the New Doodletown Pipers, Karen and Richard were introduced to many popular entertainers during the eight days of tapings. Mac Davis, Jose Feliciano, Anne Murray, Helen Reddy,

Dusty Springfield, B. J. Thomas, and the Fifth Dimension were among those booked as guests on the series. The Fifth Dimension and Carpenters traded guest spots, with Karen and Richard performing as part of that group's *Traveling Sunshine Show* television special, which was also broadcast that summer.

A review for *Make Your Own Kind of Music* in *TV Guide* detailed the gimmick that plagued the series: "Each number is introduced by the labored use of a letter of the alphabet. Twenty-six cringes a week. Did they have in mind a *Sesame Street* for adults? Possibly. But no adult over the age of nine will be either entertained or amused. . . . The musicians on this show are genuinely talented. Why didn't they leave them alone?" Another review, this one in the *Village Voice*, denounced the series's producers and detailed their mistakes, "like dressing Karen Carpenter in fashions only a little less sickeningly sweet than those worn by Trisha Nixon. By the second or third show it was beginning to look like a disaster area. The Carpenters, who are both gifted and likeable, deserve something better."

Despite the benefits of new friendships and professional associations, in addition to heavy publicity for their new LP, the duo's first encounter with television left them discouraged with the medium. It would be another five years before they agreed to host another television show. Interviewed for FM100 some years later, Karen recalled the NBC endeavor as a mistake, saying they were "violently mishandled. Our TV exposure was disastrous. We realized it immediately, and we shied away from television."

6

NOTHING TO HIDE BEHIND

A T JUST five feet, four inches tall, Karen Carpenter was barely visible on stage when surrounded by her battery of drums. "The audience was rising out of their seats to see where this voice was coming from," recalls Evelyn Wallace. "There was no one out front so they were asking, 'Where is that beautiful voice coming from?'"

By 1971, Karen's drum kit had grown to include four melodic toms. "They were built on rollers, and you could roll them right into your four-piece or five-piece kit," explains Hal Blaine, who, along with drum tech Rick Faucher, designed the set Karen used in concert. Howie Oliver of Pro Drum in Hollywood built the kit for her after she saw Blaine's setup. "There are only three kits like mine in the world," she explained in a 1974 piece for *Melody Maker*. "The other two belong to Ringo and Hal Blaine."

Blaine's original set was designed in a way that the sound of each drum decayed with its pitch "bending" slightly at the end. "It started out with me using my timbales as tom-toms and tuning them down," Blaine explains. "I loved that sound, and eventually I wanted an octave of them. I put together this drum set that everybody called the Hal Blaine monster because it was humongous. I knew nothing about design patents in those days, but I was a Ludwig drummer so I sent them all the dimensions. I was sure they'd call it the Hal Blaine set—like the Gene Krupa and the Buddy Rich, but they called it the Octa-Plus. Now that's a fine name, but Ludwig didn't even mention me. They did send me a thank-you letter."

One of Karen's worst nightmares began to unfold during the summer of 1971, one that had been mounting since the Carpenters' earliest concert engagements. "There is no balance, no center of attention," wrote Lester Bangs, reviewing an appearance in San Diego for *Rolling Stone*. "Here are six people on a stage singing and playing various instruments, and your eye just keeps shifting from one to another without ever finding a nexus to focus on."

True, the in-person Carpenters were a disjointed group and in need of a focal point. The obvious solution was to bring the group's musical focus out from isolation and into the spotlight. "Hire a drummer," wrote one music critic in Omaha, Nebraska. "Why stick a lovely girl with a tremendous voice behind a set of traps and have her pump high-hat cymbals and shoot an occasional rim shot when by rights she should be out front moving to the music while she sings?"

Taking cues from the critics, Richard and the Carpenters' management decided Karen's drums were in the way and ultimately disconnecting her from the audience. "You can't sing like that and hide behind a drum set," manager Ed Leffler told her.

Leffler and Sherwin Bash agreed Karen could be showcased more effectively at center stage. "Richard and I tried desperately to get her away from the drums," Bash recalled. "She was very reluctant. The drums were kind of a security blanket for her. This was a chubby young lady who could hide some of that chubbiness behind all of these drums. She was kind of a tomboy, and the drums were traditionally a male instrument. She was kind of asserting herself in a certain way. The girl vocalist out front was a role that she wanted to achieve, but she was insecure about getting out there. She wasn't sure she was slim enough, svelte enough, pretty enough, or any of those things."

In early 1971 Karen responded to suggestions that she should abandon her drums for a solo microphone in the spotlight. "A lot of people think that since I'm the lead singer I should be fronting the group," she said. "I disagree because I think we've got enough chick singers fronting groups. I think that as long as I can play, I want to play."

According to fellow drummer Frankie Chavez, "There weren't that many girls playing in the forefront at the time. It was a very unique thing that a girl could play *and* sing at the same time and do it well on both accounts. It wasn't a smokescreen, she could actually play!"

Richard avoided confronting Karen on several occasions, but their setup posed additional challenges when it came to the medium of television. It was difficult for camera angles, and much attention was needed in order to effectively present Karen and her drum kit for each sequence. During the filming of *Make Your Own Kind of Music* it was recommended that she stand to sing some selections. "Oh, no, no, no, no, no," she told them. "I'm the drummer here." But the directors were looking for variety in the sequences and felt watching someone sing from behind the drums was odd and would get old after a few numbers.

"Karen wasn't as concerned that people would be able to see her," explains Evelyn Wallace. "It was that she was absolutely in love with those drums, and she just didn't want to leave them. But she finally gave in. The poor kid didn't know what to do." Having been the group's only drummer, Karen had played exclusively for the first two years of live Carpenters performances. It is no wonder she lacked confidence to step into the spotlight and was reluctant to embrace the role of "star" of the group. Richard had long been the musical prodigy, and she was his tagalong. "Karen was really an *accident*," explains Frenda Franklin. "I don't think the family really understood her talent. Nobody got it. Nobody thought she was a good singer. Nobody nurtured her singing. To them she was backup."

Allyn Ferguson, who worked with Karen on the set of the television series, says her poise and self-assurance took a dive when she was singing center stage without her drums. "Her confidence was sitting behind those drums," he says. "It was a part of her, and she was a damn good drummer. When she was not behind the drums her confidence and her security just disappeared. She didn't seem to care much for her own singing. When she had to do a solo out front she was very uncomfortable and showed no confidence. She didn't know whether she was any good or not. She was not a stand-up singer in any way because she didn't believe in herself that way." For *Make Your Own Kind of Music*

Karen lip-synched the musical numbers without even a prop microphone. With her hands free she made awkward attempts at gestures of emphasis and emotion.

With the television series in postproduction, the Carpenters took a brief hiatus and drove the family's Continental Mark III cross-country to visit family and friends on the East Coast in Baltimore and New Haven. It was during this drive that Richard finally spelled out to Karen the need for her to leave the drums. "You've got to get up," he said.

"I said to Richard, 'Oh, no you don't,'" she recalled. "It hurt me that I had to get up and be up front. I didn't want to give up my playing. Singing was an accident. Singing seriously came long after the drums." The two finally reached a compromise in which Karen agreed to step out front to sing ballads like "For All We Know" and "Superstar." In return, she could remain at the drums to play on the more up-tempo, rhythmic numbers like "Mr. Guder." Before leaving New Haven, Richard hired the band's new drummer, longtime friend Jim Squeglia, whom he had once played alongside in a band called the Scepters during high school. Touring with the Carpenters, Squeglia would take on the stage name of Jim Anthony, his first and middle names.

Appearing on *The Mike Douglas Show* the following month, Karen announced her plans. "In the middle of our in-person show I'm going to go out front and do some tunes," she said. "I'm never going to give up playing, no way....I love it. I wouldn't be doing it if I didn't. People think it's a gimmick. I don't care what they think; it's not a gimmick. It's my instrument."

Out front, Karen was unsure of herself, to say the least. She was rigid, uncomfortable, and incapable of disguising her fears. "Petrified," she recalled in 1976 of her initial reaction to the switch. "You have no idea. The fear! There was nothing to hold onto, nothing to hide behind. My drums, by this time, I had so many of them all you could see were my bangs. You couldn't see the mouth, you couldn't see the hands, you couldn't see anything. We're out on the road and we're doing all the hits and the dummy is buried behind a full set of drums."

Frankie Chavez feels certain that it was torture for Karen to have been removed from her drum kit. "That broke her heart when she couldn't do both from behind the kit and had to go out front," he says. "It's different being out front. I've done both, and being out front it's as if your tether has been cut. There's a certain joy you get from playing the kit that you'd miss if you were asked to not do it anymore."

"I didn't know what to do," Karen later explained. "My mouth still worked well, but I didn't know what to do with my hands or whether to walk or stand still or sit down or what the heck to do. Before, everything was working. It was a cinch to play and sing and have a good time. But when I got out there, until I got comfortable with that, I just kind of planted myself and didn't really do anything."

With each successive tour, Karen's role as the group's drummer lessened as new drummer Jim Anthony took over on more and more songs. "I understood her reluctance," said Sherwin Bash, "but the moment we were finally able to get her out there it was all part of history. She loved being out front. She was basically the master of ceremonies for every show. She was the one that people watched. Richard never had the charisma to keep the audience's attention. It didn't matter. Even when he was speaking you didn't take your eyes off Karen."

WATCHING TELEVISION late one night in the fall of 1971, Richard came across a 1940 movie called *Rhythm on the River*, in which Bing Crosby played the ghostwriter for a washed-up songwriter named Oliver Courtney. Courtney's most famous song, "Goodbye to Love," was mentioned throughout the film but never heard. Richard was immediately taken with the title and imagined an opening line of it as a potential song: "I'll say goodbye to love / No one ever cared if I should live or die." At that point his lyric stopped.

Handing the song idea over to John Bettis, Richard and the group set off on a brief European tour. Writing of the song continued little by little with the choral ending written in London and additional work being done once they reached Berlin. "Richard didn't have the melody completely finished," Bettis recalled. "He had a verse or two but didn't quite know how he was going to form it. It's an odd melody with very long phrases. The song was tricky because of the phrasing."

Returning to the States with Bettis's contributions, Richard sat down with "Goodbye to Love" and came up with a novel idea. In constructing the arrangement he imagined the unlikely sound of a melodic fuzz guitar solo. Jack Daugherty suggested they bring in an established session guitarist and recommended Louie Shelton or Dean Parks, but Richard was relying on Daugherty less and less by this time and chose to contact a young member of Instant Joy, a band that backed Mark Lindsay's opening act for several Carpenters concerts. Karen phoned guitarist Tony Peluso, explained the project, and asked him to meet her and Richard at A&M's studio B.

Peluso was tall and thin. His hair was long and unkempt, halfway down his back. It seemed a mismatch at first. Even he was apprehensive and unsure the combination would work effectively. He could not read music but was a quick study, and when Richard gave him a chord sheet with instructions to play the melody on the first couple of bars and then improvise, the recording was complete in only two takes. The result was one of the first known uses of a fuzz tone guitar solo on a ballad. "When I got the record I actually cried the first time I heard it," John Bettis recalled. "I had never heard an electric guitar sound like that and have very few times since. Tony had a certain almost cello-sounding guitar growl that worked against that wonderful melancholia of that song. The way it growls at you, especially at the end, is unbelievable. It may be my favorite single I've ever had with anybody."

Within weeks of the radio debut of "Goodbye to Love," the Carpenters began receiving what amounted to hate mail from fans who felt the song desecrated the group's image with the incorporating of a grungy-sounding guitar. "That was the first ballad ever done with any sort of rock and roll sensibility," Bettis explained. "Aggressive electric guitar the way it was beginning to be used. There was a schism in instrumentation. It's a watershed record, sonically, because Richard put two disparate worlds together. There was a legion of Carpenters fans that wasn't ready for that, but I think it also garnered new fans."

By mid-1972, Peluso had accepted an offer to become a full-fledged member of the Carpenters' touring band. As the entourage grew to fourteen, the need for adequate transportation was filled with the acquisition of two Learjets, aptly named *Carpenter 1* and *Carpenter 2*, which were used to travel between one-nighters. It was on one such trip that Bettis came up with the song title "Top of the World." According to the lyricist, "When I got in the plane and took off I thought, 'Are we on top of the world now or what? Look at this!' I saw the visual symbolism. I was at the top of the world. I took the title and wrote it with another guy, Kerry Chater. The song never came to be anything. Somehow Richard came in contact with the title again and remembered it from the airplane experience."

Resuming work with Richard, Bettis came up with what he considered to be "the best rhyme scheme I ever executed with the Carpenters. I don't know whether anybody's ever noticed, but that was a tricky rhyme scheme to keep up: 'In the leaves on the trees / And the touch of the breeze / There's a pleasin' sense of happiness for me.'"

The Carpenters recorded "Goodbye to Love" and "Top of the World" for what became their *A Song for You* album released in June 1972. Richard heard the title song on Leon Russell's debut album and felt it would be well suited to their style. "A Song for You" is considered by many to be a contemporary standard and has since been recorded by a range of artists from Willie Nelson to Michael Bublé. The haunting melody and touching lyric combined for one of Karen's finest performances, but, although figured to be a single, it was overlooked because of its duration; it was considered to be too long for Top 40 radio. Stephen Holden of *Rolling Stone* took notice and called it "far and away the album's finest moment. It is a great song that is rapidly achieving the classic status it deserves, and Karen communicates its poignancy with effortless serenity."

Also on the album was "Hurting Each Other," which Richard first heard on KRLA in 1969. Incidentally, it was an A&M Records release by Ruby and the Romantics and one that he later came across in the stockroom on the lot shortly after having signed with the label. He played it, put it away, and was reminded of it again in 1971 while playing arbitrary chord changes on his electric piano during a sound check. His up-tempo-to-ballad formula (à la "Ticket to Ride") worked again, and "Hurting Each Other" became the Carpenters' next hit single.

Nilsson's "Without You" held the #1 spot this time as "Hurting" tried for two weeks to break through. It was the Carpenters' fourth #2 single but the sixth in a string of #1 hits on the Adult Contemporary chart.

Almost as random a discovery was "It's Going to Take Some Time." Richard first heard the song on a quad test pressing of Carole King's *Music* LP played by the engineers installing the Carpenters' new quadraphonic sound system at Newville in the fall of 1971.

Roger Nichols and Paul Williams considered "I Won't Last a Day Without You" to be a complete song with just two verses and a chorus, just as they submitted it to the Carpenters on a demo in 1971. They struggled to honor Karen's last-minute request for an additional bridge and third verse. "We finally worked it out and went in and did the demo the day before they recorded it," Nichols recalls. "They were screaming at us to get it to them and were upset with us because they were right down to the wire in the studio. What bothered me was that I heard Richard never even listened to the demo. He just looked at the sheet music and started changing it. It was kind of a sore point with me because he changed the melody in the bridge and the chord structure. After that, other people heard our version of the song—like Barbra Streisand and Diana Ross—and they all recorded the version as we had written it. I always felt that if the Carpenters had cut a better bridge it would have been a bigger song for them."

Sadly, the Nichols-Williams partnership came to an end in 1972, shortly after the Carpenters' release of *A Song for You*. "Paul wanted to be a star himself," Nichols recalls. "He was taking off and hired managers and lawyers and left me in the dust there. We stopped writing. It just wasn't happening."

The partnership between the Carpenters and producer Jack Daugherty came to an end around this time as well. Richard was enraged to read a review of their latest album in *Cashbox* magazine praising Daugherty's production abilities. Karen and Richard had remained faithful to Daugherty since he helped get their demo into the hands of Herb Alpert three years earlier, but over time this loyalty began to wane. Despite Daugherty's billing as producer, those were Richard's arrangements and Richard's productions. Some called Daugherty the Glenn Miller of the 1970s, but as far as the Carpenters were concerned he was more of an A & R man than a sound architect. He did offer production advice, but most of his time was spent booking studios and musicians, in addition to searching for potential musical material. "In the beginning Jack was the avenue between us and the Carpenters," says Roger Nichols. "He'd always say, 'Have you got anything new? What's happening? Let me hear your songs,' and so on. Later on Richard and Karen really were on the outs with him. Richard didn't need anybody to do that anymore. He felt that he was producing the records and Jack was just putting his name on them."

By 1972 Daugherty had his own secretary at A&M Records and was earning a $25,000 annual salary as staff producer for the label, in addition to his earnings from the sale of every Carpenters record. According to Allyn Ferguson, who worked with Daugherty and the Carpenters, "Jack just took a ride. He got credit for it, but he was not really a producer. He wasn't even at A&M before them. He was just the liaison between the Carpenters and A&M in the beginning, having initially brought them to Herb."

Hal Blaine claims to have stayed out of such politics, but he witnessed similar conflicts between artists and producers over the years. "I spent years with John Denver, and his 'producer' would be fast asleep in a booth. It was the musicians who made the records, but once a group gets rid of the producer and starts saying 'we can make our own records,' that's usually the beginning of the end of the group."

Asked in a 1973 UK press conference what part Daugherty had played in creating the Carpenters sound, Richard responded firmly: "Nothing. That's why he's no longer with us. We produced all those singles. It's a long story, but Jack had nothing to do with anything. He was responsible for getting Herb Alpert to hear our tape, which was very nice, but he wasn't our producer. You'll notice he hasn't had one record on any chart since he left us."

Once terminated, Jack Daugherty took the matter to court, where he claimed that the firing had destroyed his credibility in the music industry. The battle took some nine years to settle, finally going to trial in 1981. Although the court found in favor of A&M and the Carpenters, their defense cost the record company between $350,000 and $400,000. Three years after Daugherty's 1991 death, Michael Daugherty sought to vindicate his father's contributions to the Carpenters' music. "The man who produced the lion's share of the Carpenters' hits was my late father, Jack Daugherty. . . . ," he wrote in a letter to the *Los Angeles Times*. "Richard Carpenter seems intent on trivializing Daugherty's inestimable influence in the creation of the Carpenters' sound. . . . My father would have enjoyed knowing that the sound he fashioned more than twenty years ago continues to be appreciated by so many."

AN UNLIKELY friendship was born when Karen began to reach out more and more to Frenda Franklin. "Can we go shopping sometime?" Karen would ask. Or "Could I go to the hairdresser with you?" Initially Karen had been intimidated by Frenda's affluent lifestyle, fine clothing, and expensive jewelry. She seemed in awe of the woman's sense of style and sophistication. Frenda was five years Karen's senior and over time became her closest confidante and mentor. "Karen became like a baby sister to me," Frenda explains. "We became friends. Slowly."

Karen admitted she had been jealous and apologized to Frenda for having been so impolite when the two first met and begged forgiveness. Frenda was taken aback. She was astonished that someone so supremely gifted and amazingly talented could be jealous of anyone.

"You really don't have any idea, do you?" she said.

"About what?" Karen asked.

"About how good you are. If you did, you wouldn't be jealous of anybody."

Karen refused the compliment, instead reiterating her apologies for having been disrespectful. "Well, you were just *awful*," Frenda confirmed, and the two laughed over what in retrospect seemed insignificant.

Shopping with Frenda on Rodeo Drive and around Beverly Hills, Karen was unsure of the proper etiquette used in such upscale stores and boutiques. She was terribly nervous that she might say or do something inappropriate. "Now Frenny, if I go into a store and I do something wrong you'll tell me, right?" she asked.

"Let's get this straight," Frenda said. "I wouldn't want you to go in there and do a cartwheel, but Karen, they want your *money*!"

As their friendship grew, Frenda became one of the few people in whom Karen placed all confidence. "There were things Karen would never ever tell anyone, but maybe Frenda," recalls Evelyn Wallace. "She talked to Frenda a lot about things that happened with her mother." Around her parents, especially her mother, Karen became nervous about what might be said or done in Frenda's presence. The fact that Franklin came from a large Jewish family did not dissuade Agnes Carpenter from voicing her anti-Semitic opinions around her. Karen would apologize profusely for her mother's words and attempt to explain away the ignorant comments and how they stemmed from Agnes's upbringing.

"On one level, they were very good people," Franklin says of the Carpenter parents. "Harold was the greatest. What a doll. What a sweet, sweet man." Evelyn Wallace agrees, recalling Harold as a quiet man who was nice to everybody. "He was a real sweetheart, and I admired him so much," she says. "Many times I wondered how he could live with that woman the way she used to yell and scream at him. She would jump on him, and he would never ever fight back. He just sat there and took it. He wasn't a sissy but just a real nice guy. Agnes was the speaker, so he wasn't really one to get a word in edgewise."

"Agnes kind of has a mean streak in her sometimes," Harold told Evelyn in the home office one afternoon.

"Yeah, I kind of noticed that!" she said sarcastically.

"Harold wasn't allowed to have an opinion," Frenda says. "Agnes was a bulldozer. In my own way I loved her. She was Karen's mother, and she gave her life. But I was sorry that she had so many prejudices. She used really bad language, too. I'd never known anyone that called somebody the *n*-word. Those things do not go down well with me. I was shocked." The Jackson Five was the target of such talk on several occasions, and Karen was mortified when her mother would make such bigoted comments. She seemed ashamed and wanted very much to dissociate herself from what she saw as dogmatic narrow-mindedness.

"Oh, Frenny, you're still going to be friends with me, right?" she'd ask apprehensively. "You're not going to hold it against me, are you?"

"Kace [a nickname derived from K.C.], of course not," Frenda would tell her again and again. "It's nothing to do with you. Don't be silly."

This reaction from Karen was nothing unusual. She was a people pleaser with a strong desire to keep everyone around her happy, even if it came at her own expense. Her closest friends knew she was sensitive and vulnerable, and neither quality could withstand her mother's brutality. Somewhere along the way Karen had adopted a rugged exterior—an almost masculine facade—to protect herself from her mother's unapologetic harshness. She struggled with femininity, and many who were close to her say Karen always remained childlike, like a little girl who never really grew up or blossomed into a woman. In a 1974 *Rolling Stone* cover story, even Tom Nolan remarked on Karen's perceived immaturity. "Karen is in some ways like a child," he wrote, "which is not surprising. A star since nineteen, a committed musician even longer than that, she probably missed out on one or two normal stages of adaptation to 'the real world.'"

Between the years 1970 and 1975, Sherwin Bash witnessed a gradual transformation in Karen from an immature tomboy to an attractive young woman. He felt it was indeed an effort on her part to break free from the only way of life she had known in hopes of exchanging it for a life she very much desired. In his words, there was "a very strong attempt on Karen's part, whether she was consciously aware of it or not, to find a place for herself in the social strata of young womanhood." This transformation had little to do with her status as an entertainer or celebrity. She was more intent on becoming someone who "had friends, could go out on dates, and have a social life," said Bash. "And I don't believe she ever totally achieved it."

What Bash had sensed was in actuality a concentrated effort on Karen's part to shed her tomboy qualities for a more feminine persona. "She wanted to be a woman," says Frenda, who at Karen's urging assisted in a slow but steady makeover. "She so wanted to be refined. She wanted to be what she called 'uptown.' It sounds so peculiar, but she wanted what she knew she could earn and wanted all the finery that went along with her career. She looked to me for that."

The transformation would not be easy, as Karen had exhibited this tough exterior and guise for most of her life. Having grown up playing baseball with the neighborhood boys, then becoming a drummer and going on tour with an all male band, she walked and talked like one of the guys. "She used to walk across the stage like a Mack truck," Frenda exclaims. "Feminine she wasn't. We had to work on her posture a lot and her walking. . . . I worried about it because I didn't want people to take her the wrong way. That wasn't who she was. That was Karen not wanting to get hurt. I think a lot of it was a cover-up. I really do. If you put up a big, thick wall, and you're kind of a tough guy, you're not going to expose your gentleness."

Karen's makeover from Downey to "uptown" took years. In fact, it was more of a work in progress. "We went from A to Z, as you would with a baby," Frenda explains. "She was such a fast study. It was amazing. I wanted her to put her best foot forward, especially if it was on camera or in an interview. I didn't want her to be afraid and let that 'best offense is a good defense' come right out." Karen respected Frenda and took her directives very seriously. "Sit up straight," she would instruct Karen. "Talk like a lady and act like a lady. Oh, and don't come off like a truck driver!" The two would laugh. Just when Karen seemed to have reached her goal of walking and talking like a lady, according to Frenda, "There were still times the 'Downey' would come back out!"

Karen often borrowed accessories from Frenda's extensive wardrobe to complement her own. Lending her a handbag for an award show appearance, Frenda scrawled with a marker on a small index card and dropped it in the purse. Later that evening, Karen opened the bag and discovered the drawing of two huge eyes and was reminded that her friend was watching her every move and hoping for the best. Also on the card were three letters—G.U.S.—an inside joke between trainer and trainee instructing Karen to "grow up, schmuck!"

"BEING THE only girl makes you the center of attention," Karen explained in a 1971 interview for *Teen* magazine. "Let's face it, any girl likes to get attention, and the guys are all very protective toward me. It's wild, I tell you. I can't make a move. They're always watching out for me." Even so, Karen longed for the companionship of another female while on the road. "Sometimes I feel as if I've got to have another girl to talk to, but that's only natural."

Agnes and friend Beverly Nogawski kept weekly hair appointments every Friday morning at the Magic Mirror, a local beauty shop near the intersection of Firestone and Lakewood boulevards in Downey. "Did you know Karen is looking for somebody to do her hair?" Nogawski asked salon manager Maria Luisa Galeazzi.

"The idea of traveling and going places attracted the wild card in me," says Galeazzi, who accepted an offer from Karen after a brief interview at Newville. "But I didn't know what I was going to get myself into! Karen and I became friends—sort of—but I never really took the initiative to become very personal with her. . . . I didn't stick my nose in anything. If I saw things I just kept quiet. See no evil, hear no evil, speak no evil!"

Richard was immediately attracted to the feisty blond Italian. "He had fallen for Maria before they even left on the tour," recalls Evelyn Wallace. "When she would come to do Karen's hair at the house, the doorbell would ring, and before I had a chance to get up from my desk Richard was down those stairs and at the door."

Galeazzi's first gig was July 7, 1972, at University of Houston, where she went straight to work caring for the group's personal property, from travel clothes to stage outfits and jewelry. "Nothing was out of place, and everything was put away and locked up and ready to go for the next gig," she explains. "I remember the first night. My God, I was scared to death. We were a couple of stories down, way underneath the stadium, and I could barely hear the announcement to get Karen up there." Prior to the concert, an intoxicated fan jumped to the stage and sat down at Karen's drums during the performance by opening act Skiles and Henderson. "Karen, I want to marry you!" he yelled as he pounded on the instruments. The man was apprehended after assaulting a police officer. "Don't touch me!" he shouted as he continued to kick and scream his way off stage. "I'm engaged to Karen Carpenter!" Authorities found wedding rings and airline tickets for the supposed honeymoon once they booked him into the local jail.

Leaving the stadium, Galeazzi was unprepared for the farewell rituals of Carpenters fans, something Karen and Richard were accustomed to by this juncture. "I was not ready for all the fans pulling hair and clothes and trying to get into the car. They were just crazy and making the car jump up and down and everything." Neighbors Tex and Charlene McAlister witnessed the pandemonium as well when they would attend concerts with the Carpenter parents. "It was almost impossible to get out of there after a concert because the kids would go so crazy," Charlene recalls. "We were in a limo with their parents, and the fans all thought that we were Richard and Karen. 'Just raise your hand and wave,' Harold told us. The fans were all over the hood of the car. We ended up being the decoy car, and Richard and Karen were behind. It was just a regular car that nobody even looked at."

One of the more serious scares occurred as the Carpenters prepared for a concert at Oregon State University in Corvallis. As Karen and Maria left their hotel rooms they were attacked by several men and tackled to the ground. "We were walking down the hallway to go to the gig and some gypsies jumped us," Galeazzi recalls. "They came out of another room and jumped us! We were down on the ground. It's a good thing the guys from the band were not far behind us. It was really, really scary."

At times, Frank Bonito and other friends were concerned for Karen's safety and did all they could to preserve her privacy. "We wouldn't let her go to the bathroom alone," he says. "We were always very protective of her. This was around the time Patty Hearst was kidnapped and all that. Richard wasn't noticed as much as Karen was since he wasn't in the forefront." He recalls accompanying Karen to a department store once. "When she had her sunglasses on people would walk on by. Everything was fine until she used her credit card. Then we had to leave the store!"

Most Carpenters fans were kind and respected the duo's space. Others could be almost abusive. Dinner interruptions were frequent, so they would often ask for a private room or at the very least position Karen with her back to the main dining room. "They are quite gracious when asked for autographs," wrote Tom Nolan in *Rolling Stone*, "considering how often they are approached in restaurants, after concerts, while riding in limousines.... Approached during breakfast in Richmond, Virginia, by a rotund and particularly nervy fellow bearing five napkins to be individually inscribed, Karen blurted out in disbelief, 'Oh, fuck!'"

Despite the fame and recognition, Karen seemed to remain the simple, unpretentious girl Frank Bonito had walked to and from school with years before. Her trust of such friends seemed to grow with every mounting success. "Karen felt comfortable with us," Bonito says. "She was very down-to-earth and never played the prima donna. She was always interested in what we were doing in our lives. We represented history and security. We also represented how her life would be if she weren't a singer."

7

AMERICA AT ITS VERY BEST?

N THE nation's capital for a music industry awards dinner, Karen
and Richard visited the White House as guests of presidential assis-
tants James Cavanaugh, Ken Cole, and Ronald Ziegler on April 25,
1972. There they met Julie Nixon Eisenhower, the president's daughter
and a fan of their music, but President Richard M. Nixon was in a meeting with Henry Kissinger and unavailable at the time of their visit. The
Carpenters returned to the White House just months later on August 1,
this time meeting briefly and posing for photos with President Nixon
in the Oval Office. He thanked Karen for her work as National Youth
Chairman for the American Cancer Society, an organization the duo
supported with the donation of more than one hundred thousand dollars in proceeds from concert tour program sales. Conversation with
Nixon was trite. He was known to be inept at making small talk, and
Karen and Richard were quite nervous, too. Nixon asked about the
amount of sound equipment the Carpenters carried on tour. "About
10,000 pounds," they told him.

"We can probably hear you all the way here," he replied, referring
to their scheduled concert in nearby Columbia, Maryland.

In the spring of 1973 Sherwin Bash was contacted on behalf of
President Nixon with a request for the Carpenters to entertain at the
White House following a state dinner honoring West German Chan-
cellor Willy Brandt. Bash was quick to accept the invitation on the

group's behalf, and on April 30, 1973, during a hectic touring schedule of one-nighters, the exhausted Carpenters entourage flew into
Washington, D.C. Unbeknownst to them, the Watergate scandal was
on the verge of erupting. In fact, just one day prior the president had
met with key advisors Bob Haldeman and John Ehrlichman at Camp
David, where he confirmed their suspicions that they would be asked
to resign their positions.

As the Carpenters relaxed in a nearby hotel, President Nixon
addressed a nationwide television and radio audience from the Oval
Office regarding Watergate. "I want to talk to you tonight from my
heart on a subject of deep concern to every American...," he began.
"Today, in one of the most difficult decisions of my presidency, I
accepted the resignations of two of my closest associates in the White
House....In any organization, the man at the top must bear the responsibility....I accept that. And I pledge to you tonight, from this office,
that I will do everything in my power to ensure that the guilty are
brought to justice, and that such abuses are purged from our political
processes in the years to come, long after I have left office."

As the Carpenters' orchestral director Frank Pooler was transported
to the White House for his Tuesday morning rehearsal with the Marine
Corps Orchestra, agents from the Federal Bureau of Investigation
secured the files of Haldeman and Ehrlichman by placing guards outside their offices. Press Secretary Ronald Ziegler called it a "safeguard-
ing procedure." Nixon was outraged to learn of the guards and quickly
arranged for them and the files to be transferred to a less conspicuous
location. Unaware of the heightened security issues, Pooler went on
rehearsing the group he remembers as the best orchestra he ever worked
with while with the Carpenters. "Usually it took me two hours to
rehearse an orchestra," he says, "but these guys were so good we were
done in about an hour. We finished fast and got a private tour of the
rooms of the White House the tourists don't generally get."

That evening after dining at the Jockey Club, the band gathered in
their downstairs dressing rooms to prepare for the performance. Frank
Pooler realized he was the only one in the group who had yet to meet the
president. "I've got to meet him," he told Sherwin Bash. "I'm here, for

God's sake. It'll be something to tell my grandchildren." Bash directed him to the Grand Hall where a receiving line of distinguished guests, many in uniform, waited to meet Nixon. Pooler found the president to be much friendlier and better looking in real life than in pictures or on television. "Nixon was charming," he says. "He told me that his daughters had been fans of the Carpenters for a long time." As Pooler was introduced to Mrs. Nixon, he could hear the band warming up. "I'm sorry," he told the First Lady, realizing he was late, "I don't have time to talk to you!" The three laughed as Pooler rushed to lead the orchestra.

Around 10:30 P.M., the president and Mrs. Nixon entered the East Room. Addressing the crowd, which included then soon-to-be Secretary of State Henry Kissinger and his date, actress Mamie Van Doren, Nixon proclaimed, "The Carpenters are very much alive. They are young America at its very best. Mr. Chancellor," he said, addressing the dignitary, "knowing how you have such affection for young people all over the world and how you, as well as I, are working for the peace that we want for them and their children in years to come, we think that, tonight, having the Carpenters—one of the finest young groups in America—entertain us is most appropriate."

The Carpenters opened their performance with "Close to You," musically tiptoeing in an attempt to please such an esteemed audience. "We were afraid to touch anything," Karen recalled. "I was afraid to even breathe on the drums. I was barely touching them because I didn't want to offend anybody." She drummed on more rhythmic numbers like "Love Is Surrender," "Top of the World," and "Mr. Guder," but returned to center stage on the ballads. The Carpenters' new drummer, former Mickey Mouse Club Mouseketeer Cubby O'Brien, had recently joined the group following the departure of Jim Anthony.

In a variation on her standard end-of-show monologue, Karen thanked Pooler and the orchestra before going on to say, "I know I speak for all the people that are associated with Richard and me when I say that being invited to the White House to perform, or just being invited to the White House *period*, is not only a thrill, but it's indeed an honor." She then addressed Chancellor Brandt directly, saying, "Gute Nacht. Auf Wiedersehen."

President Nixon joined the band onstage as a standing ovation spread across the East Room. "We do have dancing afterward," he announced, "but we can't afford the Carpenters!"

DURING THE summer tour of 1972, the Carpenters introduced a medley of oldies, songs from the 1950s and 1960s that were enjoying a renaissance at the time. In fact, entire radio stations were switching to an all oldie format. Working toward their fifth album release, Karen and Richard realized there was only enough new material for one side of an LP. Desperation and a lack of time fueled Richard's visualization of an entire side of an album dedicated to a version of their oldies medley that would be bookended with an anthem with the message conveying "the oldies are back!" He asked John Bettis to come up with a list of possible song titles. The list of at least thirty prospective titles was narrowed to one favorite, "Yesterday Once More." The anthem was born as Richard drove up Highland Avenue on his way to A&M. He heard a melody and the start of a song lyric in his head. Arriving at the studio, he played his ideas for Karen and later came up with a first verse.

When I was young I'd listen to the radio
Waitin' for my favorite songs
When they played I'd sing along
It made me smile

Richard returned to Bettis, who created a temporary or "dummy" lyric for the chorus with every intention of reworking the words at a later time. "Well, are you going to change this now?" Richard asked as the song neared completion.

"You know what," Bettis replied, "I don't think so! I think it sounds great this way."

"Are you kidding?"

"No," Bettis said. "This 'Sha-la-la-wo-wo-wo' stuff sounds pretty good!"

A leftover song title suggested by Agnes Carpenter, "Now and Then," became the name of the new Carpenters album released May 1, 1973, the day of the duo's White House performance. An impressive tri-gatefold cover illustrated Karen and Richard driving past their huge Downey home in Richard's red 1972 Ferrari 365 GTB/4 Daytona. The "Now" side of the LP began with its debut single, which hailed from television's *Sesame Street* and composer Joe Raposo. Karen and Richard first heard "Sing" while taping a television special called *Robert Young with the Young* for NBC-TV. The catchy melodic hook left everyone on the set singing and humming the song.

Richard was so taken with "Sing" that he started arranging their version while on set at NBC studios. The finished product featured the Jimmy Joyce Children's Choir on the sing-along "la-la" sections, but it was hardly the type of single the group needed at the time. "The Munchkin Song," some fans called it. A&M did not want to release "Sing" as a single, but Richard was confident of its commercial potential. He was right, and "Sing" went to #3 on the U.S. charts. When performing the song in concert, the Carpenters often solicited the help of local children's choirs.

The crowning jewel of *Now and Then* came in the form of a Leon Russell tune from his *Carney* album. Overlooked as a single due to its duration, "This Masquerade" was one of the Carpenters' most sophisticated recordings ever, with its haunting melody, Karen's intricate drum track, and an impressive flute solo by Bob Messenger.

Rounding out side A was the Carpenters' 1972 cover of Hank Williams's country classic "Jambalaya (on the Bayou)," completed for this album and released as a single in the United Kingdom. "I Can't Make Music" was penned by occasional opening act Randy Edelman and perfectly suited for the Carpenters treatment. "The Carpenters have gone awry," wrote outspoken rock critic Lester Bangs in his review of *Now and Then*. "Side One's alright, just what you needed; more of that nice, syrupy, ultra commercial pap. 'Sing' is one of their all time best singles, and the essence of the act: 'Sing of good things not bad.' But Karen's reading of 'Jambalaya' is almost as bad as John Fogerty's, and there may be gray clouds passing over Carpenterland because she manages to sound almost *used* in Leon Russell's 'This Masquerade' while 'I Can't Make Music' is the Carpenters' hymn of despair like Traffic's 'Sometimes I Feel So Uninspired.'"

The "Then" side of the *Now and Then* LP began with "Yesterday Once More" and, as planned, the monstrous medley of oldies that Richard crafted to emulate a Top 40 radio show. Each selection segued into the next and was joined by the radio deejay antics of multitalented guitarist Tony Peluso. Narrowing down their favorites, Karen and Richard settled on a list including "Fun, Fun, Fun," "The End of the World," "Da Doo Ron Ron," "Dead Man's Curve," "Johnny Angel," "The Night Has a Thousand Eyes," "Our Day Will Come," and "One Fine Day." Their "Yesterday Once More" single went on to become the duo's fifth #2, placing them in a three-way tie with Creedence Clearwater Revival and Elvis Presley for the most #2 singles in chart history. The song also proved to be the Carpenters' biggest worldwide hit and at one point was #1 in Belgium, England, Hong Kong, Israel, Japan, Malaysia, Singapore, and Venezuela.

———— ◦◦◦◦ ————

By the time President Richard M. Nixon had declared the Carpenters to be "young America at its very best," Karen and Richard were three years into what became a futile struggle for control over their public image, and an endorsement from Nixon only worked against their cause. Early attempts to establish a true identity with the media were brought to a halt by their publicists and record label. But before they were specifically coached by management on how to handle interviewers and questioning, the Carpenters gave several revealing interviews including one in 1970 with Chicago radio legend Dick Biondi. Religion, politics, and current affairs were discussed, and neither Carpenter held back.

BIONDI: What are your feelings on the United States' involvement in the Vietnam War?
KAREN: Oh, I think I'd better let him steam first.
RICHARD: I'm completely against it.
KAREN: I think it's a complete waste . . .

RICHARD: First of all, nothing's ever going to be settled. It's like the Korean War. Nothing ever came to a complete end. It's been bubbling over there ever since. That was never won or lost. It just sort of terminated. Nothing was ever settled, and this is never going to be settled because it's not an all-out war. It's an "involvement." They don't even call it a war.

KAREN: They never even *declared* one. It's ridiculous.

RICHARD: And they're over their piddling around. One cat shoots so many one day, and then they shoot back the next day. If you're going to have a war, as much as I am against killing or anything like it, you ought to get in there and *do it*.

On the subject of censorship, Karen explained she felt it could be "very confining. It can be very destructive." Asked about her religious views she told Biondi, "I don't need to go to church and listen to some preacher tell me what to believe in. I don't dig that at all." Richard expressed his disgust with the state of organized religion and called it "hypocrisy personified."

Although the interview was one of the first to allow the Carpenters the opportunity to voice their opinions on important and relevant topics, it would be the last. Their publicist was furious. "Most people were asking them about their songs and stuff, so I went into the drugs and Vietnam," Biondi recalls. "I was very proud of myself because I could see their promotion man getting more and more upset."

According to Richard, following the Biondi interview, they were coached by the publicists to avoid controversial topics and anything not in keeping with the image prescribed for them. "We were told when you go out to do interviews, don't say anything adverse about anything. Everything is groovy. Everything is terrific. Don't say anything bad. Don't say you dislike anything. You like everything. And we went along with it."

Meet the Carpenters—A&M Records' young brother-sister hit-makers whose gentle harmony, wholesome image and natural, unpretentious personalities have virtually crashed through to make them the nation's number one recording team. Their sonorous magic has endeared them to music fans of every age and taste, and may be marking the beginning of a new musical mood for the '70s, bringing back the three H's—hope, happiness and harmony. With soft-pedaled persistence and talent galore, these melodic siblings have revolutionized the music industry.

It was through promotional blurbs such as this 1971 press release that A&M Records crafted their image of the Carpenters, and it quickly caught on. "Real nice American kids—in 1971!" wrote *Stereo Review*, saying they were "friendly people, outgoing, well-mannered, casually but tidily dressed, hard-working—and talented. No protest. No defiance. No porn. No blasphemy. No tripping." And according to the *Washington Post*: "Karen may eat a peanut butter cup for quick energy, but not an amphetamine, and there are no groupies camped out in hotels where the Carpenters stay. Autograph hounds perhaps, but not groupies. 'No,' said Karen. 'We don't seem to attract that crowd.'"

The rock press of the early 1970s in effect bullied the Carpenters, and because their music went against the grain of rock standards, they were often relegated to second-class status. Although they were not a rock band, more often than not they were reviewed by rock critics. "They were not rock," explained journalist Rob Hoerburger in a 2008 documentary, "they were not jazz, they were not country, they were not classical, but they had facets of all of that in their music. When you put all of those facets together what you get is this really amazing pop gem."

According to Paul Williams, "The Carpenters were truly one of the first great alternative bands. 'In-A-Gadda-Da-Vida' was the huge #1 album shortly before 'Close to You' and 'Begun' were hits. I was so different from them, too. I was such a raging hippie. I was pretty much a part of the counterculture yet writing songs for Karen and Richard and a lot of other middle-of-the-road acts." Williams was quite a sight on the A&M lot in those days. Often he wore tie-dyed shirts, round glasses, and work boots, with a black top hat resting atop his shoulder-length hair. Leaning on a railing outside an A&M office one afternoon, he noticed Bing Crosby waiting outside the studios for his driver to arrive. "He looked at me, said something, and pointed, like what is this world coming to?" Williams says. "He didn't know who I was then. That was before I became known as an entertainer and Crosby recorded 'We've Only Just Begun.'"

Writing for *Rolling Stone* in 1971, Lester Bangs was the first of many who found more at fault with the Carpenters' appearance than their brand of music. "I would say that they have the most disconcerting collective stage presence of any band I've ever seen," he wrote of a concert in San Diego, California. "Besides being a motley crew, they are individually peculiar-looking. Here it becomes almost cruel to go on, but there is no getting around it, especially since most of the music was so bland and their demeanor so remarkable that you could spend the entire concert wondering at the latter without once getting bored. I found the band almost like tintypes of themselves. . . . I'll never be able to hear 'We've Only Just Begun' without thinking, not of a sentimental autumn as I used to, but inevitably of that disgruntled collection of faces." Bangs also mentioned their image: "The LP cover and promo pix showed 'em side by side, identical, interchangeable boy-girl faces grinning out at you with all the cheery innocence of some years-past dream of California youth. Almost like a better-scrubbed reincarnation of Sonny and Cher."

Bangs was right, at least as far as their image was concerned. An onslaught of eight-by-ten glossy photos and unimaginative album covers made Karen and Richard appear more conservative and square than they really were. For the *Close to You* album cover they were cheek to cheek in formal wear and positioned on a rock next to the ocean. It was a rush job and one that angered Richard. Even so, management did nothing. As simple and classy as their *Tan Album* was, the inside photo looked like every engagement portrait snapped in 1971. Next was *A Song for You*, which resembled a huge Valentine card. The Carpenters' sophisticated musicianship deserved equally sophisticated packaging and promotion. In a 1993 interview, surprisingly, Herb Alpert claimed to have been pleased with the way the Carpenters were marketed by his company. "It's not enough just to have a hit record," he said. "It's to be able to promote it properly and to merchandise it properly with good taste. I think the company did a wonderful job and continues to, because we try to reflect the dignity that they both had as artists."

Despite Alpert's good intentions, early publicity attempts by the label backfired. A&M Records and their publicists succeeded only in frustrating Karen and Richard and creating a stigma for fans of their music, as detailed by journalist John Tobler in a 1974 article: "A number of people, myself included, could be seen stealing away surreptitiously into our favorite record shops and whispering our requirements to an astonished assistant, who probably thought we'd lost our minds. Shades of prohibition!" And Tom Smucker of the *Village Voice* called it "the worst case of consumer stage fright since I first bought rubbers years ago. What would the man behind the counter say when I walked up with my Carpenters record?"

In an article written some twenty years after both Tobler's and Smucker's, Rob Hoerburger explained in a *New York Times Magazine* article the wide appeal of the Carpenters, despite the stigma: "When 'We've Only Just Begun' or 'Rainy Days and Mondays' came on the car radio, kids *and* parents would turn it up.... This was musical white bread, to be sure, but it was feeding masses of a biblical proportion."

LIVING AT home with her parents and spending a significant amount of time on tour, Karen had little time to devote to romantic relationships. Since her only real interaction with men came in the form of friendships with band members and roadies, it was inevitable that she would eventually meet and fall for someone within the Carpenters' entourage. She was linked to Carpenters guitarist Gary Sims in the early days and later drummer Jim Anthony, but these were what Frenda Franklin recalls as "lightweight relationships," dismissing them as mere puppy love. "They weren't anything Karen wasn't in control of," she says.

Karen dated Alan Osmond for a brief spell, but the Osmonds and the Carpenters were in such demand during that period that the two rarely spent enough time together for a serious relationship to ensue. "She really liked Alan," recalls Franklin. "That was kind of sad because Mrs. Osmond would not allow it.... Everything was controlled by these powerful families, and trust me, the Carpenters were little leaguers next to the Osmonds. And they had the big Mormon church in back of them."

Karen downplayed the relationship with Alan in 1974 when she explained to the *Los Angeles Times*, "Contrary to what they write, Alan and I are not married. We've seen each other maybe five times. How can you date someone when you finish work at 3:00 A.M.? If you go to a lounge or coffee shop people stare. So you end up sitting in cars and talking for hours."

Karen expressed to Frank Bonito and other close friends her frustration with finding love and trying to build a relationship on the road. "It's not unusual for people in that kind of situation to have romances with the people they're working with," Bonito says. "They live a very bizarre, confined life because they are constantly traveling. Who do you meet? Even if you wanted to date someone, who do you see?"

In a 1981 BBC radio interview, Karen elaborated: "At one point, there were thirty-two of us on the road. It's a big bunch. You tend to travel in the same circles with the same people, meet the same people, and hang out with the same people. Even when you come home you never really meet anybody new. Being the only girl, outside of my hairdresser, it's not easy having thirty brothers on the road. Everybody, including management, is extremely protective. You get to the point where you don't want to go outside the hotel room because it's more difficult. You really don't meet anybody."

In 1973 Karen grew fond of another member of their entourage. Texan David Alley was close to her age and assigned to the Carpenters' tour by his employer, Showco, a Dallas-based sound equipment outfit. As a high school junior, Alley had been first chair trumpeter in the Texas All-State Band and went on to march with the Mustang Band while attending Southern Methodist University. On tour with the Carpenters, Sherwin Bash mentioned to Alley that Karen liked him. He was stunned by the news and wasted no time in asking her on a date. In no time at all he fell madly in love with Karen, and the two began spending a great deal of time together outside of rehearsals, sound checks, and shows.

"David was always a very, very nice fellow and a real gentleman," remembers Evelyn Wallace. "I had a feeling that Karen was really quite fond of him and he of her, but there was Richard in between. I think they knew that if they started dating or showed their fondness for each other that David would be gone. Karen didn't want him gone, and David didn't want to be gone from Karen either, so he didn't give her that much attention whenever he was at the house since Richard was always there."

Although Karen enjoyed David's company and felt comfortable when they were together, she did not see a future with him and seemed to distance herself at times. "Karen liked to be entertained," Maria Galeazzi recalls. "David was very serious, almost sourpusslike. He wasn't a fun guy. I am not saying he wasn't a nice guy, he just wasn't a barrel of laughs, by any means."

Also working against Alley's chances with Karen was the fact that he was dependent upon his job with the Carpenters. Karen was essentially his boss, in some respects. In fact, she and Richard hired David to manage Morsound, their own sound equipment company formed in 1974. One of Karen's crucial requirements in a potential husband was that he be independently wealthy and not reliant on her income. According to Galeazzi, Karen felt she needed her man to be of a certain status. "The person had to be somebody way up there," she explains. "Her standards were high. Some regular dude was just not going to do. I am not saying that David was a regular dude. He was successful in his own right, but she would have admired somebody that was talented in music and good looking and all that. And I think even that wouldn't have done." As Karen told the *Los Angeles Times* that same year, "It's no good when the chick is bigger than the guy."

Frenda Franklin concurs. "In the very beginning she had a huge crush on my husband, Eddie," she says. "You see, Karen had a propensity to fall in love with people that could change her life in big ways. She certainly had a giant crush on Herbie. She was like a little starstruck girl. These guys were not only handsome, they were powerful, they dressed great, they smelled great, and they were wealthy. She saw it as a way out, definitely. No question about it, it was freedom. But David Alley *wasn't* enough."

8

MOVING OUT

―――――

"**HAROLD AND** Karen were both sweethearts," remembers Evelyn Wallace. "Richard, on the other hand, was just like his mother. They could be bitchy. They *were* bitchy, even to each other once in a while. Yet Richard was still her baby."

One such exchange between Agnes and Richard occurred in Acapulco, Mexico, where the Carpenters were invited to perform two twenty-minute shows on consecutive Saturdays for the IBM Corporation's Gold Key Club, June 2–9, 1973. Outside of the performance times, the group was free to enjoy the beautiful secluded villa provided for them at Las Brisas overlooking the Bay of Acapulco. Sharing the spacious house with Karen was boyfriend David Alley. Maria Galeazzi accompanied Richard, while manager Sherwin Bash and his wife, Bobby, also stayed at the villa. Agnes and Harold were invited to Acapulco as well but were upset to learn they had been booked into the nearby Princess Hotel with the IBM executives. With their love interests on the trip, Karen and Richard sought some semblance of privacy, but this did not sit well with Agnes, who felt she and Harold were deliberately excluded. "Why are *we* in the hotel while the *strangers* are in the house?" she demanded.

"I'm not ten years old anymore!" Richard shouted back. The other houseguests looked on as the two bellowed back and forth. Once each had said their piece, everyone did their best to relax and enjoy the luxurious accommodations. They took great advantage of the private swimming pool and made several trips to Pie de la Cuesta, a long, narrow strip of beach north of Las Brisas.

By the time the group returned from Mexico, it was apparent to Agnes that Richard was in love with Maria, but their relationship threatened the family's living situation. Agnes had succeeded in keeping Richard at home with her for twenty-seven years and was not about to lose him to her hairdresser. From a parental standpoint, Galeazzi now recognizes Agnes's desire to be protective of her children, although not to the point of suffocation. "She didn't want anybody taking advantage of them," Galeazzi says. "I can understand that. If I had been their mother I would have been a junkyard dog, too. But I wasn't just a girl that came along and hooked up with him because he was Richard Carpenter. I was just a nice Italian girl who happened to be working for them, and we got together. It wasn't like I was a groupie and fell into his bed or anything." Regardless, Agnes made it her mission to excommunicate Galeazzi from the Carpenter clan, and Karen became the medium. "You *fire* her," Agnes insisted.

"Mom, she does my hair the best of anyone I've ever been to," Karen explained. "And she doesn't do just my hair, she cuts Richard's hair and the guys', too. She does our fingernails, and she always presses our costumes before we go on stage. We didn't expect her to do all that!"

"You can find someone else," Agnes said. "You get rid of her!"

Evelyn Wallace recalls this episode in the kitchen at Newville and how devastated Karen was to be given these orders. "If I heard the words 'you get rid of her' once, I must have heard them a hundred times," she says. "Karen was so nice. I think her mother weakened her."

The months that followed were very tense for Galeazzi. She made every effort to do her job and tend to Karen's needs, but she also wanted to spend her free time alone with Richard. The two enjoyed racing his Ferrari at Riverside, but Karen did her best to monopolize Maria's time with girls-only outings such as shopping trips to Beverly Hills or visits to their favorite needlepoint store. "I was always like her little shadow and supposed to be there for her twenty-four hours a day, seven days a week," she recalls. "It's not like I wasn't doing my job. When I got together with Richard I became even more conscientious about it because I didn't want to screw up."

At Agnes's urging, Karen became more demanding and impatient, and Galeazzi began to sense something was brewing. Alone time for her and Richard was scarce. "If we went anywhere it was the three of us," she says. "Every place we went it was like Karen and Richard and I, and it got old for me, let me tell you. Even the hotel rooms were always Richard's room, Karen's room, and then my room. Most of the time they'd make sure there was a door that opened up from mine into hers so that I was always there ready to assist her."

Things came to a head one evening as the three prepared to go out on the town. As always, Galeazzi stopped by Newville to do Karen's hair and makeup. When she finished, Galeazzi excused herself to return to her apartment. There she would get herself ready for the outing, but Karen stopped her. "No. Bring your stuff and get ready here," she said.

"It's just easier for me to go two miles away and get ready and then come back," Galeazzi explained.

Karen felt challenged and quickly turned to Richard. "You see? This is not working," she told him. "This is just *not working!*"

Next, Karen presented Galeazzi with an iniquitous ultimatum: forget about Richard and go back out on the road as her stylist or remain a couple and resign her position. But Galeazzi refused to conform to either suggestion. "Well, I can do both," Galeazzi replied, shocked at the nerve of Karen's challenge. "I don't understand why I have to make this choice. Be with him and, what, twiddle my thumbs and do needlepoint? If I go on the road, I am going to watch Richard dating other girls. I don't think I could stand that."

Richard visited Maria at her apartment, where the two sat at the edge of her bed and discussed Karen's demands. Both in tears, they agreed the relationship must come to an end. "He had to do what he had to do," Galeazzi recalls. "He made it understood that it was not in his power or in his best interest. I would have never pushed it, and that's why I left. I could have chosen one or the other, but I didn't because it would have been difficult for all three of us. I couldn't see myself just being his girlfriend either, so that's how it came to an end." Galeazzi returned to her job at the Magic Mirror in Downey, weighing in at a skeletal eighty-six pounds due to stress. "I lost so much weight because I was so nervous about it all."

Replacing Galeazzi was Sandy Holland. According to Evelyn Wallace, Karen spelled out her expectations in no uncertain terms, instructing the new employee to keep her distance and stay out of her brother's bed. "If Richard wants his hair cut, cut it. But whatever you do, *don't* play around with him!"

To THE outside world, Agnes Carpenter was an overprotective mother to both her children, but it was apparent to those within the Carpenter enclave that she played favorites. Evelyn Wallace recalls that when speaking of the two, Agnes always made reference to Richard before Karen. "From the time Karen was little, everything was 'Richard, Richard, Richard.' It was always 'Richard and Karen' and 'if it wasn't for *Richard*, there wouldn't be a Karen,' so to speak. He was more important to Agnes than Karen."

According to Wallace, Karen was well aware of her second-place ranking in the home and perhaps even felt it was justified. Agnes's adoration for her firstborn—to the point of idolization, according to some—was emulated and even proliferated by Karen. "She thought Richard was God," Frenda Franklin recalls, "just like her mother thought he was God." Tangible proof of Karen's adulation of her brother remains today in a poignant needlepoint message she crafted for him: THERE IS NO K.C. WITHOUT R.C.

As Frenda explains, Agnes' inability to nurture and nourish her daughter with affection, as she did Richard, led to Karen's own inability to love herself. "[Karen's] relationship with her mother was so stilted that it caused such a great hurt inside her," Franklin says. Of Agnes she laments, "I wanted her to be different with Karen. She just couldn't love her. It was not possible. I think in her own crazy way she did love her, but not like she loved Richard. If your own parent doesn't love you, you're going to walk around with a giant hole that's not ever going to get filled."

In a 1973 concert review that criticized Richard's long hairstyle, a University of Montana columnist wrote, "Whereas Richard may not appear to be every father's favorite son, Karen is the kind of girl every mother could love." This casual remark takes on a most ironic twist when paired with Sherwin Bash's observations of the real mother-daughter relationship he witnessed within the Carpenter family: "I'm sure in her own way Agnes loved Karen, but it wasn't something she was able to express," he recalled. "I think eventually that was one of the most serious problems that Karen had.... Over the years, Karen Carpenter became beloved in the world as a very special artist, a very special voice, who reminded everybody of the daughter they wished they had. In her own home she never was told or maybe never even felt that existed from her own parents, especially her mother."

KAREN WAS twenty-four and Richard approaching the age of twenty-eight when the two decided it was time to leave home. The dilemma was how to proceed without hurting their mother's feelings. They asked Sherwin Bash for advice. Bash had worked with hundreds of music artists, and in his opinion these siblings were immature. They lacked sophistication—not musically but in their personal lives. He wanted to see them take control of their lives, move out of their parents' house, and seek the independence of two millionaires in their twenties. "Their inability to develop," said Bash, "was created by their inability to separate themselves from a dominating mother who they never wanted to offend and never wanted to hurt.... I think that severely stunted and damaged their growth."

According to Evelyn Wallace, this was not the kids' first attempt at independence. The two had rented an apartment together in Bellflower for a brief spell. "That didn't last too long," she explains. "Richard was expecting Karen to do all the cooking and the stuff his mother had done." But Karen claimed to enjoy inventing new recipes and perfecting others. "Cooking is an art and a pleasure for me; I've always loved to cook, ever since I was a child," she said in a 1971 press release entitled "Karen in the Kitchen: Who Says a Young Female Superstar Can't Be a Top-Notch Cook?" She listed her favorite creations, which included pies, cookies, shrimp dishes, and "veal and eggplant concoctions."

Sherwin offered Karen and Richard his advice for officially moving out, but instead of confronting their mother and relocating, the two came up with a way they might evade the issue entirely. They bought their parents a modest 3,000-square-foot home with four bedrooms and three baths at 8341 Lubec Street in Downey, less than two miles from Newville. "The expectation was that their mother and father would move into this new house," Bash said. "When they explained this to the mother, she absolutely refused to move out of this house. Not only did she refuse to move out, she couldn't understand why they would want to separate and be living in two different houses."

Richard was never particularly fond of the Newville house and agreed that he and Karen would move to Lubec Street, while Agnes and Harold stayed at Newville. The decision to move in together seemed natural for Karen and Richard, whose careers came first. They were first and foremost a team and at this point saw no reason to live separately. "If we don't see each other, we talk at least twice a day," Karen said in 1981. "We always have to know what the other one is doing. We're very nosy!"

To many on the outside looking in, siblings living together as adults seemed odd and prompted allegations of incest. Brian Southall, who joined A&M Records' London team in 1973, fought off reporters' questions about this brother-sister relationship that sometimes appeared a little too close. They were, after all, a duo that sang love songs. "There were lots of suggestions about their relationship," Southall said in a 2004 interview. "There was always a worry about the questions that would come out. There were suggestions of an incestuous relationship and stuff like that, which was utter nonsense. But they *were* an odd couple."

According to Karen, over the years and especially near the beginning of their careers, many people thought she and Richard were married. "I remember once when we were looking for an apartment in California, and the landlady asked if we had any kids. 'No,' we said, telling the truth. 'That's good,' she replied, 'and I hope you haven't got any pets either.' And the photographers were always asking us to kiss! Well, you might hold your brother's hand, but you don't kiss him unless it's a family reunion."

Richard said, "Maybe it would have been easier if we *had* been man and wife," with Karen adding, "It's been a hell of a battle. We were mistaken for a married couple for so long. How could anyone fail to recognize us as brother and sister? We're so alike. When we smile we could be Siamese twins."

Unfortunately for the Carpenters, Southall was not present to screen a disastrous phone interview broadcast live on Toronto radio. "We might as well bring it out," the deejay told Richard. "I've listened to the lyrics of your songs. I know that Karen's singing them to you. I know they're about incest. You want to talk about this?" Richard was so caught off guard that he tried to explain how that was untrue. "Absolutely not," he said. "I don't even write all of those songs. They just happen to be love songs. Karen sings them. I sing and arrange. We happen to be brother and sister." Surprisingly, Richard finished the interview, at which time he slammed down the receiver, vowing to never do another phone interview.

———— ∞∞ ————

"WE'VE MADE it a rule that whoever we go out with must not interfere with our professional lives," Karen explained in a 1976 interview. "I feel if Richard is going out with the wrong girl, I tell him. He needs someone who will give him a good home, security, and children— someone who will understand him because he's a special guy."

Shortly after moving to Lubec Street, Richard began dating Randy Bash, Sherwin's twenty-one-year-old daughter. Some felt she was pushed by her father into dating Richard, but even Karen was fond of her at first and seemed to approve of the burgeoning relationship. But just three weeks in, Agnes chimed in with her critique, and Richard carelessly told Randy of his mother's dislike for her. By the time Randy joined the Carpenters on their European tour in February 1974, Richard was well aware that both his mother and sister had it in for her. Despite the young girl's attempts to be friendly and have lunch or go shopping, Karen ignored and avoided Randy for the duration of the tour. "Richard can have his girl travel with him—she has no career," Karen told the Los Angeles Times that year, her antipathy apparent. "But what about me? Is my guy supposed to lay around all day while we're on the road?"

Returning to Los Angeles, Karen was up in arms when Richard invited Randy to move in with them. "Randy came into the picture, and then all hell broke loose," says Maria Galeazzi. "Then Karen didn't mind me as much as she did her because she picked up her bags and moved right in! It came back to bite her." Karen told Richard she would not move the rest of her belongings out of Newville until "that girl" was no longer living under their roof.

After only a week of intense pressure from Karen, Richard told Randy she could not stay. Technically, it was both his and his sister's house, and they were obviously not going to agree on the matter. Although she packed her things and left, Randy continued to sleep there most every night. "She wasn't that particular in what, if anything, she ran around the house in," recalls Evelyn Wallace. After failing to successfully evict Randy from Lubec Street, Karen made it clear to Richard she no longer wanted to wake up in her own house only to find his naked girlfriend had slept over again. She was moving back home to Newville.

⎯⎯ ◦◦◦ ⎯⎯

WHEN KAREN began dating tall, handsome record executive Mike Curb, the new love interest became a much-needed distraction from her brother's personal affairs. "It evolved," Curb recalls of his relationship with Karen. "Richard and I both had sisters, and I think we were all very comfortable together." The sibling friendships began when Mike and his sister Carole joined Karen and Richard for dinners in the home of mutual friends Ed and Frenda Leffler. The couples also enjoyed evenings of conversation over food and wine at Jack's at the Beach, a favorite restaurant on the Ocean Park Pier in Santa Monica.

Mike was taken with Karen's love of life, music, and children. In return, she was impressed by his kindhearted personality, his confident nature, and his good looks. In contrast with Karen's history of sabotaging her brother's relationships, Richard was thrilled with her choice of mate this time. "I think Richard was happy that she was dating someone, and I think he liked me," Curb says. "I liked him." Richard and Mike started a tradition of music trivia matches. "He was certainly a much better musician than I, but at the time I was a successful record producer." In addition to the Osmonds, Curb produced Donny Osmond as a solo artist and was just beginning to work with the sibling duo of Donny and Marie. He was named *Billboard* Producer of the Year for 1972 in recognition of his production of both Sammy Davis Jr.'s "The Candy Man" and Donny Osmond's "Puppy Love." He would later produce Debby Boone's "You Light Up My Life," the biggest selling record of the decade.

Visiting the Carpenters at A&M Records was a treat for Curb, who enjoyed watching other artists work and the various production techniques employed. "Being a producer, I marveled at the way Richard and Karen worked together," he says. "Neither one of them ever made small talk. It was always music, records, or something she'd heard on the radio. I have never seen any two people more committed to their careers. Their records never sounded overproduced. They were perfectly produced, but they had just enough edge that they were really right for the moment and the radio."

Karen and Mike found it taxing to juggle their busy careers and still make time for dates and other opportunities to be together. "I was running MGM Records and producing records at that time, and she was constantly recording and traveling," Curb explains. "She would go away on international tours for quite a while, so we were unable to spend as much time together as we wanted to." When openings in their schedules did coincide, Karen and Mike would drive to Newport Beach or San Diego for a boat ride around the harbor.

For their dinner dates, Curb would often drive to Newville to pick up his girlfriend. "I could have been picking up the girl next door," he says, recalling her unaffected personality. "She never ever got caught up in the trappings of being a successful artist. Aside from maybe a gold record on the wall or a Grammy award on the table, it was just like you were going to your next-door neighbor's home. It was such a pleasure to be with her because she just loved music, loved life, loved her family, and was so unaffected. I never remember her going out and buying clothes or talking about trendy things. To her, her whole world was her brother, her family, the parents."

Although they sometimes went for dinner at Knott's Berry Farm in Buena Park, both Karen and Mike favored intimate surroundings. "Both of us preferred something more private," he says. "Not something where fifty people would come up to us. But I went to the Grammys with her and the American Music Awards, too, so we did some public things." One of the couple's first public outings was a double date with Richard and Randy Bash to the Grammy Awards on March 2, 1974, Karen's twenty-fourth birthday.

From the start of their relationship, Curb recalls Karen was always on a diet. "She was always concerned that when she ate her weight went to her hips, so she wouldn't eat," he says. "She always worried about her hips, and that's one of the reasons she wanted to stay at the drums." On May 22, 1974, the Carpenters were photographed at home by Annie Leibovitz for an upcoming *Rolling Stone* cover story. Karen was pleased to have lost some excess weight around her arms and buttocks, and to show off her new figure she wore a new pair of jeans and a tank top. It was a casual and laid-back approach, in contrast with the years of posing cheek to cheek with Richard, wearing matching formalwear. Karen looked radiant and was the picture of good health. Friends were noticing and telling her how great she looked, but no one saw it as obsessive in the beginning, just normal dieting.

Initially, Curb was not alarmed either, but as time went on he started to recognize Karen was establishing the eating patterns and rituals that would proliferate over the coming years. "I noticed very definitely that she was trying to lose weight by just not eating. She would order a meal and maybe eat 25 percent of her food. She was just sort of moving the food around her plate. My sister Carole had the same problem. She and Karen would just *not eat.*"

During their dinners, Karen reminded Mike her diet was such a success she could not stop and risk gaining the weight back. "You look *great*," he affirmed. "Now let's eat!" Or he would say, "You only ate a third of your plate. Let's stay until you eat it all." With his urging, she would usually eat her entire meal. Even Richard noticed that Karen seemed to behave differently and eat more sensibly in Mike's presence. "How are you getting her to eat?" he asked.

"I would actually *insist* that she eat," Curb says. "I would tell her that she looked great and that she should eat. And she would eat!"

After dinner, Mike would sometimes drive Karen to A&M, where she would meet Richard for a recording session. "She liked to record at night," Curb says. "I stayed enough to see how incredibly talented Richard was. He was amazing, and she had such respect for him. I remember just being stunned." Curb was even more amazed when he first heard Karen's voice up close and unaccompanied while driving with her to A&M. "She was rehearsing a song and looking at a piece of sheet music," he says. "When she sang in a car you could barely hear her voice, but when she got on a microphone it was like velvet. It was a very, very amazing thing. So many singers think they always have to belt out a song. Karen had one of the softest voices in the world, but when you put that voice on a *microphone*?!"

Despite the couple's commonalities and mutual admiration, dates between Karen and Mike Curb became more and more sporadic due to their career obligations, and they grew apart. "She went on a long tour, and we started seeing each other less and less," Curb recalls. "It was really two people that were just so busy. It never really broke up."

DESPITE THE fact that the Carpenters' greatest successes stemmed from their recordings, they spent the majority of their professional time on tour. The average Carpenters record took between four and five months to produce. The remainder of the year was spent playing night after night across the country and around the world, in addition to making various personal and television appearances. In 1971 the Carpenters played upward of 150 shows. During 1972 and 1973 they did 174 concerts each year. After six weeks of one-nighters—which was common during those seasons—Karen and Richard were exhausted. While they enjoyed performing, it became a never-ending succession of plane trips, motels, hotels, rehearsals, and sound checks that got them down.

The year 1974 began with the Carpenters greatest hits album, *The Singles 1969–1973*, topping the *Billboard* album charts in the United States. The collection was the duo's first and only #1 album, fueled by nine previous million-sellers, and sales would eventually top twelve million units in the United States alone. It also topped the UK album chart for seventeen weeks between February and July.

The promotional push for the *Singles* album came in the form of the duo's second #1 single, "Top of the World." The Carpenters and A&M Records had certainly underestimated the song's potential when recorded for 1972's *A Song for You*. All involved felt it was a nice album cut but never considered it for single release. Some Top 40 stations had programmed the song based solely upon requests, and in Japan it was culled as a single and quickly went to #1. Carpenters audiences had broken into applause at just the mention of the song once they added it to their live set in the summer of 1972. "All of a sudden people were standing up and cheering," John Bettis recalled. "Richard was kind of scratching his head and saying, 'What *is* all this?'"

When it came around to the *Singles* album, Richard decided "Top of the World" simply must be the next Carpenters single. "A&M took a little bit of convincing," Bettis said. "We're talking about the group that did 'Superstar,' "We've Only Just Begun,' and 'Goodbye to Love' coming along with a country number." Karen re-recorded her lead vocal, and other alterations were made to the recording before the new "Top of the World" was remixed and readied for release. "Then Richard had to hold the release of our single," Bettis said. Country crooner Lynn Anderson released her version of the song—a virtual clone of Richard's arrangement—which quickly climbed to #2 on the country music chart. "We didn't want to make anybody mad because we killed their record," explained Bettis. "We actually had to wait to release that record until Lynn Anderson's had died off the charts."

Additionally, the Carpenters' debut single, "Ticket to Ride," got a facelift for *The Singles*. The original 1969 version was a rare instance where tape captured Karen singing consistently under pitch. Drums were re-recorded, Tony Peluso added a guitar track, and Karen cut a much-improved lead vocal for the new release.

Following the hits album's success came a year of 203 concerts with sold-out tours across Europe, Japan, and the United States. A weeklong stop at New York's Westbury Music Fair was followed by two separate four-week stints in Las Vegas at the Riviera and two weeks at the Sahara in Lake Tahoe. The October run at the Riviera was recorded for an intended live album release that never came to fruition. They also participated in a televised concert with Arthur Fiedler and the Boston Pops and, as they had done in 1971, sold out 18,000 seats to fill the Hollywood Bowl.

Leaving Los Angeles on May 27, the Carpenters headed to Japan, where their shows were enjoyed by 85,000 fans. Tickets to their three weeks of concerts had sold out in less than an hour. "It was during their golden years when they were bigger than the Beatles," says Denny Brooks, a Cal State Long Beach alumnus who frequently toured as the Carpenters' opening act. "I'm an old folkie from the sixties. I really never had any great record success. I was just a good, working act. They were touring all these different countries, and instead of taking a comedian like a lot of these acts did during that time, they took me, just a guy and his guitar."

The Carpenters likened their 1974 touchdown in Japan to the Beatles on *The Ed Sullivan Show*, a mob scene of screaming fans rocking the limousines and pulling at their clothes. "It was outrageous," Brooks says. "Five thousand people at the Tokyo airport was really crazy, but it was a good time. I remember us doing one-nighters all over Japan, something like twenty-eight nights in thirty days in every single town."

Surprisingly, no one in the Carpenters' entourage ever complained to management about the grueling touring schedule the group was subjected to. Richard felt they were not so much overworked but overbooked. "I don't think he was ever truly happy on the road," Sherwin Bash recalled. But Bash continued to book them, filling each and every open date in their already bulging itineraries. "They were always huffing and puffing about having such a grueling schedule," Maria Galeazzi recalls. "These managers don't have any mind for the long run. They want to get the most of them—get it and get it now. . . . Sometimes you wake up in the middle of the night and you don't know where you are. The schedule was usually six weeks in a row, which takes its toll, not so much on the other people but on Karen."

Signs of Karen's stress would surface from time to time, as A&M Records' UK press officer Brian Southall remembers. He received a warning from others at the label in advance of the Carpenters' arrival in London that year. "Karen's the one you don't cross," he was told. "Karen was on an edge," Southall later recalled. "You crossed her at your peril. That was sort of the warning we were given before we started." One evening during a sold-out charity show at the Talk of the Town nightclub, the band was having fun and enjoying some spontaneity in their performance during the last night of the show. "But that was not allowed to happen," Southall observed. "[Karen] was on them like a ton of bricks. The show had to be *exactly* the same as every other show they had done. It was the first time that I had realized that the ad-libs were actually not ad-libs, they were the same ad-libs from the night before. . . . The guys in the band weren't drunk, they weren't falling about. They just wanted to have a little bit of spontaneity. It was frightening to watch when these guys got torn apart."

Maria Galeazzi witnessed the reprimands during her time on the road with the group, too. "Richard was very intense and very dedicated," she says. "He was more methodical and would explain, 'We have to do this the next show or that the next show.' Karen would be more like, 'You screwed up!'"

By 1974 everyone needed a break. Richard and Sherwin have both claimed they never saw the Carpenters as a trendy act that would come and go, but their career appears to have been handled in such a way that someone felt exploitation was the necessary means to success, even if it only proved to be in the form of short-term financial success. But even the financial successes were not of great substance. Their attorney, Werner Wolfen, put pen to paper and later informed the Carpenters they would not see a cent of profit until they had performed a minimum of 150 shows in any given year.

Concert reviews from this period agreed that the Carpenters needed time to relax and regroup. One such review for a show at the Sahara Tahoe appeared in *Variety*: "Not much showmanship... they sorely need advice on stage presentation and pace.... Attending a show is no more than listening to an album." It was true. A Carpenters concert was almost more of a recital of hit songs. From Karen and Richard came rigid directives to their band that every note must sound exactly as it did on the LP. "They were consummate musicians," says Denny Brooks. "There wasn't a lot of patter between songs, they just kept knocking out hit after hit after hit."

Although little time remained for recording, Karen and Richard managed to release three singles in 1974: "I Won't Last a Day Without You" (by then two years old and the fifth single culled from their mammoth hit album *A Song for You*), "Santa Claus Is Comin' to Town" (a track they put to tape in 1972), and one new recording, "Please Mr. Postman." Following closely on the heels of the success of their *Now and Then* album and its side of oldies, the Carpenters decided to record "Postman" as a stand-alone oldie. When the Carpenters' version became their third #1 single, it also marked the second time the song reached the top position on the Hot 100. In 1961 the original recording by the Marvelettes was the first #1 record to come out of Motown Records. It was also a popular album track on the Beatles' 1963 *With the Beatles* album.

"Ev, WOULD you do me a favor?"

As she would often do, Karen came to Evelyn Wallace asking for assistance, but she usually prefaced her requests with this polite inquiry. "It kind of tickled me," Wallace recalls.

"Karen, you're my *boss*," she would respond. "All you have to do is say, 'Ev, do this,' or 'Ev, do that.' I'd be happy to. You don't have to ask me, just tell me what you want done, and I'll do it.'" Both women laughed at these exchanges.

It was Halloween 1974. Although Karen had moved back in with Agnes and Harold, it was only to be a short-term stay and a temporary solution. She asked Werner Wolfen to start searching for real estate, preferably a nice condominium and one situated away from Downey. "She wanted me to tell her mother that she wanted to look around for an apartment," Wallace explains. "Karen really wanted to move out of the house. I think her mother was getting her down to the point where she wanted out."

"Will you ask her for me?" Karen pleaded.

"Karen, I'd do anything you asked me, and I will ask her. It would be best for everybody if you can, but I don't think you're going to have much luck."

"OK," Karen said. "Just wait until I am gone."

After Karen left the house, Evelyn approached Agnes as she sat at the kitchen table. "The kids are at that age now, you know," she began cautiously. "They've kind of, well, really got it made. You know?" Agnes's brow raised in anticipation of the next words. "Karen would kind of like to find a place and move into a little apartment by herself. A lot of the kids her age have been doing it for a while now."

Agnes jumped from the table, leaving Evelyn midsentence. "Well, you'd think that I had hit her over the head with a brick," Wallace says. "She jumped out of her chair and she ran to that phone and she called Karen, and she was screaming at her and calling her a traitor and asking how she could think such a thing." Evelyn quietly picked up her purse, slipped out the door, and headed home. "I didn't want to slam the door and let her know I was going because I thought she'd come running after me," she says. "She'd think that I gave that idea to Karen to move out, but I didn't. It was a surprise when Karen asked me to do that. That was the worst thing she ever asked me to do, but I would have died for that girl. She was such a lovely person."

9

THE COLLAPSE

I N 1996, Rob Hoerburger concisely and powerfully summed up
Karen Carpenter's tribulations in a *New York Times Magazine* feature: "If anorexia has classically been defined as a young woman's
struggle for control, then Karen was a prime candidate, for the two
things she valued most in the world—her voice and her mother's love—
were exclusively the property of Richard. At least she would control
the size of her own body." And control it she did. By September 1975
her weight dropped to ninety-one pounds.

Karen's quest to be thin seems to have begun innocently enough
just after high school graduation when she started the Stillman water
diet. Although she was never obese, she was what most would consider
a chubby seventeen-year-old at 145 pounds. She leveled off around 120
pounds and maintained her weight by eating sensibly but not starving
herself. Even so, eating while on tour was problematic for Karen, as she
described in 1973: "When you're on the road it's kind of hard to eat.
Period. On top of that, it's really rough to eat *well*. We don't like to eat
before a show because I can't stand singing with a full stomach. . . . You
never get to dinner until like midnight or one o'clock, and at that time
if you eat heavy you're not going to sleep, and if you eat heavy you're
going to be a balloon."

Maria Galeazzi never witnessed any eating habits she considered to
be compulsive or irrational during her years on tour with Karen. "When

I was with her she didn't have an eating problem," Galeazzi says. "She always watched her weight because she had a problem with her hips. She was a little bit heavier around there, but she wasn't fat. She never made any comments but always watched what she ate. For instance, she would have two strips of bacon instead of four, or one egg instead of two, but not anything obsessive. I never saw her look in the mirror and say, 'Oh, I'm so fat.' Not ever. I have no idea what triggered it."

Karen was shocked when she saw photos taken during an August 1973 Lake Tahoe concert where an unflattering outfit accentuated her paunch. This prompted her to seek the assistance of a personal trainer, who made visits to her home and recommended a diet low in calories but high in carbohydrates. Instead of slimming down as she had hoped, Karen started to put on muscle and bulk up following this new regimen. Watching the Carpenters' appearance on a Bob Hope television special that fall, she remarked that she had put on some extra weight. Richard agreed she looked a bit heavier. She was quite discouraged and vowed she was going to "do something about it."

Karen's first order of business was to fire her trainer, and she immediately set out on a mission to shed the unwanted pounds on her own. She purchased a hip cycle, which she used each morning on her bed, and because it was portable the equipment was packed and taken with her on tour. "She was working on it," remembers Denny Brooks, who was along for several Carpenters tours during the mid-1970s. "She was a little thick through the hips and thighs and middle. I know that concerned her," he says.

"She lost around twenty pounds and she looked fabulous," recalls Carole Curb. "She weighed about 110 or so, and she looked amazing. . . . If she'd just been able to stop there then life would have been beautiful. A lot of us girls in that era went through moments of that. Everybody wanted to be Twiggy. Just about everybody in the world has some sort of eating disorder—they eat too much or they eat too little. Karen's just got carried away. She just couldn't stop."

Having witnessed Karen's meticulous routine of counting calories and planning food intake for every meal, Richard complimented her initial weight loss during a break from recording as the two dined at the

Au Petit Café, a favorite French bistro on Vine Street near the A&M studios. "You look *great*," he told her.

"Well, I'm just going to get down to around 105."

"A hundred and *five*? You look great now."

Karen's response worried Richard. In fact, this was the first time he paused to consider that she might be taking the diet too far.

"With their success and being up on stage, she attempted to slim down and look a little better in a feminine sort of way," said Sherwin Bash, recalling her as a stocky tomboy prior to 1974. "Karen lost probably twenty pounds and looked terrific.... This didn't satisfy her because she needed more. She needed attention, love, care, and all the things that go with the success of losing that weight. Failing to get it, she continued to lose weight and became painfully thin.... Obviously she was looking at herself and seeing somebody that no one else saw; someone who was unattractive and overweight."

As Mike Curb had witnessed a year earlier, friends and family began to notice extreme changes in Karen's eating habits, despite her attempts at subtlety. She rearranged and pushed her food around the plate with a fork as she talked, which gave the appearance of eating. Another of her strategies involved offering samples of her food to others around the table. She would rave on and on about her delicious meal and then insist that everyone at the table try it for themselves. "Here, *you* have some," she would say as she enthusiastically scooped heaps of her own meal onto others' plates. "Would you like to taste this?" By the time dinner was over, Karen's plate was clean, but she had dispersed her entire meal to everyone else. Agnes caught on to this ploy and began to do the same in return. "Well, *this* is good, too," she would say as she put more food onto her daughter's plate. This infuriated Karen, who realized she would have to find other ways to successfully avoid eating.

THUMBING THROUGH a copy of *Reader's Digest*, Evelyn Wallace discovered an article detailing a teen girl's obsession with dieting. "She was doing the same things that Karen was doing, like playing with her food or leaving it," Wallace says. "She was somehow always getting away with not eating." The following is excerpted from the January 1975 issue of the *Digest*.

> The young high school sophomore weighed 135 pounds—about five pounds more than average for her height—and decided to diet. But when she reached her proper weight, she went right on depriving herself of food. Eight months later she entered a hospital weighing seventy-four pounds, the victim of self-inflicted starvation. Her bizarre affliction is known as anorexia nervosa.
>
> An emotional disorder that affects thousands of young women during high school and college years, the disturbance appears to be increasing rapidly. Dr. Hilde Bruch, professor of psychiatry at Baylor College of Medicine in Houston, believes that the national preoccupation with slimness plays a part in anorexia nervosa but that the condition is too complex to be defined simply as diet consciousness. The patient's refusal to eat, followed by grotesque emaciation, is the physical symptom of a deep-seated psychological disturbance. Most psychiatrists agree that the cure is twofold: putting back the weight to get the patient out of immediate danger and reaching the underlying emotional problems through psychotherapy.

Although she usually tried to steer clear of personal matters involving her employers, Wallace immediately recognized the parallels between this girl's story and Karen's, and she was alarmed. She went to Agnes with the magazine and read the article aloud. "I think Karen has what this little girl did," she told her. "Really, someone should be *doing* something about it or she'll end up the same way."

Evelyn did not feel it was her place to confront Karen on the matter but suggested to Agnes that Karen might need to see a doctor before the matter worsened. "I didn't want [Karen] to be angry with me and get the idea that I was trying to play doctor, and so I never mentioned the article to her. I showed it to Agnes and told her it was up to her." The magazine remained on the parents' bedside table for several weeks. "I don't think she ever showed it to Karen."

Cherry Boone O'Neill, oldest daughter of entertainer Pat Boone and member of the singing Boone Family, was suffering in a manner very similar to Karen. "I had never heard the term 'anorexia' or even the phrase 'eating disorder' until I was twenty years old in 1974," she says. "When I was seventeen, our pediatrician said he had seen people with my condition before and would have to hospitalize me if I didn't gain weight, but he never mentioned the name of the condition at that point. Finally, after struggling with both anorexia and bulimia for years and thinking that I was an isolated freak, I read an article in a news magazine that described anorexia and bulimia, and it made me realize I was not the only one struggling with these problems. The article didn't really tell me how to overcome my challenges, but it made me feel less alone, and it gave my condition a name. It identified the enemy."

By the time Karen's weight dropped to near ninety pounds, she looked for ways to disguise the weight loss, especially around those she knew would make comments or pester her to eat more. She began to layer her clothing, a strategy Sherwin Bash noticed in the early part of 1975. "She would start with a long-sleeved shirt and then put a blouse over that," he explained, "and a sweater over that and a jacket over that.... With all of it you had no idea of what she had become." But Evelyn Wallace was shocked when she caught a glimpse of Karen's gaunt figure as she sunbathed topless in back of the Newville house one afternoon. "They put this screen around her so nobody else could see her," Wallace explains. "She *loved* to go lay out in the sunshine. I don't know whether it was to get a tan or get away from her mother. Anyhow, I happened to go out to the kitchen for something and I saw her out there. She just had on her little bathing suit shorts. You couldn't tell whether it was a girl or a boy. She had absolutely no breasts."

IN FEBRUARY 1975 Karen met Terry Ellis, a friend of Ed and Frenda Leffler. Ellis had formed the British record label Chrysalis in 1969. Although he was based in London, where he helped guide the careers of Jethro Tull, Leo Sayer, and others, Ellis had recently bought a home in Los Angeles and was working to expand his label's presence in America. With the intent of matchmaking, Frenda introduced the two over dinner. As Ellis recalls, "I was a single guy, she was a single girl. Frenda said, 'You two lovely people should meet!' I liked Karen a lot on that first meeting. It was very difficult *not* to like Karen."

Karen was equally enthralled. Thirty-two-year-old Ellis was tall, with long, sandy blond hair to his shoulders and striking facial features. "He was *very* handsome," recalls Frenda. "He was a bon vivant. He drove a Bentley and was a man about town. He was just private jets all the way."

The dinner date with the Lefflers became the first of many, and a new relationship soon blossomed. According to Ellis, "We liked each other, made contact later, and started to see each other." Ellis observed that, unlike the rest of the Carpenter family, Karen was quite demonstrative and seemed to thrive on physical touch. "She was very loving and tactile, and she *loved* to be hugged." Those close to the couple sensed a strong chemistry between the two. Most important to Karen was that Richard approve of the man in her life, and he did. He and Terry Ellis quickly became friends.

Early in their relationship, Ellis encouraged Karen to take some time off to rest and relax with him on vacation in the south of France and on Tortola in the Virgin Islands. Arriving at Ellis's island home, Karen was horrified by a lack of creature comforts. With Terry out of earshot she phoned Frenda to rant about her surroundings. "Frenny, it's hard to believe they've even got *phones* over here," she said. "There's not even a television set!"

Frenda worried Karen would board the next plane back to Los Angeles. "You could never put Karen anywhere where there wasn't television," she explains. "She was regimented. Most people would adapt. Not Karen."

With Ellis's experience and expertise in the field of entertainment management and the record industry in general, it was only a matter of time before he became a part of Karen's professional as well as personal life. "I was an outsider, and it really wasn't my business," he says, but when he attended his first Carpenters concert he was flabbergasted by the lack of professionalism he witnessed in their stage show. "I watched them perform, and my mouth dropped because she was a terrible performer," he says. "She hadn't the slightest idea about how to use a stage.

She did everything wrong. She wasn't using her vivacious personality or her wonderful smile. She wasn't using the fact that the audiences absolutely worshiped her. She'd sing a song, and when the guitar player or drummer played a little solo she'd turn her back on the audience and sort of click her fingers and had no interrelation with the audience. Anybody who goes near stage when they're six years old learns that you never, ever, ever turn your back on an audience. I just simply couldn't believe they had so-called top-class management and nobody had taken her by the hand and said, 'Karen, let's work on your stage show.' They could have hired somebody to produce their show."

Terry could not hold back. He was an expert in concert construction and was accustomed to evaluating his artists after every show in an effort to continuously better their performances. Back at the hotel, Karen was shocked by his blunt analysis. "Karen, I'm sorry to say this, but you were *terrible*," he said. "Now, that's the bad news. But the good news is that you're never going to be that terrible again! Tomorrow I'm taking you onto the stage, and I am going to teach you some fundamentals."

The two walked the stage as Ellis explained that Karen should never stand in front of Cubby O'Brien or Tony Peluso with her back to the audience during their solos. She should face the audience, walk toward them, and interact.

"What do you mean?" she asked.

"Go to the front of the stage and reach your hand out," he instructed.

"Well, why should I do that?"

"Well, the audience will like it!"

"Well, what will they do?"

"Well, they'll jump up and they'll hold your hand."

"No they won't!"

"Yes, Karen, they will. And they will absolutely love it!"

Ellis continued, explaining to Karen that she had ignored the audience members seated in the balcony the night before. "Walk out to the edge of the stage and look up to the people in the balcony and wave at them," he said.

"Oh, I can't do *that!*"

"Well, yes you can, Karen. They'll love it."

"And what will they do?"

"They'll *wave back*, Karen!"

"No they won't," she said. "They won't!"

She argued, but Karen took the stage that night and took command in a way she had never done before. The interaction with the audience was a natural for her, but for some reason she had avoided such communication in the past. "She was like a kid in a candy store," recalls Ellis. "She discovered something that made life more exciting and more fulfilling."

As Evelyn Wallace recalls, "All of a sudden, here she was moving her arms and walking from one side of the stage to the other so that everybody could see her. It didn't take her long to realize she had to move around and interact more."

Karen's sudden on-stage blossoming took Richard by surprise. According to Terry Ellis, he reacted badly to the change in the dynamic, which was curious since it was at his urging that Karen left the drums for the forefront in the first place. "Richard had been so used to being the focus of everybody's attention that it came as something of a shock to him and something he found difficult to handle. It upset him. He couldn't understand why she was getting attention and he wasn't. At one point in Las Vegas, he was having a bit of a rant about how unappreciated he was and that nobody knew what he did—and he wasn't wrong about that. He was the musical genius behind the Carpenters, but nobody was taking any trouble to ensure that he got the credit he deserved. Karen was the focus of attention. She was the girl with the golden voice; the voice of an angel."

When Ellis arrived in Las Vegas for a series of shows, he discovered Richard was furious after having been introduced as 'the piano player with the Carpenters' during a panel discussion for *Billboard* magazine. "Have you discussed this with your managers?" Ellis asked. "Are they *doing* anything about it?"

"Well," Richard said, "no."

In Las Vegas the Carpenters were augmented by a large orchestra backing their own group. At the beginning of every show the conductor would lead the orchestra in playing an overture just prior to Karen and Richard's entrance. Ellis made one suggestion to Richard. "Rather than you just shambling onto the stage playing the piano, let's let the audiences know who and what you are. Let's have you come out at the first on the stage and *you* conduct the overture!" In Ellis's opinion, an orchestral conductor was a position of command, responsibility, and authority. "That immediately establishes you as someone who is a bit special and not just the piano player." Ellis was happy to help but felt he might have overstepped some boundaries in coaching Karen and Richard. He blamed management—particularly Sherwin Bash—for not having addressed these issues much earlier. "Basically, you're both being held back by your manager," he told them.

"Karen and Richard were kids from Downey, and the show business world was a bit overpowering to them," Ellis explains. "They were excited and felt very lucky that they seemed to have had some breaks. They had a fairly well-known manager, and they felt they were very fortunate to have him, but he did a terrible, terrible job. There was no career plan. There was no one thinking about the long term prospects for the Carpenters or for Richard or for Karen. I don't think anybody was sitting down with them and saying, 'Let's talk about your career and work out how we're going to make this last until you're fifty, sixty, or seventy years old.'"

By the time *Horizon* saw release in June 1975, two years had passed since the Carpenters' previous studio album. Disappointing to some was its brevity, clocking in at just under thirty-five minutes in duration, but the tremendous advances in sound quality due to new and improved recording techniques prevailed. The debut *Offering* album was completed using only eight tracks, while the Carpenters' next four LPs were recorded on sixteen. *Horizon* was the first to take advantage of A&M's graduation to twenty-four-track recording, and it did not go unnoticed. Stephen Holden of *Rolling Stone* called it their "most musically sophisticated album to date," saying it "smoothly adapts the spirit of mainstream Fifties pop to contemporary taste.... Karen Carpenter has developed into a fine vocal technician, whose mellow interpretation of the Eagles' 'Desperado' and Neil Sedaka's 'Solitaire' evidence professionalism on a par with such Fifties stars as Jo Stafford and Rosemary Clooney.... Richard Carpenter has imposed more elaborately orchestrated textures than before and wisely mixed them at a level that doesn't distract attention from Karen's intimately mixed singing."

Within two weeks of its release, *Horizon* was certified gold. Although it reached the top of the charts in the United Kingdom and Japan, the album missed the U.S. Top 10 when it peaked at #13. According to Richard, the single "Only Yesterday" was one of their better technical achievements, in which he employed a Phil Spector "wall of sound" approach. Even so, the song's success cost him and John Bettis the thousand dollars they bet a studio engineer that it would not be a hit. According to Bettis, sitting down to write "Only Yesterday" he thought to himself, "Oh boy, here we go again—another *yesterday* song." He was able to avoid the sad and somewhat melancholy approach taken in "Goodbye to Love" and "Yesterday Once More," turning this song into an upbeat, optimistic love song and one about "being in love *now*," he explained. "And yesterday was not so good because you weren't here."

In 1991, while remixing various tracks for a Japanese karaoke compilation, Richard discovered an unmarked, forgotten *Horizon* outtake on a multitrack tape for "Only Yesterday." It was Karen's work lead with piano, bass, and drums for the David Pomeranz tune, "Trying to Get the Feeling Again," recorded in 1975. It became the title track for a Barry Manilow album released four months after *Horizon* and a hit single for him in 1976. The Carpenters' version was abandoned when Richard decided the album had plenty of strong ballads. It remained unfinished and was somehow never cataloged into A&M's tape library. Adding a twenty-four-piece string section, acoustic guitar, electric guitar, and synthesizer, Richard completed their version of "Trying to Get the Feeling Again" for *Interpretations: A 25th Anniversary Celebration* released in 1994.

Legendary arranger Billy May's lush treatment of the Andrews Sisters' "I Can Dream, Can't I?" was one of several big band ballads Karen recorded during her career, and according to Holden of *Rolling Stone*, "such a gem of updated schmaltz, it makes me wish that veteran masters of the studio like Gordon Jenkins, Ray Ellis, Nelson Riddle and Percy Faith would be encouraged to collaborate with other best selling middle of the road acts of the Seventies."

Jazz critic Dave Gelly agreed and took notice of Karen's careful attention to microphone technique. "She sings very close to the microphone, starting at around Julie London or Peggy Lee volume, that's to say, not much more than a whisper. Then, she gradually opens up to about Jo Stafford level. No tears, no dramatics—just plain, unfussy and beautifully done."

Ken Barnes's review for *Phonograph Record* called *Horizon* "soft-rock Nirvana," going on to say, "It's certainly less than revolutionary to admit you like the Carpenters these days (in rock circles, if you recall, it formerly bordered on heresy). Everybody must be won over by now.... If all MOR were this good, one might not resent its all-out appropriation of the airwaves.... As for the Carpenters, they've transcended the genre and stand in a class by themselves."

KAREN'S NEW slim figure required that she purchase a new stage wardrobe, and she opted for a number of low-cut silky gowns, some strapless or even backless. Sherwin Bash was horrified to see her bony shoulders and ribs. Even her hip bones were visible through the thin layers of fabric. He asked Karen to rethink the wardrobe choices before going on stage. "I talked her into putting a jacket on over the bare back and bare arms," he said, "but the audience saw it."

There was often a collective gasp from the audience when Karen would take the stage. In fact, after a few shows, Bash was approached by concerned fans who knew something was terribly wrong but assumed she had cancer or some other disease. Even critics took note of her gaunt appearance. A review for *Variety* praised Karen's exit from the drums but commented on her deteriorating appearance. "She is terribly thin, almost a wraith, and should be gowned more becomingly."

It became increasingly obvious to Terry Ellis that his girlfriend's dieting was far more complex than a simple attempt to shed a few pounds. Even in the few months since the two had met, Karen had withered before Terry's eyes. "When she went onstage she usually had some backless outfit on," he recalls. "You could see her shoulder blades and ribs sticking out. You could tell that she was much thinner than she ought to be."

Five days of shows at Connecticut's Oakdale Theater in Wallingford were attended by many of the duo's childhood friends. Agnes and Harold flew in for the week and were met at their hotel by Carl and Teresa Vaiuso, who drove them to the show. The Oakdale was just fifteen miles north of New Haven's Hall Street, where the couples had first met and raised their families nearly twenty years earlier. "[Harold] was beside himself," Teresa recalled. "As soon as we picked them up, that was the first thing he said. He said, 'She's not fooling me, I know what's wrong with Karen. She has anorexia nervosa.' That was the first time I ever really heard that. I thought, 'What is he saying? Could this be true?' And sure enough, when we went to see her, that's exactly what she had. The father was right."

According to John Bettis, no one really understood why Karen wasn't eating. To those around her the solution seemed simple: *eat.* "Anorexia nervosa was so new to me that I didn't even know how to pronounce it until 1980," he said. "From the outside the solution looks so simple. All a person has to do is eat. So we were constantly trying to shove food at Karen. . . . My opinion about anorexia is it's an attempt to have control; something in your life that you can do something about, that you can regiment. I think that just got out of control with her."

Cherry O'Neill confirms that control was most definitely a factor in her own struggles. "When you start denying yourself food and begin feeling you have control over a life that has been pretty much controlled for you, it's exhilarating. The anorexic feels that while she may not be able to control anything else, she will, by God, control every morsel that goes in her mouth."

In contrast with Karen's dieting rituals, Terry Ellis was a connoisseur of both wine and fine dining. He enjoyed participating in long, leisurely dinners at many of the top restaurants across Europe. Karen would order her usual salad and push the greens around the plate while drinking water with dozens of lemons.

It was not long before Ellis witnessed the habits the rest of Karen's friends and family had observed for many months. She pretended to eat a lot, when in reality she was allocating the food to those around her. On one particular instance, out to dinner with the band, Karen ordered a huge slice of cake at the end of meal. "She made a big deal out of telling everybody how she'd ordered this cake, how it looked amazing, and how she was really looking forward to it," Ellis recalls. "It was like, 'Look at me, I'm eating this big piece of cake!' When it arrived, she nibbled a corner of it and said, 'Wow, this is fantastic,' and started working her way around the room, going to the band saying, 'Boy, this cake is delicious! You've got to try a piece.' By the time she'd finished there was very little left on the plate."

Band members and others made aware of her condition agreed that Karen fit the description of anorexia to a T. Backstage they witnessed her exhaustion. She was lying down between shows, something she had rarely, if ever, done before. They were shocked to see how she could be flat on her back one minute and on stage singing the next. Even when doing back-to-back shows, Karen displayed "a tremendous amount of nervous energy," said Sherwin Bash. He was a no-nonsense kind of man who freely spoke his mind and had no qualms confronting Karen on the issue of anorexia, even calling it by name, and he did not back down. "The fact that she was anorexic was discussed innumerable times. . . . There was every attempt to get her to seek professional help, but I believe her family was the kind of family that the mother would say, 'We can take care of ourselves. We don't need to have someone. This is a family matter.'"

According to Ellis, at times Karen seemed to seek the attention of her family and did not mind it coming at the expense of their frustrations with her disorder. When she dieted, or "overdieted" as he explains, there was a rush of attention from the family, especially Agnes. "Karen had never had attention before, so she liked it. The experts say that one of the things that seems to drive young girls to diet and overdiet is that they were oftentimes the kids that never got attention. It's a way of getting the love from their family that they never got before."

FOR THE summer tour of 1975, manager Sherwin Bash paired Karen and Richard with veteran pop singer Neil Sedaka, who was also managed by BNB Associates. Sedaka, experiencing a comeback and the success of his new single "Laughter in the Rain," would be their opening act. His unbridled energy and onstage antics made him popular with audiences but also made the Carpenters' portion of the show seem a bit dull and disappointing to some. They were pros at presenting their impeccable musicianship in concerts, but there was very little focus on theatrics.

During their first shows together at the Riviera Hotel and Casino in Las Vegas, it was already apparent to the Carpenters that Sedaka's portion of the show was better received by the audiences than their own. "In contrast to my thirty-five minutes, their act was quiet and subdued," Sedaka wrote in his 1982 autobiography *Laughter in the Rain: My Own Story.* "While I was obviously thrilled to be on stage, the Carpenters seemed to walk through the act."

As the tour continued on to New England, the press seemed to agree. "Sedaka Steals Show from Carpenters," read a *New York Daily News* headline. Management began hiding the reviews from Karen and Richard, but Sedaka immediately felt resentment coming from the duo. "I don't know what happened," said Bash. "From the very beginning there wasn't a good feeling between Karen, Richard, and Neil. He was doing things or saying things which they were not comfortable with. . . . I could not soothe all the ruffled feathers."

By summer's end the Carpenters' latest single—their version of Sedaka's own "Solitaire"—was climbing the charts, and the tour returned to the Riviera for another two-week run. On the second night, Richard announced to the band that, due to time constraints, he was pulling the finale, in which Sedaka joined Karen and Richard onstage. All hell broke loose the following night during Sedaka's opening act when he took a moment to nonchalantly introduce and welcome guests Tom Jones and Dick Clark, who were seated in the audience. It was an unwritten rule that this sort of introduction was to be left to the headliner. For Richard, this was the last straw. He was already upset to have learned Sedaka was using the Carpenters' orchestra. And several keys had been broken on Richard's piano during Sedaka's act. Now he was breaking protocol by introducing celebrities in the audience. "When I left the stage," Sedaka recalled, "I heard Richard Carpenter screaming, 'Get that son of a bitch out!'"

Karen was crying, "Neil, I'm so sorry about this."

Sherwin Bash was in Germany making arrangements with promoters for the upcoming European tour when the call came in from the Riviera. "I got a phone call one night from Richard absolutely hysterical." Bash agreed it was a huge blunder and asked Richard if he wanted to fire Sedaka. "You *bet* I want to fire him," Richard retorted.

"I was in Berlin, not exactly around the corner from the Riviera Hotel in Las Vegas," recalled Bash. "I called and had half of the people in my office in Los Angeles fly up there to no avail. Richard would not agree that this was not the end of the world. He just totally lost it over this." The next day Sedaka was informed that Richard wanted him to leave the tour immediately. His remaining days would be paid off.

By the time Terry Ellis reached Richard by phone it was too late. "We fired Neil Sedaka," he said.

"*Excuse me?*" Ellis roared. He was certain the backlash would be terribly damaging for the Carpenters.

"Neil Sedaka was and is a very talented guy and a very seasoned veteran in show business," Ellis says. "He'd been writing hit songs for twenty years at that point; he'd been around show business for a long time, and he knew what he was doing. The poor guy was just doing his job! He was going onstage and doing his absolute best. He had a real show he'd put together, and they didn't. He brought the house down every night because he knew how to do it—and they didn't. This upset Richard, and he decided that Sedaka was getting out of place—he wasn't supposed to do that—he was supposed to support, not upstage. The guy was doing his job! He was being paid to be the very best that he could."

Following the advice of several fellow entertainers, Sedaka held a press conference telling those present he was "in a state of shock. It was Richard who first suggested I tour with them. It was a wonderful trip. Every performance was filled with ovations. . . . They felt I was too strong. I guess I was going over better than they had expected." He justified the introduction of Tom Jones and Dick Clark saying, "They are both close friends of mine, and I've written songs for Tom. It's the first time I've ever been asked to leave because of *good* performances. I feel badly that such talented people would have such insecurity. Ironically, they have a current hit record, 'Solitaire,' which is my composition."

Sedaka stressed there was no resentment or bitterness, only sorrow. "I don't want to bad-mouth the Carpenters," he said, refusing the invitation of fellow performers Steve Lawrence and Eydie Gorme to tell their Caesar's Palace audience exactly what happened. Before leaving Las Vegas, Elliott Abbott rebooked Sedaka at the Riviera as a headliner, making it obvious which side he took in this battle. Sedaka parted ways with Sherwin Bash and BNB Associates, forming his own management agency with Abbott. Werner Wolfen flew to Las Vegas in an attempt to pacify Richard, who was by then upset with the manner in which Bash had handled the situation. He blamed Sherwin for planting the seed to fire Sedaka during their phone conversation. Richard's solution was to fire Sherwin and hire Terry Ellis as the Carpenters' new manager, but Wolfen was hesitant to do so. He felt there was a possible conflict of interest since Karen was dating Ellis. Even so, Richard insisted Bash be terminated immediately. "It wasn't Karen, it was Richard," Bash recalled. "He arranged with an attorney to have me discharged. And Neil Sedaka, feeling that nobody was representing him in all of this, arranged with his attorney and had me discharged as well. So over introducing Tom Jones and Dick Clark, I was fired by both artists."

Upon returning to home base in Downey, an overwhelmed Richard Carpenter was caught off guard when Terry Ellis refused his offer to manage the Carpenters. He explained he would do so only on a temporary basis, agreeing to stay until a replacement was found. As Ellis predicted, the story of the firing spread like wildfire through newspaper and radio reports. "The Carpenters 'Nail' Neil Sedaka!" "Sedaka Fired for Being Too Strong." Music critics and deejays began to poke fun at the Carpenters when playing or reviewing their music. Joel McNally wrote in the *Milwaukee Journal* that the Sedaka incident was "the first time in recorded history that the Carpenters have been heard to utter a curse—even if it was only 'Grimy Gumdrops.'"

The Carpenters Fan Club worked to respond to hundreds of letters following the Sedaka episode. Evelyn Wallace kept quiet but was embarrassed to learn Richard had lost his temper and caused such a scene. "I didn't think much of him at the time for doing what he did," she says. "I'm sure Richard wanted to introduce those guys, but he could have said something like, 'I'd like to thank Neil for introducing so-and-so,' and that would have shown he was the bigger man."

In a statement to fan club members, Richard offered the following explanation:

> It often happens in our business, not only with the Carpenters, but also with other headliners, that the choice of the opening act proves to be unsuitable for personal or other reasons. Under those circumstances, the headliner has no option but to terminate the engagement of the opener. This was the situation with Neil. Please be assured that we *did not* fire Neil Sedaka for doing too well. In fact we were delighted that he was receiving a nice response from the audience. It was a result of other circumstances of which he is totally aware that made it necessary for us to terminate his engagement.... It is a disappointment to us that he found it necessary to make statements concerning same to the press. Personally, the Las Vegas/Sedaka issue is an old matter, and right now I am much more concerned with Karen's health and writing new songs.

Reviews for the Riviera shows continued to come in, most written before the pandemonium ensued. According to *Variety*, "Current fortnight with Neil Sedaka is the best combination for them so far.... Audience reaction is overwhelming at times." It went on to praise Sedaka's performance, saying it "generates enough excitement in his opening forty minutes to indicate future headline status...prompting a standing ovation opening show." Another reviewer referred to opening night at the Riviera as "Sedaka's night."

—◦◦◦◦—

COMPOUNDED BY the stress of the Riviera engagement, Karen's failing health could no longer be ignored. In addition to her skeletal appearance, she was mentally and physically exhausted. Fall tours set for Europe and Japan only promised further deterioration for her weakened body and spirit. "I kept telling myself, 'I'm not really sick. I'll be better tomorrow,'" she explained to Ray Coleman in an article for *Melody Maker* entitled "Karen: Why I Collapsed." "When you have a show to do you just bear on through it. But it kept getting worse, and the last two days [in Vegas], I don't know how I got through. . . . It's annoying to feel that I couldn't withstand what I was doing to myself. You tend to say, 'Hey, no sweat. I can handle it,' but this time I couldn't."

Although she made it through the Vegas shows without a major incident, upon returning to Los Angeles Karen checked into Cedars-Sinai Medical Center, where she spent five days while doctors ran tests and worked to strengthen her severely weakened immune system. Upon discharge she was ordered to eat, rest, and refrain from working until the end of October. This would be the first of several hospital stays. Most were concealed, some even from her family. "There were so many hospitalizations," Frenda Franklin recalls. "There were so many near misses."

In this case the doctors declared Karen was in no shape to tour overseas as planned. The concerts would have to be rescheduled to allow her additional time to rest at home where she could attempt to recover and put on some weight. "She is suffering a severe case of physical and nervous exhaustion," said Dr. Robert Koblin in a statement to the press. "She had a hectic four-week schedule lined up in Europe, but I could not allow her to go through with it. In my opinion it would have been highly dangerous to her long term health."

Melody Maker reported that the Carpenters' tour would have been the highest-grossing tour in Britain and that approximately 150,000 people were set to see them during the planned twenty-eight day European trek. Ticket sales for the fifty shows, which sold out in a matter of hours, were refunded. It was reported that the Carpenters may have easily lost upward of $250,000 due to the cancelled concerts. In Japan, promoter Tats Nagashima said the tour would have grossed upward of $1.2 million and set numerous records in that country. On behalf of A&M Records, a concerned Jerry Moss phoned overseas tour promoters and guaranteed whatever losses such concert cancellations would incur.

Karen took the losses quite personally, apologizing profusely to management, those at A&M, and especially Richard. "I felt bad for Richard because my illness held him back," she said the following year. "And he felt bad for me, too, because he considered that it was his fault in driving me so hard. Then we both got mad because we had not put on the brakes earlier and stopped all the pressures that eventually led to my exhaustion."

Terry Ellis accompanied Richard to London and Tokyo where the two held press conferences explaining the cancellations. Richard addressed the UK media with the following statement.

Karen is really in a state of exhaustion, both mental and physical, but mostly physical. We had a tour in April and a tour in May, a five-week summer tour, two two-week engagements in Las Vegas, and it really left us no time to get much rest. The last week in Vegas she was down to eighty-six pounds.... The whole European tour in all was fifty concerts in twenty-eight days and I wouldn't have wanted her to do it even if through a miracle she got through it.... Karen's really upset at not being able to do this, and I am too, of course. I just wanted to come over in person and apologize.... We will be back as soon as is possible.

"Girls just can't take that life without something going wrong," Terry Ellis added.

Reflecting on this remark, Ellis says he never noticed that women find the touring life physically more demanding than men. "It sounds as though I was complicit in the 'anorexia cover-up' for Karen."

Gossip and rumors greeted the men when they arrived in Europe and Japan, with some reports saying Karen was battling cancer, others hinting she was suicidal. "When Richard returned he didn't want to tell me of the whispers that were circulating," Karen recalled. "It was all so much crap. Not once had suicide entered my head. I was depressed, yes, but my God, not enough to commit suicide. I value life too much for that. No, the real alarm was over my frightening loss of weight. At first I lost the weight I intended to lose, but it went on even though I began eating like mad to counteract it."

Under Agnes Carpenter's close watch, Karen slept fourteen to sixteen hours a day. "My mother thought I was dead," she told Ray Coleman. "I normally manage on four to six hours. It was obvious that for the past two years I'd been running on nervous energy." Her weight eventually climbed to 104 pounds.

Hearing of Karen's illness and ordered bed rest, Frank Pooler went to Newville and spent the afternoon with her. "She was very sick and said it was something with her colon," he says. Per Karen, the diagnosis was spastic colitis, sometimes referred to as irritable bowel syndrome. "I had no idea that she was having eating problems," says Pooler.

Karen confessed to Pooler during his visit that she was depressed because of the situation with Neil Sedaka. "I just think that kind of made her heart sick," he remembers. "She just didn't want to do anything else."

Karen was surprised when letters from worried fans poured in to Carpenters headquarters. "People never think of entertainers as being human," Karen observed. "When you walk out on stage the audience thinks nothing can go wrong with them. They see you as idols, not as ordinary human beings. We get sick and we have headaches just like they do. When we are cut, we bleed. My breakdown was caused by a combination of troubles that came as thick as the layers of a sandwich cake. Everything happened at once."

The fan club commented on Karen's condition in their December 1975 newsletter.

> Please be assured there is no truth in the rumor that Karen is a victim of cancer. Coupled with severe physical and mental exhaustion, due to overwork, dieting and lack of rest, she developed Colitis (i.e.

inflammation of the colon.) Her collapse was inevitable after the rigorous schedule of the past summer months, and her willing spirit was eventually dominated by Mother Nature who compelled her to take a well deserved rest. Thank God she exudes her vivacious, happy personality once again.

10

I NEED TO BE IN LOVE

"TERRY AND I, we're in love," Karen told Evelyn Wallace as the two stepped into the office at Newville one afternoon.

"That's great, Karen!" Ev exclaimed. "I'm glad to hear that you've found somebody."

Karen surprised everyone in late 1975 when she moved into Terry's Beverly Hills home. "Her moving out of Newville nearly knocked me over," Wallace recalls. "Mainly because I didn't think Agnes would let her out the front door."

Richard claimed to have no qualms with Karen's decision to move in with Terry. Even so, it was Karen's wish to remain discreet. "I didn't even know they lived together," says Carole Curb. "In those times, if girls did it they didn't talk about it." But Karen's mother was indeed upset. "Agnes was furious," says Frenda Franklin. "Furious!" Not only was her daughter living with a man out of wedlock, which went against her strong, traditional belief system, she was leaving Downey for the first time. "I suggested that she should come and live with me," Ellis says, "which I suppose was a big mistake on my part. Her mother just freaked out. It wasn't part of her plan."

It was soon obvious to Ellis that Agnes considered him to be a threat to the family's authority over Karen. In fact, the biggest threat was the possibility that he might persuade Karen to go solo and perhaps even move to England, disbanding the duo and leaving Richard on his own. According to Frenda, Terry did want to make Karen a solo artist and had the capability to do so. "Since he owned Chrysalis Records he could have made that happen. They all just freaked so they started their hatchet job on him." Ellis disagrees with the idea that he would have encouraged Karen to go solo but agrees that Agnes was on guard. "The family—and by 'the family' I mean her mother—saw me as a threat to her relationship with Karen and her control over Karen," he says. "My reading of the situation was that her mother saw me as such a threat that she more or less made Karen choose between me and her."

Whether or not Agnes sabotaged the love affair was of little relevance. Within no time it became apparent that the social gap between the couple was far too wide. Karen was "in love with being in love," Frenda claims, "but then when there were demands, like 'I want you to come live in England,' it just freaked her out. Terry was very continental, and he would have taken her away. That would have been good in the end, but it was too soon for her to jump ship like that. She couldn't have lived in England on his level. It was a world of private jets and islands of Tortola. . . . It was the world she wanted but was not even close to being ready for."

As much as Karen wanted to be "uptown" she was still very much a middle-class American girl who liked to relax at home in the evening and watch television with her snack on a TV tray. "There were no televisions in that house," Frenda explains. "You laugh? It was not funny with her." Within a matter of only a few weeks, Karen became restless in Ellis's palatial Beverly Hills home. "I can't go on like this," she told Frenda. "I have to get out of here!"

As they would do periodically, the Lefflers came to Karen's rescue, bailing her out in times of great despair. With Ellis out of town, Karen packed her things and left without warning. "She didn't even have the maturity to end that the right way," Frenda says. "She wanted to have it, but she just didn't have it in her. She just left. She was afraid. We had to go get her. She was pretty broken when she left." The relationship with Terry Ellis ended as quickly as it had begun, but Karen was too ashamed to face him. Instead, she phoned him shortly after moving out.

"This just can't work," she told him. "We aren't right for each other, and it's too difficult. We just have to stop seeing each other."

Ellis sensed this was the work of Agnes and the hypnotic hold she seemed to have over her daughter. "Her mother gave her such hell that she just moved straight back," he says. "It's difficult to know if that's what Karen wanted or if that's what Karen had to have or what was forced on her by her mother and her family." He disagrees that Karen was ill prepared for or ill suited to his lifestyle. "When Karen was with me, we traveled somewhat and went to France, and she really enjoyed it," he says. "When I was with her away from her family she would *come alive*! There was a lot of depth to Karen that you could see privately, but as soon as she got back into the family situation she would change.

"Very early on Harold and Agnes found that Richard had this extraordinary talent. He was a musical genius—no question about that—he was and is, but from the point they realized he had this talent, the whole family's energy was devoted to Richard's career. They moved coasts in order to give him more opportunities, and everybody in the family was told, 'We have this unique talent in the family,' 'Richard is a genius,' and 'We all have to sacrifice in order to insure that he gets the best opportunities to expose his talents.' So at a very early age Karen was told that her job in life was to support Richard. That continued all the way up through their careers until they became huge stars and beyond. If you were to go into the family environment, where I was a lot, there was that same dynamic of 'Everybody's here for Richard' and 'It's really Richard who's the star.' Even when Karen had become the star, that dynamic still existed, and she would fall in line."

Frenda feels certain that Karen was content not being the star of the family. "That wasn't what made her ill, I am positive of that," she says. "It was just being ignored. That's different. You don't have to be the star, but you can't just be pushed to the side and have no value."

Karen spoke briefly of her relationship with Terry Ellis in an interview for the *Daily Mirror*. "We had a thing going for a while, but we weren't exactly matched. We are still good friends," she said, but confessed, "I don't think I have ever really been in love," a comment she would later regret. "Everyone keeps saying that I'll know when it happens. Well, I'm waiting. Love is something I want very badly to feel. There is nothing more I want out of life right now than to be married and have children. That would be wonderful. But it must happen naturally and, I hope, in the next couple of years."

As Evelyn Wallace recalls, Agnes relished in welcoming Karen back to Newville with a bit of an "I told you so" attitude. "It's a good thing you came back home," she told her. But Karen was unhappy. The breakup with Ellis was terribly painful; it was the closest thing to a long-term relationship she had experienced. Not only was it the end of romance, it was the end of the Carpenters' professional relationship with Ellis, and—perhaps most crushing—it was another botched attempt by Karen at breaking free and leaving home. She was twenty-five years old and returning home to live with her parents in Downey, but Karen vowed that this return to Newville would be short-lived. "She really wanted to move out of that house," Wallace recalls. "I think her mother was getting her down to the point where she wanted out. She wanted to get her own apartment."

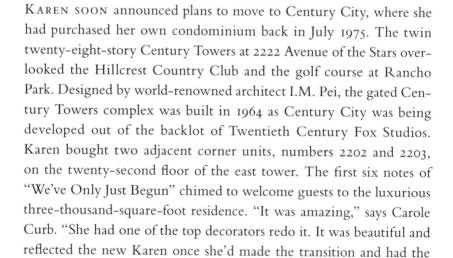

KAREN SOON announced plans to move to Century City, where she had purchased her own condominium back in July 1975. The twin twenty-eight-story Century Towers at 2222 Avenue of the Stars overlooked the Hillcrest Country Club and the golf course at Rancho Park. Designed by world-renowned architect I.M. Pei, the gated Century Towers complex was built in 1964 as Century City was being developed out of the backlot of Twentieth Century Fox Studios. Karen bought two adjacent corner units, numbers 2202 and 2203, on the twenty-second floor of the east tower. The first six notes of "We've Only Just Begun" chimed to welcome guests to the luxurious three-thousand-square-foot residence. "It was amazing," says Carole Curb. "She had one of the top decorators redo it. It was beautiful and reflected the new Karen once she'd made the transition and had the successes and everything."

"Well, what do you like?" decorator John Cottrell had asked Karen.

"You better sit down," she cautioned. Karen's decorating tastes were eclectic and a fusion of contemporary, country, and French styles. "I want it to look classy, in a funky kind of way," she told him. "I want it to be top-notch, top class, yet I want people to feel like they can put their feet up on anything. I don't want it to look [stuffy], yet I want it to be beautiful."

"Oh dear," Cottrell said.

In the end, the Lucite- and chrome-accented living room was offset by a country style kitchen. Personalizing Karen's new uptown residence were the many stuffed animals she positioned neatly across the huge bed. The bedroom was designed around an Advent VideoBeam home theater system with a seven-foot-wide screen, just like the one Richard had installed at Lubec Street. Carole Curb recalls that Karen's bedroom closet was a fine example of her friend's quest for perfectionism. "Karen was very, very meticulous," she says. "The clothes hangers were all the same and a quarter-inch apart. The pants were all together, the blouses all together. It was like an amazing boutique with everything arranged in order."

Another frequent visitor was fellow singer Olivia Newton-John. She and Karen first met in 1971 at Annabel's, a nightclub in London's Berkeley Square, and over the succeeding years developed a close friendship. "Karen was a very friendly, outgoing girl," Olivia says. "We hit it off since we are both down-to-earth people. We connected on that level, and we both liked the other's voice. We talked about doing a duet for fun, but it never eventuated because we were both so busy with our own things. We both had such crazy lives that we understood each other. Usually our schedules were so crazy that we just managed to meet for lunch, or I'd go to her place in Century City. Her place was *immaculate*. It was really a very beautiful apartment with the most amazing view. I remember thinking, 'Oh, she's so lucky. She's got this amazing pad all to herself.' She was very clean, very tidy. Obviously she had issues and probably could have had obsessive-compulsive disorder."

Interspersed among the chic and stylish decor was Karen's collection of Mickey Mouse and Disney memorabilia. "She had a lot of child in her," Olivia recalls. "She loved childhood things, she was funny and she was quirky." As Karen would often do, she invented several nick-names for each of her closest friends. Olivia was affectionately referred to as Livvy or ONJ (which Karen pronounced Ahhnj). According to Frenda, Karen had nicknames for everything. "The whole *world* was a nickname," she says. "It was like she actually had her own language. She'd say, 'Did you talk to the 'rents?' Those were my parents. If you didn't know what she was thinking about, you'd think she was from another country. She'd be fantastic at text messaging!"

Karen's new residence was only a few miles from the Leffler home on Tower Road, and Frenda welcomed her to the neighborhood and helped her establish a new sense of community. At Century Towers there were doormen who took a liking to Karen and made her feel at home. Just around the corner on Pico Boulevard was Owen's, her favorite market. "She made it a little neighborhood," Frenda says, "like her own little Downey. She loved to go on little errands with me or wherever I went, and she wanted to learn all the nice places for the locals and things that were native to Beverly Hills and Los Angeles."

When the two entered Edelweiss Candy on Canon Drive, Karen was thrilled to see the candy being hand dipped and made on the prem-ises. She rarely enjoyed such confectionery delights but was fascinated with the preparation and presentation of all types of food. "Oh my God," she told Frenda. "Now *this* is a candy store!"

JANUARY 1, 1976, brought a new contract with A&M Records and the naming of Jerry Weintraub of Management III as the Carpenters' new manager. Weintraub was an entertainment powerhouse whose career began as a talent agent for MCA Records in the 1950s. By the time he came to manage Karen and Richard he had worked with such clients as Elvis Presley, Frank Sinatra, and Judy Garland, in addition to having helped guide John Denver to the enormous success he was seeing by the mid-1970s.

Weintraub's first order of Carpenters business was to map out a plan for the duo with longevity as the foundation. They were primarily a recording group, but prior to 1976 their schedule had left them with very little time to spend in the studio. Five years of incessant touring had left Karen and Richard burned out, exhausted, and without personal lives. When not on endless tours of one-nighters across the United States they could be found in Europe or Japan for even more concerts, television appearances, and interviews. "It was sickening," Karen told *People Weekly* in a cover story for the magazine. "Suddenly it wasn't fun anymore."

As the Carpenters' new manager, Weintraub vowed to change the group's direction by limiting the number of concerts they would perform each year and making certain there was plenty of time in the recording studio. Despite these attempts, their next studio album, *A Kind of Hush*, did little to mask the poor health and fatigue that had plagued the duo the year prior. Failing to break into the Top 30 in the United States, it marked the beginning of a descent in their popularity. The title track and debut single was an insubstantial cover of the Herman's Hermits hit and one of two castanet-heavy oldies, the other being Neil Sedaka's "Breaking Up Is Hard to Do." Giving a new meaning to the word "oldie" was "Goofus," written in 1931 and previously recorded by Les Paul, the Dinning Sisters, and Chet Atkins. Calling the album "an overdose of pretty," music critic Joel McNally felt *Hush* was an appropriate title for an album that displayed such little dynamic contrast. "At this point it is the odds-on favorite to win the Grammy," he joked, "the Nobel Peace Prize and the *Reader's Digest* Sweepstakes."

The album's savior came in the form of a Carpenter-Bettis original and what John Bettis considered to be "Goodbye to Love: Part Two." "I Need to Be in Love" began as only a song title and a few bars of melody by Albert Hammond, who was writing songs with Bettis in England. Although their version of the song was never completed, the title was presented to Richard Carpenter, and it came to life in a way Bettis likened to "a little ball of twine" the duo "unrolled and knitted into a sweater."

Karen declared "I Need to Be in Love" to be her autobiographical anthem from first listen. "When he wrote the lyrics to that thing I was just flabbergasted," she said. "The first verse of that says, 'The hardest thing I've ever done is keep believing / there's someone in this crazy world for me / the way that people come and go through temporary lives / my chance could come and I might never know.' I said, 'Oh my God, it's so true.'" Bettis felt the lyric told not only Karen's story but his own and Richard's as well. It was penned during a phase when all three were looking for love with no success. "'I Need to Be in Love' is probably the most autobiographical and my favorite lyric ever written for Karen," he explained. "If there was ever anything that came out of my heart straight to Karen's I would say that was it. I was very proud of it for that."

Karen enjoyed making lists: to-do lists, shopping lists, and even lists of lists. She would often lie awake in bed with a notepad and pencil, planning every detail of the coming day, as she explained to Ray Coleman in 1975. "My mind starts going, 'This has gotta be done, that's gotta be done, you've gotta call this.' Then I find myself with a flashlight in bed writing down about fifty things that have to be done by 10:00 the next morning. It's not the best way to be. It's better to hang loose, but I'm just not that type of person." According to friends, she also made tangible lists of attributes she was looking for in a prospective husband and was not willing to settle for anything less than her own preconceived ideal. "It's really hard to meet people in this business," she told *People* magazine. "But I'll be damned if I'll marry somebody just to be married."

"What are the requirements you're looking for today, Karen?" she was asked during a 1976 interview.

"Well, I have my list here," she joked, "but I'll have to stand just in case it hits the floor!" Little did the interviewer know she had actually put pen to paper to list her requirements in a man. She valued independence and desired a relationship with someone who would understand and appreciate the challenges of her career. "Obviously I would want to cut down on the work," she said, "but you don't have to get married and sit in the house. I couldn't. There's no way I would ever stop singing or performing or doing whatever I want to do. But I want to do it with somebody and share it. I want somebody to share my joy with."

She answered the same question for another journalist later that year: "I want a husband who can accept my success, because I could not give it up and stay at home all day. He must also be pretty well off. I don't want to fight the fear of a man having to live with my money. I've seen that ruin too many marriages. And it's got to be somebody dominant because I am far too domineering myself. I'm a bulldozer. . . . So far nine out of ten of them haven't lasted. I know instantly whether it's going to work out. Most of the men I go out with panic on sight. They become scared to death of me. They're envious of my car or they get upset if we go into a restaurant where I might be recognized. . . . So where is the right guy? Still, I'll say one thing: When I marry it will be for good."

From 1976 on, Karen named "I Need to Be in Love" as her favorite Carpenters song. "It really hits me right at home," she said. "Certain nights on the stage it really upsets me. I sing it and I'm almost putting myself into tears." Despite its beauty, the single fell short of the Top 20, coming in at #25. An obvious choice for its follow-up was "Can't Smile Without You," which went on to become a smash hit for Barry Manilow in 1978. Instead it was overlooked in favor of "Goofus," the final single culled from *A Kind of Hush*. Peaking at #56, it was the Carpenters' lowest-charting single of their career to that point.

BUILDING ON changes established by Terry Ellis during his brief stint as interim manager, Jerry Weintraub set out to completely revamp the Carpenters' stage show, which had followed roughly the same format since 1974. "When we first went on the road, all we really cared about was reproducing our record sound," Karen said. "We got that; it sounded just like the record. We didn't care or we didn't know it was also important to perform or be in this showbiz thing."

In addition to the writing and directing team of Ken and Mitzi Welch, Weintraub brought in famed Broadway choreographer Joe Layton, who felt that the Carpenters had played the role of good musicians for too long. There was no need to replicate the recordings in concert for the same fans that had their records at home. "Layton was a genius," explains Michael Lansing, who joined the Carpenters as a roadie in 1976. "With Ken and Mitzi, Joe produced a new show under Weintraub's creative hand, and they threw everything out the door."

Karen's drumming became more of a novelty than ever before with the addition of a lengthy drum spectacular. "She would run from one drum to the other without missing a beat," recalls Evelyn Wallace. "The people would just scream!" The addition of a portable raked stage allowed the entire setup to be angled toward the audience. "It is just drums," Karen explained. "I don't sing a note. We end up with twenty-three drums on the stage. I love to play and I love to sing, but I wouldn't want to give either one of them up." For this percussion feature Karen often donned a pair of blue jeans and a T-shirt with the words LEAD SISTER across the front. She'd earned this nickname in 1974, after a Japanese journalist mistakenly referred to her as the "lead sister" rather than "lead singer."

Despite her love of drumming, Karen had without a doubt emerged as the voice and face of the Carpenters. Most who witnessed the professional relationship between her and Richard recall it as more of an artist-producer relationship than a duo. This might have been the appropriate juncture in their careers for Karen to have received solo billing with Richard maintaining his behind-the-scenes role as producer. Instead, the campaign to establish an equality of importance between the two continued, most notably on stage. "Ladies and gentlemen," said the emcee, "Mr. Richard Carpenter." As Terry Ellis had suggested a year before, Richard opened the show alone, entering to a roll of timpani and an orchestral overture in which he took the baton at center stage as conductor. In addition, a large mirror was hung just above his piano and angled so that the audience could watch as his hands move up and down the keys. "You want to make sure you watch that mirror," Agnes instructed Evelyn Wallace as the family awaited the start of a show in Las Vegas.

"What mirror?" Evelyn asked.

Wallace would never admit it to Agnes, but she saw absolutely no need for the mirror and, in fact, found it to be narcissistic. "People went to see *Karen*," she says. "The audience went to hear *Karen's voice*, not to watch Richard play some song he had written."

But even Karen strongly disagreed. Second only to her mother, she was Richard's biggest fan. "He's so talented that it makes me weep that everybody just walks right by him," she told Ray Coleman in 1975, by which time she was part of the latest effort to establish Richard as the genius behind the Carpenters' sound. "They never give him any credit, but he does everything. He's the brain behind it and yet I get cracks like 'What does the brother do?' Or I get the impression that it's really nice that I've brought my brother on the road....I really get upset for him because he's so good and he never opens his mouth. He just sits back and because I'm the lead singer I get all the credit. They think I did it, and all I do is sing. He's the one that does all the work. There isn't anything I wouldn't do for him to give him the perfection that we both want."

Regardless of the overwhelming love and mutual respect between the siblings, Richard could not help but become jealous of the fuss the record-buying public and concertgoers made over his sister. "Karen is the star," he had explained in 1973. "She's the one who gets the letters and requests for autographs. I don't get much attention. Everyone's mostly interested in Karen. She's the lead singer and the featured part of the act. My end is selecting material, arranging, orchestrating, production, names of the albums, selecting personnel for the group, the order of the show, and how to improve the show. The audience doesn't realize what I do. They don't know I've written several hit songs. It's always Karen, which is fine. It's the same way with Donny and the Osmonds. But to me, I know what I've done. Even though a lot of people and critics don't like it, the fact is it's very commercial. It's well produced and it feels nice to me that I selected an unknown song and made it a hit. That makes me feel good, and sure, it feeds my ego."

The habitual tribute to the oldies remained a part of the new stage show, although it was sometimes exchanged in favor of a medley of songs from the popular Broadway musical *Grease*. In this sequence, Richard tore onto the stage on a motorcycle, and Karen entered wearing pink spandex, a bouffant wig, and an overstated fake bust. New to the show was a grandiloquent Spike Jones–inspired parody of "Close to You," complete with kazoos and pot and pans. Karen loved the dramatics added to their new show. "We're hams," she told Ray Coleman while in Germany in 1976. "We enjoy dressing up and the production. Have we gone over the top? Well, the answer's in the audience; it's been well received so far. Ask me next year."

Most shocking was the finale of "We've Only Just Begun," in which Richard left his fixed stance behind the piano to join Karen at center stage, an effort on the part of the writers to, again, balance his importance with hers. "They pretend for a split second to be lovers, looking straight into each other's eyes," explained Ray Coleman in his review of one of their German concerts. "A rarely seen moment of near passion from a brother-sister act not noted for warmth, in spite of the romantic beauty of their songs.... I felt the flesh creep uncomfortably at the sight of grownup brother and sister acting out this slightly incestuous scene as just 'part of the act.'" The positive side to their "mindboggling" performance, according to Coleman, was that the duo finally seemed to have "planted the kiss of life on a two year old corpse and that their audacity has won. Their 1974 show was boring. The 1976 show is over-ambitious.... The new show forces a reaction. Nobody sleeps during this concert. The Carpenters are alive and well—and working hard, as always. They know no other way."

Calling the music "polite plastic pop," British critic Mike Evans was also unmoved by all the over-the-top attempts at entertaining. "The curtain went up on a tinseled shrine to American kitsch, a mini Las Vegas, all red lights and glitter," he wrote. The songs were "flawlessly sung and expertly performed with hardly a trace of emotion in the whole performance."

Perhaps Karen and Richard were working too hard. The new show had been scripted by the Welch duo, and every word and gesture—even the ad libs—were written out and rehearsed to robotic perfection. "Theatrics Overshadow Carpenters' Music" was the headline following a concert at Oklahoma University's Homecoming. "They were not only tied down by a script, they were bound and gagged by it.... It is unfortunate that they got saddled with the Pollyanna image early in their careers and have decided to cater to it."

———— ✕ ————

ON TOUR, both Karen and Richard kept to themselves. While the band members were sightseeing in various cities and bowling down

(above) Nathan Hale eighth grade class of 1963: Karen is in row 3, fifth from right.

Frank Bonito

(left) Karen with classmates. From left: Frank Bonito, Anthony Viollano, Debra Cusack, and Karen. Frank Bonito

Eighth grade graduation day, June 1963: Mitchell Porylo, Karen, Carol DeFilippo, Frank Bonito, and Sophie DeFilippo.

Frank Bonito

Class pictures, 1965 (left) and 1967 (right). Downey Historical Society

(above) Concert choir, 1966–67. Karen in second row, middle.
Downey Historical Society

(above right) Singing in the annual Viking Varieties talent show at Downey High School, March 1965. Downey Historical Society

1965–66 Downey High School drum line: Randy Malquist, Karen, Nancy Roubal, John Higgins, and Frankie Chavez.
Downey Historical Society

With Wes Jacobs at Viking Varieties, March 1966. Downey Historical Society

(below) Early Carpenters promotional photo, 1969. A&M Records

In rehearsal (above)
and in concert (below),
Long Beach, California,
December 1970.

Frank Pooler

Karen as the American Cancer Society's national youth chairman. The Carpenters donated proceeds from concert tour book sales to the ACS.

American Cancer Society

National Youth Chairman

At home on Newville Avenue with Agnes, Harold, and Richard, early 1971. Robert Trendler/Globe Photos

A serious pose from a duo usually known for their "toothy twosome" personas. A&M Records

Karen at age twenty-one.

A&M Records

On location for Tom Jones's *London Bridge Special*, Lake Havasu, Arizona, February 1972.

A&M Records

With Frank Pooler backstage at the Chevron Hotel, Sydney, Australia, May 1972.

Frank Pooler

The Carpenters during their second visit to the White House and first time visiting with President Richard M. Nixon, August 1972.

Nixon Library/National Archives

The Carpenters softball team comprised band members, roadies, and opening act Skiles and Henderson. A&M Records

Photographed in director's chairs the duo received as gifts from an appearance on *The Carol Burnett Show*, 1972.

A&M Records

Hollywood Bowl, 1974. Sherry Rayn Barnett

On the lot at A&M Records, 1975.

(right) On stage at the Westchester
Premier Theater in Tarrytown,
New York, May 22, 1975.

The "lead sister" in her
element at Toronto's
O'Keefe Centre,
August 1976.

(above) With guest star John Denver in a "Pocahontas"
skit, later deleted, from *The Carpenters' Very First
Television Special.* ABC-TV

(left) A casual look for a 1976 photo session. A&M Records

Filming a Suntory Pop soft drink commercial for Japanese television, 1977. Suntory

Singing "White Christmas" on *The Carpenters at Christmas* TV special, 1977. ABC-TV

Karen at age twenty-seven.

A&M Records

December 3, 1978: Joining the choirs and orchestra from California State University, Long Beach, Karen performs at the *Winter Festival Concert* in the newly completed Pacific Terrace Theater in Long Beach, California. This would be the Carpenters' final American concert appearance. Leo Hetzel

Concert program.

Author's Collection

Karen photographed during one of several West Coast sessions for the solo album. Here she is listening to playbacks in studio A on the A&M Records lot in Hollywood, early 1980.

Bonnie Schiffman

At A&M Records.

Bonnie Schiffman

Dancing and drumming in "I Got Rhythm,"
a production number from the Carpenters' final
television special, *Music, Music, Music,*
filmed March 1980. ABC-TV

elow) With guest stars Ella Fitzgerald and John Davidson in *Music, Music, Music.* ABC-TV

One of several *Made in America* photo sessions, 1981. A&M Records

hotel hallways, as they were known to do, the siblings were usually secluded in their own hotel rooms. "They were an odd pair," recalls frequent opening act Denny Brooks. "I didn't think they felt comfortable in their own skin. I loved the band, but Karen and Richard just weren't the type of folks that I would really hang out with."

Roadie Michael Lansing, however, found himself quite taken with Karen and made it his mission to make her as comfortable on tour as possible. He brought in carpeting for her dressing room and always made sure her television reception was adequate, even if it meant running wires from the TV set to various metal objects around the space. "I saw her in every kind of conceivable fashion," Lansing says, "from bra and panties in the dressing room to stage outfits ready to walk on." He and roadies Jackie Hylen and Dave Connley would retrieve Karen's huge wardrobe case, which she nicknamed Blackula, from her upstairs bedroom at Newville, slide it down the stairs, and load it into the brown Dodge van marked with the gold-lettered "Carpenters" logo. From there they would transport the wardrobe to the Carpenters' Morsound warehouse in Studio City, where it was loaded into one of two semi trucks that followed the group from city to city.

In Karen, Lansing sensed a depth of character he feels many others looked past. "I think she was misunderstood by so many people," he says. "Karen was much more sensitive than she let on. She really enjoyed just being normal and was so down-to-earth. Talking to Karen was like talking to anybody else. She didn't have airs about her. She was really a fun girl, but I think she wanted to have a lot more fun in life than she did."

To pass time on tour Karen would work on various needlepoint projects and watch videocassettes of her favorite television programs, such as *I Love Lucy* and *Marcus Welby, M.D.*, while stylist Sandy Holland put her hair in rollers. Unlike many other singers, she spent very little time preparing her voice for concerts. "I've discussed this with a lot of singers," she said in 1978. "They say, 'How do you prepare for a show?' I say, 'I get dressed and walk downstairs. What do *you* do?' 'Oh, I do pushups, and I exercise my tonal thingies.' I'm saying, 'My Lord, you wear yourself out before you go on!'"

As the Carpenters rescheduled European tour was underway in the fall of 1976, Agnes and Harold Carpenter joined the group in England for the Palladium engagement and enjoyed sightseeing during rehearsals and sound checks. "The mom ran the show," recalls Denny Brooks. "I mean she ran the whole show. They had management and they had agents, but basically all the big decisions were made by Agnes when she was along. I liked Harold a lot. He enjoyed being along on the road. He was a very charming guy and a hoot to have around. In his distinctive slow drawl he would say, 'Well, boys, where are we gonna hang the feed bag tonight?' The parents didn't have an itinerary. They just followed the yellow brick road and got on the planes with us and went wherever their kids went."

Also along on this tour was Richard's eighteen-year-old girlfriend, first cousin Mary Rudolph, daughter of Agnes's sister Bernice. "I'd stayed at their family's house in Baltimore when Mary was just a teenager," recalls Maria Galeazzi, who lived next door to Mary's older brother and Carpenters roadie Mark Rudolph. "Her brother and I were very close, and from what Mark said, Mary pursued Richard quite a bit. It was like nonstop." Michael Lansing recalls that Mary joined the group as wardrobe and prop assistant and to the press was known as "Mary Pickford," an effort to deter attention from the couple's common roots. "We'd all go bowling or to the movies or just hang out. Mary was dating Richard at the time, but nobody said anything. Nobody ever said a word!"

According to friends, Karen was "livid" and "furious" about her brother's relationship with the girl she had only known as their kid cousin. She was especially upset by the amount of time Richard was spending with Mary on tour. "I never had a boyfriend on the road," Karen had told Ray Coleman in 1975, avoiding mention of then boyfriend Terry Ellis. "Not only didn't I agree with it, but I never met anybody I wanted to have on the road. It's the same thing with the guys bringing wives or women on the road. We tend to think when you go out [on tour] you go to work."

While in England, Karen did her best to distance herself from Richard and Mary and found herself surreptitiously meeting with John

"Softly" Adrian, head of press and promotion at A&M in London. Assigned by the label's regional chief Derek Green, Softly was asked to personally assist the Carpenters for the duration of their London stay. "You'll need to look after Karen when she gets here," Green told him. The handsome, suave thirty-three-year-old former model, who acquired his nickname after appearing in a television series called *Softly, Softly*, was already a fan of the Carpenters. In what he explains as having been an attempt to familiarize himself with the Carpenters and their show, Softly had flown to Germany prior to the group's arrival in London. "We always did that with our artists," Softly recalls. "You couldn't be working with them and not know who they were."

"Why are you sitting there all alone and being so snobby?" Karen's flirtatious handwritten note became an invitation for Softly to join her for breakfast at the Albany Hotel in Glasgow. He smiled from across the room before joining her and recalls being surprised by Karen's normality. Captivated by her sweet disposition, he made a silent vow that the two would become romantically involved. "The attraction was instant, and I would like to think it was mutual," he says, "but we were kind of shy of each other a bit, to be honest."

Softly soon realized it would be more difficult to infiltrate the Carpenters' circle than he imagined. "She was always surrounded by people—family managers and record executives," he recalls. "She had several moats, and you were going to have to cross them to get anywhere near her. She was like a little girl to me, really. A little girl who happened to have an extraordinary voice. Karen was very kind and very sweet, but she lived in a glass bowl. She had sixty-five people telling her what to do and fifty-seven hangers-on and managers and submanagers, and it was like a bloody fiasco."

Softly admits his position with the record label was his only way past the moats. "I had to pick her up at the hotel and take her to interviews and look after her, so I was very close to her during that time. You get to know people rather quickly when you're working that closely with them, and I think she trusted me to take care of her." As he had hoped, a brief interlude of puppy love ensued, and he and Karen began to see more of one another as time allowed. "It was one of those short, very enjoyable, very lovely romances," he says. "Hardly anybody knew about it, really. It was very sweet. That's all, really. It was just very sweet."

Despite their affection for each other, concealing their feelings was imperative. No one would have approved of a relationship between a Carpenter and an A&M staff member. Despite their precautions, word of Karen's involvement with Softly ultimately reached A&M executives and the Carpenters' management. Frenda Leffler was along for this leg of the tour and became concerned about the intentions of this man who seemed to have showed up out of nowhere. "What would you do with all that money?" she asked him.

"I'm doing just fine without it now, actually," he responded. "I could care less about her money."

Despite Softly's claims of truly loving Karen, Frenda and others in the entourage saw him as a bit of a playboy and did not take him seriously. It was not until Karen invited him to join her in Los Angeles for Christmas that everyone became disturbed. In their opinions she was simply infatuated and not thinking this through. "It was a momentary thing, and Karen didn't really see the reality of it," Frenda recalls. "He showed her a lot of attention, and he was a cute guy, but it just wasn't right for her. He was put out of commission rather quickly. The powers that be jumped on it, and Karen didn't have anything to say about it."

Back at A&M headquarters in London, Derek Green was alerted of the budding romance between Karen and his employee. Softly's character and intentions were being scrutinized, but Green assured those who questioned his character that he was indeed a fine man and anything but a gigolo. But after much urging, Green called Softly into his office, where he explained that if he were to go through with his plans to visit Karen in Los Angeles, he would no longer have a job at A&M. With the offer of plane tickets for a Caribbean vacation, Softly was told to go away, relax, and forget all about the fantasy of ever being with Karen Carpenter. "Basically our relationship was sabotaged by many of the people surrounding us," Softly says. "It was nipped in the bud, and I was threatened with my job. I went off to the Caribbean and got married after three months. It was what you might call a rebound."

At the time, Softly figured this was most likely some sort of scheme by Karen to secretly end their impending relationship. It seemed too good to be true anyway. His pride was hurt, and he quietly disappeared from the final leg of the tour. When Karen learned he had left the tour for a tropical vacation, she was sure he had run off with some other woman. In the end, both were persuaded to believe that the other had lost interest, and the relationship came to an end. "They were a controlling bunch," Softly says of A&M and the Carpenters in general. "She was the golden goose, and people protected her. They didn't want anybody, particularly an outsider she might be fond of, to take her away from the family. I think it was that people got scared that I might become her manager or something, which was totally ridiculous. I was not qualified to do that anyway."

Upon her return to Los Angeles, Karen sent a handwritten greeting card to Softly saying, "Thanks for looking after me." He doubts she ever learned how their relationship had been disrupted. In fact, the two never spoke of the fling again. Softly was only told of the conspiracy some fifteen years later when Derek Green broke his silence. Softly was upset to learn of the control Karen seemed to have been subjected to all those years ago. "She was a sad little girl, basically. She couldn't seem to do anything for herself or make any decisions. Everything was done for her. She had her mom and dad and brother and managers, and she was lost in this whole thing."

⁂

WITH NO serious romantic interests in sight, Karen enjoyed a few sporadic dates with musician friend Tom Bähler and several entertainers including Barry Manilow, actor Mark Harmon, and comedian Steve Martin. "Steve really liked Karen, and of course she thought he was an absolute scream," says Evelyn Wallace. "They were going out, and Karen had picked out what she was going to wear. Then word got around to Richard that Karen was going to go out that night with *the* Steve Martin. It wasn't long before he got in touch with Karen and said, 'Oh, I just got the studio, so we're going to be recording tonight.' Knowing that Karen had a date, he somehow all of a sudden got the studio and they were going to go up and record. See, even when she was on her own and living in the condo, Richard had a string on her. She was never ever her own boss."

Like the celebrities she dated casually, Karen found it extremely difficult in her situation not only to meet people but to find somebody "real," as she would often say. "I want desperately to find the right man," she said in 1976, "but it really has to be someone who is understanding and extremely strong. The average guy could never live under the pressure and all the other absurdities that go along with being in the limelight. You can't force these things. When you do, it always turns into a nightmare. I know a lot of people who have, and they always ended up the loser. I'll go on doing what I'm doing, and if I meet someone who turns me on, we'll go from there.... I'm not afraid of being an old maid. The idea doesn't scare me a bit. Happiness shouldn't be contingent on another human being. We've been programmed for so long that your value goes down if you don't end up with a husband or a wife. That's a sickness that has sprouted many unhappy people."

As former manager Sherwin Bash explained, it's extremely difficult for a successful female artist to find a man who can deal with her celebrity status. "I don't know anyone who wants to be Mr. Diana Ross," he said. "Do you want to be Mr. Barbra Streisand? I don't think our male egos work that way, so to find that person is not that easy."

Karen shared with friends her desire for life as a wife and mother. "You see, I so much want to start a family," she told an interviewer in 1976. "I really want kids. Maybe I'm old fashioned, but I could not have children without first being married. I believe in the institution of marriage very strongly. I'm family oriented and I'm proud of it. I had a happy childhood, and I would like to do the kind of job my parents did."

Carole Curb affirms that having children seemed to be her ultimate goal in life. "Even though she had an amazing voice and was very driven, I think ultimately she just wanted to have a husband and kids and the white picket fence." Childhood friend Debbie Cuticello agrees. "She wanted children desperately. She wanted a family, the little white picket fence, the dog, and the two-car garage."

Until that time came, Karen lived vicariously through best friend Frenda Leffler, even climbing atop Frenda's hospital gurney on her way into the delivery room. Unbeknownst to everyone, Frenda was carrying twins. With the arrival of the second baby, Karen looked up toward the ceiling and exclaimed, "Thank you God! You sent one for *me!*" She settled for the title of godmother to babies Ashley and Andrew—the "kidlets" she would call them—and Ashley soon acquired the nickname Ashley Famous. She presented each with a silver dish that she had hand engraved with the message: WHEN I COUNT MY BLESSINGS I COUNT YOU TWICE. LOVE, AUNTIE KAREN.

In anticipation of starting her own family, Karen mulled over names for her future children. It was decided that a son would be named for Richard but that everyone would call him Rick or Richie. For a daughter she chose the name Kristi.

11

JUST LET US KNOW WHAT
THE PROBLEM IS!

ROM "(THEY Long to Be) Close to You" in 1970 through
"I Need to Be in Love" in 1976, every Carpenters single (not
including B-sides) reached #1 or #2 on the Adult Contemporary
chart, "a streak that nobody has come close to beating," according to
Christopher Feldman's *Billboard Book of #2 Singles*. On the pop charts
the duo racked up a string of sixteen consecutive Top 20 hit singles
and five Top 10 albums. They won three Grammy Awards in these six
years and were presented with an American Music Award. But these
amazing feats would do little to soothe the pains of the decline in record
sales and popularity the Carpenters would experience in the latter half
of the decade. The slope—particularly steep at home in the United
States—was most upsetting to Karen, who seemed to take each success or failure personally. "Each time you get a hit record you have to
work twice as hard to get another one," she said in 1977. "This business
changes every minute. If you don't spend all your time staying on top
of it or thinking you're staying on top of it, you're going to be gone.
And that's a full-time job."

Though Karen and Richard were still very well known, and their
concerts were a huge draw, record sales began to fall. *A Kind of Hush*
eventually went gold but was not the commercial success of previous

Carpenters albums. Herb Alpert had hinted to Karen and Richard that the album was not on par with their earlier releases. Although Alpert could have held up production in favor of better material, the Carpenters were satisfied enough and pushed for its release.

Allyn Ferguson, who worked with the Carpenters in the early 1970s, witnessed the downhill slide of many artists, even legends like Elvis Presley and Frank Sinatra. "It happens to everybody," he says. "It has nothing to do with the people themselves. They're doing the same thing they always did. The public gets tired of them. It's a strange thing how the American public is not only fickle, but they respond to a lot of different things that are not musical at all, like the publicity and the attention that everybody's giving them. It's like a mob mentality. When the idol starts to have the image disappear, American fans just move on to the next one. That's a part of show business. We have a great term in showbiz—everybody's a 'star fucker,' which means if you're not a star anymore everybody just turns their back. It's very fleeting, and there are tragedies. I think Karen was one of those tragedies, and I could name dozens of other people who can't deal with the fact that it's not like it used to be."

The Carpenters largely blamed their wholesome image for the decline in interest in their music. The image issues that plagued the duo from their debut would likely have faded if allowed to do so, but the fact that both Karen and Richard were vocal about their frustrations only seemed to draw attention to their "Goody Four Shoes" personas. They had been called "milk-fed," "squeaky-clean," "vitamin-swallowing," "sticky-sweet," and "Pepsodent-smiling" ad nauseum. The 1974 *Rolling Stone* cover story was one of their first determined efforts to add some grit to their public perception and shed the myth that they were perfect angels. "The image we have," Karen said, "would be impossible for Mickey Mouse to maintain. We're just normal people."

Their quest for acceptance continued with a 1976 cover story for *People Weekly* in which they admitted neither was a virgin and both voted in favor of legalizing marijuana. "It's no worse than alcohol," Karen said. In *Melody Maker* she told Ray Coleman the story of a journalist who asked Richard if he agreed with premarital sex. "When he said 'yes,' the woman wouldn't print it! We were labeled as don't-do-anything! Just smile, scrub your teeth, take a shower, go to sleep. Mom's apple pie. We're normal! I get up in the morning, eat breakfast in front of the TV, and watch game shows. I don't smoke. If I wanted to smoke I would smoke. I just don't like smoking, not because of my image."

What came next was a backlash not unlike that against Tony Peluso's fuzz guitar solo on "Goodbye to Love" in 1972. But they were prepared for the reaction and defended themselves accordingly. "It had to be done," Karen told London's *Daily Mirror*. "We had to shed the goody two shoes image. It was too much. We're normal, healthy people. We believe people should be free to do what they want to do. Richard is thirty, and I am twenty-six. But the letters we got when we said we weren't virgins read as though we had committed a crime. People must have been dumb to have believed that we were that good. I don't drink because I don't enjoy it much, but when Richard and some of the band boys cooled down with beers on stage there was an outcry. And when Richard was seen smoking an ordinary cigarette, the reaction was terrific. And when we said we thought pot ought to be legalized, in came a shoal of letters saying we were drug addicts. . . . We had to speak out and tell the truth about us as it is. It's hell living like a pair of angels."

Like Karen, Olivia Newton-John had her share of image-related issues in the mid-1970s. "That 'white bread' image was something else Karen and I had in common," Olivia says. "We never felt we were taken seriously as singers." Newton-John was the occasional sounding board for Karen's dismay and disappointment concerning the Carpenters' decline in sales and popularity. "They'd had incredible success and then they were going through that slack period we all do," she explains. "It's part of life."

<hr />

AFTER *A Kind of Hush* it seemed that both Karen and Richard lacked the energy and determination that had shined through on their earlier efforts. It also became more difficult to write and select material radio programmers and audiences wanted. "For the last three years there has been a definite resistance to our product, and I don't know why,"

Karen explained to *Radio Report* in 1978. "We've been doing our best to turn out the finest product we can. Richard keeps changing direction. We've covered practically every aspect that is capable of being put to disc with the exception of classical. We haven't done that yet."

Experimentation, diversity, and perhaps even desperation birthed the Carpenters' next studio album, *Passage*, released September 23, 1977. *Billboard* called it their "most boldly innovative and sophisticated undertaking yet," pointing out that "the material constantly shifts gears from calypso, lushly orchestrated complex pop rhythms, jazz flavored ballads, reggae and melodic, upbeat numbers."

Passage opened with the daring "B'wana She No Home," a Michael Franks tune with a vocal arrangement by jazz great Gene Puerling, the sound architect of vocal groups including the Hi-Lo's and the Singers Unlimited. "B'wana" was one of several songs on the album that were essentially live recordings. "When recording, we usually begin with bass, drums, piano, and build from there," Richard explained in the album's liner notes. "But on several of these tracks, almost the whole thing was recorded live all at once. Certain pieces call for that."

Passage spawned the debut single "All You Get from Love Is a Love Song," one Karen felt was a surefire hit. "We thought it was really going to make it," she said, "but it got hardly any airplay at all." It was a strong album cut but not nearly as strong a single as they needed at this stage. Monitoring airplay became a focus for the Carpenters more with this album than any previous. Some at A&M even began resorting to payola, meaning that payments or incentives were given in exchange for placement on playlists and prominent airplay during a given inter-. val. Even Carpenters fans were enlisted to assist and sent gifts as tokens of appreciation for helping monitor the number of spins a particular song was seeing on a particular station.

Richard first listened to "Calling Occupants of Interplanetary Craft" at the urging of Tony Peluso on a 1976 album by the Canadian group Klaatu. "[He] wanted to do that more than anything in the world," Karen recalled. "When we got done with it, it had turned into an epic. We figured out that we spent more time on 'Occupants' than we did our third album. That was a job. It was a masterpiece when

Richard got done with it." In addition to introducing the song to the Carpenters, Peluso reprised his role of a bemused deejay during the recording's opening dialogue segment.

For their endeavor, Karen and Richard brought in sixty-year-old Englishman Peter Knight, whose work on the Moody Blues' *Days of Future Passed* album had impressed the Carpenters nearly ten years earlier. According to harpist Gayle Levant, working with Knight was a thrill for her and the other studio musicians. "He was a phenomenal arranger," she says. "It was absolutely a joy to play his charts. Those magic moments happen when you hear a chart and you just know that you're working with a man who is magic." It was also Knight who arranged and conducted the orchestra on the *Passage* album's other epic, the sweeping anthem from Andrew Lloyd Webber's *Evita*, "Don't Cry for Me, Argentina." A&M's Jerry Moss disagreed with the Carpenters' decision to record "Argentina," saying it was a socialist anthem, but Richard believed strongly that it was well suited for Karen and in no way meant to be a political statement. For many years, copies of the album produced and sold in Argentina omitted the selection.

Contractual agreements precluded the Los Angeles Philharmonic from being credited as such, so liner notes humorously credit the "Over-budget Philharmonic" instead. With more than a hundred instrumentalists and an additional fifty in the chorus, the recording was done on A&M's Chaplin Stage (and wired into studio D) before an audience of representatives from Los Angeles–area press and media. College friend and tubist Wes Jacobs was visiting Los Angeles and sat in on the colossal recording session.

Although rarely complimentary of the Carpenters' product or live performances, Robert Hilburn, rock critic with the *Los Angeles Times*, praised *Passage* for its "experimental touches that added refreshing character to their musical foundation. On their version of 'Don't Cry for Me, Argentina' there's a maturity to Karen's vocal that was far beyond anything in the early years." Hilburn obviously overlooked "Superstar," "Rainy Days and Mondays," "This Masquerade," and countless others, but his admiration was better late than never. But on "Argentina," there was a sense of depth and understanding. Like many of her recordings, the lyric was autobiographical when placed in context with the personal struggles she faced over the years.

And as for fortune and as for fame
I never invited them in
Though it seemed to the world they were all I desired
They are illusions; they're not the solutions they promised to be

"Sweet, Sweet Smile" was the album's final single and one that took aim at the country music market. "This is the first time we've gone all out after a country hit," said A&M's assistant national promotion director Lenny Bronstein in an interview with Paul Grein. The song was also issued with "Reason to Believe," "Jambalaya," and "Top of the World" in a four-song promotional *Country Collection* EP sent to country stations and regional promoters. "We always try to get one country song on our albums," Karen told *Country Music* magazine in 1978. "Not for any specific purpose but because we like it. We don't go in and say we've got to record a song that will get on the country charts. We always just go in with what we like." Although "Sweet, Sweet Smile" reached only #44 on the pop chart, it went Top 10 on the country chart and peaked at #8. The crossover success and interest from country radio led Karen and Richard to consider recording an all-country album for 1978, but the plan never made it past Jerry Moss, who reminded them that a hit pop album was their priority.

"I Just Fall In Love Again" was an obvious choice for single release from *Passage*, but it was too much in the vein of the traditional Carpenters love song formula, complete with oboe interludes and a fuzz guitar solo. They seemed to consciously move away from such predictability with this album, which incidentally contained no original material. Canadian singer Anne Murray, herself a pop-country crossover, had a Top 20 hit with "I Just Fall in Love Again" the following year.

Passage was the first Carpenters album to be released without any photographs of Karen and Richard, a stark change from their usual smiling portraits. Even the trademark "Carpenters" logo appeared only on the lower portion of the back panel. Popular Los Angeles illustrator

Lou Beach, commissioned to do the *Passage* artwork, was given the title and free reign. "I was exploring the limits of the new color Xerox machines," recalls Beach. "That art came out of a session at the copy center. It was the best-paying record cover job I'd ever had."

While the Carpenters considered *Passage* to be a creative success, commercially it flopped, becoming their first album to fall short of gold status. Ardent Carpenters follower Ray Coleman had felt the duo's two previous albums were inferior, but he proclaimed that *Passage* was an "indecisive" career low. "After all these years of admiring their excellence, we have come to expect something special from Carpenters albums," Coleman wrote in his review for *Melody Maker.* "This one just will not do.... Karen's melting vocals—always their most powerful asset—are lost when they tackle "Man Smart, Woman Smarter" and "Don't Cry For Me, Argentina."... It's a tragic comment on such talent, but Carpenters fans can safely ignore this release; let's wish them a speedy return to musical decisiveness."

Often accused of not allowing the Carpenters the necessary studio time to produce a quality album, former manager Sherwin Bash explained the duo's need for patience once their records sales took a downturn. "Too many artists forget that you don't have to do everything in five years," he said. "But you can space it out and take your time. Take time to recharge those batteries and sit down and think about the next album. If you're going to write it, you're lucky to come out with an album every one or two years. In today's life, even if it isn't for three years the world won't forget. The world doesn't need another album, they only need *great* albums. I could never convince Richard of this."

Karen was fiercely proud of the material she and Richard recorded and was troubled by discouraging reviews, especially from those who had long been on their side. "In this business you've not only got to prove yourself but you've also got to prove them wrong," she had declared in 1976.

Luckily, the Carpenters' presence on the international music scene was strong, with "Calling Occupants of Interplanetary Craft" becoming a huge hit in Japan and "Sweet, Sweet Smile" a smash in Germany. But the fickle American audiences left Karen and Richard scrambling to produce something they would buy. "We just don't know what Top 40 radio is looking for," Karen told *Radio Report*. "One minute they say they're looking for a traditional Carpenters record. We give them one of those and they don't want it. They say they want something different, so we give them 'Occupants' and they don't want that either. We give them country and Top 40 again resists. If somebody would just let us know what the problem is, then we could take it from there. Everybody has a different answer."

Karen was unable to separate these professional discouragements from her personal life. She was so focused on achieving and succeeding in the outside world that her inner world and inner beauties were not valued. Although she claimed to want nothing more than a traditional family life with a husband and children, business came first. In fact, when interviewed in 1975, she told Ray Coleman that if it came to a choice between private life and fame, hers would be fame. "We're very dedicated to our business," she said. "Our life is our music, creating it. We try to do everything with as much perfection as we can. We have certain beliefs, certain loyalties to ways of doing things."

"She was very, very career conscious," recalls Olivia Newton-John. "It was very important to her, she took it very seriously and she took it personally. I'd always had relationships and boyfriends. To me, my career wasn't the be-all and end-all of life, but for her it pretty much was at that point."

⌒⌒⌒

"You are the Perry Comos of today," Jerry Weintraub told the Carpenters. Yet another aspect of Weintraub's visions involved bringing the duo into American living rooms via television. He felt this was a sure way to guarantee permanence for their careers. From specials featuring performers such as Como, Frank Sinatra, Barbra Streisand, and Petula Clark to regular series starring performers such as Judy Garland, Tom Jones, Sonny and Cher, and Glen Campbell, musical variety shows were a staple of American television in the 1960s and 1970s.

At first, Karen and Richard were unconvinced. Their 1971 summer series *Make Your Own Kind of Music* had been a disaster in their opinions, primarily due to a lack of control over the sketch material. "We stayed away from television for quite a few years until we signed with Jerry Weintraub, at which point he got us our own shows," Karen said. "That's really what we needed. We needed to have full control of what we wanted to put and present on television."

After negotiating a deal with ABC-TV program director Fred Silverman in 1976, Weintraub formed Downey-Bronx Productions with the Carpenters to produce their television specials and remained actively involved throughout the production. He attended most rehearsals and tapings, offered feedback, and made suggestions to director Bob Henry. "Jerry was always an extra set of eyes and ears looking out for Karen and Richard," remembers Jerry Jaskulski, associate producer for several of the Carpenters' specials. "Bob Henry was in charge overall, and they trusted him when it came to the visual presentation of the show. They were always kept aware of all planning and did have veto power if they didn't like something. Richard was certainly in charge of making the musical decisions. Karen could be demanding when it came to her own performances, as she should have been. She also had a great sense of humor. The mere fact that she chose to play the drums shows that she enjoyed letting loose."

After three weeks of intense rehearsals with guest stars John Denver and Victor Borge, *The Carpenters' Very First Television Special* was taped September 30–October 2, 1976. The December 8 airing came in at #6 for the week in the Nielsen ratings and garnered an offer from ABC-TV for additional specials on the network. For their 1978 holiday television special, *The Carpenters: A Christmas Portrait*, Karen and Richard were joined by legendary song and dance man Gene Kelly and other guests. "By the time we did that special they were certainly more relaxed and familiar with the routine," says associate producer Jerry Jaskulski.

Karen agreed, saying, "Each one, in our opinion, has gotten better because you grow. You learn very quickly in television how to do certain things and what you do and what you can pull off and what you can't pull off. There are a lot of things that time doesn't permit you to do the way you want to. If it were up to us we'd spend a week just recording, but you can't do that with television. Luckily, we've come off as close to perfection as we have attempted. Some things we had to let go against our judgment. On the whole we've been real, real happy. We've had the opportunity to work with so many, many good people."

Guest stars on the television specials ran the gamut from legends like Ella Fitzgerald and Gene Kelly to Grade B stars including Jimmy and Kristy McNichol, Suzanne Somers, and John Davidson. While the comedic efforts were entertaining in moderation, the writing was poor to say the least. "The Carpenters should have demanded better scripts, guest stars, sketch ideas, and staging concepts," wrote Paul Grein in a 1991 reassessment of the duo's work. "If they didn't have the power to make those demands, they should have."

Hindsight reveals a number of poor choices in terms of scripts and scenarios. Given Karen's history with an eating disorder, it was a bizarre decision by producers to stage one of her song sequences in a kitchen wearing an apron. "I've found over the years the best way to get a party going is to make sure that people have enough food to eat!" From there Karen went from appliance to appliance, all the while singing and dancing—and baking. "The reason we chose to have Karen in a kitchen environment was to present her to be more like one of the girls," Jerry Jaskulski says. "We wanted to show her as a typical family member and make it easier for the women in the audience to relate to her. Prior to that they had only seen her singing and playing the drums. We all knew Karen had an eating problem, but no one ever thought it would end so tragically."

Unfortunately the producers' narrow-mindedness meant Karen usually portrayed one-dimensional caricatures during their television specials. Her dialogue lacked depth, and as a result she often came across as gullible or naive, at times even a little ditzy. Richard loathed the attempts at comedy and later regretted the emphasis on those sketches and their canned laughter over higher-caliber musical routines. But Karen was the star, and she seemed to enjoy these productions, which gave her the opportunity to sing, dance, drum, and even try her hand at acting, which sparked her interest in starring in a movie. "It's something I would really like to do," she said in 1978. "I love to act and sing. I'm not sure how or when but I'd like to do a musical." In fact, Karen had hinted at this idea as early as 1971, evidenced by this A&M Records press release.

> As for Karen, the far-flung future ("at least five years from 'now'") holds possibilities of singing and acting in a musical comedy. "I've always loved Broadway-type musicals like *Camelot, Finian's Rainbow* and *The King and I*. I'd like to do something like that, eventually." With her vibrant beauty, her electric stage appeal and her voice—which definitely blends pure sweetness with a hunt of sophisticated sultriness—this seems like another dream that could well be gloriously realized. For the Carpenters, dreams seem to turn to reality with the snap of their magical fingers.

Karen loved female comedians like Lucille Ball, Carol Burnett, Phyllis Diller, and even more dramatic actresses like Barbra Streisand, who had seen much success with musicals like *Funny Girl* and *Hello, Dolly!* "Streisand just floors me," she said in 1976, just two months prior to the release of Streisand's *A Star Is Born*. "She's so good. I would like to do something like that."

The natural comedian in Karen was evident to all who knew her. "She was really droll," says Carole Curb. "She made everybody laugh with this amazingly witty and sarcastic sense of humor." According to Frenda Franklin, "Karen did the best Barbra Streisand imitation you've ever heard in your life. She really, really could have been an actress. She wanted to act. She even wanted to study acting. Today it seems as though everybody wants to do everything in the business, but in those days if you sang, you sang. You were lucky that you got the opportunity to sing. But Karen wasn't looking at it like, 'Oh, I want to be a movie star.' She just knew that she had something else to offer."

In the fall of 1956 during a visit to the Music Corner, one of New Haven's popular record shops, Harold Carpenter had purchased Spike Jones's *Xmas Spectacular* album for his children. It was an odd and varied mix of trademark Spike Jones novelty songs and serious choral music arranged by Jud Conlon. A progressive vocal arranger at the time, Conlon came onto the scene in the 1940s and is often credited with pioneering the tight, close harmony sounds used in popular music at the time. He and his "Rhythmaires" backed Bing Crosby, Judy Garland, and others on a number of popular recordings.

"There was one album that I remember from the day I was born," Karen said. "It was Spike Jones's Christmas album. There are some zany things on there.... Spike Jones was a master at zany stuff. A lot of people don't know that it takes more talent and more perfection to pull off crackpot things than it does to do a lot of serious things.... This album was a combination of nutty and serious. We grew up with that album and just loved it to death."

Since signing with A&M Records in 1969, Karen and Richard had wanted to record a Christmas album of their own. They both loved the Christmas season and the abundance of great holiday music, but due to touring and recording schedules they had only been able to fit in two seasonal offerings over the years, "Merry Christmas, Darling" in 1970 and "Santa Claus Is Comin' to Town" in 1974. In preparation for *The Carpenters at Christmas*, their second special for ABC-TV, recording sessions commenced in August 1977. It was quickly decided that these recordings would serve as the foundation for an entire album of Christmas music to be released in conjunction with the television special's airing.

The early Spike Jones recordings proved to be the inspiration for Richard, who admittedly patterned much of this project after the *Xmas Spectacular* LP both he and Karen had enjoyed so much as children. They immediately set out to hire Jud Conlon to do their arrangements, only to find that he'd died in 1966. Their next call went to Peter Knight. It was Knight, along with veteran arranger Billy May, who helped bring the concept to life with the help of an eighty-piece orchestra and seventy-voice choir. A five-minute overture of nine selections was orchestrated with the strings, making way for the grand entrance by Karen's voice.

Frosted window panes, candles gleaming inside
Painted candy canes on the tree

Santa's on his way, he's filled his sleigh with things
Things for you and for me

Sammy Cahn's festive lyric for "The Christmas Waltz" was the perfect match for Karen's warm delivery, which melted into a creative rendition of "Sleigh Ride." Lesser-known titles like "It's Christmas Time," "Sleep Well, Little Children," and "The First Snowfall" were culled from the Spike Jones album. Arranger Billy May, who had previously lent his talents to the Carpenters' *Horizon* in 1975, was responsible for helping re-create the Spike Jones charts in a way best suited to Karen's vocal range. This included the pairing of songs like "Winter Wonderland" and "Silver Bells" in an unforgettable medley with "White Christmas."

It became obvious that there was not time to complete and release the album prior to the airing of the 1977 television special. As a consolation, A&M released "The Christmas Song (Chestnuts Roasting on an Open Fire)" as a special holiday single that year. Karen's is one of the only performances of the tune that truly rivals the warmth and presence of Nat "King" Cole's classic recording. In the same vein were "Have Yourself a Merry Little Christmas" and "I'll Be Home for Christmas," two songs so identified with Judy Garland and Bing Crosby, respectively. Surrounded with the choral and orchestral sounds of a glorious 1940s MGM musical, Karen was as natural and at home with these songs as either a Judy or a Bing. The songs took on new ownership in the capable, worthy hands of Karen Carpenter.

Recording continued off and on between other sessions, tours, and television tapings, and the Carpenters spent a total of fourteen months producing what became *Christmas Portrait*. Midway through the process they took their Christmas selections to the Las Vegas stage at the MGM Grand, complete with a huge tree and nearly eighty musicians. Their usual Vegas orchestra was augmented with a twenty-four-voice choir.

Construction of the album continued in the New Year. "Merry Christmas, Darling" was by then a recurrent holiday favorite on the radio, but Karen was never pleased with the huskier sound from the lead vocal recorded when she was only twenty years old. Her voice had matured and developed immensely, so she opted to re-record "Darling" in 1978, as she had done with "Ticket to Ride" in 1973. The Carpenters also took time to record several nonfestive songs amid the Christmas sessions, including "When I Fall in Love" and "Little Girl Blue" for their 1978 ABC-TV special *The Carpenters—Space Encounters*. The tunes were so similar in style that only the latter was included. "When I Fall in Love" was later included in their 1980 special, *Music, Music, Music.*

The sacred selections intermingled with the secular on *Christmas Portrait* included "Christ Is Born," a lovely musical setting Richard first heard on *The Perry Como Christmas Album* in 1968, the traditional carol "Silent Night," and the vocally demanding Bach-Gounod version of "Ave Maria." Karen's love for the Christmas season and its music was always evident when asked about the album, which was planned for a double LP set at one point. "To sing these songs is something that gives me more pleasure than I can really put into words," she said. "I think we came out with something like twenty-nine songs. We've got at least another twelve in the can that we couldn't finish.... We were dying because we couldn't stuff them on the record. We'd have had to leave the label off!"

In contrast with *A Kind of Hush* and *Passage*, reviews for *Christmas Portrait* were overwhelmingly positive. "They've synthesized everything to ever come out of Sunset Boulevard at Yuletide into two sides of a perfect piece of plastic," wrote James Parade of *Record Mirror.* "[I]t will bring you Disney, Snow White and her snow, whiteness whiter than white, sleighbells...shimmering strings, snowflakes scurrying, ring-ting-tingling, jingling and lots more besides.... Buy this record for instant atmosphere and have yourself a merry little Christmas."

Christmas music was the ideal showcase for Karen Carpenter, and in many ways her renditions were the perfect union of songs and singer. "*Christmas Portrait* is really Karen's first solo album, and it should have been released as such," explained Richard in 2004. "But I don't believe A&M would have been too keen on that, especially since no conventional album had been released by us that year."

12

THE BIRD HAS FINALLY
FLOWN THE COOP

GNES CARPENTER was a worrier. She had trouble getting to
sleep each night and had sought the help of a doctor in the early
1970s. "When she'd go to bed, she'd think about what she
had to do or things that had been done that shouldn't have been done,"
explains Evelyn Wallace. "She'd always have something on her mind.
She couldn't get to sleep, so they had to give her something strong."

Agnes first noticed Richard's state of exhaustion and inability to
sleep in the fall of 1971 after the group returned home from their European tour. He was worried about completing their next album, *A Song
for You*, in the allotted time. "I was up just about every night," he recalled
in 1988. "I wasn't getting any sleep, and I did not look too hot when I
stepped off the plane. I'd never had a pill before or since except for this. I
was really in need of some sleep and quite nervous and concerned."

Quaaludes were prescription sedatives commonly used to treat
insomnia at the time, and Richard did not hesitate when his mother
offered them to help him sleep. "Taken properly they were a very
good pill," he later explained. "She took them until they discontin-
ued them—one a night the way you're supposed to. She never had any
problem with them."

For a number of years, Richard took the quaaludes as directed. "It was very difficult to sleep on the road," recalls Maria Galeazzi, who began taking quaaludes with Richard during their romance. "I just sort of bummed off of him. It wasn't every night. It was now and then when he couldn't sleep."

According to Evelyn Wallace, "If Richard didn't go to sleep the minute he hit the pillow, he'd get up, and he'd end up fooling around at the piano or get something to eat in the kitchen. Those wear off after a while if you keep busy enough. He'd go up to bed, but he still wasn't sleepy. He'd take another one and sometimes a third one. He was just taking too darn many of them." Richard found that he enjoyed the high the quaaludes gave him—a convenient but risky side effect of sorts—but he was never much of a party animal. For some time he knew nothing about the use of quaaludes as a recreational drug, but the more he took, the longer it would take for the drug's effects to wear off.

Gradually Richard became more and more severely addicted. As his condition worsened his playing began to suffer, and he lost all confidence in his abilities as a pianist. By late 1978 the addiction had taken hold. Disguising the problem became more difficult for Richard because his speech was slurred, and he could barely sign his name because he was unable to hold a pen in his trembling hands. This meant that playing certain intricate piano parts was out of the question. "One side of me was saying, 'You fool! You're killing yourself, you can't function and you're letting your sister and parents down,'" he wrote a decade later in *TV Guide*. "But the other side convinced me I couldn't get by without those pills. . . . I tried a couple of detox programs, but even if you get the stuff out of your system, it's hard to lick the problem. By 1978 I was in trouble, no two ways about it."

Richard hit rock bottom in September when they played the MGM Grand in Las Vegas. He spent most days in bed or dealing with anxiety issues and panic attacks. He would emerge early in the evenings, just long enough to do the show. All he could think about was getting off the stage and going back to bed, where the vicious cycle continued. It was between performances on Monday, September 4, that Richard abruptly informed the band and their crew that he was quitting.

"That's it," he said. "I'm not playing another night." Although it was never Richard's intention, this run at the MGM Grand would prove to be the Carpenters' last professional engagement, save a few public appearances in 1981. Even then, the band reunited only to mime their instrument playing while Karen and Richard lip-synched to their studio recordings.

Los Angeles session singer Walt Harrah, who was brought in to fill in for band member Dan Woodhams after a serious automobile accident, was disappointed to see his stint with the Carpenters end prematurely. "I did their last MGM show where Richard just quit," he recalls. "It was a two-week engagement of something like twenty-eight shows, and he quit after four or five days. I guess he was sick of it. He was very private. He was very aloof and alone and kind of depressed, but so was Karen. It could have had to do with her physical condition. She looked like a Holocaust victim."

With Richard dealing with his addiction and the aftershocks felt from his swift termination of the group's Vegas gig, the last thing he wanted to do was prepare for another appearance. Yet the Carpenters were on the bill for a concert with Frank Pooler, his choir, and the university orchestra. The show was to be held December 3, 1978, in the Pacific Terrace Theater at the Long Beach Convention Center with proceeds benefitting the Carpenters Choral Scholarship Fund at California State University Long Beach. As the date approached, Richard began removing songs from the program when he realized he was unable to perform them. "My hands were shaking too much," he explained some years later. "I told Karen I was dropping 'It's Christmas Time' because I didn't think it would go over well. And I told her I was dropping 'The Nutcracker' because I didn't think the university orchestra could cut it. I pared that damn program down to almost nothing because I couldn't play most of it. Poor Karen. She was buying all of this, even though she knew I had a problem."

The Carpenters took the stage late in the show that Sunday afternoon with guest conductor Doug Strawn leading the choir and orchestra. Karen's entrance on "Sleep Well, Little Children" was uneventful, and Richard was incapacitated. He did manage to fulfill his promised rendition of themes from *Close Encounters of a Third Kind* and *Star Wars*, a medley somewhat out of place in the context of a Christmas performance.

"The Carpenters finally arrived on the stage far too late in the show to make much difference, and stayed for too short a time," wrote Charles Carney in his review for the *49er*, a student newspaper. "Their presence should either have been established during the early portion of the show and woven throughout, or extended for a longer time at the end. As it was, their arrival broke the carefully designed momentum that had been building during the first two-thirds of the show and catapulted it into the predictability of a Las Vegas lounge act." The Carpenters' lackluster appearance in Long Beach was saved only by Karen's rich and warm tones on "Merry Christmas, Darling" and "Silent Night" and a performance of "Ave Maria" rivaling that of the album version.

During the following week, Karen and Richard were scheduled to depart for London, where they were set to appear on *Bruce Forsyth's Big Night* on BBC rival ITV. Richard was in no condition to perform, much less travel overseas. He was practically bedridden and tried to convince Karen that these promotional appearances in London could wait, even though two new albums, *The Singles 1974–1978* and *Christmas Portrait*, had just hit the UK market. "We're going!" she told Richard, determined to follow through with the engagement.

Arriving at the group's rehearsal space in North Hollywood, Karen was met by the band members but not Richard. She called him immediately and discovered he was still in bed and refusing to make the trip. When she visited him later that day, Richard explained how his addiction had gone too far. Although she was aware of his condition, he had always made excuses and she'd usually believed him. "You get pretty devious," he later recalled. "The same way anorexics do. But it finally got so bad that I couldn't get out of bed, and I had to say, 'Karen, I've got a problem here.'"

Due to her tenacious spirit—or perhaps just out of sheer stubbornness—Karen flew to London with the band to make good on their promise to perform. Covering for Richard, she told Bruce Forsyth's audience that he was under the weather. "Two days before we were going to come over, he caught himself a real nice case of the flu," she said through a nervous smile. "So he's flat on his back in Los Angeles, and he's really upset that he couldn't come."

Musically, the show went off without a hitch, thanks to the support of friend Peter Knight and Jeff Wesley, the latter filling in for Richard on keyboards. Taking liberties with the melody, Karen's performance of "I Need to Be in Love" was perhaps the most tender and intimate reading of the song ever. She also performed "Please Mr. Postman," "Merry Christmas, Darling," and the ambitious grouping of "Winter Wonderland," "Silver Bells," and "White Christmas" as a duet with Forsyth.

Word of a possible split between the Carpenters spread across Europe with the airing of the Forsyth show, but Karen did her best to dispel such rumors. "Karen wants everyone to know that she is not going solo," Tim Ewbank wrote in the *Sun*, with Karen explaining that "Brucie's show is setting a sort of unfortunate record for us. It is the first time that the Carpenters have been billed to appear anywhere without both of us going on." Ewbank inquired about her health, to which she replied, "I'm fine now. I've got my energy back and I'm raring to go!"

Indeed, this was one of the first occasions in her entire career that Karen had been away from home without Richard by her side. From her hotel suite at the Inn on the Park in central London, Karen sent her brother a postcard of encouragement, postmarked December 12, 1978: "It's all coming off like clockwork—the album is getting hotter by the minute. The music end is tops. Miss you—Love, KAC1." (Karen's abbreviated signature referred to the personalized California license plate attached to her 1972 Mercedes 350.)

While in London, Karen requested that John "Softly" Adrian assist her. Softly was by then a married man and maintained a safe distance from Karen. Their conversations consisted mostly of small talk. "You haven't said 'thank you' for your wedding present, Softly," Karen said playfully.

"What present?" he asked.

"The present I sent you," she said. "I sent you a crystal punch bowl with glasses!"

Softly was puzzled. The only contact he was aware of came in 1976 when Karen sent him a note saying "The bird has finally flown the coop"—this after her move from Downey to Century City.

"Karen, I didn't get any present from you," he said.

"Hmm," Karen pondered. "Well, I gave it to someone at A&M. Obviously they didn't send it to you." The mystery surrounding the orchestrated ending of their relationship some two years earlier seemed to continue but without their knowledge. The two shared one last hug at London's airport as Karen boarded a plane bound for home.

Soaring record sales in Europe did little to cheer Karen. The reality of her personal problems and those of her brother hit home once she returned to Los Angeles just in time for Christmas. A year earlier they were celebrating on stage in Las Vegas, but in 1978 the holidays were anything but happy in the Carpenter household. Heated arguments ensued with Richard becoming increasingly dismayed by Karen's withering figure. "He was not all that kind to Karen," recalls Evelyn Wallace. "But at times he'd even argue with his mother, which was taking his life in his hands!" Karen would retort with comments about the consequences of his addiction. To Richard, these were not welcome observations from someone on a similar path of self-destruction. "She was so concerned," Frenda Franklin explains. "You see, Karen was very sensible about everybody else. In the case of Richard, there was nothing to debate. It was terrible. She just couldn't wait any longer to get him help. He wasn't happy with her, but she took the strong role and did what she had to do as a sister."

Richard was called to a meeting at the office of Jerry Weintraub with Werner Wolfen and others present. "Before you know it, in the middle of the meeting Richard was sound asleep in the chair," recalls Wallace. "They knew Richard was on something even then."

On the morning of January 10, 1979, Richard popped ten pills before boarding a plane bound for Topeka, Kansas. "Karen forced him," Frenda says. "She took him on an air ambulance to Menninger's." There Richard checked into the chemical dependency unit with Karen and Wolfen at his side. Both Richard and Werner felt this would be a great opportunity for Karen to address her issues as well, but she was not serious enough about her eating disorder to do anything significant about it. Instead she returned to Los Angeles—full of nervous energy—and began looking for projects to occupy her time while Richard was in rehab. "It was OK for a little bit," she told the *Los Angeles Times*, "but then I was anxious to go back to work."

During her first return visit to see Richard at Menninger, Karen hesitantly shared her plans to go into the studio to begin recording a solo album. Just two weeks into the six-week program, he was in no condition to hear this sort of news and was understandably livid. "He was madder than hell," recalls Evelyn Wallace. "He did *not* want her to go to New York and record on her own. I think that he realized that Karen could sell more records than he could."

By this time, Richard was certain Karen was battling the disorder brought to his family's attention by Wallace three years earlier, and he confronted her about her own well-being and deteriorating physical appearance. "What the hell are you talking about? Going and doing a solo album?! Why don't *you* go and check into something like this that is meant for anorexics!" He reminded Karen of their upcoming tenth anniversary in the music industry. "We can go into the eighties the same way we went into the seventies. We have our talent. We have our record contract."

Karen shut down. She adamantly denied her own issues. "No," she insisted, "there's nothing wrong with me. I don't have anorexia nervosa; I have colitis." In her diary entry for January 24, 1979, Karen wrote: "Confrontation about album."

In public, Karen refused to admit that her physical state was due to anything more than exhaustion from years of overwork. In private, however, Karen took her illness seriously enough to seek professional help—but not without Frenda Leffler by her side. "I had known for a while that she had some sort of a mental illness," Frenda explains. "I knew it wasn't just that she didn't want to eat because she didn't want to eat. She just couldn't conquer this. We were somewhat aware of what it could be, but they just didn't know how to treat it. We didn't have a

Menninger type of thing for her. If we had the great centers for eating disorders they have today, everything could have been different. " With Karen's blessing, Frenda had researched and made appointments with several Los Angeles–based psychiatrists, several of whom dealt with food issues. During each visit, Karen insisted Frenda remain with her while she met with the doctors. "Let me just go in the other room," Frenda said, sensing one doctor's exasperation during a consultation.

"No, Frenny," Karen exclaimed in a panic. "Take me, too!"

"I'm just going to the outer office," she said, assuring Karen she would be fine. "I'll be right out there. You don't have to worry."

"I'm going with you," Karen said, jumping from the couch and heading for the door, leaving Frenda to apologize.

Another cry for help went out to singer Cherry O'Neill when Karen phoned her for advice. "She didn't sound panicked, but she felt that she really needed some help," O'Neill says. "Karen was having particular problems with laxatives, and she didn't believe she could ever get to a point where she was not dependent upon them." O'Neill felt Karen needed a change of scenery. She understood the benefits of getting away from family and the obligations of work. "You need to get away from the pressures of L.A. and show business and concentrate on your own life and survival," she said.

"I'm going to do it," Karen told her. "I'll get well. It's just so damn hard." Evelyn Wallace entered the office during one of the calls in time to overhear Karen say, "Well, I don't want to *die*." Wallace quickly grabbed her things and exited once she realized the serious tone of Karen's conversation.

Cherry sent Karen a copy of a typewritten manuscript for her forthcoming book, which made its way to Ev's desk. *Starving for Attention* was O'Neill's autobiographical look at her battle with anorexia and her eventual recovery. "Whether Karen read the whole thing or not, I don't know," Wallace says. "I think she left it on my desk purposely. Otherwise she would have gotten rid of it or she would have hid it in some of her stuff. Why would she leave that on my desk? I think she wanted me to read it."

BY 1979 Karen's voice had dominated the airwaves for nearly a decade alongside other great pop female vocalists, including Barbra Streisand, Anne Murray, Helen Reddy, and Olivia Newton-John. These singers maintained individual identities as solo artists, garnering a great deal of attention to their personal strengths and abilities, but the public identified Karen as part of a duo. Year after year she was overlooked when Grammy and American Music Awards nominations were announced in categories recognizing female vocalists. Although she rarely voiced disappointment, Karen had yet to receive accolades for her talents as an individual singer.

Karen would mention from time to time that she would like to record a solo album and receive recognition as a solo artist. She had received numerous requests to guest on albums by other artists but always declined out of respect for Richard. In fact, just months earlier she had turned down an invitation from KISS member Gene Simmons, who asked her to sing on his self-titled solo album (which ultimately featured appearances by Helen Reddy and Donna Summer). But Karen had gradually reached a point in her career where she wanted to be known as Karen Carpenter, not just the lead singer from the Carpenters. "That is the ultimate compliment," she had told Ray Coleman back in 1975, "to have respect not only from your fans but also your peers and other singers. To have that kind of reputation and have it stay, it would be fantastic. And it's really nice to know that other people think that something you have is that special."

There was no doubt in Frenda's mind that Karen knew she was good. She was always confident in her talent and abilities. "I think she knew that she had an ability to really touch people," she recalls. "I also think she wanted to do her own thing, and that was a big, big problem. She had talked about it for a long time. It wasn't about hurting anybody. It was about exploring her talents." Frenda encouraged Karen, seeing a solo project as a huge step toward the independence and autonomy Karen so desperately needed. "It was her Emancipation Proclamation," she says. "There's no question, it was her coming out party. That's exactly what it was. But she had no idea the price she was going to pay."

Karen seemed optimistic about her musical options, despite Richard's debilitated state. "Everybody is trying new things," she said in a radio interview during her visit to England in December. "Needless to say, the disco thing is so hot right now. Even a lot of the disco things are pretty, you know. Donna Summer has done some beautiful songs." She also expressed a love for the music of the Bee Gees, whose *Saturday Night Fever* album became one of the best-selling soundtracks of all time.

When asked about future projects and the possibility of both she and Richard working separately, Karen spoke of her brother's interest in scoring a film and hinted of a possible solo project for herself. "We have often thought about it," she said in 1978. "We have discussed it—not necessarily interrupting the Carpenters as a unit but to add on to that. One of the things that Richard's wanted to do for years is produce other people, and if he did something like that I might do a solo album or get into acting, but at the same time keep the Carpenters going because we don't ever want to let that go. We've been discussing a lot of things. There's so much to do, and it's a lot of fun to keep changing."

To the Carpenter family, a solo venture for Karen threatened the Carpenters as a duo. This was especially difficult for Agnes Carpenter, who saw the idea as her daughter tampering with the established formula she had devised. She was fearful a temporary split might lead to a permanent separation and the end of her son's career. "You have to remember, these were uneducated, unsophisticated people," says Frenda of the senior Carpenters. "They were going to stay with the tried and the true. Agnes had washed those cars so that Richard could perform. That was her vision and her goal. That was it! And you stayed with the plan. Anything that deviated or threatened was bad. So Karen was bad."

Initially, Herb Alpert and Jerry Moss supported the idea of a solo project for Karen, as did manager Jerry Weintraub. It was Alpert who recommended producer Phil Ramone, "the Quincy Jones of the East Coast," according to Rob Hoerburger for *Rolling Stone*. Ramone's career with such artists as Billy Joel, Bob Dylan, and Paul Simon was thriving. His recent production of Joel's *52nd Street* album won the Grammy for

Album of the Year for 1979. Karen was hopeful the producer would consent. Ramone, too, had a great deal of respect for Karen as a vocalist and was a self-professed fan of the hits she created with Richard earlier in the decade. "The greatness of her is that within five seconds of hearing that voice on the air you know it is Karen," Ramone says. "Hers is still one of the most instantly identified sounds in the world."

Ramone first met the Carpenters in 1970 when working on an album with Burt Bacharach on the A&M lot. "Herb asked me to come in his office," he recalls. "He said, 'Oh, you've got to hear these two young people we signed recently.' I went crazy. The next time that I heard about them, Burt said they had covered 'Close to You.' Fast-forward a little bit, Burt goes out on a tour and the opening act was the Carpenters. That's when I saw them in New York at Westbury Music Fair."

Jerry Weintraub made the call to Ramone proposing he work with Karen and explained that Richard was taking a year off due to overwork and exhaustion. Phil agreed enthusiastically but was unaware of Richard's bout with quaaludes and his stay at Menninger. "I knew nothing," he says, although he sensed something might be going on beneath the surface. The call from Weintraub was followed by calls from both Alpert and Moss, with both men expressing their support but reminding Phil they were not looking to replace the Carpenters.

Karen's initial meeting with Ramone was a short and informal one that took place at the producer's duplex on Burton Way in Beverly Hills. "Karen didn't want anybody to know that she was even thinking about doing a solo album," recalls Karen Ramone, then Karen Ichiuji and Phil's girlfriend. "She was so hard on herself. She was basically hyperactive, and she really wanted to continue her music. She didn't know whether or not Richard would come out of Menninger's and say he wanted to work again. I think she was really trying to prepare herself for any scenario that might happen. She got all thumbs up by everybody—Herbie, Jerry Moss, and Jerry Weintraub—everybody. She had a huge support system when she started this thing."

Arriving at Karen's Century City condo for the first time, Ramone was caught off guard when the doorbell chimed the first six notes of "We've Only Just Begun." "Isn't that an amazing bell?" Karen said as she answered the door. "I had a guy make it for me, and it's *exactly* as I sang it!"

Phil was puzzled by Karen. He knew her only as the naive girl he had seen in publicity photos and on album covers. He was familiar with the duo's biggest hits and was well aware of their reputation for attention to intricate details in the music, but Ramone's goal was never to achieve the Carpenters' echelon of perfection with Karen. In fact, his plan for her was to follow no set plan at all. "It was a lot of experimenting," he recalls. "We were trying to make an artist's complete dream."

Karen flew to New York on February 16, 1979, for further meetings with her producer, just a week prior to his receiving the Record of the Year Grammy for Billy Joel's "Just the Way You Are." Ramone interrupted Karen when she began talking about recording tracks in Los Angeles at A&M and how she planned to record with all the musicians and engineers she and Richard had known and trusted for years. "No, no," he told her. "You have got to come back to New York. A&M's a great studio to cut in, but it will confuse the issue."

After much consideration, it was agreed that Karen would fly to New York to record with Ramone at his own A&R Recording Studios in Manhattan. "Coming to New York was a big thing for her and for me," he says. "We talked about what the approach should be. How do you make a record when your whole reputation is built on your life as a Carpenter? I personally didn't want to touch anything in that world. I thought of her as an actor who had been typecast, like Judy Garland was typecast after *The Wizard of Oz*. She made all those *Andy Hardy* movies. Recording artists get typed, too. I said to Karen, 'It is like comedians who want to do a serious role as a singer and singers who want to be comedians. You must be cautious here.'"

———— ∞∞∞ ————

DESPITE HAVING put his stamp of approval on a solo project for Karen, Jerry Weintraub's concern for her health and well-being remained. He was intrigued when he came across a television interview with Steven Levenkron, a psychotherapist specializing in eating disorders, promoting *The Best Little Girl in the World*, his new novel about "the obsession that kills." Weintraub was immediately impressed with the therapist's convincing tone and perceived knowledge of the subject matter, and felt Karen would surely benefit from meeting with Levenkron. Little did he know, Karen was already familiar with Levenkron after having become engrossed with the book at first reading. Weintraub's call to the therapist was returned after several days, at which time he explained his concern for Karen and the struggle that had become apparent some four years prior.

With Richard present, Karen phoned Steven Levenkron in New York from Weintraub's office on March 27, 1979. She purposely moved away from the men and spoke softly in an attempt to keep the conversation private. During their brief exchange Karen felt she had been able to convince the therapist that she was not suffering with anorexia nervosa but a gastrointestinal problem, specifically colitis. Levenkron urged her to find a qualified gastrointestinal specialist and wished her good luck. Returning to Richard and Weintraub, Karen lied, saying that Levenkron could tell she did not have anorexia from their conversation. They were skeptical but pleased to know she had made a significant step in just making the call, an act that hushed the two, if only temporarily.

To further appease Richard and Weintraub, Karen checked into Cedars-Sinai in Los Angeles for a few days of diagnostics. Exhausted and, of course, underweight, she must have thought that going to these lengths would calm the fears of those around her—or at least appear to be an effort on her part to get well.

The April 1979 fan club newsletter told of Karen's solo venture, sparking concern from fans afraid this meant an end to the duo. At that time, no one really knew for certain, not even Karen and Richard themselves. In an attempt to calm fears, the club's next issue included the following statement.

To dispel any rumors that the group has split up, Karen wishes to assure you this is not so. The reason for the temporary lapse in their recordings is that after ten arduous years of concentrating on per- fecting music to the Carpenters standards we expect, Richard felt the need for a long vacation which probably will extend into the

New Year. Karen reaffirms they will resume work on their album whenever Richard feels ready. He is really enjoying the freedom from pressures, and we must not be selfish in denying him the time off he deserves.

According to Evelyn Wallace, "It was stuff like that we just kind of skirted around. A person's always allowed to take time off. You don't have to tell people what it's for."

Phil Ramone recalls that Karen was very frustrated once rumors of a Carpenters breakup began to spread. "That was the thing that drove her crazy," he says. "The 1970s saw the breakup of Peter, Paul and Mary, Crosby, Stills and Nash. They were all going out on solo careers. People thought if you left a group you never came back or would never work together again. They could never leave the roost. Not in that family."

In a 1981 interview with Paul Grein, Karen expressed in no uncertain terms that her solo album was never meant to signal an end to the Carpenters as a duo. "It was never planned for me to drop the Carpenters and go cut a solo—that would never happen, ever! If Richard hadn't gone on vacation, I never would have done the solo album."

With flights and studio time booked, Karen's loyalty to Richard still weighed heavily on the eve of her departure for New York. Having completed Menninger's six-week program, Richard spent much of 1979 visiting friends around the country, relaxing, and putting on some of the weight lost during the crisis. He avoided the stress of the business and even his home life, taking up residence in the Long Beach home of Gary Sims and Dennis Strawn, brother of Doug. On the evening of April 30, Karen phoned Richard at Sims's house, hoping to get his blessing before embarking on the project. She knew very well he did not and would not approve, but she made the call regardless. Distraught and in tears, she told him, "I can't go do this unless I know that you're behind it."

In an attempt to pacify Karen, Richard offered his blessing. But before their conversation ended he asked that she promise him one thing: "Do me one favor. Do *not* do disco!"

13

POCKETS FULL OF
GOOD INTENTIONS

———————

ITH GREAT anticipation and a mix of emotions, Karen
boarded a plane bound for New York on the morning of
May 1, 1979. Production meetings commenced the following day with Phil Ramone asking, "Ideally, what would you like
to do?"

"Well, I *love* Donna Summer," Karen replied, explaining how Summer's latest single "Hot Stuff" was her current favorite. "I'd give *anything* if we could do a song like that!" This certainly surprised Ramone.
Disregarding her brother's plea, she went on to explain that, in addition
to singers like Aretha Franklin and Barbra Streisand, she loved just
about anything of the disco genre.

Karen took up residence in a posh suite at the Plaza Hotel on Fifth
Avenue. She was fascinated by the panoramic views of the New York
skyline and the idea that there were butlers assigned to every floor, but
within weeks the novelty of the revered Central Park address wore
thin. "We were talking about stupid expenses and the hotel," Ramone
recalls. "I said to Karen, 'Why would you want to do that? If we're
going to work together, why don't you come live at my house? We've
got plenty of room.'"

Ramone proceeded to move Karen into the master suite of the relaxing estate he shared with girlfriend Karen Ichiuji in Pound Ridge, a small town on the New York and Connecticut border. The quaint surroundings of this rural community were much like Hall Street from Karen's childhood. The two Karens quickly became close friends. Ichiuji was a singer herself who recorded under the name Karen Kamon and would later contribute the song "Manhunt" to the popular motion picture soundtrack for *Flashdance*. Phil called her K.K., but Karen preferred her own silly nickname of Itchie. Living together allowed producer and artist to discuss plans for the solo project around the clock. "She was a workaholic," Ramone says. "That house was a very creative house for me, and it was for her, too."

Karen and Phil set out to establish a common vision. Their hour-long commute from Pound Ridge to Manhattan's A&R Studios, located at 322 West Forty-Eighth, allowed the two to peruse demos for the project. "The laughs and silliness we shared on those trips forever made us friends," Ramone recalled in his book, *Making Records: The Scenes Behind the Music*. "While we were driving, Karen would be the DJ, playing all the songs that had been submitted for her consideration. She'd sit with a legal pad, listen intently and rate them. 'Should this be on the A list, or the B?' she'd ask."

During these initial stages, Ramone extended an invitation to friend Rod Temperton to come to New York to write for Karen. The former keyboardist for the funk/disco band Heatwave accepted and moved into Ramone's guest house with only a keyboard and a set of headphones in tow. "All you had to do was make coffee and give him cigarettes," says Itchie. "Our house became this big musical commune." Temperton offered Karen several of his own compositions, including "Off the Wall" and "Rock with You," but at that point the songs were just grooves at the piano, still in their most raw form. She declined both charts, saying they were too funky. According to Itchie, "Everyone else loved the idea," but the project was young and lacked direction. Within a few months, Ramone introduced Temperton to Quincy Jones when the two attended a barbecue held at the home of the pop music titan, and the songs were soon pitched to Michael Jackson.

Karen visited Jackson in the studio during his 1979 solo sessions while he laid down tracks for "Get on the Floor," a song he had cowritten with bassist Louis Johnson. "Phil wanted to show her what Michael's album was like," recalls Itchie. "He was so upset that Karen didn't want to do any of Rod's material at first." Ultimately she chose two Temperton originals for her project, "Lovelines" and "If We Try," the latter being a particularly satisfying match for her smooth and flirtatious vocals. "Once Rod started arranging for her, they got along so well," Itchie adds. "She loved the harmonies they created, and they were so right for each other musically. She felt comfortable working with him, and it was kind of like being with Richard in a sense, artistically."

The two Temperton songs Karen passed on became huge hits for Michael Jackson on his *Off the Wall* solo album. Also featured on the album was his recording of "She's Out of My Life," a song by Tom Bähler long rumored to have been written in response to the end of the composer's own brief relationship with Karen Carpenter in 1978. "Some believe that I had written that as a result of mine and Karen's breakup," Bähler says. "The fact is, I had already written that song by the time Karen and I became romantic. That song was written more about Rhonda Rivera, who later married my friend John Davidson. Rhonda and I had been together for two years, and it was after we broke up that I started dating Karen."

Over time, Karen developed a great sense of security as she recorded with Phil Ramone. It was not the same as working with her brother, but she felt comforted and protected by him in the studio. "If he hadn't been as gentle and sensitive as he is, I couldn't have done it," Karen said. "He knows how close Richard and I are." Aside from the early contract with Joe Osborn's Magic Lamp Records, Karen had worked exclusively for A&M Records and under Richard's guidance. "I was scared to death beforehand," she said. "I basically knew one producer, one arranger, one studio, one record company, and that was it. It was a different surrounding, working with different people with different habits. I didn't know how they worked; they didn't know how I worked. I'm used to blinking an eye and an engineer knows what I want or Richard knows what I'm thinking. . . . I'm used to being part of a duo. Richard's like a third arm to me."

For Karen's sessions, Ramone recruited members of Billy Joel's band. At the time the men were in the middle of recording *Glass Houses*, their fourth album together with Joel and one that produced his first #1 single, "It's Still Rock and Roll to Me." Unlike many of the polished studio musicians Karen was accustomed to working with in Los Angeles, this band was raw—likened to a garage band—and chosen by Ramone for their boundless energy. "Was Billy's group perfect?" Ramone wrote in 2007. "No—but that's what I loved. They were a real band that worked together night after night, playing his music with passion."

At the age of seventeen, drummer Liberty DeVitto and fellow Long Island teens Russell Javors and Doug Stegmeyer formed the band Topper, which eventually evolved to become Billy Joel's band. "Phil thought we'd be an interesting core group of musicians to work with her because of the relationship we had with him and Billy as an artist," recalls Russell Javors. "We were the kinds of musicians that would push the envelope when we worked with an artist, too. I'm sure it was a different kind of atmosphere than Karen was used to working in. We were very vocal about what we thought and what we did. It was a bunch of guys rather than a group of session musicians."

For Karen's album, the band was tracked at A&R's studio A1, located at 799 Seventh Avenue. "It was kind of a family situation," Javors says, "but this was a whole different kind of family than she was used to. We were kind of 'New York' and Karen was nothing like that. We were a rowdy bunch of bar band guys. Karen became part of the fold, and we didn't hold anything back. She certainly got into it, and it felt like she was one of the guys. I think she had fun."

Bob James, renowned smooth-jazz artist, keyboardist, and former musical director for Sarah Vaughn, was enlisted by Ramone to arrange, orchestrate, and play keyboards for the project. "Karen was an arranger's dream," says James, who admits he found himself a bit starstruck at times in the studio. "It was a flattering but also very intimidating assignment. That sound coming through my headphones in the studio was very inspiring and exciting. I remember thinking, 'Wow, I'm actually in the studio playing the piano for Karen Carpenter!'"

Javors was surprised by the tiny sound he heard coming from Karen in the booth. "When you hear her voice on a record it's so big and so full. In the studio it was kind of like a whisper. She didn't really belt it out. She was up close to the mic, and it wasn't this tremendous voice that you'd hear. It was just a very intimate, focused voice. I was amazed at the ease and how softly she really sang." DeVitto concurs "She almost whispered into the mic, but Phil was able to capture that and have it sit on top of the music. He never lost sight of Karen."

In one of their daily phone calls, Karen told Frenda Franklin that she was in awe of this diverse assembly of musicians. "They treated her like an equal in the studio, and she loved the process," Franklin says. "She had the best time!"

At times the band members saw evidence of Karen's sheltered Downey life and would even poke fun at her, which she seemed to enjoy, given her own knack for humor. "She'd never been on an airplane by herself before," Javors recalls. "Then she had these road cases with different sweat suits and Nike sneakers, and they were all the same color and all lined up in a row. She came from a different world." Even Phil would join in and tease Karen, especially when she would show up to a session wearing pressed and starched blue jeans. "This girl loved to be fussy and get it done right," he laughs. "Karen was fastidious, and I would tease her ruthlessly. She had every satin jacket given out by the record company—and a matching pair of sneakers for each one!"

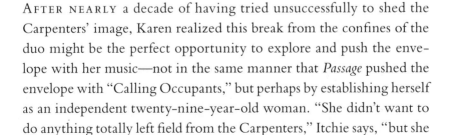

AFTER NEARLY a decade of having tried unsuccessfully to shed the Carpenters' image, Karen realized this break from the confines of the duo might be the perfect opportunity to explore and push the envelope with her music—not in the same manner that *Passage* pushed the envelope with "Calling Occupants," but perhaps by establishing herself as an independent twenty-nine-year-old woman. "She didn't want to do anything totally left field from the Carpenters," Itchie says, "but she wanted to say that she was an independent artist. The Carpenters had their image, and she didn't want to present an image that clashed with that, but she did want an image that set her apart. I saw what Phil was doing. Basically he was trying to help her grow up a bit, gain the confidence to be a woman, and state what she felt and what she thought."

Olivia Newton-John sensed that Karen was torn between following this desire and staying loyal to her family. "She was incredibly ensconced by or tied into her family and Richard and the whole situation," she says. "She wanted to break out as a human being and as a woman and live an independent life. She also wanted to feel her way musically into other areas. . . . I think it was really important for her to feel that it wasn't just Richard or just the production that had made the Carpenters a success. She was just as important and needed to find her own feet and find her own style."

According to Ramone, "Karen was twenty-nine, but she couldn't be a woman who could think like a woman and express herself. . . . Some people still thought that I was taking her down a street she didn't want to travel. We weren't out to shock people. I was not interested in putting out a shock record on her behalf. That would be so wrong for me. But some people were shocked. You can't make a record in fear of what everyone's going to say. You can't make a record that doesn't speak from your heart."

The environment was one of "admiration and appreciation for Karen and her talents," says Russell Javors. "People had such strong feelings about their legacy and what they'd done and the way they did it, but this was *Karen*, and it should complement anything that she'd already done. Nobody was doing it in the spirit of 'we'll show you, Richard,' or anything. Phil was trying to push the envelope a little bit but let her do it naturally."

Song titles like "Remember When Lovin' Took All Night," "Make Believe It's Your First Time," and "Making Love in the Afternoon" led to accusations that Ramone was force-feeding Karen sexual lyrics and themes to create a new persona, but according to those closely involved, he gave Karen complete choice and control. "Phil was trying to pick material that would allow her to push the envelope, but it was never forced on her," says Javors. "He's a nurturer. He kind of opens the road up to you, and you either take it or you don't; but he's not somebody who says, 'You go down this road.'…She was very intimately involved in everything that was going on, and this was 100 percent her project."

A number of Karen's song choices contained lyrics with overtones of sexuality, some less subtle than others. "I Love Makin' Love to You" was written by Evie Sands, formerly with A&M Records, and recorded for her *Estate of Mind* album on the Capital/Haven label in 1975. "When I heard Karen was going to cover it," Sands recalls, "I imagined her take on it would be similar to mine or closer to the mellow Barbra Streisand version. It turned out to be a perfect blend of both." Although Karen and Phil finished the ambitious arrangement of Sands's tune, complete with lush background vocals and an outstanding brass section, it was ultimately set aside. The risqué lyric is likely to blame.

There's no lightnin' or thunder, any seventh wonder
Mightier than what you've got
Keep it up forever, no one does it better
Baby, get it while it's hot

For the infectious "Making Love in the Afternoon," Chicago front man Peter Cetera joined Karen in the studio on the song he had written. "Peter was a fan of Karen's voice," recalls Ramone, who produced the *Chicago 13* album around that time. "Cetera wrote the song for her." Billed as a duet, Cetera's role was more of a backup singer to Karen's lead. According to Itchie, "A true duet would have stepped over the line by stepping on Richard. Harmonizing is one thing, but a duet? No. That would have been trespassing."

According to Itchie, "Everybody had input as far as the album was concerned.…I remember Billy Joel coming in the studio and saying, 'Uh, excuse me, but why am I not doing keyboards?'" Paul Simon stopped in as well. "They treated her like a major mega artist," Itchie says. "I think she really needed that in becoming her own self. It really got her started building a backbone. It was her environment, and everybody was there to support her, and she absolutely loved it."

Paul Simon recommended to Karen his own "Still Crazy After All These Years," a song originally produced by Phil Ramone on the Grammy Album of the Year for 1976. "It expressed a lot of what she wanted to say," Ramone recalls. "But she had Paul rewrite a line. It used to be 'crapped out, yawning' and she did 'crashed out, yawning.' We talked about how that song wouldn't be a Carpenters song!" Karen's vocal on the mellow, jazz-inflected "Still Crazy" was self-assured, relaxed, and alluring. She also recorded Simon's "I Do It for Your Love" and, in true Carpenters fashion, the oldie "Jimmy Mack," a Motown hit for Martha and the Vandellas in 1967. The initial rhythm tracks and work leads for these two showed little promise, and both went unfinished. Another outtake, a real diamond in the rough, was "Something's Missing in My Life," a stunning ballad by Jay Asher and Paul Jabara and recorded by Jabara as a duet with Donna Summer on his 1978 album *Keeping Time*.

Karen felt challenged by the intricate background vocal arrangements, many of which took on a brass-influenced instrumental feel. Bob James was responsible for several arrangements, including "If I Had You," the most funky, demanding, and ambitious of all. Like Ramone, he felt obligated to move Karen out of the Carpenters mold. "I wanted to give her something different and challenging," James explains. "I was very intrigued to find out how she would react to an arrangement that was deliberately moving away from the Carpenters sound." Karen's inimitable style on the sophisticated "If I Had You" resulted in an original and captivating piece of ear candy with a complex, multilayered call-and-response ending, the brainchild of Rod Temperton.

Although Karen had conveyed to her brother the vocal challenges she faced when singing Bob James's arrangements, she spoke very little about Richard to the guys in the studio. "I don't recall Karen *ever* mentioning him," Russell Javors says. According to Frenda, despite having given Karen the go-ahead, Richard was "not supportive" of the project after it got underway. "I don't want to pick on him," she says. "He wasn't exactly in good shape. His and Karen's timing was always off, but I know during that whole time when Karen did the album and stayed with Phil and Itchie, he was never supportive.... We were all hoping that because she finally was able to do this that it could be the catalyst to really turn everything around. Nothing else was doing it."

Sitting down at the drums next to Lib (as she and others referred to Liberty DeVitto), Karen joked, "Let me show you what I got," before tearing into the kit. A second-generation Italian-American, DeVitto taught himself to play drums after having seen the Beatles on *The Ed Sullivan Show*. He claims to have been a closet Carpenters fan even prior to meeting Karen. "I never bought a record but knew all their songs," he says. DeVitto was attracted to Karen from the start, and his feelings grew the more time the two were together. "To be honest with you, I fell in love with Karen," he says. "I was married at the time, but I felt like I wanted to be with her. Silly, I know. I had no idea how she would have felt about that so I just kept it to myself." When asked his views on Karen as a drummer, the comic emerged: "Is this the part where I am supposed to get in trouble by saying, 'She was all right for a girl'?"

Karen was drawn to the drums as if by some gravitational pull. Occasionally she would go to the studio before the others arrived and sit down behind the battery of drums. "Those days are over," she told Ramone. "I'm not sitting behind the drums and singing anymore."

Sensitive to this downhearted moment he replied, "Well, you never know."

"It doesn't help my rear end," she told him.

Ramone thought Karen looked good during the first recording sessions and did not sense any unusual eating habits. Even so, her comment at the drums that day stuck out in his mind. He had been cautioned about her eating disorder by others. "But there were no clues at all at first," he says. "If there were dead giveaways they came later. Everything seemed logical and fine. Sitting down at a meal was to sit down to have a meal. I know a lot of nitpickers. She wasn't a fusspot."

In her free time, Karen enjoyed going with Itchie to Serendipity, a favorite Manhattan restaurant, and out to the Bottom Line, a popular Greenwich Village music club. She also liked eating seafood but only with an abundance of lemons. "She had a little bit of fish with her lemons!" Itchie laughs. "Then we would eat stone crab claws at Joe's Pier Fifty-Two across from A&R Studios every night until the stone crab season was over." The trio of Karen, Phil, and Itchie also attended a baseball game at Shea Stadium in Queens where Karen immediately noticed the initials "K.C." on the scoreboard. "Look, it's for me—K.C.!"

"Come on, Karen," Ramone chuckled. "That's Kansas City, the *team!*" A few minutes later Karen was thrilled to hear the announcer say, "Please welcome Karen Carpenter from the Carpenters," as strains of "We've Only Just Begun" echoed across the park.

"Oh, here comes Lucy and Ethel," the guys in the band would tease when Karen and Itchie would arrive at the studio together. According to Itchie, she was the Ethel to Karen's Lucy in almost every scenario. Karen's collection of *I Love Lucy* videotapes often traveled with her. A favorite episode was "The Ballet," in which Lucy trained with Madame LeMond, an authoritarian ballet teacher. "I think we should go to the barre," LeMond said.

"Oh good," Lucy replied, "'cause I'm awful thirsty!"

After becoming entangled in the barre, Lucy cried out "Ahh-ba, Ahh-ba," in hopes of freeing her leg. Watching this, Karen and Itchie would laugh until they cried. The "Ahh-ba" exclamation became a part of the twosome's banter with one another. "Sometimes Karen was *really* tired and *really* had to be 'on' for a performance or whatever," Itchie explains. "She'd yell out 'Ahh-ba!'" In observance of their inside joke, Karen bought Itchie a wristwatch. On the underside was engraved AHH-BA!

Karen sometimes phoned childhood friend Debbie Cuticello asking to spend the weekend at her home in Guilford, Connecticut, an hour from Phil's estate. "She wanted the chance to get away and enjoy some good Italian home-cooked meals," Cuticello recalled in 1983. "I remember the big limo driving down my driveway, and I wondered what her thoughts would be about the quiet little town of Guilford. She loved the quiet and the comfort."

Some weeks later, Debbie and her husband, C.J., made the two-hour drive into Manhattan to visit Karen at A&R Recording Studios, where she and Ramone played several songs for the couple. Debbie was especially taken with the contemporary sound of the recordings. "It was wonderful, like an angel's voice," she says. "I was impressed."

The reception at home on the West Coast was less enthusiastic. With a handful of songs completed, Karen flew home to Los Angeles, excited to play the new recordings for her family and friends. This was one of several returns to Southern California during the solo project, each of which proved to be a setback as far as her energy and progress in the studio with Ramone was concerned. Friend Carole Curb felt Karen was torn between these two lives. The decision to move to New York and record a solo album was actually a huge weight on Karen's shoulders. "I just heard that she had decided to go off on her own," Curb says. "It was a big decision to make, and I think all these things contributed to a lot of anxiety. It's hard to leave the nest."

Needless to say, the nest was thrilled to have Karen back but not as excited once they heard the material she had been recording. "Agnes did not like the idea that Karen came out and did this project at all," Itchie says. "She was a very rough person as it was, but then she didn't particularly care for me. Whenever I would go to their house I would speak to Harold, not Agnes. Karen was much closer to her dad, but there wasn't really a whole lot of communication, but he would be loose with me, whereas Agnes was a Gestapo agent. With Agnes there was not a list of dos and don'ts. It was just don'ts."

Although Agnes was disappointed in Karen for attempting an album without Richard, overall she put very little stock in the solo endeavor. According to Evelyn Wallace, "As far as Agnes was concerned, regardless of how many records Karen would have made, to her mother they'd never be as good as Richard's."

Phil Ramone was surprised by the negative response from the family and, in time, those at A&M as well. "I feel like I've taken your daughter out on a date and was supposed to be home by midnight but came in at 12:01 A.M.," he told Jerry Moss. "It's like you met me at the door saying 'I hope you didn't change my daughter.'"

"What could I change?" Ramone asks now. "There are accusations that come at you, like when I worked with Julian Lennon they said, 'You made him sound like his dad.' Man, if I am that good then why couldn't I do it for me? You cannot do something for somebody unless they want it done. We weren't out to change the world, but we were certainly representing her coming of age. And I mean that in the best possible way."

⸗∞⸗

RICHARD'S SUMMATION that Karen was not well enough to have embarked on such a grand plan was confirmed as she became weaker and thinner over the course of the project. Additionally, signs began to point to the possibility that she was resorting to bulimic practices, ridding her body of food she would ingest to give the appearance she was eating healthily. "She was very thin," Russell Javors recalls. "My wife and I had dinner with her one night, and she ate a hell of a lot then excused herself. That was the first person we'd seen go through that ritual."

Itchie witnessed the same. "At one point she started to gorge herself," she says. "It was amazing. She ate twice as much as me. She said that she had colitis, and I said, 'Oh, so do I.' I would go to the bathroom every single time she did. She would be so pissed because she was very uncomfortable having all this food in her."

In the spring of 1980, sitting at home with Phil and watching a video of herself on Olivia Newton-John's recent *Hollywood Nights* TV special, Karen's warped sense of body image surfaced. Dancing and singing alongside Olivia, Linda "Peaches" Greene (of Peaches and Herb), Toni Tennille, and Tina Turner, Karen looked radiant but too thin. "Oh, God, look how *heavy* I am," she said. Ramone, baffled by what he'd just heard, jumped up from the couch, paused the videotape, and grabbed a nearby crayon. He proceeded to draw lines around each of the ladies' bodies and observed that hers was like a pencil. "You're just two lines," he told her. "You don't *see* that?"

"No, look how fat I am. Look how big my hips are!"

Ramone was incredulous and unable to convince Karen she was by far the thinnest of all the women on stage. Things took a turn for the worse one evening when Phil heard a loud "thump" sound come from his kitchen. Alarmed, he ran in to discover Karen passed out on the floor. She was so thin and frail he worried she might have broken a bone. He carefully moved her to the couch and phoned paramedics.

By the time they arrived, Karen was lightheaded but alert. She refused to go in the ambulance and was concerned when she realized the paramedics were aware of her identity. On her behalf, Phil pleaded that they not release her name. Karen said the collapse was most likely due to her having taken half a quaalude earlier in the evening. It was unfathomable that she would have the pills in her possession after having dealt with Richard's addiction.

Following this scare, Karen attempted to ease the Ramones' worries by promising to start eating properly, but just days later Itchie found laxatives hidden around the house. She found them in Karen's room—in her luggage, her pillowcase, and even her shoes—and throughout the house behind cupboards and in a fruit bowl. Karen assured her that she wasn't using them and just needed them there for security. Phil, Itchie, and their friends were extremely concerned. They knew something was very wrong but admit no one knew what they were dealing with. "The clues were there," he says. "The treatment wasn't."

As friendly and warm as Karen was to those involved in the project, Russell Javors sensed what he calls "a tinge of sadness about her. You could kind of sense that there was something going on. All the clues were there. . . . But the project was about music and not eating disorders. When you're involved in a situation like that, first and foremost, you're there to make a record. You're there to make music."

RECORDING FOR the solo album wrapped in January 1980, by which time Karen had spent the customary $100,000 allotted by A&M Records, plus an additional $400,000 of her own. With the album in the mixing phase, A&M Records began a promotional campaign and assigned the album a catalog number, readying for a spring 1980 release. Several on the A&M lot recall the record was being talked up as a smash hit, and Phil Ramone noticed a renewed sense of optimism in Karen, who was finally exhibiting self-assurance in her work. "She was getting more and more confident," he says.

"So Kace, do you like the way Liv looks here?" Itchie asked, showing Karen the record jacket for Olivia Newton-John's recently released *Totally Hot* LP.

"Oh, look at ONJ!" Karen exclaimed, smiling at the cover photo shot by French glamour photographer Claude Mougin. While she was fond of the look, Karen had trouble picturing herself made up like Olivia, who had been photographed wearing black leather and intense eye makeup. Phil felt Karen's photos should make a statement in congruence with the album's sensual lyrical content. He contacted Mougin to shoot Karen's album cover and promotional photos, which were captured during a two-hour session on February 2, 1980. Karen was accustomed to doing her own hair and makeup or having an assistant along with her on the road, but she rarely received a glamour treatment such as this. Being made up for this *Vogue*-style photo shoot was exciting, but Karen seemed nervous and panicky. "Maybe we should get you some herbal tea, Karen," Itchie suggested.

Unbeknownst to Karen, Itchie crushed up a Valium tablet and added it to her cup of tea. "I spiked her chamomile tea," Itchie recalls. "I put honey and five milligrams of Valium, and she never even knew! She calmed down and was absolutely gorgeous."

When the photo proofs were delivered, Karen was amazed by the transformation; she looked sexy and provocative. She was ecstatic when she showed them to Itchie. "Itch, will you *look* at these?" she said, her eyes wide and mouth open in astonishment.

"Yeah, so how do you feel about them?" Itchie asked.

"I look *pretty*," Karen said in astonishment. "I actually look pretty."

"But Kace, you've always looked pretty," she was assured.

Having selected eleven songs from more than twenty they recorded, Karen and Phil arranged a series of meetings to present the new album to those at the label. The first playbacks were held at A&R Studios in New York with London's Derek Green representing the A&M label at the request of Jerry Moss. Champagne toasts and cheers of "congratulations" flowed freely as everyone celebrated the exquisite and sophisticated sounds Karen and Phil had succeeded in crafting. "It was the coming of a great new artist," says Itchie. "In New York, everybody had their arms open and was excited—the whole nine yards!"

All that remained was a West Coast playback at A&M in Hollywood for Alpert and Moss. At Karen's request, Richard was asked to be present for the unveiling. According to Ramone, "The hardest thing in the world is to have to play back a record to your company that has known you and thinks of you in only one world. Karen certainly had confidence in what we were about to play, but she was nervous as hell. Overall, I think her deepest fear was Richard. He definitely did not like the record."

Song after song, Herb, Jerry, and Richard sat pokerfaced. It was a "den of silence," according to Ramone, who began to bite his nails. He grew increasingly troubled with the passing of each song and sensed Karen's mounting disillusionment, too. She expected cheers and hugs to celebrate each new track, as she had received in New York, but the three men remained impervious. "It's easier when you have ten or twelve people in the room," Ramone says. "My life has been made up of listening and watching and feeling an audience, even if it's just four people. There was much discomfort, and they really had a hard time finding something to love."

"How could you do a *disco* record?" one asked following the play-back. "Why would you attempt a song like that?" another wondered. "Well, somehow you've got to omit something," they said. "We're not happy." Karen was ill prepared to defend the album and was disillu-sioned by the requests to do so.

"Was this the wrong album for her? No," Ramone says. "Was it not what the expectancy was? Yes. But I think if we'd made an album that was like what the Carpenters were doing at that time, then that would have been shot down even more. Richard decided that he wanted to get going with the Carpenters again—and the label got behind him on that. I think we were in a situation where people did not want to break up this team that was about to re-sign with the label."

Karen had previously played tracks from the album for Frenda, who was ecstatic—but mostly for Karen's sake. "I liked it," she tepidly sum-mons up. "It was *different*. I can't say it was the perfect album, but when you have the Carpenters sound in your ear, you have to kind of divorce yourself from that and go on with it."

When Karen played the album for Mike Curb, he was struck by her noticeable anxiety. "She was back in Los Angeles and called wanting me to hear the album," he recalls. "I went over, and she played it for me, but she seemed very reticent to do the album and reticent to release it—reticent in terms of the effect it might have on her family."

According to Olivia Newton-John, "It's very hard to follow a Carpenters record. The Carpenters' sound and productions were exquisite. She would have gone through criticisms, no doubt." Karen played the album for Newton-John with Richard present. "I remember Richard said, 'You've stolen the Carpenters sound.' That was kind of ironic because she *was* the sound of the Carpenters. Her *voice* was 'the Carpenters.'"

From the project's beginning, Frenda was certain there would be disapproval from A&M and especially Richard. According to her, his negative opinion of Karen's solo work signaled a turning point in the siblings' relationship and one that Karen never seemed to get over. "He told her it was *shit*," Frenda says. "All Karen ever wanted was his approval. It could have turned everything in her life around, but it wasn't there. What's sad is that he has to live with that, and I don't think it even fazes him. I *do* think he should be excused to some extent because he had his own problems, but God Almighty, what does it take to just be kind? They could see she was melting away like a snowman in front of their faces, but they couldn't do it. It was brutal."

Karen's hopes and dreams for the solo album were shattered. After an exhilarating year of creativity, exploration, and hard work, the entire project was rejected by those she loved and respected most in her family and professional life. "We came in with all these high hopes, and then nobody actually liked it," Ramone says. "Of course, they had the right to not like it, but it was never in our minds that this could fail. But it was over. The game was over! There wasn't going to be a part two or attempts to try and figure it out. This wasn't going to be something we could add a few more songs to and make it OK. Sometimes a mix can change things or save the day, but they didn't think that would help. The whole thing was a flop. Karen was completely down in the dumps, and so was I. There was nothing that could cheer us up. What was there to say? At the time we didn't see it as them against us. For us it was all about what *we* did wrong. '*What* did we miss?' '*How* did we miss?'"

Karen and Phil left the A&M lot that day under a veil of disillusionment. "She was absolutely destroyed by the rejection," Itchie says. "You have to understand she was soul searching. She had always felt inferior. She was trying to grow up and start focusing on herself as an artist, a person, a human, and a woman with needs, and it all just went to pieces. It was like somebody just stepped on her and just erased everything she'd worked for."

14

WHITE LACE
AND PROMISES BROKEN

ETURNING TO Los Angeles and no longer juggling the
demands of a bicoastal existence, Karen found time to reunite
with friends like Olivia Newton-John, who suggested a relaxing getaway to the Golden Door health spa in San Diego. There they
were joined by mutual friend Christina Ferrare, an actress and wife of
auto industry executive John DeLorean. During their stay at the spa,
Karen told the women how she finally felt ready to find a husband and
settle down, and spelled out her ever-growing list of requirements in a
man. This was met with laughs from the other women, who told her
she would be extremely lucky to find someone possessing even half of
those prerequisites.

It was around this same time that Karen was astonished to learn
that ex-boyfriend Terry Ellis had become engaged. She had always
regretted the way she ended their relationship and had even hoped they
might one day rekindle their romance. After weeks of introspection
and the continued urging of Itchie, Karen decided to call and invite
Terry to lunch. After all, in her mind he was only engaged. He was not
yet married, so perhaps there was still a chance to renew his interest in
her. "Listen, I've made a big mistake," she began. "I really made a big
mistake in ending our relationship. Can we get back together again?"

"Well, Karen, I'm engaged," he told her. "I'm going to be married."

Along with Olivia Newton-John and Christina Ferrare, Carole Curb was one in a small group of trusted girlfriends who always kept their eyes and ears open in hopes of finding "Mister Right" for Karen. "I have somebody I think you'd like to meet," she said.

"Yeah, *sure* Carole," she replied, the sarcastic rolling of her eyes perceived across the phone line.

Though Karen valued Carole's good taste and sensitive discretion, she felt as though she had heard it a thousand times before. Moreover, she wasn't thrilled by the idea of a blind date, even one arranged by a well-meaning cupid. "But he's nice, good looking, and he's philan-thropic," Curb urged reassuringly.

This latest prospect was Thomas James Burris of Newport Beach, whom Carole had met while attending a dinner with her brother, Mike Curb, whose career path had made several unexpected turns coincid-ing with the dissolution of his own relationship with Karen. Following the 1974 sale of Metro-Goldwyn-Mayer and the MGM Records label by Las Vegas resort mogul Kirk Kerkorian, Curb's work in the record industry was only part time, and he eventually became involved in government. In 1977 he married Linda Dunphy, daughter of popular Southern California news anchor Jerry Dunphy, and by 1980 Curb was lieutenant governor of California and national vice chairman of the Ronald Reagan presidential campaign. The Curbs knew Tom Bur-ris as an enthusiastic Reagan supporter and active member of another organization overseen by Mike Curb, the Commission of Californias, which promoted relations between California and Baja California. "My sister Carole played a role in the matchmaking," he recalls, "but I did not. It was the busiest time of my life back then. But I did know Tom, and he sure seemed like a nice guy."

Thirty-nine-year-old Burris met a number of Karen's require-ments in a potential husband. "He was very attractive, very nice, and he seemed very generous," Carole says. "He had just donated some ambulances to some of the hospitals in Baja California." Burris was not in the music business. A native of Long Beach, Tom had dropped out of school at the age of thirteen and went to work as a mechanic's assistant. In 1958 he joined the Marine Corps and after being discharged worked in a Long Beach welding shop. He later worked as a steel contractor and general housing contractor before becoming the self-proclaimed "industrial developer" who founded Burris Corp. in Long Beach in 1964. In 1975 he moved the business to Corona, California, where he built the city's first planned industrial complex on Pomona Road. An avid NASCAR fan, Burris was a handsome man with blond hair and blue eyes, seemingly affluent and successful, but he was not single. In fact, Burris was the married father of an eighteen-year-old son. He clarified to Carole that he and his wife were separated and their divorce was underway.

Karen first met Tom Burris on a double date with Carole and then husband Tony Scotti on Saturday, April 12, 1980. The couples enjoyed dinner at Ma Maison, the West Hollywood bistro that launched the career of celebrity chef Wolfgang Puck. Having just returned from the East Coast, Karen was a bit jet-lagged. In fact, she wanted to cancel the date, but Agnes Carpenter urged her to attend. Over dinner, Burris told Karen that he was not familiar with the Carpenters or their music. "He really didn't know who I was," she said. "I hadn't known him an hour, but I said to him on the first date, 'What, have you been under a rock for ten years?'" Even so, Karen bought Tom's story and found herself instantly attracted. "I automatically liked him. I liked his way, his look, his style, and his *car*," she laughed. "It was the first time I had actually been attracted on the first date."

At the end of the evening, Karen phoned Frenda Leffler, who had helped ready her hair and makeup that afternoon. "So, how did it go?" Leffler asked.

"Oh, Frenny," she exclaimed, "he reminds me of Chard!" (In addition to "R.C.," "Chard" was one of Karen's many nicknames for her brother.)

After the first date Tom Burris mysteriously disappeared. Karen was disappointed when she did not hear from him right away and blamed herself for running him off. "She told us all about this guy she met and how she really liked him, but she hadn't heard from him" says Frank

Bonito. "What he did was he went off to Las Vegas or somewhere and got a divorce." But Tom soon returned to the scene with gusto, at which time he and Karen embarked upon a whirlwind romance. "It seemed to go really quickly," Carole Curb recalls. She was pleased to see the new couple having a great time together. "What was not to like?" she says. "He had a silver Rolls-Royce, and he was very charming. They got along well and seemed to kind of bond. He seemed really nice."

Best friends Frenda and Itchie did not share Carole's optimism. "I disliked him from the second I met him," Frenda says. "I thought he was a phony and a blowhard. He was egotistical and arrogant."

Itchie tried to remain positive despite some suspicions. She had heard from friends that Tom's background had checked out, and Karen seemed excited. Reportedly, he was not a gold digger. "I liked him at first—sort of," she says. "But I didn't really believe him. He was blond and he was cute but overly manicured and a little too good to be true. He always had a plastic smile and would never look me in the eye." Itchie was shocked when Karen told her, "I think he's going to pop the question," just one day after Tom met her and Phil.

"Now, wait a minute, Kace," she replied. "I just met him. And so did *you* for that matter! Does he know about the anorexia? Does he know what to look for? Does he know the signs?"

"No, no, no, I'm over it," Karen assured her. "I'm eating and I'm really, really happy!"

Itchie was panicked but backed off, not wanting to discourage Karen. "She had searched so long for the perfect guy. I really didn't want to rain on her parade."

Phil Ramone concurred with his wife and Karen's other friends. "It was like he was *too* perfect," he says, "but that was an attractive thing for her."

"So what did you think?" Karen asked Phil after he joined the couple for dinner.

"I don't like his hair," he said teasingly. "He's too perfect. It's *Tom Terrific!*"

Karen soon took Tom to meet the Carpenter family at home at Newville. "She brought him into the office and introduced us all,"

Evelyn Wallace recalls. "He was a really nice looking man, and he was very, very polite. I could see nothing wrong with him. I think she really loved Tom. Maybe it was just a crush, I don't know, but she *seemed* to be in love with him." Like Evelyn, the Carpenter family was initially charmed by Tom. "He gets along fabulously with my family," Karen told *People Weekly*.

Whether it was his good looks, personality, or what Karen told them about his career and real estate successes, the family seemed to be won over by Burris—even Richard at first. "Tom instinctively knew what to do," recalls Itchie. "He started palling around with Richard, although even Richard seemed a little apprehensive at the time."

Tom laughed when he told the family how he had been unfamiliar with the Carpenters and their music before having met Karen. "I didn't know *anything* about the Carpenters," he said.

This left Evelyn Wallace skeptical. "You mean you've never *heard* them?" she asked. "They're on the radio a lot. You haven't heard them on the radio?"

"Oh, I am too busy," he replied.

Recalling the conversation with Burris, Wallace is angry she did not see through what she now recalls as an act. "I know in my heart that he knew darn well who Karen Carpenter was...and that there would be a lot of money there." Friends agreed and cautioned Karen that Tom could possibly be an opportunist. "Is he deaf or something?" Itchie asked. "Has he never turned on a radio or a television? I mean, *come on!*"

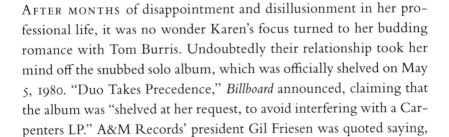

AFTER MONTHS of disappointment and disillusionment in her professional life, it was no wonder Karen's focus turned to her budding romance with Tom Burris. Undoubtedly their relationship took her mind off the snubbed solo album, which was officially shelved on May 5, 1980. "Duo Takes Precedence," *Billboard* announced, claiming that the album was "shelved at her request, to avoid interfering with a Carpenters LP." A&M Records' president Gil Friesen was quoted saying, "Karen thought about it long and hard and decided that the duo takes precedence; that was the priority in her life, and there was no way she wanted the solo project to interfere."

According to Evelyn Wallace, Phil and Itchie wanted more than anything to see Karen's album through to completion for Karen's sake. "They would have done anything to get it done for her, but Richard wasn't willing to give up one minute." In fact, he had returned to work and even booked studios for various Carpenters-related projects, including their impending "comeback" album. Their *Music, Music, Music* special, which became their final for ABC-TV, was set to air in a matter of weeks, and Karen's album was low on the list of priorities.

According to Phil Ramone, "Once Richard didn't like the album, the traditional response in that family was, 'We're not going to like it either.' Nobody would jump forward to say, 'Now wait a minute, this is what Karen wanted to say, and we should accept that.' And once you've put it on the shelf, you've put it on the shelf." He and Itchie wanted the album on record store shelves and to see Karen singing in clubs and performing concerts to promote her new music. According to Itchie, "The artists who had come forward and supported her thought it was really a strange deal considering who they were and who she was. Once again the attention got focused on Richard, what Richard wanted and what Richard needed."

Musician Russell Javors was worried to hear of the unenthusiastic response from Richard and A&M. "Poor Karen," he says. "She was an artist, and she was just trying to work and to explore her craft, and she had every right as an artist to do that. Collaboration is only as good as the sum of its parts, and you have to let each one of those pieces explore what it is that they do. There have to be equal parts. Nobody can be controlling. Karen was every bit as important to those records—if not more so—than the other part. She had the right to explore it. Richard had his own issues at the time. I am sure that he was not thrilled about this project, but if he were in good enough shape to work they would have been working together. Not her with us."

In a 1993 interview Richard explained how he often felt wrongly accused in the case of the solo album and reaffirmed it was Karen's choice and not his urging that put a stop to the album's release. "I get the blame for this, you know," he said. "People who are 'anti-Richard/pro-Karen' seem to take everything that was wrong with Karen and blame it on me. They say that I talked her out of releasing this record because I was ready to start our new album. It was sheer nonsense. All you have to do if you don't believe me is talk to Herb, talk to Jerry, or talk to Derek. . . . They believed that it didn't have any hits on it, and they weren't going to release it. It had nothing to do with me."

A&M officials agreed unanimously with the album's cancellation. Despite his enthusiasm at the New York playbacks, Derek Green felt the album was "a dog" from a commercial standpoint. "To everybody's credit, the record was stopped," he told Ray Coleman. "The responsibility to the greatest extent with an artist like that would rest with the producer. And it was a mismatch."

Asked over the years about the album's shelving, Herb Alpert almost always answered with nervous hesitation, choosing his words carefully. According to him, the album did not have an effect on him in the same way that a Carpenters album would. He also described Karen as being indecisive and explained how she would go back and forth between loving and hating the album. Other times he conveniently forgot the details. "I don't *exactly* remember why, but I'm sure she wasn't real comfortable with it."

According to Jerry Moss, the men were simply thinking of Karen's best interests. "We didn't think it would get a really great reaction," he said. "We didn't want to have Karen go through that, you know."

In public and to the press, Karen put on her game face, nonchalantly glossing over the project's demise. "It's a good album," she said in 1981. "It just dragged on so long. It seemed all of a sudden to be getting in the way of us going back to work again. . . . It got to a point where I had to make up my mind because Richard wanted to go back to work and . . . I wanted to go back to work, too, as the Carpenters. . . . I'm sure there would have been people who would have been shocked, and a lot of people who would have loved it. I didn't put it away because I was dissatisfied. We ran out of time."

"I WANT to spend the rest of my life with you," Tom Burris told Karen two months into their relationship. She was unsure how to interpret such a declaration so she phoned Karen Ichiuji for advice. Already hesitant to support her friend's blind faith in Tom, Itchie was shocked to learn of the couple's quickly progressing love affair. "I think Tom proposed," Karen said.

"You don't just *think*," Itchie said, explaining that a proposal of marriage should never be a vague or indefinite statement.

Karen's uncertainty was resolved a few days later on Monday, June 16, when Tom officially asked her to marry him and presented her with a ten karat pear-shaped diamond ring. Although she had been anticipating the proposal, she did not accept right away. Tom was still married, and his divorce would not be final for another two days. Seeking her mother's advice, she asked, "Should I marry him?"

Agnes offered little assistance, telling her daughter she was old enough to know what she was doing. "That's all up to you," she said. But Karen knew what she wanted all along. She was under Tom's spell and not about to let this opportunity pass her by. She returned to Tom, accepting his proposal on June 19, the day after his divorce became final. To celebrate their engagement, Burris presented his fiancée with a new Rolls-Royce Corniche convertible to match his own. "Hey Itch!" Karen said, waking her friend with an early morning phone call. "You wanna be a B.M.?"

"A *what?*"

"Tom proposed! We're getting married next year. Do you wanna be a B.M.? You know—a bridesmaid!"

Interestingly, syndicated astrologer Joyce Jillson forecasted Karen's engagement several weeks prior. "Pisceans have marriage on their minds...," she wrote in the "Celebrity Trends" portion of her May 21, 1980, column. "Karen Carpenter could announce her engagement under these lucky Piscean aspects."

The couple's plan for a year-long engagement hastily narrowed when they announced in July their plans for an August ceremony. "They just seemed to want to move quickly," Carole Curb says. She was shocked but says she felt they were surely old enough to know what they were doing. "I just hoped for the best."

The push to be married alarmed Karen's friends. According to Itchie, "That's when everybody's antennas went up." Despite Karen's excitement over the engagement and fast-approaching wedding, Tom was a stranger to them and one who seemed to be on the fast track to marrying their close friend. Karen assured them of his successes in the world of commercial real estate development and talked about his multiple homes, racecars, yachts, and even an eleven-passenger Learjet, but they sensed something was awry. According to Frenda, "It was like, 'I-met-you-will-you-marry-me?' Karen was just all caught up with this. Never ever could any of us have anticipated that it was going to be what it really was.... What I didn't know was that he didn't have a nickel. I believed the stories she told me. Why wouldn't I? It was coming through reliable sources, Mike and Carole, who are certainly not fly-by-nights." Frenda doesn't blame the two, however: "Had they known the truth, would they ever have introduced her to this horrendous person? No!"

By this time Karen was determined to be married at any cost, regardless of warnings from loved ones. Without her knowledge, the family hired a private investigator to look into Burris's background. "If only we'd done a better job checking him out," Frenda says. "His intentions were very clear right in the beginning. This was a plan, but who could have possibly known? Don't think all of us didn't tell her, but when somebody's not listening, they're not listening."

CASTING HER strong personal opinions of Tom Burris aside, Frenda Leffler set out to assist her best friend in coordinating all things wedding related. Karen wanted her big day to be exactly like those of Frenda and her sister Alana Megdal, who both wed in huge Beverly Hills society events with armies of bridesmaids and groomsmen and every tiny detail executed in the grandest of styles. But with only weeks to organize this magnificent event there was no time to waste.

"Frenda took over right away," Evelyn Wallace recalls. "She took care of everything." Agnes Carpenter was upset to discover many of the big decisions had been made without her input. She claimed to have wanted to spend mother-daughter time assisting Karen, but plans were already underway by the time she volunteered. "Usually, when your daughter gets married, you want to be with her and help her," explains Wallace.

"Agnes did absolutely nothing. Frenda did everything. She helped her get the dress, pick out the cake, and even did the invitations."

"Showering Karen with Love and Affection" was the theme of a wedding shower thrown by Frenda, by then named as Karen's matron of honor, and bridesmaid Carole Curb. The event took place on Sunday, August 3, and gathered more than a hundred women at the exclusive Hillcrest Country Club bordering Karen's residence at the Century Towers. Olivia Newton-John was in attendance, as was Itchie, who flew in for the weekend with fiancé Phil Ramone. Ramone treated Karen and Tom to a Billy Joel concert that weekend at the Forum in Inglewood, California.

The Hillcrest's clubhouse garden room was decorated in shades of lavender and peach with an abundance of lilies and orchids flown in from Hawaii. "Karen loved a good party," recalls Frenda. "She was a vision in yellow organdy that day. Like a spring daffodil." Her two-piece yellow outfit and sun hat were designed by Bill Belew, who was also commissioned to create her wedding gown. Belew had been the costume designer for a number of television specials, including the Carpenters' recent *Music, Music, Music*, for which he would later receive an Emmy nomination.

Maria Galeazzi, Karen's former stylist and Richard's ex-girlfriend, was among the guests at the Hillcrest. She was invited a few weeks earlier when she happened upon Karen as they both were shopping in Beverly Hills. "When I saw her I was shocked," Maria says, recalling that day on Rodeo Drive. "People said she had lost weight, but I had not seen her. She looked so thin."

Agnes seemed happy to recognize Maria among the sea of unfamiliar faces at the country club. "Oh, Maria Luisa," she said. "You have no idea what Richard's been through!"

Agnes was referring to her son's addiction to quaaludes, a problem that Maria witnessed during her time with Richard in the early 1970s. "I didn't go nuts with those pills," she says. "When I got off the road I didn't take them anymore. I guess he just kept on going. I was shocked to hear that part." Maria was not nearly as surprised to hear that Richard was still dating his cousin Mary Rudolph. "What do you expect?"

Grammy
Issue
The Carpenters

At the Thirteenth Annual
Grammy Awards, March 16, 1971.

(right) Carpenter family Christmas card
sent to fan club members, 1972.

(below) Newville at Christmas, 1972. Ken Bertwell

Between shows in
Acapulco, June 1973.

(below) At a softball game
with Richard in Valley Forge
Pennsylvania, July 1973.

(left) At Pie de la Questa with Richard and
Maria Galeazzi. "If we went anywhere it was
the three of us," Maria says. "Every place we
went it was like she and I and Richard. It got
old for me, let me tell you."

With boyfriend Mike Curb on a boat in San Diego Harbor, 1974. Mike Curb

Striking a comedic pose on stage for a fan at the MGM Grand, Las Vegas, 1976.

Rhonda Ramirez

1975 tour program.
Author's Collection

(below) With the Leffler
"kidlets," Ashley
and Andrew, Karen's
godchildren. Frenda Franklin

(above) Karen shows off her diamond ring to wedding guest Olivia Newton-John. Frank Bonito

(right) The beautiful bride on her wedding day, August 31, 1980.

Frank Bonito

Agnes Carpenter and son share a dance as the Michael Paige Big Band entertains at the Beverly Hills Hotel wedding reception.

Frank Bonito

With Tom Burris,
fall 1980. Globe Photos

At Radio Cidade, Rio de Janeiro, November, 1981.

Sydney Junior/Brazilian Carpenters Friends Club

(left) Terribly thin and looking exhausted, Karen
prepares to depart Rio's Jobim International
Airport, November 1981.

Vitor Bruno/Brazilian Carpenters Friends Club

(above) Karen's final public appearance came January 11, 1983, at CBS Television City, where she and Richard (fourth row, second and third from left) attended a photo shoot with past Grammy recipients. "Look at me, I've got an ass!" she exclaimed to Dionne Warwick.

(right) The original Carpenter crypt at Forest Lawn Memorial Park in Cypress, California.

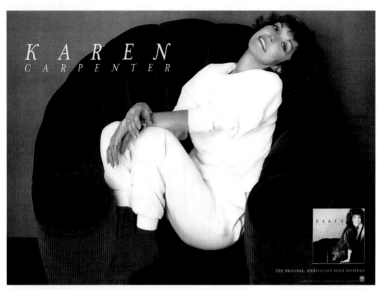

Promotional poster for the 1996 release of *Karen Carpenter*, the original, unreleased solo sessions. A&M Records

The Carpenters' star on the Hollywood Walk of Fame, 6931 Hollywood Boulevard.

Randy Schmidt

(above) The Carpenter Exhibit on display in the foyer of the Richard and Karen Carpenter Performing Arts Center on the campus of California State University at Long Beach. Randy Schmidt

(right) Cynthia Gibb and Mitchell Anderson star in the 1989 biopic *The Karen Carpenter Story*. CBS-TV

she says. "They'd thrown daggers at everybody he'd hooked up with. Now he had resorted to staying within the family."

According to friends, Karen was mortified by her brother's involvement with their cousin. Itchie had noticed early on that she was strongly against the relationship. "I thought it was because of the gene thing, but after many confrontations Richard finally just screamed out, 'For God's sake, we had the tests! They were *fine*. We can have wonderful, healthy children!' Karen just did *not* want Richard to marry her."

Karen asked Itchie to play matchmaker for Richard on numerous occasions. "It didn't matter what country or what city we were in, she was scrambling for someone for him. I didn't even know Richard when I had to start coming up with these dates for him. Even I was thrown into that mix. She tried to fix Richard and *me* up!"

"Now I *know* you're out of you mind!" Itchie told Karen, laughing uncomfortably at the mere suggestion she date Richard.

"But I want a sister," she answered back.

"Well, we can still be sisters, but quite frankly, Kace, there is no way I would ever get involved with Richard."

Olivia Newton-John was always near the top of Karen's list of potential dates for Richard. In fact, some recall she considered her to be the "dream match" for her brother. "I always had a boyfriend," Olivia says. "But for Karen to think that I was perfect for Richard was probably the biggest compliment that she could pay to me because she *adored* him."

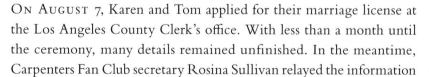

ON AUGUST 7, Karen and Tom applied for their marriage license at the Los Angeles County Clerk's office. With less than a month until the ceremony, many details remained unfinished. In the meantime, Carpenters Fan Club secretary Rosina Sullivan relayed the information via newsletter.

Mr. and Mrs. Harold Carpenter of Downey, California, are very happy to announce the forthcoming marriage of their only daughter KAREN ANNE to THOMAS JAMES BURRIS, eldest son of Mr. and

Mrs. James Burris of Orange County, California, on Sunday, August 31, 1980, in Beverly Hills, California. . . . As emotions run high and excitement reaches fever pitch, the heart strings take an extra tug as we learn of Richard's intention to compose a very personal message for the bride to sing to her bridegroom during the marriage ceremony. . . . What a poignant moment that will be.

As Burris explained to the members of the press, "Richard is writing a special song for us. She'll say 'I do' then come out singing. It's going to be interesting." Calling on longtime collaborator and friend John Bettis, Richard wasted no time churning out a big Broadway-style show tune. He then commissioned Peter Knight, who flew in from England to finish the arrangement and orchestration. This was much more of a task than Knight anticipated, as the song was an epic, jumping moods and octaves. Needless to say, it did not lend itself to the rush order Knight was given when he signed on. Initially, Karen intended to sing in person during the ceremony, but she and Richard ultimately chose to pre-record the song, including her lead vocal. "We were planning on doing it live, but it would have required a huge orchestra," Karen recalled. "When I really thought about it . . . I said no, I don't want to do it live. . . . I don't really think I could have focused. And it's a very difficult song to sing. . . . I was having trouble standing up."

Karen undoubtedly lost her footing when just days before the wedding rehearsal Tom dropped a bombshell—one significant enough to end their relationship. The couple had made every plan to start a family as soon as they were married, and Karen was thrilled at the idea of finally becoming a mother. But it was not until the last minute that Tom shared with her how he had undergone a vasectomy procedure prior to their meeting. Her plan of carrying his children was simply not going to happen. Karen was dumbfounded. Tom offered to reverse the procedure, but their chances at a family would be significantly lessened. Regardless, Karen felt betrayed. Tom had lied to her; he had withheld this information for the duration of their courtship and engagement, knowing full well that starting a family was at the top of Karen's list of priorities. This was the deal breaker. The wedding was off.

Karen was in hysterics when she called Frenda. The matron of honor ran to her side and did her best to comfort her. As much as friends hated to see her in such horrific pain, they silently felt relieved that this nightmare seemed to be coming to an end. With Frenda at her side, Karen picked up the phone and called her mother. She cried to Agnes as she explained the deceit that left her with no choice but to cancel the ceremony. But her mother's power over her was never stronger. Agnes told her she would do no such thing. Family and friends were traveling from all over the country to attend the event, and Harold's brother and sister-in-law were even flying in from London. Moreover, the wedding expenses had already cost what Agnes considered to be a small fortune. "We'll deal with it later," she said. "The invitations have gone out. There are reporters and photographers coming. *People* magazine is going to be there. The wedding is *on*, and you *will* walk down that aisle." Karen was in disbelief. Surely deception of this magnitude justified an end to her plans of marriage to Tom? But Agnes remained firm. "You made your bed, Karen," she told her. "Now you'll have to lay in it."

———— ⌖ ————

THE LUXURIOUS five-star Beverly Hills Hotel on Sunset Boulevard was the site of what promised to be the society wedding of the decade on Sunday, August 31, 1980. For Karen it promised little. Evelyn Wallace was upset to learn of Karen's turmoil some time later. "As she was walking down the aisle, she knew that Tom was not the person he said he was," she explains, "but she carried on. She wasn't marrying the guy she thought Tom was, but she didn't stop the wedding. She carried on like she was really, really happy that day."

Although photographs from that day show a seemingly radiant and glowing bride, few knew of Karen's inner conflict. She had adopted her mother's position and resolved to deal with the problems later. She had long been a master at concealing her true feelings, and this was perhaps her finest performance. "I don't know how she's doing it," Itchie told a friend as the women observed Karen smiling for the cameras. "Kace, are you playacting or are you really happy?" Itchie asked, but Karen's only response was her silent stare.

"She was the typical bride, a little nervous," recalls Debbie Cuticello, who was not privy to news of the previous week. "She was very excited, very beautiful, and just beaming. The wedding was like a fairy tale. It was a Cinderella event for me. There were lots of things we had to do beforehand, like getting fitted, getting the dresses, and doing the rehearsal." Bill Belew's design team, consisting of members of both the ABC-TV and NBC-TV wardrobe departments, oversaw the fittings. "We all had these amazing lavender dresses with these big sun hats," Carole Curb recalls. "It was just sumptuous."

Frank Bonito and his wife were in attendance as well. "Karen let all the girls try on her ring. My wife had a pear-shaped diamond, too, which was of course much smaller." Still, Bonito feels Karen was unaffected by her fame and fortune, regardless of diamonds and other luxuries. On her wedding day she came to him saying, "Frank, this diamond around my neck's not falling right. Would you just knot the chain behind my neck?" As he recalls, Karen was often quite casual about things. "Then she took her ring off to wash her hands, and this ring almost went down the sink drain! I said to her, 'Oh my God, Karen, if that thing goes down the drain we'll be pulling the pipes apart!'"

Greeted with the fragrance of thousands of sweet-smelling gardenias, the five hundred wedding guests began arriving shortly after noon in preparation for the 1:00 P.M. ceremony. "I invited everybody in the city, and everybody in the city showed up," Karen said.

Named for its elegant chandeliers, the Crystal Ballroom's art deco theme was concealed by a facade of silver trellises. Adorned with white orchids, gardenias, violets, and lemon leaves, the framed lattice displays helped simulate a 1930s old English garden setting. The room's chandeliers were interspersed with huge baskets of orchids suspended from the ceiling.

The Who's Who list of celebrities included many of those attending the wedding shower a month earlier, in addition to Casey Kasem, John Davidson, JoJo Starbuck, Dionne Warwick, Burt Bacharach, Herb Alpert, Dorothy Hamill, and Toni Tennille and husband, Daryl Dragon. Head usher Mike Curb arrived in Beverly Hills with an entourage of state police escorts. In addition to his role as lieutenant governor of California, Curb was acting governor of California during Jerry Brown's campaign for president in 1980.

Phil Ramone arrived wearing a tuxedo. "Karen told me it was absolutely formal," he explains. "'I expect you to wear a tux,' she said. The only guys wearing tuxes were me and the waiters. That's how she got back at me for saying I didn't like Tom's hair. Now that's what I consider great humor!"

Organist Frank Brownstead offered Johann Sebastian Bach's "Sheep May Safely Graze" as members of the wedding party took their places. The mother of the bride, escorted by her son Richard, was outfitted in a lavender chiffon gown and picture hat similar to that of the groom's mother. Then, sweeping strings and a most familiar voice came seemingly out of nowhere. As the crowd shifted in their seats in hopes of seeing the bride as she sang, most soon realized the song was pre-recorded. The production was surprisingly polished for a rush job. Even a hasty Carpenters recording was perfection. Down to the wire, the recording was done three days earlier, with the master delivered just hours before the wedding rehearsal. Karen's singing conveyed John Bettis's lyric to great effect and with a soaring sense of optimism and determination.

Because we are in love we reach for our tomorrows
And know we won't be lonely in laughter and in sorrow
Where love abides there is the place we'll keep our home forever
You and I, because we are in love

Frenda's three-year-old twins, Ashley and Andrew, along with their cousin Brooke Megdal, led the seemingly endless trail of bridesmaids and groomsmen down the red-carpeted aisleway to the tune of Wagner's "Bridal Chorus." The bride's attendants, wearing waltz-length lavender chiffon gowns with green sashes, included close friends Connie Chapman, Linda Curb, Debbie Cuticello, Sandy Holland, Karen Ichiuji, Alana Megdal, Carole Curb Scotti, Elizabeth Van Ness, and Karen's cousins Mary Rudolph and Joan Will. Noticeably absent from the bridal party was Olivia Newton-John, who attended the ceremony with *Xanadu* choreographer Kenny Ortega. The film had been released just weeks earlier, and a trip to its Australian premiere prevented Olivia from accepting Karen's invitation to be a bridesmaid. "I wanted the attention to be on Karen anyway," she says.

Richard Burris served as his brother's best man. Other groomsmen and ushers, dressed in traditional morning coats, included Mark Armbruster, Effie Beard, Tom's son Mike Burris, his brothers James Burris and Vern Burris, Jolyn Gissell, Casey Kasem, Ed Leffler, Tony Scotti, and Jerry Van Ness. The ring bearer's pillow was created by Bill Belew from remnants of all the gowns the designer had made over the years for the Carpenters' television specials.

After placing a kiss on his daughter's extended hand, Harold Carpenter escorted Karen down a path of white gardenia topiaries and baskets filled with pink chrysanthemums to the altar, where she was met by the groom. Karen's wedding gown was made from fifteen yards of crisp, white mousseline de soie and modeled after an eighteenth-century English riding ensemble. The long-sleeved dress and jacket with its stand-up collar displayed a sparkling floral design of seashells and sequins. Her silk veil was affixed to a classic-style picture hat made up of a beaded Juliet cap and detachable white chiffon brim. She carried a bouquet of lilies of the valley, white orchids, and white pikake.

Accompanied by the forty-voice Tom Bähler Chorale, under the direction of Peter Knight, Richard sang David Williams's "The Wedding Prayer." Behind Karen's veil, her eyes were closed and her head bowed in silence as if in her own solemn moment of prayer.

> *Bless thou the ring, bless thou the promise*
> *Strengthen our love throughout each day*
> *All happy moments, all times of sadness*
> *Teach us to trust and share them all with Thee*

Well-known television evangelist Dr. Robert H. Schuller, pastor of Garden Grove Community Church, officiated the ceremony, just two weeks before the dedication of his famed Crystal Cathedral, the first-ever all-glass church facility.

"Tom made fun of Schuller during the ceremony," recalls Walt Harrah, who sang in Bähler's chorus. He and others were unnerved by the groom's behavior. Speaking out in his distinctive, commanding voice, Reverend Schuller asked Burris, "Do you take this woman?" In response, the groom proceeded to mimic the pastor. "When he said, 'I do,' he just *mocked* him, and the whole place laughed," Harrah says. "It was really bizarre."

Evelyn Wallace felt Tom was not taking the vows seriously. "He probably knew exactly what was going to happen once he got Karen. All he was in for was the money. He wasn't thinking of her; he was thinking of her money. That's all."

In contrast, Karen delivered her vows in a very solemn and serious manner—almost stern. "So help us God," she repeated, giving a long, firm glare and nod to her groom. "Amen."

Following the ceremony, guests sipped cocktails as they mingled in the Maisonette Room, while Karen and Tom met with the media for a press conference in the Persian Room. Richard was also present and photographed in somewhat of an awkward trio with the newlyweds. According to one reporter, he looked "more like a father giving away his daughter."

The Crystal Ballroom was transformed into a giant banquet hall and the site of the $25,000 wedding luncheon, which began around 3:00 P.M. "The big attraction was Olivia Newton-John," recalls Frank Bonito. "That was not long after the time when *Grease* was big, so there was lots of discussion about where Livvy would sit. We all told Karen, 'Oh, Olivia can sit at *our* table!'" At one point during the reception a security officer approached Bonito as he snapped photos with his camera. "Kindly stop taking pictures of Miss Newton-John," he cautioned when Frank was unable to produce press credentials.

"I am a guest of the bride, and she asked me to take them for her," he fibbed.

The elegant banquet tables were decorated with lavender tablecloths and arrangements of purple orchids, Alba lilies, and African violets. The menu included Karen's favorite, shrimp salad, and a main course of chicken chasseur with broccoli polonaise, rice pilaf, strawberries

Romanoff, and Parducci Chablis wine. Karen and Tom cut the five-tiered chocolate and mocha cream wedding cake, adorned with traditional bride and groom figures on top, and Mike Curb proposed the first toast to the couple. "Excuse me, waiter!" Jerry Weintraub called out to Phil Ramone periodically throughout the meal, poking fun at his tuxedo predicament. Providing the live dance music was the Michael Paige Big Band, inviting the newlyweds to lead the first dance, which was of course to "We've Only Just Begun."

15

BEGINNING OF THE END

OLLOWING A brief stop in Baja California, the honeymooners flew to the Tahitian island of Bora Bora, where they planned to spend ten days on what promised to be "the most romantic island in the world." Known for its white sand, dazzling turquoise waters, and unique overwater bungalows, Bora Bora had all the ingredients for the perfect romantic getaway for two. But instead of two, these travelers numbered four. Considering that Karen Carpenter's marriage to Tom Burris was essentially over before it began, it is understandable that she might not have had any qualms inviting her husband's brother Rick and his wife to join them on their honeymoon. She had extended the same bizarre invitation to her aunt Bernice and other family members as well, but all declined.

Arriving on Bora Bora, a location chosen by Tom, Karen immediately began to complain about the setting, which she likened to a forsaken, deserted island. She called it Boring, Boring and blamed her loathing on having grown accustomed to hotels with room service and twenty-four-hour concierge service while on tour. True, there were no phones, radios, or televisions in the resort guest rooms, but when Karen rescheduled their return flights and ended the honeymoon early, it had little to do with her dislike for the accommodations. She wanted to get back home to Los Angeles as fast as she could.

Karen and Tom made their home at 61 Linda Isle in Newport Beach, just across the Lido Channel from another of their residences at 117 Via Yella. In addition to Karen's Century Towers condo, the couple also kept a large house in Bel Air and even one in Mexico—a vacation getaway situated in the gated celebrity enclave El Pedregal, the first residential community in Cabo San Lucas. "Karen bought their house in Newport Beach, and she was paying for *all* of these homes," Itchie Ramone recalls. "All the antennas were starting to go up between Frenda, Livvy, Carole, and myself. We knew what was going on."

For a period of time Karen played the part of the happy newlywed, at least to anyone she thought she could fool. "I love it," she said of her marriage during a phone interview broadcast to Japanese radio audiences. "I'm having a wonderful time. I'm very, very happy."

The couple's time in Newport Beach was short lived. Karen preferred to stay at their two-and-a-half-acre rented estate in Bel Air, where Frenda Leffler was close by. From the time Karen moved to Century City she had established a small circle of friends and acquaintances. "She made friends in Century City," Frenda explains, "but she still had never really been on her own. This was Bel Air now, and she was a married lady and on her own."

<hr />

"NOBODY'S BEING stolen," Karen assured the press during a public appearance in the fall of 1980. Richard and Tom did their best to uphold smiles for the cameras but were ill at ease. Work on the Carpenters' next album had ceased with the couple's engagement and wedding plans, but Richard had stayed busy making preparations for Karen's return to the recording studio. Jerry Moss suggested that the duo stick with their tried-and-true Carpenters formula, which they had abandoned in some ways for the mishmash selections on 1977's *Passage* album.

Perhaps in an attempt to recapture the 1973 success of Joe Raposo's "Sing," the Carpenters told Paul Williams they wished to record his and Kenny Ascher's "The Rainbow Connection" from the highly successful 1979 film *The Muppet Movie*. "I saw Karen after I won the Oscar for *A Star is Born*," Williams says. "She was really sweet about that and also said that 'Evergreen' was a great song. Then the same thing happened with *The Muppet Movie*. They loved the songs from that movie and wanted to record 'Rainbow Connection.'" But Richard was bothered by the syllabification of the song, notably the opening phrases written for Muppet character Kermit the Frog to sing. "Richard wanted me to change some of it," Williams recalls, "but this song was nominated for an Academy Award! The song is written in Kermit's speaking rhythm, and I wouldn't change it. It was written for Kermit; it should be recorded the way that Kermit recorded it."

Although the Carpenters went on to record "The Rainbow Connection," they took artistic license and altered the rhythm and melody to suit their wishes. Even so, Karen was displeased with the outcome, and her work lead was filed away with the album's other outtakes. It was not until 1999 that Richard completed the recording, which ultimately saw release on the *As Time Goes By* collection. "I really wanted them to do 'Rainbow Connection,'" Williams says, "but I didn't like the changes they made in it. Still, it's always a treasure to hear her sing my words."

A surprise call came in November 1980 from legendary guitarist Les Paul. He wanted to meet Karen and Richard, who were busy working in A&M's studio D. Like Lester William Polsfuss, his given name, Evelyn Wallace grew up in Waukesha, Wisconsin. "He was a neighbor of ours when I was a kid," she says. "He went to the same school as we did and lived just down the street." Wallace phoned Richard at A&M and explained Les Paul would like to sit in on a Carpenters recording session. Karen and Richard had often cited Les Paul and Mary Ford among their earliest musical inspirations, making this meeting especially meaningful. They discussed with him their recording techniques and the evolution of the overdubbing process, which Les Paul essentially pioneered.

A few months later on January 20, 1981, Karen arrived at A&M Studios wearing a new patriotic-themed running suit with large block letters across the chest: MADE IN AMERICA. Although the Carpenters had Republican ties, neither was known to be political. But this was Inauguration Day, and Ronald Reagan was sworn in as the fortieth

president of the United States. Richard noticed the suit and immediately said, "Well, there it is!" He felt "Made in America" was a perfect
name for the duo's forthcoming album. Karen agreed.

Released June 16, 1981, *Made in America* was the Carpenters' first
traditional studio album in nearly four years. Although the inner photo-
graph showed Karen looking comfortable and seemingly fit, it had been
heavily retouched by A&M's art department. The original, untouched
photo reveals her bloodshot eyes and drawn appearance. In just the few
short months between that John Engstead photo session and the album's
release, Karen had lost even more weight.

The standout track on *Made in America* was "Touch Me When We're
Dancing," the obvious choice for debut single. When the demo for
"Touch Me" arrived from Welk Publishing, Karen and Richard needed
only one listen to know it was the right song to launch their return
to Top 40 radio. And it did. The debut single was released a week
prior to the album's release and soon peaked at #16. "Touch Me" had
all the ingredients of a 1971 Carpenters hit packaged neatly in a 1981
production. "When all the ingredients gelled, the result was irresist-
ible," wrote John Tobler in a review. "That's what we have here, a
perfect Carpenters confection, reminiscent of the classic days of the
early Seventies."

"(Want You) Back in My Life Again" was one of the most
1980s-influenced recordings in the Carpenters catalog. Incidentally,
the synthesizers were manned by two well-known artists in their own
right—Daryl Dragon, the "Captain" of Captain and Tennille, and Ian
Underwood of the Mothers of Invention. With its strong, melodic,
singable hook, "Back in My Life Again" seemed a wise choice for the
second single, but it did not fare as well as "Touch Me." Reminiscent
of "Top of the World" was "Those Good Old Dreams," a country-
tinged collaboration by Richard and John Bettis released as the album's
third single. "When It's Gone (It's Just Gone)" was another tune with
a country ballad feel, sounding a bit like "Two Sides" from *Passage*.
Randy Handley's poetic lyric tells of an aching, unrequited love. Judging from the effectiveness of Karen's interpretation, it sounds as if she
penned it herself.

Where's the word for the sadness
Where's the poetry in the pain
Where's the color in the stain where the tears have fallen
It's gone, it's just gone

Karen still loved oldies, and somehow an "oldie-but-goodie" seemed to find its way onto every Carpenters album after 1973's *Now and Then* medley. *Horizon* had "Please Mr. Postman." *A Kind of Hush* opened with the title track and closed with Sedaka's "Breaking Up Is Hard to Do." Then "Man Smart, Woman Smarter" from *Passage* reached all the way back to a 1956 Harry Belafonte album, and Karen even cut a work lead of "Jimmy Mack" by Martha and the Vandellas during her 1979 solo sessions. "Richard and I always talked about bringing back songs," says Mike Curb, who was treated to a preview of the Carpenters' next oldie. "I've gotta play a song for you," Karen told him. "You'll get a kick of out it. It is really fun! It'll bring back memories." After playing the recording of "Beechwood 4-5789" down the phone line she asked, "So, what do you think of this as a single?"

Curb was encouraging and unable to bring himself to tell her it lacked Top 40 potential. "That was the last song she played for me," he says. Whereas "Postman" was a case of the right song at the right time, "There's a Kind of Hush" was overkill, and remaking the Marvelettes' "Beechwood 4-5789" was a waste. A promotional video for "Beechwood," shot on A&M's Chaplin Stage, further relegated the song to the most syrupy sweet category of bubblegum pop. Karen looked ill at ease—to say the least—as a thirty-one-year old woman sporting a poodle skirt and swaying her way around a faux malt shop. "Beechwood" was released on Karen's birthday, March 2, 1982, and became the Carpenters' lowest-charting single at #74 and their final appearance on the U.S. singles chart during Karen's lifetime.

From listening to demos and writing new material through to the mastering process, *Made in America* took over a year to create, twice as long as the average Carpenters record. Considering the wealth of quality leftovers and outtakes from their 1980–1981 sessions, namely "The Uninvited Guest" and "Kiss Me the Way You Did Last Night," both of which saw posthumous release, *Made in America* could have fared much stronger. In his review for *Billboard*, Paul Grein explains: "Innocuous ditties like 'Postman' and 'Beechwood' don't begin to tap the depths of Karen's voice. She needs a meaningful lyric to really show her stuff."

The Carpenters' new album and their contributions to A&M Records were celebrated by Herb Alpert and the entire label on the evening of June 29, 1981, at a party in their honor on the grounds of the Bel Air Hotel. An audience of more than two hundred guests watched as Alpert welcomed Karen and Richard back to the music scene, presenting two matching plaques that displayed their eleven studio albums for A&M. He also announced that the Carpenters' record sales as of March that year had topped seventy-nine million units.

MADE IN America concluded with "Because We Are in Love (The Wedding Song)," written for Karen's wedding, but by the time the album hit shelves, Karen's marriage was already on its last leg. "She thought she'd married the right guy," Maria Galeazzi says, "but this one took her for a ride." Friends of the couple, including Carole Curb, began to hear "bits and pieces that didn't feel good and didn't sound right. I heard that there were some monetary things that popped up with Tom that none of us knew about. That didn't sit right with her. All that glitters isn't gold."

According to Itchie, Karen had learned the truth of Tom's financial status the morning of their wedding. "They were all in the process of investigating, but there wasn't enough time," she says. But Karen was more upset to learn of her family's probing and refused to heed the warnings from Werner Wolfen and others. "Artists are prone to fall in love with somebody who can spend their money without them knowing it," explains Phil Ramone. "Karen was pretty frugal, to say the least. Some of the older-thinking artists watched every penny. The Carpenters had a pretty good money advisor, so I am surprised that Tom got through that fence."

Most had assumed Burris's lifestyle and net worth were comparable to that of Karen's. The expensive cars and other possessions gave him the appearance of a multimillionaire, but what others did not realize was that he was living well beyond his means. On several occasions he treated the Carpenter parents and their friends to a short yacht trip around Newport Harbor, even instructing Evelyn Wallace on steering technique. "Oh, I have six boats," he boasted to her.

"Tom had wanted Karen to think that he was Mr. Money Guy, but it wasn't long after they got married that he started asking her for money," recalls Wallace. "He'd give her some excuse, and she'd give him the money. He'd ask for $35,000 and $50,000 at a time. Finally it got down to the point where all she had left was stocks and bonds."

As Itchie recalls, "Tom couldn't afford the houses, the cars, her wedding ring; he couldn't pay for *anything*." Karen began to share with friends her growing misgivings about Tom, not only concerning his finances but also his lack of feelings for her. He was often impatient, and she admitted being fearful when he would occasionally lose his temper. "He could be very cruel to her," says Itchie. But Karen's longing to be a mother proved to be stronger than her desire to leave her husband. At the house in Newport Beach Karen expressed to Tom her desire to get pregnant and start a family. Of course a vasectomy reversal would be required, and he had promised to go through with the procedure, but in this particular moment Karen just wanted to be intimate with her husband. She never could have dreamed that his response would be so brutal. She was still crying hysterically when she called Itchie for support. According to Karen, Tom had told her he wouldn't even consider having children with her and called her "a bag of bones." Karen was well aware that her weight had plummeted since her wedding to Tom the previous year, but hearing such callous words in response to a physical advance toward her husband was unbearable.

Karen and Tom saw their first anniversary come and go with little merriment. During the last week of August the two set out on a journey taking them more than six thousand miles round-trip in Tom's cumbersome four-wheel-drive Dodge Ramcharger, equipped with CB radio and refrigerator. Although the Carpenters rarely toured or traveled in what would be considered excessive luxury, this trip found the Burris couple roughing it, to say the least. Following a stay in the San Juan

Mountains near Durango, Colorado, Karen and Tom schlepped north-ward. They stopped at Canada's hiking capital, Lake Louise in Banff National Park, before visiting the city of Vancouver. Relieved to return to Los Angeles, Karen recovered from what she considered to have been a disaster of a vacation.

Itchie flew to Los Angeles to find out for herself what was happen-ing in her friend's marriage and offer her love and support to Karen. They met for lunch at their normal hangout, Hamburger Hamlet, but Karen asked the host for a different table than their usual. "We didn't sit at our regular table, which was odd," Itchie recalls. "We sat in the dark, and she wore huge, dark sunglasses."

"OK, what do you want me to do, Kace?" she asked, realizing things had gone too far. "You can't go on living like this."

According to Itchie, this marriage was "the straw that broke the camel's back. It was absolutely the worst thing that could have ever happened to her. She was just so loving and so wonderful, and then the next thing you know you're sitting there across the table from your best friend all bruised up. How do you do that? She was pretty much wrecked." Karen initially passed it off, but she then could not make it through the meal. "She couldn't eat, she was crying, and we had to leave. We didn't want anyone to recognize her."

At the urging of friends and family, Karen met with legal counsel to revise her will on September 1, 1981. She could not yet bring her-self to file for divorce but was obviously moving in that direction. "I give all household furniture and furnishings, household equipment and appliances, and silverware located in the residence occupied by my hus-band and myself to my husband," she stated in the codicil. "I give any residence occupied by my husband and myself as our home at the time of my death to my husband." Karen willed everything else to Harold, Agnes, and Richard, listing estimated assets totaling between five and ten million dollars. ¹

Friends suggested she and Tom seek marital counseling. Instead, the Carpenters prepared to leave for Europe and South America. Itchie went along to keep Karen company on this series of Carpenters pro-motional tours, which began in Paris, France, where Karen's laxative addiction became an issue. "Laxatives were her major companion," Itchie says. "When we were in Paris we made quite a scene in a pharmacy across the street from our hotel about her needing to buy more laxatives. I suggested natural food groups that might relieve her 'constipation,' but she always won those arguments."

Following a brief stop in Amsterdam, the Carpenters arrived at London's Heathrow Airport on Wednesday, October 21, 1981. They made numerous promotional appearances while in London, both in person and on television. On Thursday they taped an interview for *Nationwide*, a popular news magazine on BBC television. Barely one minute into their visit, host Sue Lawley surprised Karen by casting light on her darkest secret. "There were rumors that you were suffering from the slimmer's disease anorexia nervosa," Lawley said. "Is that right?"

"No, I was just pooped," Karen said with an intense frown. "I was tired out."

"You went down to about six stone in weight, I think, didn't you?" Lawley asked.

"I have no idea what 'six stone in weight' is," Karen replied, becoming noticeably uncomfortable and increasingly agitated. She struggled to fake a laugh, rolling her eyes at the interviewer, who quickly converted the amount to approximately eighty-four pounds. "No," she said, shaking her head adamantly. "No."

In actuality her weight was hovering around eighty pounds even then. The interviewer's continued efforts to pinpoint a reason for Karen's skeletal appearance prompted Richard to come to his sister's defense. "I don't really feel that we should be talking about the weight loss," he told Lawley and producers. "Maybe it's better to take a pass on the whole thing. It's really not what we're here for."

"I am just asking you the questions people want to know the answers to," she replied.

All involved regrouped, and the interviewer offered to pursue a new line of questioning geared toward Karen's marriage, an almost equally unpleasant topic but one that Karen could fake her way through. Richard agreed to allow the questioning to continue. A labored exhalation was captured by Karen's lapel microphone as Lawley instructed the

Carpenters to relax. "Now, we have to pretend all that didn't happen," she joked.

"Yeah, I feel *terrific*," Karen chuckled with heavy sarcasm. And the interview continued. By this point Karen had become what author Ray Coleman called a "professional anorexic," perfecting the deceit while assuring all those around her she was just fine. While she was considered by those who knew and loved her to be one of the most honest and open individuals they ever met, she was rarely truthful when it came to anorexia nervosa.

RETURNING TO Los Angeles, Karen and Richard joined the Carpenter family to celebrate Harold Carpenter's seventy-third birthday. Family and friends gathered on the evening of November 9, 1981, for dinner at Sambi of Tokyo, a favorite Downey restaurant. After dinner, the party continued at Newville, where Karen and Tom went upstairs and, as Richard recalled, "had it out."

Evelyn Wallace recalls no sign of tension during dinner but explains, "In the restaurant, Karen wouldn't do that. She would be a lady in a restaurant." After some time, an exasperated Tom barreled down the stairs exclaiming, "You can keep her!" As he raced away from the house in his car, cousin Joanie ran upstairs to comfort Karen, hugging her and telling her how much she loved and cared for her. The guests downstairs were speechless. Karen was humiliated and inconsolable.

Although the family cites this episode at Newville as the last time Karen saw her husband, Frenda visited Karen back in Bel Air around this time and was shocked to find the couple in the process of making a twenty-thousand-dollar upgrade to a house they did not even own. This was oddly uncharacteristic of Karen, who had a reputation for being thrifty, a trait passed down from her parents. With Tom away, Frenda expressed concern to Karen over the unnecessary expense of home improvements. After all, it was a rented house, and the couple was on the verge of separating. "Karen was very frugal," Frenda recalls. "She wasn't frugal if she bought you a gift or something, but she earned her own money, and she paid a price for that money. She wasn't cavalier about it, which I respected. I thought that was a wonderful way to be. She had some areas in which she didn't have much sense, but she *did* have sense in the area of finances. If it had been five hundred dollars I wouldn't have said anything, but this was a lot of money."

Arriving back home, Frenda was not surprised when the phone rang and it was Karen. It had not even been twenty minutes, but the two talked "fifty million times a day," she says. But this call was different. Karen was in a panic. "Oh my God, Frenda! Oh my God, oh my God," she said, her voice quivering in fear.

"Kace, what is it?"

"There was a man that came to the door and I let him in and he said something about the Corniche."

"Don't tell me it was a burglar," Frenda scolded. "Kace, you should never have let anybody in!"

"No, no, no. They really *were* from the car agency," Karen explained.

"Well, what's the problem then?"

"Well, Tom never even bought me the car! It's leased. And he hasn't paid the lease in two months, and they were here to repossess the car. They offered to let me make restitution, and I said, 'No, just take it!'"

"Kace! Oh my God. I'm coming to get you."

"No, no, no," Karen told her. "I want to talk to Tom about it when he comes home."

"All right," Frenda said, "but I am going to get a hold of Eddie."

When Tom returned home Karen confronted him about the leased car. He became furious when he learned it had been repossessed by the dealership. Additionally, he wanted more money and her signature on yet another loan. Mustering up all the strength she could, Karen looked her husband in the eye and said, "Tommy, I am not a bank. I am *not* a bank."

Ed Leffler was on the golf course with friends that day and not easy to reach. As Frenda tried to contact her husband she heard three tiny taps from her brass door knocker. She opened the door to find Karen, who had driven across town after a falling-out with Tom. "She was in a hump, slumped over," Frenda recalls. "Oh my God, I was hysterical.

I tried so hard to be calm because I had two babies there, but I had to help her in the house. I will never forget that day as long as I live. I said, 'That's it. It's over!' She never went back to that house again. We cleaned it out. That was the end of it."

Karen moved in with Frenda for a short time and then back to her condo at Century Towers, telling friends and family she was afraid to return to the Bel Air estate due to recent burglaries in the neighborhood. "She wouldn't go back," Frenda explains. "She couldn't go back. We wouldn't *let* her go back. That was the end, and I know she never saw him again after that. That really was the beginning of the end of her life."

———— ⧜ ————

KAREN'S DISASTER of a marriage only served to exacerbate her mental illness and physical descent. "You expect a marriage to go through its ups and downs," says Phil Ramone. "Unfortunately hers read exactly like the solo album, but it was her life. Its failure was exactly the same. That's too much for any human being to take. Any way you look at it, that disaster was the final nail." According to Itchie, "Karen tried to put a smile on her face all the time. No one wants to own up to having been deceived, especially with her life in the spotlight. Her wedding had been the centerfold of *People*. In truth, her marriage didn't really last more than about three months."

Too embarrassed and ashamed to return home to Downey, Karen relied on Frenda and her parents, Ben and Melba, for support during this time of deep depression. "She would sit and my mother would cradle her like she was an infant," Frenda recalls. Mealtime at the Leffler house became a dreaded and terribly painful experience for all involved. "I'd make everything that she liked. Everything. She loved white fish, and she loved the way I made it. Then I made peas. I made everything that I knew she'd like, and she ate one pea!" Adding to the Lefflers' frustration was the fact that Karen would carefully divide, sort, and compartmentalize the food on her plate. "I couldn't help but notice," Frenda says. "She'd make little patterns out of it. I'd watch it. Even that was artistic. Even in the mania she was an artist."

Frenda would sit patiently at the table with Karen long after the rest of the family had finished their meals and left the dining room. She tried every approach she could think of to encourage her friend to eat. "Now Kace, we can't do this," she would say. "Don't make me feed you like a baby!" But Karen just sat quietly. "OK, then open your mouth. Here comes the choo-choo!"

When Karen did manage to eat a few bites she would immediately say she felt sick and quickly disappear to the nearest bathroom. "She couldn't keep food down," Frenda says. "It was a serious depression, no question. I knew she was severely depressed when singing was the last thing on her mind. When you have a passion for music like she had, and all at once you can't even think about it, something is definitely wrong. It was not about music anymore. It was not about fun anymore. It was about trying to eat something. Survival." The absence of food and nutrients left Karen very weak, and she tired easily. This worried Frenda, but there was an underlying determination that showed through at times. "It was frightening," she recalls, "but as sick as Karen was, she'd still want to give the twins their baths. She'd rub their little backs in circles. See, she still tried to do some of the things she loved doing."

While many around Karen felt her obsession with dieting had taken over, those who knew her intimately say that was not the case. There came a time when she did not want to lose more weight, but by then she knew the disorder was out of her control. She wanted to stop and was even ashamed of how she looked. As she had done years before, Karen began layering her clothes to disguise her skeletal frame. She would tell others she was cold and then add a sweatshirt to a turtleneck sweater. "She'd put on so many layers of clothing because she didn't want people to know she was *that* thin," Frenda says. "My feeling always was that she wanted to disappear. I certainly know that's not a medical diagnosis, but that is what it seemed like."

"RICHARD, I realize I'm sick and I need help." As 1981 came to an end, Karen was more freely expressing this realization to family and friends.

She went to her brother and finally admitted things had gone too far. Something had to be done—and soon.

"How do I get over this?" she asked a group of girlfriends who gathered for lunch at the Beverly Hills Hotel. She expressed to them how she felt a great deal of responsibility on her shoulders. In addition to her efforts to maintain a successful career, she spent a lot of time worrying about family issues. Her friends sensed that Karen was constantly trying to keep all members of her family happy, with no time left to take care of herself. She wanted to get help but felt guilty even considering the idea of putting everything on hold to address her personal problems. "Maybe I should just wait for the perfect time," she said.

"Life can't always be that perfect, Kace," Frenda told her from time to time. "It just can't be. You can't be all things to all people all the time. You're just one little girl!"

"Her face was all eyes," Carole Curb recalls. "She looked like she weighed somewhere between eighty and ninety pounds. As I look back I can tell she was reaching out. She'd succeeded in everything else, and she wanted a scientific formula for how she could get over this. I think that she just couldn't quite pull it together. In retrospect, she was pleading for help, which we all wish we'd given more of." Over the years, Curb struggled with her own weight issues and an ongoing battle with anorexia. "In that era we all had little bouts of that. It was really in vogue then. Maybe it's never been out of vogue. Mine wasn't anything like hers. I never got down to eighty pounds. But she would ask me questions about it, and I would try to give her answers."

Karen's food issues had been obvious to Olivia Newton-John for several years by this time, but Newton-John admits it was difficult for her to identify with or comprehend what her friend was experiencing. "Anorexia was not something that was talked about or known about in those days," she says. "People were very thin, but you didn't realize what it was. When I looked at Karen I saw this face with these big, beautiful, soulful brown eyes and this funny, quirky personality.... She was a clown on the outside, but you know how clowns are— they are sometimes sad on the inside and funny on the outside—that was Karen."

Karen also reached out once again to Cherry O'Neill. "The fact that I had blazed the trail of recovery before her gave her hope to think she could do the same," O'Neill says. "I think she was looking for encouragement and inspiration along her own journey toward wellness. Karen was acknowledging her own eating disorders and was actively seeking help. I think she knew that she needed to get serious about dealing with her problem, but she didn't want to talk with just anybody. As a public figure, she knew that she was dealing with pressures and expectations that were much different than most people struggling with eating disorders. Perhaps she thought I could identify with those pressures and expectations better than most other people."

O'Neill sensed that Karen sincerely wanted to get better. "She was very blunt and straightforward in the way she spoke about it, and she knew she could do it." What fascinated Karen was that Cherry had seemingly recovered by that time. She was also happily married with a young child, the life Karen still longed for, even though deep down she knew it could never be with Tom Burris. She spoke little of her marital issues or her separation from Tom. Instead Karen remained focused on the matter at hand. "What was behind her was in the past, and she was trying to focus on her future and on moving forward," O'Neill says. "She just felt like she had tried her best and was sorry the marriage failed. She didn't like failure and probably felt it reflected on her personally. That is another hard pill to swallow for perfectionists, and almost all anorexics are."

As she had told Karen several years earlier, Cherry O'Neill believed Karen needed to make some radical changes to her surroundings and suggested she leave Los Angeles for a quieter, more sedate environment where she could work through her issues and take plenty of time to properly heal. "I actually recommended she consider coming to the Northwest and seeing the doctor who helped me," she says. "The pace was so much slower, the values less superficial, and the natural beauty absolutely awe-inspiring and invigorating."

But in Karen's world, one name was synonymous with anorexia treatment, and that name was Steven Levenkron. Since the time she spoke with the therapist by phone from Jerry Weintraub's office several years earlier, his successful book *The Best Little Girl in the World* had become a highly acclaimed television movie, which aired in May 1981. Levenkron's high profile was a huge factor in helping make this decision. Plus, a move from Los Angeles to the Big Apple sure seemed radical enough in terms of distance. In reality, the two cities could not have been more similar as far as pace and environmental pressures were concerned.

With Karen's consent, Itchie Ramone phoned Steven Levenkron, telling him of an anonymous celebrity she represented. He considered his extensive list of clients to be held under the strictest confidence and was annoyed to talk around a situation such as this. He refused to discuss the possibility of someone in need of his help and demanded this "unnamed famous person" call him directly. "Well, it's Karen Carpenter," Itchie finally revealed. Levenkron immediately recalled the brief conversation with Karen two and a half years earlier, when she'd assured him she was fine and did not have anorexia. Itchie told him that was simply not the case and that Karen had lied to him, but she was very sorry and desired very much to meet with him.

The following day, Karen called Levenkron herself from Los Angeles, informed him she had purchased a plane ticket to New York, and began detailing her plan for recovery—she would be arriving that Saturday and would see him for three hours. When the therapist explained that he was a family man who did not keep hours on weekends, Karen broke down. "This will only take you a couple of hours," she promised. Taking back control of the conversation, Levenkron firmly explained that Karen was entirely wrong to think she would be cured after one quick consultation. Enumerating the minimum requirements for treatment, he told her to sit down and really think about whether or not she was ready to fight. If her answer was an honest "yes," then he would be willing to help her. But she would need to move to New York, at least temporarily.

Karen immediately phoned Itchie, tattling on Levenkron for upsetting her. But Itchie supported the therapist's suggestions and affirmed that she should consider relocating to New York. Like Cherry O'Neill, she felt Karen would greatly benefit from time away from Los Angeles and the strict schedule of work and life there. Itchie's encouragement prompted a return call from Karen to Levenkron, just three hours after the first. Her new plan was to move to New York and see him an hour a day, five days a week. He agreed.

Sharing the news with family and friends, Karen was met with much support and without questions, although Evelyn Wallace did her best to talk Karen out of relocating to New York. "Karen, there are wonderful doctors right here in L.A. that could help you," she said, "and they have lovely hospitals here, too." Wallace's attempts proved futile. "She wanted to get as far away from her mother as she could," she explains. "New York was a place she figured her mother couldn't be running up to all the time."

Although Karen confided in Evelyn regarding her illness, the two never spoke specifically of anorexia. Despite her attempts at honesty, Karen refrained from using the words "anorexia nervosa." Frenda Franklin recalls, "She just didn't like those words."

16

DANCING IN THE DARK

L EAVING BEHIND the pieces of her broken marriage, Karen set forth on a year-long recovery mission, relocating to New York City's Regency Hotel in January 1982. Manager Jerry Weintraub was acquainted with the owners of the hotel and arranged for Karen and Itchie Ramone (by then married to Phil) to share a two-bedroom suite with a living room and kitchenette. Itchie secured a private telephone line, in addition to a big screen television with video machine. Karen's weekly TV appointment was every Friday night with prime-time soap opera *Dallas*, while Itchie's must-see was *Dynasty*.

Monthly hotel bills were upward of six thousand dollars, not including room service tabs and phone bills. Although Karen was known to be a penny-pincher, she felt that these expenditures were for the most part justified. Therapist Steven Levenkron received one hundred dollars for each hour-long session five days a week, totaling two thousand dollars month. "I liked Levenkron, at least in the beginning," Itchie says. "He was the new kid on the block, but he did have some answers. No one really knew why someone would get the disorder or how to treat it. We didn't have answers to any of our questions about the disorder, so we were really looking to him to quote 'save' her."

Arriving at Levenkron's office at 16 East Seventy-Ninth in Manhattan, Karen weighed in at an alarming seventy-eight pounds. Although her family cited 1975 as the onset of anorexia nervosa, she felt its inception was a more recent occurrence. From her therapist's brown leather sofa, Karen explained how her anorexic behaviors began "the day she walked away from Menninger's after leaving Richard there." In a 1993 interview the therapist explained, "She had to take this brother who she loved and lock him up in a psychiatric hospital. . . . That's where she equated the beginning of her anorexia."

A week into their daily sessions, Karen admitted to Levenkron she was taking an unfathomable number of laxative tablets—eighty to ninety Dulcolax a night. The ingestion of large quantities of laxatives did not surprise Levenkron. In fact, it was a common practice for many anorexics. "For quite some time, I was taking sixty laxatives at once," admits Cherry O'Neill. "Mainly because that was how many came in the box. . . . I would ingest the entire contents so as not to leave any evidence."

What did stun Levenkron was Karen's next casual disclosure. She was also taking thyroid medication—ten pills a day. He was shocked, especially when she explained that she had a normal thyroid. He demanded she bring him the bottle, which she did during the following session. Dated August 17, 1981, the prescription for Synthroid had been dispensed by Newport Center Pharmacy and issued in the name of Karen Burris. Realizing she was using the medication to speed her metabolism, Levenkron immediately confiscated the vial and remaining pills. Of all the terrible forms of self-abuse he had witnessed with his patients, this was the first case of thyroid medication abuse he had seen in his dozen years in the field.

KAREN AND Itchie enjoyed this time together at the Regency Hotel and took advantage of what oftentimes seemed like a recurring sleep-over between teenage girlfriends. "OK, so who would your perfect guy be?" Itchie asked.

"Mark Harmon," Karen answered, referring to the actor with whom she enjoyed a couple of dates in the late 1970s.

Although Harmon was in show business, he was not a "Hollywood hoo-ha" as Karen referred to some men. According to Itchie, "Mark would have been the absolute perfect guy with all the qualifications on her list. He was a star in his own right but really down-to-earth, and he was basically a family guy, which was exactly what she was looking for. But to tell you the truth, I don't know that Mark could have ever survived the sharks around her."

With notebook paper and pen in hand, Itchie jotted down a list of the qualities Karen desired in a man. "We were writing down every single little thing that she wanted in a guy as a mate or as a partner," Itchie recalls. Obviously Karen was somewhat separating herself emotionally from Tom Burris, and rightfully so. Her requirements were similar to those she had expressed before her marriage to Burris, but she was determined to never be taken advantage of again. She still desired a man who was articulate, bright, intelligent, and witty. He had to be good looking and be a spiffy dresser. She wanted someone who hailed from a good family and preferred someone who was not in show business. He could be a celebrity but only if he was unpretentious. But above all she wanted someone who would love her unreservedly and unconditionally.

As she settled into her new surroundings, Karen again phoned Cherry O'Neill, who was relieved to hear she had finally taken the first step toward seeking professional help. She was also pleasantly surprised to learn Karen went so far as to remove herself from Los Angeles and what she calls "the ever-present pressures of the music and entertainment business, as well as the expectations of family, agents, managers, and record company executives." But O'Neill believed New York City was just as fast-paced as Los Angeles. "I really felt like her being there was not enhancing or complementing the recovery. She would have benefitted from a more pastoral, less urban, more low-key environment where she would have no alternative but to slow down and focus on herself, her health, and her recovery."

Cherry was also concerned with what she knew of Levenkron's therapeutic approach, which she explains as an effort to have his patients "develop something of a dependence on him as they wean themselves from their family of origin or spouse who may have contributed inadvertently to the eating disorder." In Karen's case it seemed that both family and spouse had aggravated her situation.

According to Levenkron's 1982 book, *Treating and Overcoming Anorexia Nervosa*, the patient must become totally dependent upon the therapist. "The therapist must develop a care-taking relationship with someone who views relationships as always competitive." This sort of dependence was not easy for Karen. She was more comfortable offering care and concern to others. Receiving care seemed to leave her feeling helpless and somehow unworthy. O'Neill tried to encourage Karen, even though she knew Levenkron's plan would take much longer than she had allotted. "She had entered therapy with an agenda and time frame in mind that did not allow for that process to run its course. Once the patient has transferred their dependence onto him, he tries to teach them how to create their own sense of identity, and he helps them disengage from their dependence on him with new behaviors, habits, and thought patterns in place. But that takes a lot of time!"

KAREN RETURNED to Los Angeles for two weeks in April 1982. Most who saw her thought she looked dreadful, but despite her haggard appearance she seemed quite energetic. She even took time to cut several tracks with Richard at A&M Studios during the visit. In what became her final recording session, she laid down work leads for two new Carpenter-Bettis tunes, "At the End of a Song" and "You're Enough," in addition to a Ruby and the Romantics oldie, "Your Baby Doesn't Love You Anymore," and a Roger Nichols composition entitled "Now." Richard felt Karen sounded as marvelous as ever, despite her ill health and frailty, but hindsight reveals a weakness to her vocals. Her interpretation, phrasing, and enunciation were beautiful—near perfection, in fact—but something was missing from the timbre.

Frenda tried her best to reason with Karen, citing her voice and the need to keep it healthy and vibrant. "Kace, you've been so lucky for so long," she told her. "But you're going to ruin this gift. I don't care for myself. In fact, I wouldn't care if you never sang again. You have enough money to live on for the rest of your life. It's not for any of those reasons. It's for you. I think you'll be lost without it. If you don't eat something, one of these days you're going to open your mouth and nothing's going to come out!"

When she returned to New York Karen took every advantage of the beautiful spring weather and began a new exercise routine—to and from her sessions with Levenkron—a brisk two-mile round-trip walk. This was yet another method to burn extra calories. Occasionally she would stop by a needlepoint store she'd found on Madison Avenue. Sometimes she was recognized on the street and asked for her autograph, but to those who had not seen Karen in a number of years she was nearly unrecognizable. Comedian David Brenner, who worked with the Carpenters in Las Vegas, was enjoying lunch with a friend at an outdoor café on Madison Avenue one afternoon. "Hi, David," he heard from a passerby on the sidewalk near his table. Brenner looked up and smiled, said "hello" to the woman he assumed to be a fan, and returned to his meal. "But, David, it's me," she interrupted. "We worked together!" Bewildered, he looked up again but had no idea what this stranger was talking about. "It's me, Karen," she said with a laugh. Brenner then recognized the voice and smile.

"Karen!" he said as he stood to hug her. "I'm so sorry. I didn't *recognize* you. You've lost a *lot* of weight." She didn't reply to his observation but explained she was visiting friends in New York. "Great, well, let's have lunch sometime," he said.

"That's about as stupid a thing to say to an anorexic as could be said—'let's have lunch,'" Brenner says, "but I had no idea she had this disease. Ironically, it was the last time I ever saw her."

Former Carpenters manager Sherwin Bash saw Karen in New York in mid-1982 as well. He was walking through Central Park South when he heard a familiar voice. "Shermine Bush!"

"She would never call me Sherwin Bash," he explained. "It was always 'Shermine Bush.'"

Bash turned around to see Karen running to meet him. "I took her in my arms and gave her a kiss," he recalled. "She had her sweater and her jacket and everything on, and through it all I could feel the bones. She said she was doing fine and that she was at the point where she was well aware that she was a victim of anorexia. She said she was doing better and she was under a therapist's care."

In her daily calls to both Frenda and Agnes, Karen reported on life in New York City and her recent visitors. Anticipating her daughter's call, Agnes would always answer on the first or second ring. The two talked at length, but Karen rarely spoke with Harold. "Agnes never once asked Harold if he wanted to talk to Karen," Evelyn Wallace recalls. "She just talked and talked and then—bang—she'd hang up the receiver." On one occasion, Harold answered Karen's call from the office. "Well, just a minute, let me get your mother," he said.

"Oh, no, no, no, Dad," she replied. "You're the one I want to talk to. I *never* get to talk to you. Please stay on the line."

Evelyn suggested Harold take the call in the privacy of the music room. She knew if Agnes discovered Karen was on the line she would surely take the phone away for herself. That afternoon, the two were finally able to enjoy a long-overdue conversation between father and daughter. "I think that she really loved her father," Wallace says. "She didn't have to say anything, but you could tell when she was around him. She just had this happy look when she'd talk to him, and it was always with the sweetest voice. I know she thought the world of her dad, but with her mother, that was another story."

According to Frenda, Harold did his best to compensate where Agnes was lacking. "He really, really, really loved her," she says. "If she had never sung a note he loved her. Pudgy or whatever, he loved her."

Being more than two thousand miles from home, Karen relied on a small but close network of relationships on the East Coast. "Please come and stay in New York," she would beg longtime friend Debbie Cuticello. Debbie and husband C.J. went to Karen's suite at the Regency several times before taking her out for dinner but always made the return trip to their Connecticut home the same evening. "I would bring Karen here once every two or three weeks, and she'd spend the weekend with me," Debbie says. "I was much happier to have her here with me in quiet Guilford than being in New York City."

Karen enjoyed weekends with the Cuticello clan, which by this time included the couple's baby son, Jamie. Babysitting while C.J. and Debbie went to church or out to dinner allowed Karen time to play surrogate mom. Like Frenda Leffler's twins, Jamie Cuticello was quite special to her, and she showered him with love and attention, in addition to gifts including her own needlepoint creations. She also seemed to enjoy the domestic aspect of the family's home and assisted in preparing meals, washing dishes, and helping with other household duties. "She absolutely adored children," recalls Itchie Ramone. "She would have been such a wonderful mom. Mothering was totally instinctive. She even taught me how to iron!"

While visiting Guilford, Karen told Debbie the meetings with her therapist were going better than expected. According to her, it was only a one-year process, and she seemed to be "breezing" through. Her therapist felt she could finish in six months—maybe even four. This seemed to be a very self-deceiving declaration. In fact, Karen was well aware that successful treatment would take years, not months. Following her own quick-fix plan, she told friends and family what they wanted to hear and moreover what she wanted to believe.

Outwardly Karen seemed committed to the idea of therapy, but as evidenced by her daily walking regimen, she was not as committed to making important changes that would result in real progress and positive results. Friends including Carole Curb say Karen continued to dabble in—if not delve into—even stricter anorexic practices while under Levenkron's care. "She was still walking a lot, and she was exercising," Curb says. "And then she was into throwing up and taking water pills that make you lose water weight. Debilitating things like that."

Several months into his sessions with Karen, Levenkron began to suspect that she had fallen off the wagon. He phoned Itchie, soliciting her help with a matter she would long regret. "When she leaves the room, go into her bedroom and check under her mattress," Levenkron instructed. "Check underneath her bed, in her bathroom, and anywhere else you can think of." The therapist wanted confirmation that Karen had stopped using and thrown away all laxatives, diuretics, and other medications. Even the half quaalude she was known to take on occasion was too strong for her tiny body. "But it really helps me to sleep," she told Itchie, who insists that Karen was in no way abusing quaaludes.

"I felt so horrible, but it had to be done," Itchie says. "She had been saying to Levenkron that she had stopped the laxatives and stopped the 'ludes. I said, 'There's just no way. She's just too thin!' I called

Levenkron back and said, 'Look, I found all these things. What am I supposed to do?'"

With Karen in tow, Itchie delivered her findings to Levenkron's office the following day. Learning of the conspiracy and that her friend had collected evidence against her, Karen became incensed. "When I told her what I had done, I really felt like I'd betrayed her," Itchie recalls. "All I could say was, 'I really, really want you to get well.'"

Following that meeting, Itchie realized that in cooperating with Levenkron she had lost her best friend's trust. "It caused a major, major upset," she says. "In retrospect it caused a bit of a setback. She really started to have trust issues with me. I said, 'Look, I am really sorry.' And I truly was. I was invading her privacy; I had no idea what I was doing, and I just panicked because I loved her.... After that I just felt that she had to do it for herself from that point on."

But Levenkron was right. Karen had done exactly as he predicted. Like many of the women he worked with, she resisted the very treatment she was seeking. He was not fooled by her tactics and let her know, just as he let hundreds of other patients know: "You are the victim of a disease and not the designer of a creative way of being special." A message entitled "For the Afflicted" appeared in his book and remains a revealing look at the language used by the therapist in meeting with his patients. "You suffer," he wrote, "and are condemned to defend that suffering so that you will feel powerful rather than ashamed. If you defend that suffering eloquently enough, you may be regarded as manipulative and deceitful, instead of desperate. Surely words that connote being powerful are more desirable labels than words that suggest helplessness."

Dependence did not come easy for Karen; it suggested incompleteness and vulnerability. Like many with an eating disorder, Karen would oftentimes argue that she was not in need of any care. She felt she was plenty successful the way she was. Levenkron disagreed and did so using language that cut to her core. He told her she was "incompetent" and unable to keep herself alive. Levenkron's goal was for her to relearn dependence and see it as a healthy dependence upon him. "The victims must learn how to become patients," his book reads.

"The patients must risk trusting, and being receptive to support, guidance, care and even affection."

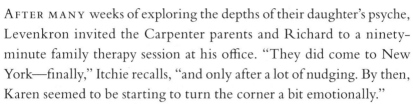

AFTER MANY weeks of exploring the depths of their daughter's psyche, Levenkron invited the Carpenter parents and Richard to a ninety-minute family therapy session at his office. "They did come to New York—finally," Itchie recalls, "and only after a lot of nudging. By then, Karen seemed to be starting to turn the corner a bit emotionally."

The stigma surrounding mental illness and a need for therapy was frightening for the family, especially Agnes, who felt Karen was simply going overboard as far as dieting was concerned. If only she would stop being so stubborn and just eat. Over the years, the family tried every possible approach to get through to her and make her eat. "Everyone around her did everything that they could have humanly done," Richard said in 1993. "I tried everything—the heart-to-heart, the cajole, the holler.... It can just make you crazy. I tried everything. Obviously it wasn't about to work, and I was upset."

Levenkron explained that the family's attempts to threaten or bribe Karen out of her behaviors would never make them go away. According to his book, "Failure of the family to understand this produces division within the family that in turn results in feelings of anger and guilt. The family atmosphere is chaotic, reinforcing the anorexic's belief that she and no one else knows what is best for her."

Agnes was what Levenkron termed an "oppressive-dependent" mother. At first she appeared to be overbearing, but that same domineering presence is oftentimes a cover for her fear of losing her daughter—or at least control over her daughter. Levenkron suggested to the family that Karen was in need of a more tactile, demonstrative kind of love. Karen bawled uncontrollably during the meeting. She told them how terribly sorry she was for having put them in a situation where they felt a need to defend her upbringing, and she went so far as to apologize for ruining their lives.

"I think Karen really needs to hear that you love her," Levenkron told the family.

"Well, of course I love you," Richard told her unreservedly.

"Agnes?" The therapist tapped the mother's shoe with his own.

Rather than address her daughter, Agnes explained how she preferred to be called Mrs. Carpenter. "Well, I'm from the north," she continued. "And we just don't do things that way."

"Agnes couldn't do it," says Itchie Ramone, who discussed the meeting with Karen and Levenkron after the family left. "*She couldn't do it!* . . . In therapy you're basically stark naked. Then your own mother can't reach out to you? And the way she doted on Richard! Most children would try to dance as fast as they could to make their parents love them, but it was at that point that I think Karen decided it was time to take a step back."

When Levenkron lightheartedly suggested to the family that Karen might come out of treatment and realize she no longer enjoyed singing, that was it for Richard. His distrust of the therapist was forever solidified. In his mind, there was no question of Karen's deep-seated love for singing. She loved performing and recording more than anything in the world. As she explained to Ray Coleman in 1976, "I gotta sing. I love that crowd." Karen had always considered herself fortunate to be able to make a living doing something she loved. "A lot of people don't get the chance to do that," she explained in a 1981 interview. "They spend their whole life doing a job they hate. . . . We walk in and sing and have a good time and make albums, go all over the world."

After the meeting with Levenkron, Richard became angry with the treatment plan, which he thought to be worthless. "At that point, he didn't have a lot of respect left for Levenkron," Itchie says. "At first everybody was grabbing for any information Levenkron might have that could help Karen. Then all of a sudden in a few months it turned around to where everyone was asking, 'Is this guy for *real*?'"

Richard was upset that Karen had not checked herself into an inpatient facility as one would do to conquer substance abuse, like a Betty Ford Clinic but for eating disorders. According to Levenkron, he also wanted to put Karen in an inpatient facility immediately after she arrived in New York, but she refused to even consider it. The therapist proceeded to work with her in what he called a "less-than-perfect treatment modality," according to his interviews with Ray Coleman. He went on to say the modality ended up being a nonissue, however, because the damage that would eventually kill Karen had already been done. "In the end," he explained, "what killed her was all her behavior previous to coming to New York."

The Carpenter family returned to Downey and, although greatly alarmed, chose to keep their distance after this painful encounter with Levenkron. Wishing to consult exclusively with Karen during this time, they made no further attempts to contact her therapist. "What I find interesting," Levenkron stated in 1993, "is that in the entire time Karen was in New York, I got zero calls from the entire family. I have never treated anyone with anorexia nervosa that their family didn't call somewhat regularly because they were concerned." Likewise, Richard claimed to have never received a call from Levenkron.

Karen and Itchie were surprised to learn that Levenkron was not an actual doctor. "We used to call him 'Dr. Levenkron' all the time," Itchie explains. "Then we found out that he wasn't even a real doctor. Any medical issues she had, we had to go see this other doctor who was a medical doctor at Lenox Hill Hospital."

According to Evelyn Wallace, "She picked the wrong guy to go to. He wasn't even a doctor! It seemed like Levenkron was simply trying to talk Karen out of having anorexia, but she'd talk to him and she'd go back to the same routine. He was some kind of a counselor. I don't know what you'd call him. Call him a liar! That's what he was."

Wallace could only do so much from afar. She wanted to see Karen with her own eyes and be able to hug her and show her love and support. Although she refused to travel by plane, Evelyn called an area train station to inquire about a round-trip ticket from Los Angeles to New York. "I think I'll go visit Karen," she told Agnes one afternoon.

"Oh no, you can't do that," she responded.

"Oh? Well, I wouldn't stay long or bother her or anything," she explained. "Just visit."

But Agnes was adamant that she not try to see Karen. "The doctor said she can't have any more visitors!"

This puzzled and even angered Evelyn. She knew Karen was not in any sort of confinement. "She was alone in a hotel room," Wallace says. "I was so mad! I thought, 'What in the heck has she got, something *catching?*'"

By the fall of 1982, Karen showed no real signs of progress. In fact, her walks to and from sessions with Levenkron kept her body weight dangling beneath the eighty-pound mark. Itchie Ramone called Levenkron and voiced her concerns. "Look, Karen's getting thinner and thinner and thinner," she exclaimed. "Plus, it's obvious she doesn't have her usual energy anymore. When do you expect this turnaround? She's just skin and bone!"

The therapist agreed that Karen seemed extra tired and was not responding as quickly as he had hoped and vowed to try another approach. Leaving her next session with Levenkron, Karen asked Itchie if she could borrow a swimsuit. "What?" Itchie asked. "There's no pool in the hotel. Besides, it's cold out!"

"No, I have to wear it tomorrow for Levenkron," Karen answered.

The two stopped by the Ramones' apartment to pick up a size 2 light green bikini belonging to Itchie. Karen changed into the bikini and emerged smiling. Itchie was mortified and unable to hide her reaction. "What's the matter?" Karen asked. "It fits."

"Uh, yeah, it fits," she said hesitantly. "You can use it tomorrow, I guess."

Returning to Levenkron the following day, Karen was asked to change into the bikini and stand in front of the office mirror. He urged her to survey and evaluate her body. "She didn't really see any problem with how she looked," Itchie recalls. "In fact, she thought she was gaining a little weight. But she was seventy-nine pounds. That was one of the times where I would go home and lock myself in my bathroom and cry."

Karen, too, was growing impatient and discouraged that she was not progressing as quickly as she had hoped. Her impending self-imposed deadline was on the horizon, and she had nothing to show for almost a year of therapy. "My mother is going to kill me if I haven't gained weight," she told Evelyn Wallace and reportedly expressed the same to her therapist.

In mid-September Karen phoned Levenkron and told him her heart was "beating funny." She was quite upset, anxious, and confused. She complained of dizziness to an extent that she was unable to walk. He recognized her symptoms as those of someone suffering extreme dehydration. He knew she needed immediate medical attention but was unable to refer Karen to a hospital based on his own credentials. Instead he asked Dr. Gerald Bernstein to meet him and Karen for an evaluation.

At what might very well have been her lowest point ever, both physically and emotionally, Karen was admitted to New York's Lenox Hill Hospital on September 20, 1982, to begin hyperalimentation, or intravenous feeding. "When they do that they're really seriously worried that you're going to die," Frenda explains. "That's why they do it. It's a last resort."

Two blocks east of Central Park, Lenox Hill Hospital is an intensive care hospital on Manhattan's Upper East Side. "In the beginning she was definitely a Jane Doe," Itchie recalls. Attempting to check in as Karen Burris, she was recognized by the receptionist as the singer from the Carpenters. She was "terrified but determined," according to Dr. Bernstein, who conducted a series of tests that revealed a critically low blood potassium level of 1.8. The normal range is 3.5 to 5.5. Upon admission to the hospital Karen was, in Levenkron's words, "seventy-seven pounds of dehydrated skeleton."

The next morning Karen went into surgery to have a small-bore catheter implanted within the superior vena cava (right atrium of the heart). An unexpected complication was discovered later that day when she complained to the nurse of excruciating chest pain and X-rays revealed the doctors had accidentally punctured one of her lungs in their attempts to insert the tube. She phoned Frenda at the first opportunity. "I could hardly understand her," she recalls. "I went running on the red-eye to New York. It was just a nightmare!"

As Karen recovered, Itchie took on the arduous task of re-creating the suite from the Regency in her hospital room. "Lenox Hill was an absolute nightmare for me," she says. "I turned her hospital room into a multimedia room. I thought the nurses were going to kill me! I had to set up the TV equipment, a refrigerator, and bring in tons of videos, a cassette player, you name it." Listening to piles of cassette tapes and song demos helped Karen pass the time when she was alone and surrounded by four orange walls. "She was always drumming everywhere," Itchie recalls.

Between various needlepoint projects she watched reruns of *I Love Lucy* and even took time to finally read the manuscript for Cherry O'Neill's forthcoming book, in which O'Neill referred to anorexia as a "sophisticated form of suicide that afflicts millions of young women." The parallels between these two women's stories were apparent. Like Karen, Cherry grew up in a musical family with singing siblings and shared similar desires to please everyone around them. Both women grew up in Christian households with what O'Neill refers to as "authoritarian-type parents."

Near the book's conclusion Karen read how Cherry's newfound freedom spurred a long-overdue confrontation with her mother: "When are you going to stop treating me like a child? Why can't you relate to me as an adult? I'm twenty-four years old and even though I'll always be your daughter, I'm *not* a baby anymore!" The words mirrored Karen's own cries for autonomy. She deeply feared the idea of ever having to face up to her mother, and her attempt at confronting Agnes several months earlier in Levenkron's office had ended up being more of a pleading for forgiveness. But now she knew that she would have to confront Agnes in the future to get her attention.

"I did it!" Cherry wrote in triumph. "I actually said what I felt for years but could never reveal. I declared my independence, embraced my adulthood, and confronted my mother with a truth to which both of us had been blind. The little bird who fought so furiously—and belatedly—to learn to fly refused to have her wings clipped." *Starving for Attention* was in many ways Karen's personal story but with an added "happily ever after" ending. It seemed more like a fairy tale than nonfiction.

As her lung began to heal, Karen's body quickly responded to the artificial means of feeding. The hyperalimentation process completely replaced all of her nutritional needs, and a precise daily calorie intake was dispensed through the catheter. This loss of control was known to oftentimes spark fear in patients, but Karen was assured the goal was to *help* her gain weight, not *force* her to gain weight. Doctors who oppose hyperalimentation argue that it does not teach the patient to eat properly and therefore does not personalize their experience. Karen gained twelve pounds in only a few days. This rapid increase alarmed Itchie, who called Frenda, Jerry Weintraub, and Karen's doctors back home in Los Angeles. "*Please* help me," she told them. "Karen's gained twelve pounds in less than a week! Where does it go from here? She's gaining much too much weight too soon. It's just going to be too hard on her heart!"

Debbie Cuticello and her mother, Teresa Vaiuso, visited Karen at Lenox Hill. "They say I have anorexia," she told them. "But look, I have all my teeth, and I have all my hair," she joked, as if suggesting the diagnosis was in need of revision. Both mother and daughter were distraught to see the once vibrant and youthful Karen in such a debilitated state. She looked too old and frail for someone just thirty-two years old.

Mike Curb was disheartened to see the beautiful young girl he had dated in this predicament. Although Karen walked around the room during his visit, she wheeled intravenous drip bags and an infusion pump beside her. "She was so thin that it almost brought tears to my eyes," he says. "I didn't know what to say then. I was more than shocked; I was heartbroken and devastated."

Solid foods were slowly reintroduced as the level of assistance from Karen's IV lessened, and she continued to gain weight steadily. Unlike many other patients she seemed pleased and excited to show visitors her progress. Richard flew in to visit on October 25 and was expecting to see evidence of the improvement she spoke of in her calls. The sounds of the dripping IV and beeping monitors provided the soundtrack for this family reunion. Cards, gifts, Mickey Mouse toys, and various stuffed animals decorated the room but did little to warm the cold and sterile surroundings. Like most who saw her there, Richard was more shocked and saddened. She was still horribly emaciated and barely identifiable by this stage. "You see how much better I look?" she asked.

Richard nodded in agreement but only to appease his sister. In an attempt to divert the attention away from her situation, Karen told him of other patients who were much worse off. But he was not sidetracked, finally breaking his silence. "Karen, this is *crap*," he said. "Don't you understand? This is crap! You're going about this all the wrong way. This guy isn't getting anything accomplished because you're in a *hospital* now!"

Three days later, on October 28, 1982, from her room at Lenox Hill, Karen scrawled her name across a petition for divorce.

⸙

BY NOVEMBER Karen was eating three meals a day at Lenox Hill and trying to stay positive about the weight gain, by then approaching the thirty-pound mark. The return of her menstrual cycle, which had ceased during the previous year, seemed to signify an improvement in emotional and physical well-being. "The extent of her bravery has to be stressed," recalled Dr. Bernstein. "These patients have enormous fear as they look at the pounds coming on." Looking at her developing arms she told her therapist, "I'll just have to keep remembering that they're supposed to look like this."

On the phone with Frenda, Karen bragged about her weight gain. "I've gained!" she said. "I'm going to come home for Thanksgiving, and I'm just going to knock everybody's socks off!"

Yeah, but by hyperalimentation, Frenda thought to herself. That's not eating it on, that's a tube. Just because you gain, that means nothing!

Karen was upbeat when discharged from the hospital on November 8, 1982, but as Cherry O'Neill recalls, "It was during a time when Levenkron was out of town that Karen chose to check herself out of the hospital. She terminated her therapy before she should have. She knew that people were depending on her for another album, and she was giving herself an imaginary deadline of Thanksgiving being the time she had to be 'well' so she could meet everyone else's expectations of her." As Dr. Irving George Newman, a Hollywood internist and father of musician Randy Newman, once told Cherry, "There are no contracts when health is concerned." She shared this advice with Karen but was sure it fell on deaf ears. "That is hard medicine to take, in and of itself, especially for those of us who never want to let other people down. Therapy and recovery don't work that way. It takes several years to develop the behaviors and thought patterns involved in eating disorders. It takes a while to untangle them and turn around to start moving in another direction."

Dr. Bernstein signed the paperwork allowing for Karen's release from Lenox Hill in time to return home for Thanksgiving in Downey. He sensed that she was very positive and optimistic as she left the hospital that day. "She was a little anxious about the future," he recalled, "but also very eager to get back to L.A. and sing."

Karen remained in New York for two weeks after checking out of the hospital. She returned to the Regency Hotel, this time with the aid of a personal nurse and explicit instructions against walking to and from Levenkron's office. It was during this time that Richard phoned Phil Ramone, concerned his sister might overdo things following the release from the hospital. "Promise me that you won't go into the studio," he said. "I am telling her I won't either. You've got to stand alongside me, and she's got to eat. She looks like a skeleton."

Ramone agreed he and Itchie would watch over Karen and was puzzled that Richard would think they would even consider recording together at this juncture. "He asked me not to record, but why would that happen? We'd shelved the album!"

Karen's return to hotel life left her homesick again, and she called Werner Wolfen to arrange her return trip to Los Angeles. He strongly advised her against abruptly ending the treatment, but she would not be swayed. She had checked out both mentally and physically. "I don't care," she told him. "I'm going home. I'm cured. That's it."

On November 16 Karen visited Steven Levenkron for the last time and presented him with a farewell gift, a framed personal message in needlepoint. The large green-threaded words YOU WIN—I GAIN served as tangible proof of the long hours Karen had spent alone in the hospital. Learning of her plan to leave, Levenkron reminded Karen she was abandoning the program much too soon and that treatment takes at least three years. He even suggested a therapist in Los Angeles so that she might continue a routine of some sort upon her return home, but she declined. She promised to call him and swore she would not take any more laxatives or diuretics. Agnes and Harold met up with Karen at Levenkron's office that day. The couple had flown to New York City to bring their daughter and her twenty-two pieces of luggage home.

It was obvious to most that Karen's treatment was inadequate and ending too soon. Frenda felt the timing was one of the biggest hindrances. "She tried to get help," she says. "She went to New York to try. It just wasn't the right way to do it. If this had happened in today's world I think Karen would have lived. I think we would have had a good shot. They know so much more. We were dancing in the dark."

17

TOO LITTLE, TOO LATE, TOO SOON

ROM THE office window, Evelyn Wallace caught a glimpse of the limousine as it pulled up in front of Newville. She ran to meet Karen as she approached the door, and the two embraced. Even though Karen's weight was above one hundred pounds, Ev was shocked to see she looked as frail as ever. "She didn't look one ounce over what she did when she left," she recalls. "I knew not to squeeze her too hard, and I didn't. I just put my arms around her. I could feel every bone in her back."

Karen ate heartily on Thanksgiving Day, much to the delight of her family, and she even called Itchie Ramone that night to tell her of all she had eaten. "She said to me, 'I ate this and that and all my favorite things,'" she recalls. "She was very proud of herself then. We were all very proud of her. It seemed like progress."

In the weeks following her return to Los Angeles, Karen went back to shopping and socializing without delay. Although she spoke with Steven Levenkron regularly by phone, most of her friends believed she had no real intention of returning to his care. At home, she ate very little and slept a lot. This worried Agnes, but she had been cautioned to "keep quiet," says Wallace. "She had been warned by Levenkron to not be jumping all over Karen. Agnes was told that Karen was trying her best to get healthy again and that she should just leave her alone and not be yelling at her and reminding her that she was sick. 'Just leave her alone,' he said."

On December 17, 1982, Karen gave what became her last public performance, singing for Frenda Leffler's twins Ashley and Andrew, their cousin Brooke Megdal, and the children's classmates at the esteemed Buckley School in Sherman Oaks, California. "I never dreamed it would turn out to be the last time—never, never, never," Frenda says. "How could that be possible? But it was. She was so thin. There was just nothing left of her." Ed Leffler was worried about Karen, given her recent traumatic hospital stay in New York, and tried talking her out of making the appearance. "But she wanted to do it for the little children," Frenda explains. "Except for our kids, these children had no idea who she was. To them she was just a nice lady who came to sing."

Wearing a festive cardigan over a turtleneck with red slacks and matching shoes, Karen sat on a platform at one end of a small auditorium before the audience of forty or fifty children watching attentively with their chins on their fists. As Frenda recalls, Karen's joy was palpable that day. "She loved singing more than anything in the world," she says. "Who better to sing for children? She was a natural mother. If life had been different and kinder I know she would have had a wonderful family. It meant so much to her, and she would have excelled at loving her family with the same love she gave to every performance she ever gave. Even that would have been perfection. She didn't know any other way."

Although others felt she was still quite fragile and thin, Herb Alpert saw Karen shortly after the New Year and recalled her looking terrific and healthy. She bounced into his office saying, "Hey, look at me, Herbie! What do you think? How do I look?" She was excited and twirled around to show off her new figure. Alpert agreed that she looked happier and healthier than he had seen her in some time and felt she appeared to have won the battle. "I am so happy," she told him. "I'm ready to record again, and Richard and I have been talking about getting the group together and performing."

On the evening of January 11, 1983, publicist Paul Bloch drove Karen to CBS Television City, where they met Richard for a special photo session celebrating the twenty-fifth anniversary of the Grammy Awards. They posed for group portraits alongside other past Grammy winners, including Glen Campbell, Dionne Warwick, and Helen Reddy. Karen spoke to reporters and mingled with friends including Debby Boone, Johnny Rivers, and Toni Tennille during what became her last public appearance. She looked tired, worn, and much older than a woman of thirty-two. Afterward she and Richard stopped for dinner at St. Germain on Melrose in Los Angeles, where Karen had an appetizer, entrée, French bread, and wine.

On January 14, Karen met Richard and former college friend Dennis Heath for dinner, again at St. Germain. She startled the two when she stopped eating, put down the knife and fork, and looked at them as if frightened or in pain. She struggled to speak but couldn't. After a lengthy visit to the ladies' room, Karen returned and assured Dennis and Richard she was fine. After dinner the three drove to nearby A&M Studios, where they listened to playbacks from the April 1982 sessions.

Debbie Cuticello called Karen on the evening of January 25 after having watched an Olivia Newton-John concert special on HBO. Incidentally, Karen had joined Olivia on the road for several stops during that 1982 *Physical* tour. The two had even discussed the possibility of Karen drumming during a few concerts, but because of her deteriorating health that idea was never realized. In 1982 she was far too weak for such an endeavor, but by 1983, Debbie Cuticello thought she sounded great—at least over the phone. "She was full of energy, vigor, and excitement and seemed to have pulled herself together and was ready to start a new lease on life. I asked her to send me some new photographs, and she said she would."

Despite Karen's efforts to convince friends and family she was cured, her eyes told a more truthful story. The usual rich, warm, twinkling brown eyes were shadowed by a lifeless black. Even her nervous energy seemed stifled. She was taking more naps than usual and sometimes lying down by 7:00 in the evening. When Richard reported to Werner Wolfen that he did not think she looked well, word got back to

Karen, and she was furious. She tracked Richard down and found his Jaguar parked outside the Broadway, a department store in Downey's Stonewood Center. Richard exited the store to find Karen's Jaguar XJS parked next to his XJS. Reluctantly he approached Karen, who was visibly incensed, and with great articulation and eloquence she chastised her brother in the parking lot that evening. "I want you to know that I am doing my best here," she insisted, reminding Richard he did not recover overnight when he came home from Menninger. He responded that, although he may have acted a little strangely, he was most certainly well. He did not believe she was well, and he told her so.

The confrontation continued when Karen demanded another meeting with Richard, this time with Werner present. There she explained that she felt unfairly attacked and that she had not been given the chance to fully recover. Questioning their belief in her ability to do so, she began to cry. "It's not that I don't believe in you," Richard told her, "it's just that I love you so much."

On Thursday, January 27, Florine Elie drove to Century City for her weekly cleaning of Karen's condo at Century Towers. There the housekeeper made an unnerving discovery. "When I was working up there, I found Karen," Elie says. "She was lying on the floor of her closet." She gently shook Karen and rubbed her back. She awoke but was groggy. "Karen, is there something wrong?" she asked.

"No, I am just so tired," she replied, looking up in a daze at Florine.

"Maybe you better go lie on your bed," she said, helping Karen up and tucking her into bed. "You'll be more comfortable this way." Florine checked on Karen again before leaving. By then she was awake and was adamant that she was OK. Even so, this worried Florine, so she called Karen to check on her the next morning before reporting to work at Newville.

Tuesday, February 1, found Karen once again dining with her brother, this time at Scandia on Sunset Boulevard. They were joined by stage producer Joe Layton, and the trio discussed plans for the Carpenters' return to touring. Karen ate with enthusiasm and after dinner returned to Century Towers. This was the last time Richard would see his sister alive.

The next day Karen drove to Werner Wolfen's office at Irell and Manella, just a few blocks down Avenue of the Stars. There she and W (her nickname for the attorney) reviewed her final divorce decree. "Well, did you get the better of him?" she asked Wolfen playfully. Further revisions were necessary, so she made another appointment to sign the papers that Friday afternoon, February 4, at 3:00 P.M. Wolfen recalled she wanted desperately to finalize the divorce so that she could begin rebuilding her life without Tom Burris.

Later in the day Karen spoke with Itchie Ramone, who was pregnant with her and Phil's first child. From the time she learned of the pregnancy Karen had begun preparing for the arrival of the baby she called "ours" when talking to the Ramones. "K.C. went crazy buying strollers, a playpen, a swing, a highchair, a car seat, and you name it," Itchie says. "Everything, by the way, was in blue. She was certain the baby would be a boy." Karen shared her plans for the week. She would sign the final divorce papers Friday and then prepare to leave for New York. "That weekend, February 6, she was going to hop on a plane and be there for the birth," Itchie recalls. "But first, she was finally going to sign her divorce papers and pay Tom off. She was ready to pay him the money and send him on his way—one million dollars. That's what she said: 'I'll give you the million dollars, now get lost!'"

On Thursday, February 3, Karen spoke with Richard by phone and asked his advice on videocassette recorders, as she was planning to purchase a new one. He recalled that she yawned a lot during their conversation. That afternoon Karen drove to Downey, where she planned to buy a new stackable washer/dryer for her condo. Hers was in need of repair, but she refused to call a service technician or simply order a replacement. She certainly had the resources to do so, but as she often did, Karen remained loyal to Downey, where she felt she would get the best deal and hometown service. "Both Karen and Agnes shopped at the best stores, and she shopped at the bargain stores," says Debbie Cuticello. "They were never ostentatious. They were always very cautious with their purchases. I'm not saying cheap; I'm just saying they remember their roots. They remembered where they came from."

Stopping by Newville to pick up Agnes, Karen said a quick hello and hugged Evelyn Wallace in the office before setting on a mother-daughter shopping trip. Unable to find stackable units in stock at Gemco, the two postponed their search, and Karen agreed to sleep over and continue the search at the local Sears store first thing Friday morning.

"We're going down to Big Boy. You want to come?" Agnes often invited Evelyn to join the family for dinner. Ev declined the invitation this time but encouraged them to go and have a nice dinner since Karen was visiting. The three drove up Florence Avenue to Bob's Big Boy, where Karen ordered her usual shrimp salad and asked for an extra serving as well. Afterward she told her parents she was still hungry and stopped for a taco. "Boy, that was good," she told them as she finished the snack by the kitchen counter at home.

Settling in, the family gathered in the den to watch a rerun of *Shogun*, the 1980 NBC miniseries starring Richard Chamberlain. At the end of the evening Karen went upstairs to Richard's old room, where she often slept when visiting her parents. She preferred the room to her own since it had a television and videocassette recorder. This particular night she watched a taped episode of *Magnum, P.I.* and then phoned Phil Ramone before bed, finalizing travel plans for her New York trip the following week. Karen mentioned to Ramone that she had recently listened to her solo recordings. Her voice softened in hesitation as she continued. "Can I use the *f*-word?"

"Yeah."

"Well, I think we made a fucking great album!"

Ramone agreed and encouraged Karen to look upon their work together as a positive milestone in her career, regardless of the way it was received by others. "You will make many more records with your brother," Ramone told her, "but don't lose the landmark just because it's not out in the marketplace."

Shortly after midnight, Karen went over her to-do list with Frenda by phone, and the two finalized plans for the next day. "OK, I am going to go try to find a washer/dryer," she said. "Then I'm going to drive in. There shouldn't be a lot of traffic." According to Frenda, Karen enjoyed keeping up with traffic reports. "Then we're going to go get the red fingernail polish!" The two had a noon appointment for a manicure. She was excited and planned to have them finished with bright red polish in celebration of her divorce. "Then we're going to go up to Werner's and sign everything."

Frenda was in agreement. "Honey, I am with ya. It's going to be a *great* day!"

Judging by her voice, Karen was exhausted. "You know, Fren, I am so tired," she said. "I don't know what it is. I just feel like my chest is tired."

The two said their goodnights, but Frenda was worried. She phoned Agnes downstairs. "Do me a favor," she said. "Would you go up and check on her for me?"

Agnes phoned her back a few minutes later. "Well, I think she's all right, Frenny," she reported. "She's going to be OK. I pulled the covers up over her."

Although Agnes and Frenda had their differences, they shared a common concern for Karen's well-being. "We still were all on the same page," Frenda says. "We all wanted to save her. That was our goal."

ON FRIDAY morning, February 4, Karen awoke and went downstairs to the kitchen, where she turned on the coffeepot her mother had prepared the night before. She went back upstairs to get dressed. Around 8:45 A.M. Agnes Carpenter heard the heavy mirrored closet doors slide open above her and Harold's bedroom. "Karen's up," she said, getting up and heading to the kitchen, where she habitually prepared hot cereal and coffee each morning.

On the kitchen counter she saw the percolator Karen had hooked up and the place settings she had prepared—two cups for coffee and two bowls for the cereal. "Before she had always set it for herself, too," Evelyn Wallace says, "along with a bunch of pills the doctor gave her to take. This particular morning it was just a cup for Harold and one for Agnes; nothing for Karen."

Rather than shouting for Karen when the coffee was ready, Agnes picked up the multiline phone and dialed the upstairs bedroom phone, but its ring, heard faintly in the distance, went unanswered. Agnes went to the foot of the stairs and called to her daughter. She continued calling for Karen as she climbed the stairs, but there was no response. Entering the room, Agnes found Karen's motionless, nude body lying facedown on the closet floor. Her eyes were open but rolled back. She was lying in a straight line and did not appear to have fallen. "She had just laid down on the floor and that was it," Agnes recalled. "I picked her up and I called to her and held her." She screamed to Harold to call for help.

"She was out on the floor when I got there," recalls Florine Elie, who arrived just after Agnes discovered Karen unconscious. "It must have been just before 9:00. She was out on the floor, and I am pretty sure she was dead there at the house."

The Downey Fire Department received Harold Carpenter's call at 8:51 A.M. and dispatched Engine Company No. 64 as well as a nearby paramedic unit. "They were there so fast, pulling me off," recalled Agnes, who herself attempted to resuscitate her daughter.

The three firemen from Downey Fire Squad 841 and two paramedics from Adams Ambulance Service in Santa Fe Springs found Karen to be unconscious but detected a slight pulse. "It was a chilling scene," paramedic Bob Gillis recalled to reporters. "Karen looked frail and very thin. She was completely nude." A faint pulse was detected in her neck with her heart beating only every ten seconds. "This is a sure sign of a dying heart," Gillis said. The crew moved her from the closet to the bedroom, where they began performing CPR and finally asked that Harold escort his distressed wife from the room.

Agnes rushed down the stairs and phoned Richard. Like many musicians, Richard was a night owl and still sound asleep when the call came in around 8:55 A.M. So panic-stricken was Agnes that her son had trouble understanding her hysterical cries. Finally realizing Karen was unconscious, Richard threw on a T-shirt and blue jeans and tore out of the house.

Arriving for what she thought to be an ordinary day at work, Evelyn Wallace was startled to see emergency vehicles outside the house and grew worried about Harold Carpenter. "Harold was the first one I thought of," she says. "He had heart trouble and had to take a number of pills for his heart." Hurrying into the house, Evelyn was met with Agnes, sobbing as she held tightly to a railing that separated the entry from the living room. "Agnes, what's the matter?" she asked.

There was no response. "Agnes couldn't talk. She was crying and just waved me up the stairs. I went upstairs and saw they had Karen on a gurney. I could tell they were working on her heart."

Driving frantically from Lubec Street, Richard hoped it was only a collapse, perhaps even one severe enough to persuade Karen to take her condition more seriously. He began to cry as he rounded the corner onto Newville in time to witness paramedics exiting the house with the gurney. With full lights and siren, the ambulance transported Karen's lifeless body and her shaken mother, still in her robe, to Downey Community Hospital. Richard and Harold were instructed to follow cautiously.

Arriving at 9:23 A.M., the unidentified patient was reportedly in full cardiac arrest, not breathing and without a heartbeat. "All we knew was that we were getting a thirty-two-year-old female in full arrest," says Pat Tomlin, RN, who worked in the emergency room. "When she arrived, the first thing that shocked me was her size. She was so frail and fragile looking."

Paramedics told the ER staff, "This is the lady who came from the Carpenter house in north Downey," perhaps a subtle attempt to establish identity without compromising her privacy. In the field the team of paramedics had been unsuccessful in establishing an intravenous line after several attempts, so Tomlin continued the effort. Nurse manager Vivian Carr sat with Richard and Harold, who joined Agnes in a conference room adjacent to the emergency room. Inside, the crew went to work in further attempts at saving Karen. As personnel took their places, Dr. Irv Edwards reached for a laryngoscope and began the intubation process. A young respiratory technician and Carpenter family friend stepped forward with the respirator and began securing the bag and mask. "Oh my God!" she screamed. "It's *Karen!*" The woman's voice cut through the room's intensity, and she began to sob hysterically. The others were quite perplexed by the outburst.

"What's going on? What's wrong with you?" Nurse Tomlin asked her.

"It's Karen," she replied. "It's *Karen Carpenter!*"

Several members of the ER crew, including Tomlin, leaned over the bed for a closer look. "Holy shit," she cried. "It is!" She was shocked to realize this body belonged to the youthful girl she knew only from the Carpenters' album covers. Tomlin knew the words to most of the Carpenters' hit songs, and the lyric to one of them immediately ran through her head: "So much of life ahead...And yes, we've just begun." Tomlin sent one of the staff members to notify the hospital manager. "We knew this was going to turn into the nightmare from hell, publicity-wise."

Dr. Edwards was less concerned with the pending media circus and recalls only thinking of the Carpenter family. "This was an incredibly young woman who was too young to die," he says. "What a terrible, terrible, terrible family tragedy this was. They were an extraordinarily popular and much beloved family in Downey, and she was a hometown celebrity."

The medical team at Downey Community spent twenty-eight minutes attempting to resuscitate Karen. "We worked on her for quite a while but then ended up calling the code," Tomlin says. At 9:51 A.M., Karen Anne Carpenter was pronounced dead.

Dr. Edwards emerged from the emergency room and entered the room where Harold, Agnes, and Richard were huddled. The rueful words stumbled from his mouth: "I'm sorry, but Karen is dead." This was a heartrending but not uncommon task the doctor was required to carry out time and time again. "It's never easy to tell a family that someone they love and is dear to them has died," he says. "Richard was fairly composed. Incredulous, but somewhat composed. The parents were absolutely in a state of disbelief."

"Are you *sure* she's gone?" they asked. "Can't you do *anything* to bring her back?"

"We took some time to explain things to the parents," Edwards recalls, "and grieve with the family." Richard was angry. Agnes and Harold were numb. Their faces filled with tears before asking, "May we see her?"

DISPATCHED TO Downey Community Hospital at 9:55 A.M. for a "possible overdose," patrolman J. Rice of the Downey Police Department spoke with Dr. Edwards and his staff, who advised him of Karen's history of anorexia nervosa and depression. "She was extraordinarily thin and what I would describe as gaunt looking," recalls Dr. Edwards. "She did have the appearance or the persona of a person who had anorexia nervosa. In part of my evaluation of Karen we did test her blood sugar, and it was very, very elevated." Tests revealed a blood sugar level of 1,110, which equated to approximately ten times the norm. In Dr. Edwards's opinion, the immediate cause of death was a "hyperosmolar diabetic coma."

Patrolman Rice questioned Karen's parents at the hospital before escorting them home. The family's agony and anguish during the three-mile drive back to Newville without Karen was immeasurable. By the time Harold, Agnes, and Richard returned, the street had been barricaded by local authorities who were stationed at the corner to assist in providing some sort of privacy for the grief-stricken family. National and local media soon swarmed the neighborhood. Heartbroken fans overtaken with sorrow and disbelief gathered behind police lines after hearing the news: "Singer Karen Carpenter, who helped put soft rock at the top of the charts, is dead at the age of thirty-two of a heart attack."

Running errands in anticipation of spending the afternoon with Karen, Frenda Leffler was driving up Palm Drive in Beverly Hills when she caught a special report on the radio. "I almost ran into a tree," she recalls. "Of course I didn't believe it. I went home and I was just in a daze. I opened the back door and I saw Eddie, who was never home early. . . . He looked at me and said, 'She's gone.' Even though we should have known, you don't want to believe that something is really going to happen. You want to think that your loving her was going to make everything all right. But the last blow with this marriage was just more than her little body could take."

Olivia Newton-John also heard the news on her car radio as she traveled down a Los Angeles freeway. "It was a terrible shock," she says.

"I was meeting someone I didn't even know for a business lunch at the Melting Pot on Melrose. I was still in shock, and when I sat down I just burst into tears.... It was just horrendous and such a shock. Poor girl, she'd been through a lot. We were supposed to have lunch the next day."

Returning from a business meeting of her own, Itchie Ramone arrived home to the sounds of ringing phones and the voices of a small group of friends crowded around her husband in the middle of the couple's living room. "Have you listened to the radio this morning?" he asked.

"No, I just went to the meeting and came out. Why?" She was alarmed to realize the room had fallen silent. "What's going on?" she asked.

"It's about Karen," Phil said cautiously.

"Oh good God, what has she done now?" she laughed, but Phil remained serious.

"What's wrong? Phil, what's the matter? Is she ill? Is she in the hospital? What's wrong with her?"

"It was her heart," he said.

"It was her *heart*? Is she dead? Did she die?"

As Karen had predicted, Phil and Itchie welcomed their new baby boy, B. J. Ramone, the following week on February 7.

At Cal State Long Beach, Frank Pooler was in a rehearsal when his assistant heard the news reports over the radio. "Come on, let's go over to the office," the assistant told him. "I've got some sad news for you. Karen just died."

Pooler attempted to reach Richard, who proved to be incommunicado. "I went down to the house that night. It was all cordoned off with cops so I just gave them a letter for Richard. I volunteered the choir for anything they might want to have sung at the service."

John Bettis was in a writing session in Nashville. "Those things don't hit you right off," he recalled. "It's almost as if you're watching a TV show or something. It's an out-of-body experience." He immediately called Richard and was surprised to get through. "I don't know how you feel, but I'm mad as hell," he told Richard, later regretting the words he came to feel were egocentric. "The selfishness of my first reaction has haunted me because I actually felt as if Karen had taken something from me that I didn't want to be without. My first reaction was, 'How selfish of you.' Isn't that odd? Since then I've had the other emotions, but that was the first one. I felt cheated."

Richard agreed. "My immediate reaction was anger," he told *People Weekly* in 1983. "Anger at the waste of her life and the loss of her talent. Then the grief set in. The shock was tremendous—I knew she was ill but not that ill." He also admitted to being angry with himself, the therapists, the doctors, and the hospitals.

In Connecticut, C. J. Cuticello raced to get in touch with his wife, Debbie. "Before you turn on the radio or do anything, this is what has happened," he said.

Shaken and stunned by her husband's words, Debbie spent the day recalling her special memories of Karen. "Disbelief," she says. "That was a hard day. That was tough." Bittersweet were her emotions as she went to the mailbox the next day only to find the photos Karen had sent after what proved to be their final phone conversation a few days earlier.

C.J. also broke the news to Frank Bonito, who was employed as a medical social worker at the time. "Channel 8 News has been trying to get you," the receptionist in his office mentioned.

"I had no idea as to why," Bonito says. "C.J. contacted me and he told me. Thankfully he got to me before the TV news. You see this on the news all the time where they call someone up and say, 'Did you hear that so-and-so died?' That is not the way you want to hear about it!"

Songwriter Paul Williams was in Washington D.C. "I was at Wolf Trap with Elizabeth Taylor and doing a big benefit. The news of the day was that Karen had died. Everybody was just stunned. I remember being devastated for everybody, for all of us, for her, and for everyone," he says. "I think that most of us around A&M and those who'd had contact knew what was going on, but the feeling was that she was doing a lot better." At the Cap Centre's Wolf Trap Gala, Williams sang "We've Only Just Begun" as a tribute to Karen. "An angel sang this song for me," he told the crowd of more than twelve thousand. As he tried to hold back his emotions, tears filled his eyes, and the stage lights were brought down.

Also in the nation's capital was Carole Curb, living in Paris at the time but visiting her brother Mike, who'd relocated to D.C. the month prior. "I was on the way to the airport to fly back to L.A. to visit my parents, and I heard it on the radio," she says. "I remember falling to the floor of the limo. I just fell on the floor." Mike Curb was in route to London and heard the news in the airport. "I was so jolted when I heard she'd died that I was just in a state of total shock. I almost fainted. The feeling I had was that she was working her way through it. A lot of people go through a tough time after a bad marriage. . . . I remember how frail she had looked the last time I had seen her, but then my sister had a lot of those same issues. My sister is still alive, so why isn't Karen still alive?"

News reports began hinting that the cause of death was believed to be associated with anorexia nervosa, but this information did little to lessen the astonishment of even those reporting the story. C. P. Smith of the *Orange County Register* wrote: "It's hardly surprising when one of rock's hard-livers dies at an early age. The passing of a Janis Joplin or a Jimi Hendrix is perhaps understandable in a macabre fashion—it's as though the nature of their gut-level music made death into more of an occupational hazard than anything else. But the passing of Karen Carpenter at the age of thirty-two came as a complete shock."

INVESTIGATORS WITH the Downey Police Department drove house-keeper Florine Elie to Karen's Century City residence, where they searched the premises looking for anything unusual or suspicious. "They went through the house and rumbled around," she recalls. "I just sat there and waited on them." They confiscated several bottles of prescription medication and various items unknown to Elie before returning her to Newville, where the mood was somber, to say the least. "They were real sad," Elie remembers. "They didn't talk or do hardly anything."

A bottle of Ativan tablets, commonly used to treat anxiety disorders, was turned over to investigators. The pills were prescribed by

Dr. George Monnet on January 10, 1983, and filled at the local Gemco pharmacy. Monnet later told the investigators he suspected Karen might have also been taking Lasix, a potent diuretic, and not taking the required potassium supplements. In his opinion, this might have caused a cardiac arrhythmia.

On the afternoon of February 4, Los Angeles County medical examiner Dr. Ronald Kornblum conducted autopsy number 83-1611. It began at 2:30 P.M. and lasted two hours. Pending results of further lab tests, the immediate cause of death was marked "deferred." Word from National Medical Services, a Pennsylvania-based clinical toxicology and forensic testing firm, came early in March. The autopsy report became final on March 11, and the certificate of death was amended to list the cause of death as "emetine cardiotoxicity due to or as a consequence of anorexia nervosa." The anatomical summary listed pulmonary edema and congestion (usually caused by heart failure) first and anorexia second. Third was cachexia, which usually indicates extreme weight loss and an apparent lack of nutrition. The finding of emetine cardiotoxicity (ipecac poisoning) revealed that Karen had poisoned herself with ipecac syrup, a well-known emetic commonly recommended to induce vomiting in cases of overdose or poisoning. A letter detailing National Medical Services's lab findings was composed March 23, 1983. After testing both blood and liver, it was determined that 0.48 micrograms/g emetine, "the major alkaloidal constituent of ipecac," was present in the liver. "In the present case," they explained, "the finding of 0.5 micrograms emetine/g, with none detected in the blood, is consistent with residua of the drug after relatively remote cessation of its chronic use."

In a press release detailing Karen's autopsy report and cause of death due to emetine cardiotoxicity, the coroner failed to cite ipecac by name. "It never occurred to me to mention ipecac," Kornblum later told *People Weekly* journalist Gioia Diliberto in her exposé detailing the dangers of the syrup. "In my mind, emetine and ipecac are the same things."

Karen's therapist Steven Levenkron claimed to know nothing of Karen's use or abuse of ipecac. He was reportedly shocked to even hear the word "emetine" as part of the official cause of death. In their phone calls following her return to Downey in November 1982, Levenkron had quizzed Karen about weight maintenance and laxative use. She assured him she was maintaining her new 108-pound figure and had completely suspended use of all laxatives. He never dreamed she was resorting to something much more lethal.

Although she had kept the ipecac secret from Levenkron, Karen had shared with Cherry O'Neill that she was resorting to the syrup on occasion. "She did mention ipecac and admitted to using it to make herself throw up," says O'Neill. "She said she could never make herself throw up so she resorted to using syrup of ipecac to purge. I don't think she knew the dangers of using that substance for more than just emergencies. Not many people knew back then. The combination of self-starvation, the poisoning effect of ipecac over time, and not strengthening her heart and body with regular exercise probably became a lethal combination for her. I remember being concerned that she took ipecac and laxatives to purge, which are probably the most dangerous methods. I was also told that she resumed her use of diuretics upon returning to Los Angeles, and it was obviously more of a drain on her body than she was able to endure."

Itchie Ramone had feared Karen was resorting to ipecac and, after hearing of the autopsy findings, was reminded of a phone conversation the two had the day after Thanksgiving 1982 when Karen's voice sounded weak and raspy. "What's wrong with your voice?" Itchie asked her.

"Oh, I was throwing up a bit," she said. "I think I ate a little too much."

"Oh, no," she thought to herself. "*Please* tell me it's not ipecac!" The Ramones had kept a bottle of ipecac in their kitchen cabinet for years, just in case of emergencies, and it went untouched for the duration of Karen's stay during the recording of the solo album. She believes Karen may have begun using the syrup sporadically in late 1980. "Karen hated to throw up! But I know it started a bit after she met Tom. It was sort of an introduction with ipecac, and it was not a constant. The laxatives were. When she was in New York in 1982 she was not taking ipecac. That habit must have formed after she got home. I was just shocked."

In a radio interview taped shortly after Karen's death, Levenkron discussed the autopsy findings: "According to the L.A. Coroner, she discovered ipecac...and she started taking it every day. There are a lot of women out there who are using ipecac for self-induced vomiting. It creates painful cramps, it tastes terrible, and it does another thing that the public isn't aware of. It slowly dissolves the heart muscle. If you take it day after day, every dose is taking another little piece of that heart muscle apart. Karen, after fighting bravely for a year in therapy, went home and apparently decided that she wouldn't *lose* any weight with ipecac, but that she'd make sure she didn't gain any. I'm sure that she thought this was a harmless thing she was doing, but in sixty days she had accidentally killed herself. It was a shocker for all of us who treated her."

In one of Steven Levenkron's most recent books, *Anatomy of Anorexia*, the author boasts of his above-average recovery rate in working with those suffering from eating disorders. "In the last twenty years I have treated nearly 300 anorexics," he wrote. "I am pleased to state that I have had a ninety percent recovery rate, though tragically, one fatality." That was Karen Carpenter.

SADDENED BY the death of his friend and client, hairstylist Arthur Johns recalls being shocked but not all that surprised to learn of her death. "It just seemed like nothing was going right in Karen's life," he says. "From the failed marriage to going to New York and being hospitalized, it seemed like it was one thing after another." Shortly thereafter, Johns received a call from Agnes asking if he would prepare Karen's hair and makeup prior to the public viewing. "Her mother was so pleading and so upset," he recalls. "I found myself saying yes before I even realized how big and how emotional this might be for myself. And it was." Johns called on a good friend to accompany him to the mortuary, where he worked to style Karen's hair one last time. "I was so young myself. Before this I had not done anybody that had died."

Hundreds of friends and fans attended a visitation held Sunday evening, February 6, under the direction of Downey's Utter-McKinley Funeral Home and held at the Forest Lawn Memorial Park Mortuary in Cypress. Guests filed past the white casket adorned with red and white roses to view Karen's body, which was clothed in a rose-colored two-piece suit. A thin, sheer veil draped across the casket's opening, and a barrier of floral arrangements helped keep visitors at a distance in hopes of somehow masking Karen's gaunt form. Agnes, Harold, and Richard, along with other family members, greeted those paying their last respects to Karen throughout the evening. "Most kept their visits short, some chatting quietly about pleasant memories, others bowing their heads in silence," reported the local newspaper.

Among the mourners was Tom Burris, who, according to Karen's closest friends, had come forward saying that he was still Karen's husband (which was legally true, as Karen had never signed the final divorce papers) and threatening against releasing her body to the family. "We had problems with him after Karen passed away," Frenda Franklin recalls. In a statement to *People* magazine Burris claimed he and Karen "always got along" and "always cared about each other. Karen was dealing with her anorexia and her career; I was dealing with my real estate problems. I feel totally guilty, like I'd like to reverse everything. I tried to work with her. I got her in touch with a doctor, but she wouldn't admit she had an eating problem. We both tried, but we just couldn't work it out."

Tom Burris tossed his wedding ring into the casket alongside Karen's body, an act later explained by Ray Coleman to be a sign of affection. Others were unmoved by this display.

Burris later called the Newville house and asked Agnes for Karen's personal wedding album. "Get it wrapped up and send it to him," she told Evelyn Wallace.

"Agnes, why are you sending this to him?" she asked. "I don't think Karen would want him to have that. I wouldn't give it to him!"

But Agnes was "hard-hearted," she says. "She made me wrap that up and mail it to him. I was just fuming to think that she would give him that wedding album. He probably sold it for several thousand dollars."

Itchie Ramone confronted Tom several months later when he surprised her with a phone call shortly after Karen's passing. "I'm *really* sorry I even picked up the phone," she told him. "Tom, the only thing

I have to say to you is if we are ever in the same room at the same time, you'd better make sure you see me first."

———— ∞ ————

LINING UP as early as 10:00 A.M., fans surrounded the gray stone walls of Downey United Methodist Church on the morning of Tuesday, February 8, awaiting the 1:00 P.M. funeral service for Karen Carpenter. Members of the Downey police force, in addition to private guards from Shaw Security, directed dozens of limousines through the crowds of mourners and curiosity seekers lining Downey Avenue. Olivia Newton-John, wearing a black dress and sunglasses, was among a list of celebrities in attendance, which also included John Davidson and Burt Bacharach. "We just missed Dionne Warwick," yelled one spectator as her friend put away her camera. Overflow seating was moved to a large room holding approximately 250 people, and another 400 were led to a courtyard where they were able to hear the service on speakers. "It was simply horrible," remembers Carole Curb, who sat alongside Terry Ellis and his wife. "We just held hands and cried," she says. "We were all heartbroken," Ellis adds.

Karen's New Haven childhood minister Reverend Charles Neal gave the eulogy. "Into every nook and cranny of this global village the sad news travels yet, and the world weeps. For Karen's story is one that has graced this world with life, with love, and with song."

Neal recalled first meeting Karen when she and Richard were part of the Methodist youth ministry that welcomed him when he relocated to New Haven where he attended Yale University. He described her childhood as a balance of "blue jeans, baseballs, and ballet," going on to assess her adulthood and its many ups and downs. "Karen's life has continued to unfold—a unique and beautiful tapestry woven with all the experiences of life: a tapestry at once joyous and furious; a tapestry filled with the joys of time but also the tyranny of time; the joy of success but also the tyranny of success; the joy of life but also the tyranny of life...joy and sorrow, laughter and tears, limelight and loneliness, love and heartache, health and illness, triumph and tragedy, quietness and fury." Neal concluded his tribute with the words of John Bettis.

She sang for the hearts of us all
Too soon and too young
Our Karen is still
But her echo will linger forever

Frank Pooler's Cal State University Choir choir sang "Adoramus Te" by Corsi and backed soloist Dennis Heath on an arrangement of the Bach-Gounod "Ave Maria," transposed from the Carpenters' *Christmas Portrait* album. Pallbearers David Alley, Herb Alpert, Steven Alpert, John Bettis, Ed Leffler, Gary Sims, Ed Sulzer, and Werner Wolfen carried the casket from the church at the close of the service. A small group of close friends and family reconvened for a brief private ceremony at Forest Lawn Cypress. "It's so sad," Harold Carpenter uttered again and again to those gathered. "It's just all so sad."

According to her friends, Karen feared death and especially the idea of being buried in the ground. She pleaded that she never be "planted," a term she used in jest to describe such interment. In keeping with her wishes, Karen's body was entombed above ground in a massive, ornate marble crypt in the Sanctuary of Compassion at Forest Lawn's Ascension Mausoleum. Towering overhead was an elaborate mosaic depicting Madonna and Child by Spanish Renaissance artist El Greco. A lustrous gold epitaph was affixed to the marble shortly thereafter: A STAR ON EARTH—A STAR IN HEAVEN.

EPILOGUE

A SONG FOR YOU

CTOBER 8, 1996. Karen Carpenter's dream of becoming recognized as a solo artist was realized, albeit too late for her to experience and enjoy. Sixteen years had passed since she and Phil Ramone delivered the solo album to A&M Records, where it was scrutinized and sent to the vaults. It had also been some thirteen years since her untimely passing. Since the album was shelved in 1980, and particularly after her death in 1983, fans had been relentless in pushing for the album's release. They hoped that Karen would find some sort of posthumous vindication once the album made it onto record store shelves.

"People are *really* driving me crazy about the album," Richard had told Ramone several years earlier.

"Well, then why don't you put it out?" he urged.

Aside from Karen's, Ramone had never produced an album deemed unworthy of release, and the rejection weighed heavy on him. "Sixteen years of not having it out on the street made it very frustrating for me," he explains. "There were people who thought it was a disgrace or some crazy, silly album."

Prior to 1996 Richard had remixed several of Karen's solo tracks for a Carpenters album in 1989, then two others on a 1991 box set. The mixes were extremely well done and executed with Ramone's blessing, but he was afraid Karen's vision for the solo recordings might be lost if the entire project were subjected to this form of musical facelift. "We could have easily fixed them up and modernized them and changed some of the parts," Ramone says. "But personally, I like to think of it like a painting. It was done at a particular time, with Karen being the artist. . . . The solo album was something she really, really cared about, and as a friend who cared about her, I thought we should put out everything the way she wanted it."

The resulting eponymous album, *Karen Carpenter*, contained the eleven original recordings as approved by Karen in 1980, plus "Last One Singin' the Blues," an unmixed bonus track. "I have not remixed or done anything to the tapes," Ramone announced in the press release from A&M Records. "These mixes, the material and style, are the way Karen approved them. . . . As years passed, both Richard Carpenter and I wondered when it might be released. Together we stand proud as this was a piece that meant so much to Karen, it was truly a labor of love."

Contributing to the album liner notes, Richard declared, "Karen was with us precious little time. She was a great artist. This album reflects a certain period and change of approach in her career. As such it deserves to be heard, in its entirety, as originally delivered."

Prior to the album's release, Richard had phoned Itchie in hopes that she might unearth the album's original dedication. After consulting the notes she had saved from the project, she called him back: "Dedicated to my brother Richard with all my heart." According to Itchie, he bawled into the phone.

Despite the apparent change of heart, Richard did little to promote the album on Karen's behalf. "When it was released I thought Richard would get behind it," Ramone says. "That was the reason I said 'release it.' He didn't have to *embrace* it, but some of the interviews didn't give you the feeling of he had changed his mind."

Reviews for *Karen Carpenter* were mixed. Some reviewers made unreasonable comparisons to the Carpenters' biggest hits, as illustrated by David Brown in his "C+" review for *Entertainment Weekly*: "For anyone accustomed to hearing her virginal delivery on mope-pop standards like 'Goodbye to Love,' few things will be more disconcerting than the sound of Karen Carpenter loving to love you, baby."

Others reviewed the album without bias or preconception, like Tierney Smith of *Goldmine*, who cited Karen's warm and expressive vocals as the record's saving grace. "She brings a sweetness to the buoyant, gently ringing pop of Peter Cetera's 'Making Love in the Afternoon,' shines on the lovely understated country ballad 'All Because of You' and sounds right at home with the infectious mellow pop of 'Guess I Just Lost My Head.'"

Reviewing Karen's songs for *Rolling Stone*, Rob Hoerburger praised Ramone for recording her in what he called "leaner, decidedly unsaccharine settings... her vocals come damn close to soulful. Listening to them, it becomes apparent why singers like Chrissie Hynde, Madonna and Gloria Estefan have 'come out of the closet' and admitted they were Karen fans."

Paul Grein felt the album was not in any way the definitive portrait of Karen Carpenter, "nor was it intended to be," he clarified. "It is a provocative snapshot of her at the age of twenty-nine. Future projects, with Richard or other producers and artists, would have revealed still more facets of this complex woman and multidimensional artist."

Hoerberger agreed that, while it may not have been the album to define Karen Carpenter's career, it was on par with contemporaneous albums. "It holds up with anything that like-minded singers—Barbra Streisand and Olivia Newton-John—were recording at the time, and especially with anything the Carpenters put out immediately before or after. If there is no 'We've Only Just Begun' on the album, it doesn't really matter. Fans typically crave an artist's most personal work—even if it isn't a masterpiece.... [It] ends up a cherished souvenir from the collection of a woman who was never allowed more than a vacation from her own image."

THE WORLD in 1983 was not ready for *Karen Carpenter* the album—perhaps in 1980 but not 1983. For a period of several years following her death, appreciation for Karen's music went underground. The mere mention of her name would incite remarks like, "What a waste!" Or even questions like, "Wasn't she that singer who killed herself?" The tragedy appeared to have triumphed over the talent, and it would be years before this injustice would begin to unravel.

Within eight weeks of his sister's death, Richard Carpenter had returned to the recording studios at A&M Records, where he worked meticulously on what would become *Voice of the Heart*, a collection of outtakes and other previously unreleased songs, including several from Karen's last recording session in 1982. "It actually made the time a little bit easier," Richard shared with Paul Grein for *Billboard*. "I think if I'd just stayed home, it would have been that much more difficult. I felt strongly that the material shouldn't be stuck away on a shelf. Putting myself in a fan's position—if I'd never met Karen—I'd want to hear it."

Coinciding with the album's release, the Carpenters' star was unveiled on the Hollywood Walk of Fame on October 12, 1983. "This is a very sad day and at the same time a very special and beautiful day for my family and me," Richard told the 250 or so gathered for the occasion. "My only regret is that Karen is not physically here to share it with us, however I know she is very much alive in our minds and in our hearts." Their star, number 1,769, can be found at 6933 Hollywood Boulevard, just steps away from Grauman's Chinese Theatre.

Fueled by an intense television ad campaign, *Yesterday Once More*, a double-album set featuring twenty-four Carpenters hits, was issued in 1984. Its success prompted a tie-in video released the following year. The fourteen selections were compiled from various television appearances and promotional videos.

Richard released his first solo album, *Time*, in 1987, which featured his own lead vocals on six tracks and guest vocals by Dionne Warwick and Dusty Springfield. "Something in Your Eyes," recorded by Springfield, became a Top 20 hit on the adult contemporary charts. Richard's multitracked, a cappella tribute to Karen, "When Time Was All We Had," featured Herb Alpert on flugelhorn.

That same year, little-known filmmaker Todd Haynes directed and produced *Superstar: The Karen Carpenter Story*, a 16 mm, 43-minute film with a cast of Barbie-type dolls shot against a backdrop of miniature interiors. At first glance the film may have appeared to be a kitschy piece of mockery, but closer examination revealed a serious and sometimes touching and sympathetic account of Karen's life. Shown primarily at film festivals and small theaters throughout the United States, *Superstar*, nicknamed "the Barbie doll movie," garnered a huge underground following and by the year 2000 had earned a place at #45 on the *Entertainment Weekly* list of "Top 50 Cult Films of All Time."

Prior to the film's release, Haynes had attempted to license a number of original Carpenters recordings and other music for the production, but his requests were denied. When he proceeded to use the material for which he was denied permission, legal injunctions from Richard Carpenter ensued, and the film was withdrawn from distribution in 1990. In an open letter to Richard, Owen Gleiberman of *Entertainment Weekly* asked, "Will you please allow people to see Todd Haynes's *Superstar: The Karen Carpenter Story?*" and called it "one of the most startling, audacious and sheerly emotional films of the past decade." Gleiberman asserted that the film was not just a case study but a tribute to the duo's musical legacy. "Todd Haynes has turned Karen Carpenter's life into a singular work of art. Even for those who never cared about the Carpenters' music (but especially for those who did), it deserves to be seen."

In Richard's response, which appeared in the publication the following month, he explained that his issue with the film related not to its content but to the filmmaker's behavior. The fact remained that Haynes had distributed the film to numerous theaters after having been denied permission to utilize the Carpenters' recordings. According to Richard, "His decision to make his movie using this material amounted to a deliberate attack on the rights of those who Gleiberman now suggests ought to give their blessing to Haynes's exhibition of the movie."

The catalyst for a sweeping renaissance of interest in Karen's story and the music of the Carpenters came on January 1, 1989, with the premiere of *The Karen Carpenter Story* on CBS-TV. The revival has continued in varying degrees to this day. The New Year's Day airing took advantage of a captive holiday viewing audience, and the movie finished in first place for its rating week with 41 percent of televisions tuned in. It was the highest-rated television movie licensed by CBS in five years and second most watched for all of 1989, behind *I Know My First Name Is Steven.* "Carpenters Telepic Boosts Record Sales" reported *Variety.* According to their research, sales of the Carpenters' catalog soared some 400 percent in the two weeks immediately following the broadcast on CBS. Absent from record store shelves was a tie-in or soundtrack release. Two previously unreleased recordings debuted in the film, "You're the One" and "Where Do I Go from Here," outtakes from 1977 and 1978 respectively. Both appeared on *Lovelines,* a new Carpenters album released ten months later in October.

There had been more than twenty years of jibes and sneers—two decades of dismissing even Karen's best recordings as bland, homogenized, or saccharine sweet—but with the airing of this low-budget dramatization, prejudice against the Carpenters' recordings began to fade, revealing an extraordinary change in perception. Over time, Karen found her rightful home alongside other timeless vocalists like Frank Sinatra, Nat "King" Cole, and Sarah Vaughan. Not just that, but retro was in. At times it seemed almost cool to like the Carpenters. "Maybe it's just an overdue appreciation of a singer who, despite some terrible material, always had a pure pop voice," wrote Stephen Whitty in an article for the *San Jose Mercury News.* "Or maybe it's simply a twinge of '70s nostalgia. For baby boomers in their twenties, 'Close to You' was part of their AM-radio childhoods. But the Carpenters are back. And it's only just begun. Again."

The revival made its way from the United States to the United Kingdom, where in 1990 a "greatest hits" compilation, *Only Yesterday,* held the #1 spot for a total of seven weeks. Carpenters tribute acts surfaced in the United Kingdom as well. One featuring vocalist Wendy Roberts was even praised by Richard Carpenter, who was amazed to learn the act had sold out the London Palladium, just as the Carpenters had (many times over) in 1976.

Next came *The Carpenters: The Untold Story,* an authorized biography by former *Melody Maker* editor-in-chief Ray Coleman, who previously authored books about Eric Clapton, the Beatles, and others. Bound by restraints similar to those imposed on the writers of the 1989 TV movie, the author skirted around certain subjects and overlooked

others altogether in order to craft a book deemed worthy of the Carpenter family's stamp of approval. That same year, it was Coleman who
proclaimed the musical duo "too good to be through" in a feature for
The Sunday Times in London. "There is little doubt that Karen would
have enjoyed all the commotion," he wrote. "Fiercely ambitious, professional and proud, she was hurt by the taunts on the way up and would
have loved the irony of being considered retro-cool."

That retro-cool acceptance of the Carpenters' product was certainly
a long time coming. "It was a transformation in taste that took twenty
years," wrote Sue Cummings in *Trouble Girls: The* Rolling Stone *Book
of Women in Rock*, calling it a "renewed ironic appreciation. [Listeners]
had loved the veneer, then hated it, then found it even more compelling, on a second look, for the complexity in the places where the dark-
ness cracked through."

Also seeing release in 1995 was *If I Were a Carpenter*, a somewhat
questionable but highly successful tribute album featuring alternative
rock acts including Sonic Youth, Sheryl Crow, and the Cranberries.
The collection sparked interest in Carpenters music among yet another
generation of listeners, and co-producer David Konjoyan assured
the project was honest and in no way done with a tongue-in-cheek
approach: "While it's easy to dismiss all of this as just more quirky
campiness where the mediocrities of the past are celebrated as master-
pieces of the present—'Here's a story of a man named Brady' and all
that—there seems to be more to it than that."

Richard approved of the tribute, even making a guest appearance
on Matthew Sweet's interpretation of "Let Me Be the One." He felt
Karen, too, would have appreciated the sentiments backing the project.
"She'd like it for the same reasons I like it," he told *HITS* magazine.
"The people involved thought enough of our music or her talent to take
time out of their schedules to contribute, and that there continues to be,
after all these years, so much interest in our music."

The Carpenters revival wave crested in Japan again in 1996 with the
enormous success of *22 Hits of the Carpenters*. The collection included
two of the duo's songs that had been featured as opening and clos-
ing themes in a popular Japanese teen-oriented television drama called

Miseinen. Interest in "I Need to Be in Love" and "Top of the World" quickly pushed sales of the album over three million copies. "In the U.S., alternative rock and grunge are becoming mainstream, but in Japan, young people really don't want to listen to music that lacks melody," explained Shun Okano, product manager for the Japanese record label, in a feature for *Billboard.* "They like the Carpenters' pleasant melodies and beautiful harmonies. It sounds like something fresh and new to them."

Richard's focus moved back to the United States when in 1998 a twenty-song collection entitled *Love Songs* rode the American album chart for six months. This success was enhanced by the airing of the highly acclaimed *Close to You: Remembering the Carpenters* documentary produced for public television (PBS), as well as other television profiles on A&E's *Biography* and VH1's *Behind the Music.* Additionally, Richard released his second solo album, *Richard Carpenter: Pianist, Arranger, Composer, Conductor.* The album sent him back on tour for a series of shows with orchestras in Japan and several in Southern California. Its only single, "Karen's Theme," received moderate play on easy listening radio stations.

The Carpenters are one of only a few acts that made such an impact on the music scene in the 1970s and do not have a place in the Rock and Roll Hall of Fame. The museum has a reputation for inducting trendy acts based on the tastes of a select few executives, but even record mogul Mike Curb argues that the Carpenters were certainly catalysts for a musical trend during that decade and deserving of such recognition. "Their body of work was really good pop music with an edge," he says. "It was very fresh, pop rock and perfectly produced, but always produced with just enough edge. It didn't sound dated. It sounded fresh. When her voice would come on the radio, there was such a presence to those records that said this is not just a pop record, it's pop rock. They were competing with rock artists right and left."

Whether the duo belongs in the Rock and Roll Hall of Fame or not, interest in their music has never waned. In 2009 the Carpenters' *40/40 The Best Selection,* a forty-track compilation recognizing the duo's fortieth anniversary, debuted in Japan's Top 5. It was the highest debut ever for a Carpenters album in that territory and within a month went to #1. "Karen and Richard are the seventh American act to top Nielsen/SoundScan's Japanese chart in the past five years," revealed Paul Grein in his popular "Chart Watch" column online. "They follow Bon Jovi (*Have a Nice Day* and *Lost Highway*), Britney Spears (*Greatest Hits*), Destiny's Child (*#1's*), Linkin Park (*Minutes to Midnight*), Backstreet Boys (*Unbreakable*), and Madonna (*Hard Candy*)....Japan is the world's #2 music market, behind only the U.S."

"WERE YOU angry about Karen dying and finishing off your career as a superstar?" The question, posed by a reporter working for a 1990 *Daily Mirror* feature, surely caught him off guard, but Richard Carpenter paused only for a moment before answering: "Not angry, I'd say disappointed. There's nothing I'd rather be doing than making records with Karen. You know, when she died I actually had people saying that I should find another Carpenter. They said, 'You own the rights to the name.' I said 'You've got to be kidding.' Not for a split second would I have done that. There could never be another Karen Carpenter."

Richard has spent much of the last quarter century as a family man and patron of the arts in his community. On May 19, 1984, with best man Wes Jacobs at his side, he and Mary Elizabeth Rudolph wed in a private ceremony at Downey United Methodist Church. The couple had dated off and on for eight years. "[Richard] and Mary do not wish to commercialize their marriage," wrote Rosina Sullivan, "so there will be no pictures available through the fan club." On August 17, 1987, they welcomed their first child, a daughter, Kristi Lynn. This was the name chosen years earlier by her aunt Karen, who had hoped to one day have children of her own. The union of Richard and Mary produced four more children: Traci Tatum, born July 25, 1989; Mindi Karen, born July 7, 1992; Colin Paul, born July 20, 1994; and Taylor Mary, born December 5, 1998.

Following a lengthy period of poor health, Harold Carpenter died of heart failure in 1988 on his son's birthday, October 15, at the age of seventy-nine. Agnes Carpenter died November 10, 1996, at Good

Samaritan Hospital in Los Angeles after a lengthy illness and complications following triple-bypass heart surgery. She was laid to rest alongside her husband and daughter in the family crypt at Forest Lawn Cypress.

Tom Burris is remarried and resides with his wife and the couple's son in Lincoln, California, where he manages Aberdeen Burris Contractors. No longer at liberty to speak of his relationship with Karen, he declined to be interviewed for this book. "There's an agreement between me and the Carpenters where I don't reveal anything," he said in 2002. "That is primarily tied to personal information about the Carpenters, their finances, and things like that."

As construction of a new concert hall began on the campus of California State Long Beach, Richard Carpenter stepped forward with a one-million-dollar pledge. As a result, the 1,074-seat venue was named the Richard and Karen Carpenter Performing Arts Center. It was dedicated during a star-studded gala opening on October 1, 1994, which featured performances by Herb Alpert, Rita Coolidge, and Marilyn McCoo. The Carpenter Exhibit, a permanent display of awards and memorabilia, was added to the Center lobby in 2000, and on May 26, 2000, the university honored Richard with an honorary doctorate after his delivery of the commencement speech.

Richard and Mary remained in Downey until 2000, when they relocated their family to Thousand Oaks, California. They soon gained a reputation as generous supporters of the local arts community after pledging three million dollars to the Thousand Oaks Civic Arts Plaza. In exchange for the contribution, a park in front of the plaza was named the Mary and Richard Carpenter Plaza Park. "We weren't thinking about that amount when we had this in mind," Richard told a local reporter, "but we liked the look of where the name would go." In 2007 he and Mary were named Ventura County's Philanthropists of the Year.

In December 2003, Karen Carpenter's body, along with the bodies of her parents, was exhumed from the crypt at Forest Lawn Cypress and reinterred in a new Carpenter family mausoleum in the Tranquility Gardens at Pierce Brothers Valley Oaks Memorial Park in Westlake

Village, California. *Entertainment Tonight* explained that the cemetery in Cypress was more than an hour's drive for Richard, while the Westlake Village location was only minutes from his home in Thousand Oaks. "With room for six," they reported, "the 46,000-pound Partenope-style structure was constructed in Texas over seven months. It is polished sunset red with beautiful warmth and color and lively crystal patterns. Similar structures have a price range of $600,000."

Unaware of the move, a number of visitors arrived in Cypress that Christmas to pay their respects but were shocked to find the empty grave. Forest Lawn employees were unable to disclose any details but offered a rather palpable statement: "Miss Carpenter is no longer with us."

"IRREPLACEABLE." ALWAYS a master at crafting words into poetic song lyrics, John Bettis offered this one word recapitulation of Karen Carpenter. "*Irreplaceable*. Not just the voice, but the person. . . . She was just beginning to blossom as a person. There was so much there that very few people got to see: the sense of humor, the sense of life. There was a certain profundity to Karen. If you believe in all this old soul stuff, there was always a sense that Karen knew more than she had any right to know. She had a sense of feeling and understanding about people that was remarkable."

Olivia Newton-John cherishes her memories of Karen, their friendship, and their admiration for one another as fellow pop singers. She recalls her "perfect pitch, beautiful tone, beautiful interpretation of a lyric, and a very simple, very soothing sound" and says that the feeling in Karen's voice "can't be taught. It's a gift that she had that came from within."

Recalling Karen as an incredibly spirited person, Phil Ramone expresses regret that someone so feisty and vivacious never fully succeeded in breaking free and establishing a singular identity. "Her dreams of what a family and her life could be weren't accomplished," he says. "The top two things in her life—interchangeably—were her music and her family. There's no question how much she cared for her family, but they were a close-knit family with things that frustrated her. At the end of the day, no one really ever understood that she had some kind of an eating disorder. If life were reasonably fair, therapy would have been there for her ten years earlier. It just wasn't there."

Not a day goes by that Itchie Ramone does not think of Karen or is not reminded of her in some way. "What can one say about losing your best friend?" she asks, struggling to articulate the void. "In terms of her voice and her music, I still have her there, but I miss the company. I miss her wit. She was *very* witty! I miss us pulling jokes on each other. What can I say? She will forever remain in my heart. She was Lucy and I was Ethel."

"I feel very, very robbed. We all do," says Frenda Franklin. "Karen touched your life and embraced it with such laughter and fun and happiness. Her take on everything was so left of center, and she was *special*. It's an overused word, no question, but not in her case. She really, really was as unique a person as her voice was unique. I don't know how else to say it. You can't replace that."

ACKNOWLEDGMENTS

N WRITING this biography I have been assisted by hundreds of people and consider it to be a collaboration between the individuals who agreed to be interviewed and others who contributed to my research in a number of ways. Some shared articles, interviews, concert reviews, audio, and video footage. Others provided important documents, transcripts, photographs, and additional material. All played an important role in the telling of Karen Carpenter's life story.

Several important teachers supported my interest in the Carpenters as a youth and encouraged me to write about their lives and music: Elaine Garvin, Zonelle Rainbolt, Shannon Cunningham, Rebecca Gilchrist, and Billie Goetsch. I also wish to recognize several music educators who shared with me their passion for the art: the late JoAnn Carlson, Jennifer Wedel, Mike Plunkett, Suzanne Aylor, and Charles "Skip" Klingman.

I am grateful to Chicago Review Press for believing in *Little Girl Blue*, and to my meticulous editors, Yuval Taylor and Lisa Reardon, whose passion for this project has remained strong. Their endless support and thorough attention to detail is greatly appreciated.

Special thanks to artist Chris Tassin for his lovely rendering of Karen created exclusively for this book; to Dionne Warwick for her heartfelt foreword; to Petula Clark for her assistance; to Carrie Mitchum for inadvertently introducing me to Karen Carpenter's life story and music; to Barry Morrow, who, in addition to providing files, script revisions, and other important documents, gave this project a much-appreciated change of direction; to Cynthia Gibb and Mitchell Anderson; and to Cynthia Cherbak for sharing additional script revisions and correspondence.

My thanks to Karen's childhood friends Debbie Cuticello and husband C.J. for years of support and for the guided tour of Hall Street and Nathan Hale School in 1996; to Frank Bonito for his encouragement and contribution of previously unseen photos; to Frankie Chavez for sharing his memories of Karen and her inscription in his yearbook; to Leslie Johnston, who recalled the Spectrum era; and to choral music legend Frank Pooler for his contribution of various resources and photos from his personal archives.

Evelyn Wallace deserves a resounding thank-you, due in part to her willingness to recall enough "Karen stories" to fill eight audiotapes. I first met Ev in 1994. Three years later she personally guided me through the Carpenter estate at 9828 Newville Avenue, by then a time capsule akin to Elvis's Graceland. (The property remained in the Carpenter family until June 1997. Sadly, in 2008 a large portion of the home was demolished.) Ev was the personal connection to the Carpenters for fans of their music for nearly three decades. Collectively, her fan club newsletters serve as one of the most comprehensive resources for information about the Carpenters' lives and their music.

Words cannot express my gratitude to two of Karen's closest friends, Frenda Franklin and Karen "Itchie" Ramone. Extremely private and fiercely protective of her memories, Frenda (with rare exception) has not granted interviews regarding her friendship with Karen. As for Itchie, she became a cheerleader for my efforts with this book, just as she had been a cheerleader for Karen since the two first met in 1979. I am indebted to both Frenda and Itchie for their honesty and openness.

My thanks to Carole Curb for years of support and for encouraging Frenda to participate after six or seven years of my subtle but persistent efforts; to Mike Curb for taking time from his busy schedule as head of Curb Records to talk with me; to Maria Luisa Galeazzi, who shared numerous photographs and made herself readily available by phone and e-mail; to Terry Ellis, who surfaced just in time to share his remarkable insight and stories; to Cherry Boone O'Neill for her memories and observations; to Olivia Newton-John, whose initial phone call succeeded in permanently brightening my life; to Phil Ramone for a great interview and several much-appreciated follow-ups; and to Liberty DeVitto, Bob James, Russell Javors, and Rob Mounsey for recalling the 1979–1980 solo sessions.

Thanks to journalist Jon Burlingame, who interviewed Richard Carpenter on November 18, 1988. I appreciate Jon's willingness to dig for the tape and am especially grateful for his permission to transcribe and use the interview in this book. Thanks also to John Tobler for permission to use transcripts of his in-depth interviews with Herb Alpert, Sherwin Bash, and John Bettis.

Grateful acknowledgment is made to the following individuals and their respective institutions and organizations: Bob Garcia, former publicity director at A&M Records, for arranging a tour of A&M offices, studios, and the Chaplin soundstage in 1996; Jim O'Grady for research he conducted at the Downey City Library; Marilynn Hughes for records assistance at the Downey Police Department; Pamela R. Cornell at the Historical Research Center at the Houston Academy of Medicine-Texas Medical Center Library; Marsha Grigsby in the Office of the Los Angeles County Coroner; Michelle Dyson with National Medical Services in Pennsylvania; Bill Hosley of the New Haven Museum and Historical Society; Allen Rice of the Richard Nixon Presidential Library and Museum; David Konjoyan and Paul Madeira of the Recording Academy; Storytech Literary Consulting and Brad Schreiber; Donna Honeycutt, George Redfox, John Vincent, and Frank Williams at the Downey Historical Society; Kristie French with the Frank Pooler Collection at California State University Long Beach; Connie Griffin at the Richard and Karen Carpenter Performing Arts Center; Lauren Buisson with the A&M Records Collection at the University of Southern California Los Angeles; and Brooke Megdal, founder/director of the Loving Heart Center in Brentwood, California, for helping me to better understand anorexia nervosa and other eating disorders.

In 1994 I organized the Newville Avenue Carpenters Mailing List, one of the first and largest online networks devoted to the Carpenters. Much knowledge was shared and many friendships were born during the group's six-year existence. The fans are the experts, and I have learned so much from their willingness to share that expertise. Two generous fans in particular, Lindeigh Scotte and Cindy Ward, left us much too soon and too young. It is in memory of their giving spirits and kindness to all Carpenters fans that I dedicate this book.

Many thanks to my team of experts—Amanda Abbett, Carolyn Allen, Donnie Demers, Sue Gustin, and Chris Tassin—who spent countless hours attentively poring over my drafts, fact checking, and offering insightful comments and suggestions. I consider their knowledge and input to have been invaluable, and their patience is greatly appreciated. Also assisting in the reading of various chapter drafts were Jeffrey de Hart, Robert Ingves, and Paul Steinberg. Photo research assistance was provided by Miranda Bardwell, Donnie Demers, and Jill Anne Matusek, and special thanks to Matusek and Leo Bonaventura for their generosity in sponsoring several important photographs that might not otherwise have been possible. My appreciation also goes to Paul Ashurst, who shared copies of Karen's wedding scrapbook.

I am indebted to Pecan Creek Elementary for providing me with a creative and supportive environment in which to work. In addition to my principal, Aleta Atkinson, and assistant principal, Emily McLarty, the staff, students, and parents have been a cooperative and encouraging captive audience.

Thanks also to Laura Adam, Nancy Alexander, Randy Anglin, Viv Atkinson, Sherry Rayn Barnett, Nick Barraclough, Peter Benjaminson, Jeff Bleiel, Ken Bertwell, Joe Bine, Dana Britten-Stein, Ron Bunt, Chip Cogswell, Bradley Coker, Steve Cox, Mark Crow, Jason Douglas, Patrick Driscoll, Brenda Ehly, Heidi Ewing, Bob Finholm, Julia Foot, Ashley Franklin, Michael J. Glenn, David Grant, Becky Judd, Sydney Junior, Donovan Keogh, Carlos Keyes, Inga Kleinrichert, Jon Konjoyan, Jay Lumbee, Joshua Mahn, Cindy Martin, Rhonda Martinez, Chris May, Doug McComas, Bob McDonald, Bonnie Miller, Vicki Mitchell, Jena Morrow, Nancy Munoz, Yuka Ogura, Jonathan

Owen, Laura Pascoe, Mark Pelzel, Mary Perica, Samantha Peters, Ronald Pledge, Robert Polston, Ying Qin, Pam Quiggle, Matt Ramone, Stephen Richardson, Jaime Rodriguez, Celso Lopes Santos, Victoria Sarinelli, Bonnie Schiffman, Jennifer Schmidt, Norma Segarra, Daniel Selby, Julie Stanfield, Jeffrey Strain, Tiana Galeazzi Taylor, J.B. Thomas, Vickie VanArtsdalen, Pamela Verona, Denise Wagorn, Kimberly Wall, Cindy Williams, and Ron Zurek.

Finally, I wish to thank my family for their love and support: my parents, Linda Schmidt and Ron and Frances Schmidt; my sister, Rhonda Morrison; and my beautiful, talented, and entertaining daughters, Camryn and Kaylee.

SELECTED DISCOGRAPHY

<hr>

THE CARPENTERS released ten traditional studio albums between the years 1969 and 1981. This selected discography refers to each original conception as first released on A&M Records in the United States. Singles from each album are noted, as are peak U.S. chart positions for both albums and singles. Only the most significant posthumous releases and compilations (notably those containing previously unreleased material) are included. Also listed are Karen's solo releases and other various issues.

CARPENTERS

Offering / Ticket to Ride   (A&M 4205)   1969 (#150)
Invocation / Your Wonderful Parade / Someday / Get Together / All of My Life / Turn Away / Ticket to Ride / Don't Be Afraid / What's the Use / All I Can Do / Eve / Nowadays Clancy Can't Even Sing / Benediction

SINGLES:
Ticket to Ride / Your Wonderful Parade (#54)

Close to You   (A&M 4271)   1970 (#2)
We've Only Just Begun / Love Is Surrender / Maybe It's You / Reason to Believe / Help / (They Long to Be) Close to You / Baby It's You / I'll Never Fall in Love Again / Crescent Noon / Mr. Guder / I Kept on Loving You / Another Song

SINGLES:
(They Long to Be) Close to You / I Kept on Loving You (#1)
We've Only Just Begun / All of My Life (#2)

Carpenters (A&M 3502) 1971 (#2)

Rainy Days and Mondays / Saturday / Let Me Be the One / (A Place to) Hideaway / For All We Know / Superstar / Druscilla Penny / One Love / Bacharach-David Medley: Knowing When to Leave, Make It Easy on Yourself, (There's) Always Something There to Remind Me, I'll Never Fall in Love Again, Walk On By, Do You Know the Way to San Jose / Sometimes

SINGLES:
For All We Know / Don't Be Afraid (#3)
Rainy Days and Mondays / Saturday (#2)
Superstar / Bless the Beasts and Children (#2 / 67)

A Song for You (A&M 3511) 1972 (#4)

A Song for You / Top of the World / Hurting Each Other / It's Going to Take Some Time / Goodbye to Love / Intermission / Bless the Beasts and Children / Flat Baroque / Piano Picker / I Won't Last a Day Without You / Crystal Lullaby / Road Ode / A Song for You—Reprise

SINGLES:
Hurting Each Other / Maybe It's You (#2)
It's Going to Take Some Time / Flat Baroque (#12)
Goodbye to Love / Crystal Lullaby (#7)
I Won't Last a Day Without You / One Love (#11)

Now & Then (A&M 3519) 1973 (#2)

Sing / This Masquerade / Heather / Jambalaya (On the Bayou) / I Can't Make Music / Yesterday Once More / Oldies Medley: Fun, Fun, Fun, The End of the World, Da Doo Ron Ron, Deadman's Curve, Johnny Angel, The Night Has a Thousand Eyes, Our Day Will Come, One Fine Day / Yesterday Once More—Reprise

SINGLES:
Sing / Druscilla Penny (#3)
Yesterday Once More / Road Ode (#2)

The Singles: 1969–1973 (A&M 3601) 1973 (#1)

We've Only Just Begun / Top of the World / Ticket to Ride / Superstar / Rainy Days and Mondays / Goodbye to Love / Yesterday Once More / It's

Going to Take Some Time / Sing / For All We Know / Hurting Each Other
/ (They Long to Be) Close to You

SINGLES:
Top of the World / Heather (#1)

Horizon (A&M 4530)   1975 (#13)
Aurora / Only Yesterday / Desperado / Please Mr. Postman / I Can Dream,
Can't I? / Solitaire / Happy / (I'm Caught Between) Goodbye and I Love
You / Love Me for What I Am / Eventide

SINGLES:
Please Mr. Postman / This Masquerade (#1)
Only Yesterday / Happy (#4)
Solitaire / Love Me for What I Am (#17)

A Kind of Hush (A&M 4581)   1976 (#33)
There's a Kind of Hush (All Over the World) / You / Sandy / Goofus /
Can't Smile Without You / I Need to Be in Love / One More Time / Boat
to Sail / I Have You / Breaking Up Is Hard to Do

SINGLES:
There's a Kind of Hush (All Over the World) / (I'm Caught Between)
    Goodbye and I Love You (#12)
I Need to Be in Love / Sandy (#25)
Goofus / Boat to Sail (#56)

Passage (A&M 4703)   1977 (#49)
B'wana She No Home / All You Get from Love Is a Love Song / I Just
Fall in Love Again / On the Balcony of Casa Rosada / Don't Cry for Me,
Argentina / Sweet, Sweet Smile / Two Sides / Man Smart, Woman Smarter
/ Calling Occupants of Interplanetary Craft (The Recognized Anthem of
World Contact Day)

SINGLES:
All You Get from Love Is a Love Song / I Have You (#35)
Calling Occupants of Interplanetary Craft / Can't Smile Without You
    (#32)
Sweet, Sweet Smile / I Have You (#44)

Christmas Portrait (A&M 4726)   1978 (#145)
O Come, O Come Emmanuel / Overture: Deck the Halls, I Saw Three
Ships, Have Yourself a Merry Little Christmas, God Rest Ye Merry

Gentlemen, Away in a Manger, What Child Is This (Greensleeves), Carol of the Bells, O Come All Ye Faithful / The Christmas Waltz / Sleigh Ride / It's Christmas Time / Sleep Well, Little Children / Have Yourself a Merry Little Christmas / Santa Claus Is Coming to Town / The Christmas Song / Silent Night / Jingle Bells / The First Snowfall / Let It Snow / Carol of the Bells / Merry Christmas, Darling / I'll Be Home for Christmas / Christ Is Born / Medley: Winter Wonderland, Silver Bells, White Christmas / Ave Maria

SINGLES:
Christmas Song / Merry Christmas, Darling

Made in America (A&M 3723)   1981 (#52)

Those Good Old Dreams / Strength of a Woman / (Want You) Back in My Life Again / When You've Got What It Takes / Somebody's Been Lyin' / I Believe You / Touch Me When We're Dancing / When It's Gone (It's Just Gone) / Beechwood 4-5789 / Because We Are in Love (The Wedding Song)

SINGLES:
I Believe You / B'wana She No Home (#68)
Touch Me When We're Dancing / Because We Are in Love (#16)
(Want You) Back in My Life Again / Somebody's Been Lyin' (#72)
Those Good Old Dreams / When It's Gone (It's Just Gone) (#63)
Beechwood 4-5789 / Two Sides (#74)

Voice of the Heart (A&M 4954)   1983 (#46)

Now / Sailing on the Tide / You're Enough / Make Believe It's Your First Time / Two Lives / At the End of a Song / Ordinary Fool / Prime Time Love / Your Baby Doesn't Love You Anymore / Look to Your Dreams

SINGLES:
Make Believe It's Your First Time / Look to Your Dreams
Your Baby Doesn't Love You Anymore / Sailing on the Tide

An Old-Fashioned Christmas (A&M 3270)   1984 (#190)

It Came Upon a Midnight Clear / Overture: Happy Holiday, The First Noel, March of the Toys, Little Jesus, I Saw Mommy Kissing Santa Claus, O Little Town of Bethlehem, In Dulci Jubilo, Gesu Bambino, Angels We Have Heard on High / An Old-Fashioned Christmas / O Holy Night / (There's No Place Like) Home for the Holidays / Medley: Here Comes Santa Claus, Frosty the Snowman, Rudolph the Red-Nosed Reindeer, Good King Wenceslas / Little Altar Boy / Do You Hear What I Hear? / My Favorite

Things / He Came Here for Me / Santa Claus Is Comin' to Town / What Are You Doing New Year's Eve? / Selections from "The Nutcracker" / I Heard the Bells on Christmas Day

SINGLES:
Little Altar Boy / Do You Hear What I Hear? (promo)

Lovelines (A&M 3931)   1989
Lovelines / Where Do I Go from Here? / The Uninvited Guest / If We Try / When I Fall in Love / Kiss Me the Way You Did Last Night / Remember When Lovin' Took All Night / You're the One / Honolulu City Lights / Slow Dance / If I Had You / Little Girl Blue

SINGLES:
Honolulu City Lights / I Just Fall in Love Again
If I Had You / The Uninvited Guest (promo)

Interpretations: A 25th Anniversary Celebration   (A&M 3145403122)
                                                              1994
Without a Song (a cappella version) / Superstar / Rainy Days and Mondays / Bless the Beasts and Children / This Masquerade / Solitaire / When I Fall in Love / From This Moment On / Tryin' to Get the Feeling Again / When It's Gone / I Believe You / Reason to Believe / (They Long to Be) Close to You / Calling Occupants of Interplanetary Craft / Little Girl Blue / We've Only Just Begun

The Essential Collection: 1965–1997 (A&M 0694934162)   2002

DISC 1: Caravan / The Parting of Our Ways / Looking for Love / I'll Be Yours / Iced Tea / You'll Love Me / All I Can Do / Don't Be Afraid / Invocation / Your Wonderful Parade / All of My Life / Eve / Ticket to Ride / Get Together / Interview / Love Is Surrender / Maybe It's You / (They Long to Be) Close to You / Mr. Guder / We've Only Just Begun / Merry Christmas, Darling / For All We Know

DISC 2: Rainy Days and Mondays / Superstar / Let Me Be the One / Bless the Beasts and Children / Hurting Each Other / It's Going to Take Some Time / I Won't Last a Day Without You / A Song for You / Top of the World / Goodbye to Love / This Masquerade / Sing / Jambalaya (On the Bayou) / Yesterday Once More / Oldies Medley: Fun, Fun, Fun, The End of the World, Da Doo Ron Ron, Deadman's Curve, Johnny Angel, The Night Has a Thousand Eyes, Our Day Will Come, One Fine Day / Yesterday Once More—Reprise / Radio Contest Outtakes

Disc 3: Morinaga Hi-Crown Chocolate Commercial / Please Mr. Postman / Santa Claus Is Coming to Town / Only Yesterday / Solitaire / Tryin' to Get the Feeling Again / Good Friends Are for Keeps / Ordinary Fool / Sandy / There's a Kind Of Hush (All Over the World) / I Need to Be in Love / From This Moment On / Suntory Pop Jingle #1 / Suntory Pop Jingle #2 / All You Get from Love Is a Love Song / Calling Occupants of Interplanetary Craft / Sweet, Sweet Smile / Christ Is Born / White Christmas / Little Altar Boy / Ave Maria

Disc 4: Where Do I Go From Here? / Little Girl Blue / I Believe You / If I Had You / Karen-Ella Medley: This Masquerade, My Funny Valentine, I'll Be Seeing You, Someone to Watch over Me, As Time Goes By, Don't Get Around Much Any More, I Let a Song Go out of My Heart / 1980 Medley: Sing, Knowing When to Leave, Make It Easy on Yourself, Someday, We've Only Just Begun / Make Believe It's Your First Time / Touch Me When We're Dancing / When It's Gone (It's Just Gone) / Because We Are in Love (The Wedding Song) / Those Good Old Dreams / Now / Karen's Theme

As Time Goes By (A&M 0694931122)   2004
Without a Song / Medley: Superstar, Rainy Days and Mondays / Nowhere Man / I Got Rhythm Medley / Dancing in the Street / Dizzy Fingers / You're Just in Love / Karen-Ella Fitzgerald Medley: This Masquerade, My Funny Valentine, I'll Be Seeing You, Someone to Watch Over Me, As Time Goes By, Don't Get Around Much Anymore, I Let a Song Go Out of My Heart / Medley: Close Encounters, Star Wars / Leave Yesterday Behind / Carpenters-Perry Como Medley: Yesterday Once More, Magic Moments, Sing, Catch a Falling Star, Close to You, It's Impossible, We've Only Just Begun, And I Love You So, Don't Let the Stars Get in Your Eyes, Till the End of Time, No Other Love Have I / California Dreamin' / The Rainbow Connection / '76 Hits Medley: Sing, Close to You, For All We Know, Ticket to Ride, Only Yesterday, I Won't Last a Day Without You, Goodbye to Love / And When He Smiles

KAREN CARPENTER

Looking for Love / I'll Be Yours (single) (Magic Lamp ML704)   1966

Karen Carpenter (A&M 3145405882)   1996
Lovelines / All Because of You / If I Had You / Making Love in the Afternoon / If We Try / Remember When Lovin' Took All Night / Still in Love

with You / My Body Keeps Changing My Mind / Make Believe It's Your
First Time / Guess I Just Lost My Head / Still Crazy After All These Years /
Last One Singin' the Blues

RICHARD CARPENTER TRIO

Battle of the Bands   (Custom Fidelity 1533)   1966
Includes: The Girl from Ipanema / Iced Tea

SELECTED TELEVISION APPEARANCES

THIS LIST includes all known appearances by Karen Carpenter on American television during her lifetime. Since many of the programs were syndicated, occasional discrepancies between air dates exist. Other inconsistencies have been found in past publications (notably the Carpenters Fan Club's *Decade* publication from 1979), which have not always distinguished between the taping and broadcast dates. Whenever possible, corrections have been made here to reflect the earliest known air dates.

1966

07/03 *Battle of the Bands! (Richard Carpenter Trio, KNBC-TV, Los Angeles)*

1968

06/22 *Your All-American College Show (Richard Carpenter Trio)*
06/29 *Your All-American College Show (Richard Carpenter Trio)*

1969

09/09 *Your All-American College Show (Karen Carpenter)*

11/23   *Your All-American College Show (Karen Carpenter)*
12/01   *Your All-American College Show (Carpenters)*
12/04   *The Della Reese Show*

1970

01/18   *Lohman & Barkley's Name Droppers*
06/24   *The Virginia Graham Show*
07/20   *The Dating Game*
09/15   *The Don Knotts Show*
09/18   *The Tonight Show*
10/02   *The David Frost Show*
10/18   *The Ed Sullivan Show*
11/08   *The Ed Sullivan Show*
11/13   *The Tonight Show*
11/14   *American Bandstand*

1971

01/24   *Peggy Fleming at Sun Valley*
02/13   *The Andy Williams Show*
02/18   *This Is Your Life*
03/16   *The Grammy Awards*
03/24   *The Johnny Cash Show*
06/30   *The Tonight Show*
07/13   *Make Your Own Kind of Music*
07/20   *Make Your Own Kind of Music*
07/27   *Make Your Own Kind of Music*
07/29   *The Mike Douglas Show*
08/03   *Make Your Own Kind of Music*
08/10   *Make Your Own Kind of Music*
08/17   *Make Your Own Kind of Music*
08/18   *The 5th Dimension Traveling Sunshine Show*
08/24   *Make Your Own Kind of Music*
08/31   *Make Your Own Kind of Music*
09/22   *The Carol Burnett Show*
11/05   *The Tonight Show*

1972

01/14   *The Ed Sullivan Show*
01/19   *The Carol Burnett Show*
02/21   *Jerry Visits (Jerry Dunphy)*
03/14   *The Grammy Awards*
04/10   *The Academy Awards*
05/07   *The Special London Bridge Special*
10/05   *The Bob Hope Special*

1973

06/01   *Robert Young with the Young*
11/05   *The Tonight Show*
11/13   *The Bob Hope Special*

1974

03/02   *The Grammy Awards*
08/04   *Evening at Pops*
12/17   *The Perry Como Christmas Show*

1975

02/18   *The American Music Awards*

1976

05/22   *The Midnight Special*
11/17   *The Dorothy Hamill Special*
12/08   *The Carpenters' Very First Television Special*

1977

01/27   *The Tonight Show (Steve Martin, host)*
12/09   *The Carpenters at Christmas*

1978

02/05	*The ABC Silver Anniversary Celebration*
03/16	*Thank You, Rock and Roll*
05/17	*The Carpenters: Space Encounters*
06/27	*The Tonight Show (John Davidson, host)*
11/19	*Wonderful World of Disney: Mickey's 50*
12/19	*The Carpenters: A Christmas Portrait*

1980

03/13	*20/20*
04/14	*Olivia Newton-John: Hollywood Nights*
05/16	*The Carpenters: Music, Music, Music*

1981

07/11	*America's Top Ten*
08/10	*Good Morning America*
10/02	*The Merv Griffin Show*

1983

| 01/11 | *Entertainment Tonight* |

NOTES

THE PRIMARY interviews on which this work is based were conducted by the author between the years 2001 and 2009. Other important interviews were made available by journalists Jon Burlingame (Richard Carpenter) and John Tobler (Herb Alpert, Sherwin Bash, and John Bettis). Numerous interviews with Karen Carpenter and others were culled from diverse publications, as well as television and radio archives, and are identified in the following pages of sources. As a rule, quotations presented in *past* tense are from existing interviews and other secondary sources. Those quotes offered in *present* tense originate from the author's personal interviews, consultations, or correspondence with the following individuals:

John "Softly" Adrian, Mitchell Anderson, Carolyn Arzac, Tom Bähler, Lou Beach, Max Bennett, Ken Bertwell, Dick Biondi, Hal Blaine, Frank Bonito, David Brenner, Denny Brooks, Bill Catalde, Frankie Chavez, Cynthia Cherbak, Petula Clark, Marion Connellan, Carole Curb, Mike Curb, C.J. Cuticello, Debbie Cuticello, Liberty DeVitto, Digby Diehl, Gioia Diliberto, Veta Dixon, Irv Edwards, Florine Elie, Terry Ellis, Allyn Ferguson, Frenda Franklin, Wanda Freeman, Dan Friberg, Maria Luisa Galeazzi, Dave Gelly, Cynthia Gibb, Victor Guder, Walt Harrah, Bill Hosley, Bob James, Jerry Jaskulski, Russell Javors, Leslie Johnston, Mickey Jones, Arthur Johns, Pete Jolly, Michael Lansing, Gayle Levant, Art LeVasseur, Charlene McAlister, Tex McAlister, Brooke Megdal, Ollie Mitchell, Barry Morrow, Claude Mougin, Rob Mounsey, Maxine Mundt, Nancy Naglin, Olivia Newton-John, Roger Nichols, Cherry Boone O'Neill, Glen Pace, John Pisano, David Pomerantz, Frank Pooler, Karen "Itchie" Ramone, Phil Ramone, David Robson, Evie Sands, Bonnie Schiffman, Brad Schreiber, Randy Sparks, Stephanie Spruill, Linda Stewart, John Tobler, Pat Tomlin, Charlie Tuna, Teresa Vaiuso, Evelyn Wallace, Dionne Warwick, Paul Williams

PROLOGUE: RAINY DAYS AND *RAIN MAN*

The first draft just   RC to Burlingame, 1988.
You don't know the first   Morrow, September 30, 1987.
What would possess   Carpenter, 1988.
genetic, the same way   Littwin, 1988.
Have you told her   Morrow and Cherbak, December 24, 1987.
If there's an arch-villain   Miller, 1989.

1. CALIFORNIA DREAMIN'

Mom was known for   Dosti, 1971.
I did everything   KC to Moore, 1981.
I was a tremendous   Oppenheimer, 1972.
It was slightly embarrassing   Gautschy, 1971.
She can take care   Oppenheimer, 1972.

2. CHOPSTICKS ON BARSTOOLS

Head down the Santa Ana   Charlesworth, 1973.
He'd been playing the drums   Hardwick, 1973.
I used to march   Hardwick, 1973.
I finally had to   Hardwick, 1973.
All I ever heard   KC to Tuna, 1976.
We met in theory class   Cameron, 2009.
I can't really remember   Coleman, 1975.
It's kind of corny   Coleman, November 8, 1975.
He heard this voice   Coleman, November 8, 1975.
I remember when   Coleman, November 8, 1975.
The musical surprise   Feather, 1966.

It was really great playing   Cameron, 2009.
She didn't strike me   McGreevy, February 5, 1983.

3. STAND IN LINE, TRY TO CLIMB

They had very strict regiments   Bettis to Tobler, 1993.
We got all the way   Bettis to Tobler, 1993.
He used to perform   Bettis to Tobler, 1993.
I was heavier   Hardwick, 1973.
All the guys   Hardwick, 1973.
People hear what we accomplished   "John Bettis Interview 2007," 2007.
You had to wait   Thegze, 1972.
The customers sat   Tatham, 1976: 12.
At first, the audience   Tatham, 1976: 12.
Since Richard did all   KC to Radio Clyde, 1978.
Wow, we couldn't believe   Diehl, 1971.
What good is biology   KC to Biondi, 1970.

4. SPRINKLED MOONDUST

I had it for about   Lees, 1972.
I put on the tape   Alpert to Tobler, 1994.
encouraging them to reach   Pfenninger, 2001.
It doesn't matter   Alpert to Tobler, 1994.
couldn't keep enough albums   Goldsmith, 1970.
Offering tends toward   Nolan, 1975.
fresh and original concepts   Billboard, 1970.
The first album did   Alpert to Tobler, 1994.
Thank God it didn't fit   KC to Roberts.
It was about borrowing money   KC to Biondi, 1970.

5. YOU PUT US ON THE ROAD

[Richard] called me, and   Cameron, 2009.
The five-member group is   Hilburn, 1970.
Everything seems to be going   Kraus, 1970.
Looking back, it's a bit   Tobler, 1998: 26.
Every direction we could have   KC to Nite, 1977.
The vocal harmonies, the construction   Bash to Tobler, 1990.
I'd never seen anything   Nolan, 1974.

suburban dream home   Forbes, 1973.
They all have names   MacDougall, 1971.
We can live   Small, 1972.
library full of bank books   Bash to Tobler, 1990.
It took some doing   Bash to Tobler, 1990.
I've seen enough groupies   Gautschy, 1972.
We got along fine   Haber, 1974.
Karen Carpenter has one of   Erlich, 1971.
Each number is introduced   Miller, 1971.
like dressing Karen Carpenter   Heckman, 1971.
violently mishandled   KC to Goldman, 1978.

6. NOTHING TO HIDE BEHIND _____

There are only three kits   Henshaw, 1974.
There is no balance   Bangs, 1971.
Hire a drummer   Bresette, 1971.
Richard and I tried desperately   Bash to Tobler, 1990.
A lot of people think   Kraus, 1970.
I said to Richard   Coleman, November 8, 1975.
In the middle of   KC to Douglas, 1971.
Petrified   KC to Tuna, 1976.
I didn't know   KC to Moore, 1981.
I understood her reluctance   Bash to Tobler, 1990.
Richard didn't have   Pogoda, 1994.
When I got the record   Bettis to Tobler, 1993.
That was the first ballad   Bettis to Tobler, 1993.
When I got in   Bettis to Tobler, 1993.
Far and away   Holden, 1972.
Nothing. That's why   Legge, 1974.
The man who produced   Daugherty, 1994.
Karen is in some ways   Nolan, 1974.
a very strong attempt   Bash to Tobler, 1990.
Being the only girl   MacDougall, 1971.
They are quite gracious   Nolan, 1974.

7. AMERICA AT ITS VERY BEST? _____

About 10,000 pounds   Associated Press, 1972.

I want to talk   Nixon, 1974.

We were afraid   KC to Blackburn, 1974.

Well, are you going to   Bettis to Tobler, 1993.

The Carpenters have gone awry   Bangs, 1973.

We were told   Coleman, November 8, 1975.

Real nice American kids   Pleasants, 1972.

Karen may eat   Rosenfeld, 1973.

They were not rock   Hoerburger, 2008.

I would say   Bangs, 1971.

It's not enough   Alpert to Tobler, 1994.

A number of people   Tobler, 1974.

the worst case of   Smucker, 1975.

When 'We've Only Just Begun'   Hoerburger, 1996.

Contrary to what they write   Haber, 1974.

At one point   KC to Aspel, 1981.

It's no good when   Haber, 1974.

8. MOVING OUT

Whereas Richard may not   Van Valkenburg, 1973.

I'm sure in her own   Bash to Tobler, 1990.

Their inability to develop   Bash to Tobler, 1990.

Cooking is an art   A&M Press Release, 1971.

The expectation was that   Bash to Tobler, 1990.

If we don't see   KC to Aspel, 1981.

There were lots of suggestions   Southall, 2004.

I remember once   Short, 1977.

Maybe it would have been   Short, 1976.

It's been a hell   Short, 1976.

We might as well   Nolan, 1974.

We've made it a rule   Short, 1976.

Richard can have his girl   Haber, 1974.

All of a sudden   Bettis to Tobler, 1993.

A&M took a little   Bettis to Tobler, 1993.

I don't think he   Bash to Tobler, 1990.

Karen was on an edge   Southall, 2004.

Not much showmanship   Variety, 1974.

9. THE COLLAPSE

If anorexia has   Hoerburger, 1996.
When you're on the road   Hardwick, 1973.
With their success   Bash to Tobler, 1990.
most musically sophisticated   Holden, 1975.
Oh boy, here we go   Bettis to Tobler, 1993.
such a gem   Holden, 1975.
She sings very close   Gelly, 1990.
soft-rock Nirvana   Barnes, 1975.
I talked her into   Bash to Tobler, 1990.
She is terribly thin   *Variety*, August 24, 1975.
[Harold] was beside himself   Vaiuso, 2004.
Anorexia nervosa was so new   Bettis to Tobler, 1993.
a tremendous amount of   Bash to Tobler, 1990.
In contrast to my   Sedaka, 1982.
I don't know what happened   Bash to Tobler, 1990.
When I left the stage   Sedaka, 1982.
I got a phone call   Bash to Tobler, 1990.
It wasn't Karen   Bash to Tobler, 1990.
the first time   McNally, 1976.
It often happens   Wallace, October 1975.
Current fortnight with Neil Sedaka   *Variety*, September 3, 1975.
I kept telling myself   Coleman, November 1, 1975.
I felt bad for Richard   Short, 1976.
When Richard returned   Short, 1976.
My mother thought   Coleman, November 1, 1975.
People never think   Coleman, November 1, 1975.

10. I NEED TO BE IN LOVE

We had a thing   Short, 1976.
It was sickening   Windeler, 1976.
an overdose of pretty   McNally, 1976.
a little ball of twine   Bettis to Tobler, 1993.
When he wrote the lyrics   KC to Tuna, 1976.
'I Need to Be in Love'   Bettis to Tobler, 1993.
My mind starts going   Coleman, November 8, 1975.
It's really hard   Windeler, 1976.
Well, I have my list   KC to Tuna, 1976.

I want a husband   Short, 1976.
It really hits me   KC to Tuna, 1976.
When we first   KC to Leonard, 1976.
It is just drums   KC to Tuna, 1976.
He's so talented   Coleman, November 8, 1975.
Karen is the star   Lieberman, 1973.
We're hams   Coleman, 1976.
They pretend for a   Coleman, 1976.
polite plastic pop   Evans, 1976.
They were not only   Sinor, 1976.
I've discussed this   KC to Radio Clyde, 1978.
I never had a boyfriend   Coleman, November 8, 1975.
I want desperately to   St. John, 1977.
I don't know anyone   Bash to Tobler, 1990.
You see, I so much   Short, 1976.

11. JUST LET US KNOW WHAT THE PROBLEM IS! _____

a streak that nobody   Feldman, 2000: 140.
Each time you get   KC to Nite, 1977.
The image we have   Nolan, 1974.
It's no worse   Windeler, 1976.
When he said 'yes,'   Coleman, November 8, 1975.
It had to be done   Short, 1976.
For the last three years   Moran, 1978.
most boldly innovative   Billboard, 1977.
We thought it was   Theroux, 1978.
[He] wanted to do that   KC to Goldman, 1978.
experimental touches that   Hilburn, February 13, 1983.
This is the first time   Grein, 1978.
We always try   Naglin, 1978.
After all these years   Coleman, 1977.
Too many artists forget   Bash to Tobler, 1990.
In this business   Short, 1977.
We just don't know   Moran, 1978.
We're very dedicated   Coleman, November 8, 1975.
You are the Perry Comos   Coleman, 1994: 214.
We stayed away from television   KC to Goldman, 1978.
Each one, in our opinion   KC to Goldman, 1978.
The Carpenters should have   Grein, March 8, 1991.

It's something I would   Moran, 1978.
Streisand just floors me   KC to Tuna, 1976.
There was one album   KC to Radio Clyde, 1978.
To sing these songs   KC to Sky, 1978.
They've synthesized everything   Parade, 1978.
Christmas Portrait *is really*   "Carpenters Biography," 2005.

12. THE BIRD HAS FINALLY FLOWN THE COOP

I was up   RC to Burlingame, 1988.
Taken properly they were   RC to Burlingame, 1988.
One side of me   Carpenter, 1988.
That's it   Coleman, 1994: 239.
My hands were shaking   Carpenter, 1988.
The Carpenters finally arrived   Carney, 1978.
You get pretty devious   Carpenter, 1988.
Karen wants everyone   Ewbank, 1978.
It was OK   Grein, 1981.
Confrontation about album   Coleman, 1994: 244.
That is the ultimate compliment   Coleman, November 8, 1975.
Everybody is trying new things   KC to Radio Clyde, 1978.
We have often thought   KC to Radio Clyde, 1978.
the Quincy Jones of   Hoerburger, 1990.
It was never planned   Grein, 1981.

13. POCKETS FULL OF GOOD INTENTIONS

The laughs and silliness   Ramone, 2007.
If he hadn't been   Grein, 1981.
Was Billy's group perfect   Ramone, 2007.

14. WHITE LACE AND BROKEN PROMISES

He really didn't know   KC to Moore, 1981.
He gets along fabulously   Mackay, 1980.
shelved at her request   Grein, 1980.
Karen thought about it   Grein, 1980.
I get the blame   Carpenter, 1993.
To everybody's credit   Coleman, 1994: 271.
I don't exactly *remember*   Alpert, 1996.

We didn't think it   Moss, 2007.
It's a good album   Grein, 1981.
Pisceans have marriage   Jillson, 1980.
We were planning on   KC to Aspel, 1981.
I invited everybody   KC to Aspel, 1981.

15. BEGINNING OF THE END

I love it   KC to Japanese All-American Top 40 Show, 1981.
When all the ingredients gelled   Tobler, 1998: 94.
Innocuous ditties like   Grein, July 25, 1981.
Richard, I realize   Carpenter, 1983.

16. DANCING IN THE DARK

the day she walked   Levenkron, 1993.
The therapist must develop   Levenkron, 1982: 21.
She would never call me   Bash to Tobler, 1990.
You are the victim   Levenkron, 1982: 191.
The victims must learn   Levenkron, 1982: 193.
I did everything   Carpenter, 1993.
Failure of the family   Levenkron, 1982: 173.
I gotta sing.   Coleman, 1976.
A lot of people   KC to Roberts, 1981.
less-than-perfect treatment   Coleman, 1994: 303.
What I find interesting   Levenkron, 1993.
sophisticated form of suicide   O'Neill, 1982: ix.
When are you going to   O'Neill, 1982: 157.
I did it   O'Neill, 1982: 157.
They say I have anorexia   Vaiuso, 2004.
Karen, this is crap   Carpenter, 2007.
The extent of her bravery   Levin, 1983.
She was a little anxious   Levin, 1983.

17. TOO LITTLE, TOO LATE, TOO SOON

Hey, look at me   Alpert to Tobler, 1994.
She was full of energy   Wallace, July 1983.
I want you to know   Carpenter, 1993.
It's not that I   Carpenter, 1993.

Well, did you   Coleman, 1994: 25.

She had just laid down   Agnes Carpenter, 1983.

It was a chilling scene   National Enquirer, 1983.

Those things don't hit you   Bettis to Tobler, 1993.

My immediate reaction   Carpenter, 1983.

It's hardly surprising   Smith, 1983.

It never occurred to me   Diliberto, 1985.

According to the L.A. Coroner   Levenkron, 1983.

In the last twenty years   Levenkron, 2001: 12.

Most kept their visits short   Pickney, 1983.

always got along   Levin, 1983.

EPILOGUE: A SONG FOR YOU _____

For anyone accustomed to   Browne, 1996.

She brings a sweetness   Smith, 1996.

leaner, decidedly unsaccharine   Hoerburger, 1990.

nor was it intended   Grein, 1996.

It holds up with   Hoerburger, 1996.

It actually made   Grein, 1983.

Will you please allow   Gleiberman, 1991.

His decision to make   Carpenter, 1991.

Maybe it's just   Whitty, 1990.

too good to be through   Coleman, 1994.

It was a transformation   Cummings, 1997.

While it's easy to dismiss   Konjoyan, September 11, 1994.

She'd like it   Konjoyan, October 3, 1994.

In the U.S., alternative   McClure, 1996.

Karen and Richard are   Grein, 2009.

Were you angry   Appleyard, January 3, 1990.

[Richard] and Mary do not   Wallace, July 1984.

We weren't thinking   Barlow, 2004.

With room for six   Entertainment Tonight/ETonline.com, 2004.

Irreplaceable   Bettis to Tobler, 1993.

BIBLIOGRAPHY

Alpert, Herb. Interview by John Tobler. 1994.

————. *Yesterday Once More*. BBC-TV. 1996.

Appleyard, Christena. "How I Learned to Live Without Karen." *Daily Mirror,* January 3, 1990.

————. "My Tragic Karen: Richard Carpenter's Own Story of the Superstar Sister He Couldn't Save." *Daily Mirror,* January 2, 1990.

Armstrong, Dan. "Why They're on Top?" *Southeast News,* December 9, 1971.

Autopsy Report # 83-1611. County of Los Angeles. February 4, 1983.

Bangs, Lester. "Carpenters: *Now and Then*." *Let It Rock,* November 1973.

————. "The Carpenters and the Creeps." *Rolling Stone,* March 4, 1971.

Barlow, Zeke. "Singer Carpenter Donates $3 Million to Thousand Oaks Civic Arts Plaza." *Ventura County Star,* October 24, 2004.

Barnes, Ken. "Carpenters: *Horizon*." *Phonograph Record,* July 1975.

Barrios, Greg. "Carpenter: 'This Album is Karen's.'" *Los Angeles Times,* October 23, 1983.

Bash, Sherwin. Interview by John Tobler. 1990.

Bauer, Stephen. *At Ease in the White House*. Lanham, MD: Taylor Trade Publishing, 2004.

Bego, Mark. *Billy Joel: The Biography*. New York: Thunder's Mouth Press, 2007.

Beller, Miles. "Last Respects Paid to Karen Carpenter." *Herald Examiner,* February 8, 1983.

Bettis, John. Interview by John Tobler. 1993.

"A Billboard Pick: Carpenters—*Offering*." *Billboard,* 1970.

Blanche, Tony and Brad Schreiber. *Death in Paradise: An Illustrated History of the Los Angeles County Department of Coroner.* New York: Running Press, 2001.

Booth, Amy L. "Carpenters: A Song for You." *DISCoveries*, December 1991.

Boskind-White, Marlene and William C. White. *Bulimia/Anorexia: The Binge/ Purge Cycle and Self-Starvation.* New York: W.W. Norton, 2000.

Bresette, James. "Bring Karen from Behind Those Drums." *Omaha World-Herald*, May 22, 1971.

————. "Carpenters' Fortune is in Karen's Voice." *Omaha World-Herald*, October 14, 1972.

"Bride-to-Be Karen Carpenter Feted with Pre-Nuptial Party." Unknown Publication, 1980.

Bronson, Fred. *The Billboard Book of Number One Hits.* New York: Billboard Books, 1988.

————. *Billboard's Hottest Hot 100 Hits.* New York: Billboard Books, 2007.

Browne, David. "...And Oh So Far Away." *Entertainment Weekly*, October 11, 1996.

————. "Magic Carpenter Ride." *Entertainment Weekly*, September 16, 1994.

Bruch, Hilde. "Anorexia Nervosa." Manuscript for *Reader's Digest*, 1977.

————. *The Golden Cage: The Enigma of Anorexia Nervosa.* Cambridge, MA: Harvard, 1978.

"Builder Burris to Wed Karen Carpenter." *Corona Independent*, July 8, 1980.

"Burris, Carpenter Have Only Just Begun." *Corona Independent*, July 9, 1980.

Butler, Patricia. *Barry Manilow: The Biography.* London: Omnibus Press, 2002.

Calio, Jim. "Four Years After His Sister Karen's Death, Singer Richard Carpenter Makes His Debut as a Solo Act." *People*, October 26, 1987.

Cameron, Jacob. "Wesley Jacobs: The Career of a Lifetime." *International Tuba Euphonium Association Journal* 36, no. 2 (2009).

Carney, Charles. "Winter Festival Joins Campus Choirs and Orchestra." *The 49er*, December 1978.

"Carpenter Funeral Today." *Associated Press*, February 7, 1983.

Carpenter, Agnes. By David Hartman. *Good Morning America.* ABC-TV, November 3, 1983.

Carpenter, Karen and Richard Carpenter. *Carpenters: Decade.* Downey, CA: Carpenters Fan Club Publication, 1979.

————. By Sue Lawley. *Nationwide.* BBC-TV, October 22, 1981.

Carpenter, Karen. By Bob Sky. KIQQ Radio, December 1978.

————. By Carl Goldman. FM100 Radio, 1978.

————. By Charlie Tuna. October 8, 1976.

————. By Dick Biondi. WCFL Radio, 1970.

————. By Michael Aspel. Capital Radio, 1981.

_____. By Norm Nite. WNBC Radio, February 20, 1977.

_____. By Radio Clyde, December 1978.

_____. By Roy Leonard. WGN Radio, August 1, 1976.

_____. By Tony Blackburn. BBC Radio, 1974.

_____. Interviewer unknown. *Japanese All-American Top 40 Show.* July 11, 1981.

_____. By Mike Douglas. *Mike Douglas Show.* July 29, 1971.

_____. By Dave Roberts. *Music Star Weekend Special.* RKO Radio, 1981.

Carpenter, Richard. "A Brother Remembers." *People,* November 21, 1983.

_____. "Carpenter Responds." *Entertainment Weekly,* May 31, 1991.

_____. "Karen Was Wasting Away... I Had A Drug Problem... And We Couldn't Help Each Other." *TV Guide,* December 31, 1988.

_____. "My Sorrow at Karen's Long Battle with Death." *Mail on Sunday,* November 20, 1983.

_____. Interview by Jon Burlingame. November 18, 1988.

_____. *Only Yesterday: The Carpenters Story.* BBC-TV, 2007.

_____. *Superstar: The Karen Carpenter Story.* BBC Radio, February 4, 1993.

"'Carpenter': No. 1 Hit for CBS." *USA Today,* January 5, 1989.

"The Carpenters: An Interview." *A&M Compendium,* July 1975.

"Carpenters at Greek Theatre." *Southeast News,* July 10, 1970.

"Carpenters Biography." http://www.richardandkarencarpenter.com (accessed 2008).

"Carpenters Coming." *Melody Maker,* December 8, 1973.

"Carpenters Get Their Star: Downey Duo Given Salute." *Downey Herald American,* October 15, 1983.

"The Carpenters 'Nail' Neil Sedaka." Unknown Publication, 1975.

"Carpenters Serenade Brandt at White House." *Variety,* May 9, 1973.

"Carpenters Telepic Boosts Record Sales." *Variety,* February 8, 1989.

"Carpenters Tour Downey, Hospitals." *Southeast News,* December 7, 1971.

"Carpenters: Concerts Off." *Melody Maker,* November 1, 1975.

"Carpenters: *Passage.*" *Billboard,* October 8, 1977.

Certificate of Death: Karen Anne Carpenter. State of California. 1983.

Certificate of Registry of Marriage: Thomas James Burris and Karen Anne Carpenter. County of Los Angeles. Issued August 7, 1980.

Charlesworth, Chris. "Carpenters: It's Plane Sailing!" *Melody Maker,* September 29, 1973.

Coleman, Ray. "Carpenters Über Alles!" *Melody Maker,* November 20, 1976.

_____. "Carpenters: Good, Clean, All-American Aggro!" *Melody Maker,* November 8, 1975.

_____. *The Carpenters: The Untold Story.* New York: HarperCollins, 1994.

_____. "Karen: Why I Collapsed." *Melody Maker*, November 1, 1975.

_____. "*Passage*." *Melody Maker*, October 15, 1977.

_____. "Too Good to Be Through." *Sunday Times*, September 11, 1994.

Corliss, Richard. "Yesterday Once More." *Time*, November 4, 1996.

Crowe, Jerry. "Karen Carpenter's 'Lost' LP." *Los Angeles Times*, August 31, 1996.

Cummings, Sue. *The* Rolling Stone *Book of Women in Rock: Trouble Girls*, edited by Barbara O'Dair. New York: Random House, 1997.

Daugherty, Michael. "Calendar Desk: Carpenters' Tools." *Los Angeles Times*, October 16, 1994.

Diehl, Digby. "They Put Romance into Rock." *TV Guide*, August 14, 1971.

Diliberto, Gioia. "Karen Carpenter Was Killed by an Over-the-Counter Drug Some Doctors Say May Be Killing Many Others." *People*, May 13, 1985.

Dosti, Rose. "Karen Carpenter Feels Close to Mom, Culinarily Speaking." *Los Angeles Times*, February 11, 1971.

"Downey Youths on 'Your Life.'" *Southeast News*, February 10, 1971.

"Editorial: TV Writers Faked Review." *Billboard*, January 28, 1989.

Erlich, Nancy. "Carpenters: Carnegie Hall, New York." *Billboard*, May 29, 1971.

Evans, Mike. "Carpenters' Tinsel Circus." Unknown Publication, 1976.

Ewbank, Tim. "An Unkind Cut for the Carpenters." *The Sun*, December 1978.

Farber, Sheryl. "Karen Carpenter: Getting to the Bare Bones of Todd Haynes' *Superstar: The Karen Carpenter Story*." *Film Threat* #20. 1989.

Feather, Leonard. "Battle of the Bands." *Los Angeles Times*, June 1966.

Feldman, Christopher G. *The Billboard Book of No. 2 Singles*. New York: Billboard Books, 2000.

First Codicil to Last Will and Testament of Karen A. Carpenter. September 1, 1981.

Flans, Robyn. "In Memoriam: Karen Carpenter." *Modern Drummer*, May 1983.

Fleming, Peggy. *The Long Program: Skating Toward Life's Victories*. New York: Pocket Books, 1999.

Fox-Cumming, Ray. "Carpentry." *Disc*, September 1, 1973.

"Friends, Family Mourn Agnes Reuwer Carpenter." *Downey Eagle*, November 14, 1996.

Gaar, Gillian. *She's a Rebel: The History of Women in Rock & Roll*. New York: Seal Press, 1992.

Gautschy, Dean. "The Carpenters: They've Only Just Begun." *TV/Radio Mirror*, August, 1971.

Gautschy, Jan. "The Carpenters: Two Superstars' Young Dreams Come True." *Words and Music*, March 1972.

Gelly, Dave. *Appraisal of Karen Carpenter's Career*. BBC Radio, June 1990.

Gleiberman, Owen. "Dear Richard Carpenter." *Entertainment Weekly*, April 26, 1991.

Goldsmith, Len. "Carpenters Find Winning Number." *The Southeast News*, January 30, 1970.

Grein, Paul. "Album Recalls Karen Carpenter." *Billboard*, 1983.

_____. "An Essay." *Carpenters International Fan Club Newsletter*, June 1991.

_____. "Carpenters Cracking Country Chart Without Nashville Push." *Billboard*, April 1, 1978.

_____. "Carpenters: Building on Experience." *Los Angeles Times*, August 23, 1981.

_____. "Carpenters' Hits Resurfacing." *Billboard*, May 18, 1985.

_____. "Chart Watch: Week Ending May 17, 2009." http://new.music. yahoo.com/blogs/chart_watch/33675/week-ending-may-17-2009-three-days-is-plenty-for-green-day/ (accessed 2009).

_____. "Closeup: Carpenters—*Made in America*." *Billboard*, July 25, 1981.

_____. "Karen Carpenter Shelves Solo LP." *Billboard*, June 7, 1980.

_____. "Karen Carpenter: She Had Only Just Begun." *Los Angeles Times*, November 7, 1989.

_____. "Karen Carpenter: The Solo Album." A&M Records Press Release. October 1996.

_____. "The Carpenters: Yesterday Once More: A Critical Reassessment of Their Work." *Goldmine*, March 8, 1991.

_____. "Trust Us, This Is Real." *Los Angeles Times*, September 11, 1994.

Haber, Joyce. "Carpenters Nail Down a Spot in Pop Pantheon." *Los Angeles Times*, August 4, 1974.

Haithman, Diane. "A TV Movie He Didn't Want: Brother Guides CBS' *Karen Carpenter Story*." *Los Angeles Times*, July 25, 1988.

Hall, John. "Kids Next Door." *Los Angeles Times*, March 7, 1972.

Hamill, Dorothy. *A Skating Life: My Story*. New York: Hyperion, 2007.

Hardwick, Nancy. "Karen Carpenter: When I Was 16." *Star*, March 1973.

"Hard-Working Carpenters." *Teen*, March 1975.

Harrigan, Brian. "Carpentry." *Melody Maker*, September 6, 1975.

Harrison, Ed. "'Surprise' by the Carpenters." *Billboard*, September 17, 1977.

Haynes, Todd. *Far From Heaven, Safe and Superstar: The Karen Carpenter Story: Three Screenplays*. New York: Grove Press, 2003.

Heckman, Don. "Riffs." *Village Voice*, August 26, 1971.

Henshaw, Laurie and Steve Lake. "Carpenters' Hammer." *Melody Maker*, February 16, 1974.

Hilburn, Robert and Dennis Hunt. "Behind Carpenters' Girl-Next-Door Image." *Los Angeles Times*, February 7, 1983.

Hilburn, Robert. "Bacharach Plays Pop Fare at Greek." *Los Angeles Times*, July 8, 1970.

_____. "The Carpenters Come Home." *Los Angeles Times*, August 11, 1972.

_____. "A Lesson in Art of Emotion." *Los Angeles Times*, February 13, 1983.

Hinckley, David. "Richard Carpenter Remembers His Sister Karen." *New York Daily News*, November 20, 1983.

Hoerburger, Rob. *Carpenters: Inside the Music: The Ultimate Critical Review.* DVD. 2008.

_____. "The Carpenters: *Lovelines*." *Rolling Stone*, February 8, 1990.

_____. "Karen Carpenter's Second Life." *New York Times Magazine*, October 6, 1996.

Holden, Stephen. "Carpenters: *A Song for You*." *Rolling Stone*, October 12, 1972.

_____. "Carpenters: *Horizon*." *Rolling Stone*, August 28, 1975.

"House Review: London Palladium." *Variety*, December 1, 1976.

"Hundreds Attend Karen Carpenter Rites." *Southeast News*, February 9, 1983.

Hyatt, Wesley. *The Billboard Book of Number One Adult Contemporary Hits.* New York: Watson-Guptill, 1999.

"Inside Track." *Billboard*, October 4, 1975.

Jacobs, Jody. "It Won't Be Your Average Garage Sale." *Los Angeles Times*, July 9, 1981.

Jillson, Joyce. "Astrology." Syndicated Column. May 21, 1980.

"John Bettis Interview 2007." http://www.drownedmadonna.com/modules. php?name=john_bettis (accessed 2008).

Jones, Peter. "Talent in Action: Carpenters: London Palladium." *Billboard*, December 18, 1976.

"Karen Carpenter and Tom Burris Marry." *Beverly Hills People*, September 3, 1980.

"Karen Carpenter Anorexia Death." *National Enquirer*, March 15, 1983.

"Karen Carpenter Wed in Beverly Hills Rites." *Southeast News*, September 3, 1980.

"Karen in the Kitchen: Who Says a Young Female Superstar Can't Be a Top-Notch Cook?" A&M Records Press Release. 1971.

Kinnersley, Simon. "A Death Too Cruel." *Daily Mail*, November 1983.

Knappman, Edward W. *Watergate and the White House: June 1972–July 1973, Volume 1.* New York: Facts on File, 1973.

Konjoyan, David. "That Whitebread Inspiration Came with a Dark Side." *Orange County Register*, September 11, 1994.

_____. "Yesterday Once More: An Exclusive *HITS* Interview with Richard Carpenter." *HITS*, October 3, 1994.

Kraus, Bill and Jan Grimm. "Hammer and Nails: A Carpenters Interview." *Rock Spectacular*, Summer 1970.

Landau, John. "Carpenters: *Carpenters.*" *Rolling Stone*, June 24, 1971.

Last Will and Testament of Karen A. Carpenter. May 2, 1972.

Leaf, Earl. "The Carpenters: They Nail a New Sound." *Teen*, January 1971.

Lees, Gene. "Success Comes to Jack Daugherty." *High Fidelity Magazine*, January 1972.

Legge, Beverly. "'I Mean Nobody Could Be That Clean.'" *Disc*, March 2, 1974.

Levenkron, Steven. *Anatomy of Anorexia*. New York: W.W. Norton, 2001.

_____. *The Best Little Girl in the World*. New York: Warner Books, 1978.

_____. *A Current Affair*, February 5, 1993.

_____. Radio interview, source unknown, 1983.

_____. *Treating and Understanding Anorexia Nervosa*. New York: Warner Books, 1982.

Levin, Eric. "A Sweet Surface Hid a Troubled Soul in the Late Karen Carpenter, a Victim of Anorexia Nervosa." *People*, February 21, 1983.

Levitin, Daniel. "Pop Charts: How Richard Carpenter's Lush Arrangements Turned Hit Songs into Pop Classics." *Electronic Musician*, May 1995.

Lieberman, Frank H. "The Carpenters: A Talented Brother and Sister Act Which Represents Clean, Wholesome Entertainment." *Billboard*, November 17, 1973.

_____. "The Carpenters: Soft Rock and 14 Gold Records." *Saturday Evening Post*. October 1974.

Liebovich, Louis W. *Richard Nixon, Watergate, and the Press*. Westport, CT: Praeger Publishers, 2003.

Littwin, Susan. "Artistic Differences: The Family's Memories vs. Hollywood's Version." *TV Guide*, December 31, 1988.

"Local Coed Performs Sunday." *Southeast News*, November 21, 1969.

MacDougall, Fiona. "The Carpenters: Nailing Down Success." *Teen*, October 1971.

Mackay, Kathy. "A Carpenter Ties the Knot and Finally That Song's for Karen." *People*, September 15, 1980.

McAfee, Paul. "A City in Mourning." *Southeast News*, February 8, 1983.

McCardle, Dorothy. "A Pair of Experts at Coming Back." *Washington Post*, May 2, 1973.

McClure, Steve. "The Carpenters Are a Hit Among Young Japanese." *Billboard*, February 10, 1996.

McFadden, Ian. "Carpenters: It's Only Just Begun." *Melody Maker*, February 23, 1974.

McGreevy, Pat. "Downey is 'Stunned' by Death of Artist." *Southeast News*, February 7, 1983.

————. "Karen Carpenter Dies in Downey." *Downey Herald American*, February 5, 1983.

————. "Thirty Minutes with Richard Carpenter." *Southeast News*, October 17, 1983.

————. "Walk of Fame Star Dedicated to History's Top-Selling Duo." *Southeast News*, October 13, 1983.

McNally, Joel. "It's an Overdose of Pretty." *Milwaukee Journal*, 1976.

McQuay, Dave. "Like TV Dinner for the Ears." *Columbia Flier*, August 1975.

Medigovich, Lori B. "It Still Hurts: Richard Carpenter Remembers His Sister Karen." *Los Angeles Times Syndicate*, April 1988.

Michaels, Ken. "Rainy Days and Carpenters Always Get Me Down." *Chicago Tribune Magazine*, November 21, 1971.

Miller, Merle. "Review: 'Make Your Own Kind of Music.'" *TV Guide*, September 4, 1971.

Miller, Ron. "She'd Only Just Begun: Fine CBS Movie Tells Sad Story of Karen Carpenter." *San Jose Mercury News*, January 1, 1989.

Millman, Joyce. "The Troubled World of Karen Carpenter." *San Francisco Examiner*, January 1, 1989.

Moran, Bill. "'If Somebody Would Just Let Us Know What the Problem Is.'" *Radio Report*, May 29, 1978.

Morgan, Lael. "The Carpenters: They've Only Just Begun." *Los Angeles Times*, January 8, 1971.

Morrow, Barry, and Cynthia A. Cherbak. *A Song for You: The Karen Carpenter Story*. Draft. December 24, 1987.

————. *A Song for You: The Karen Carpenter Story*. Shooting Draft. February 12, 1988.

Morrow, Barry. *A Song for You: The Karen Carpenter Story*. Draft. September 30, 1987.

Moss, Jerry. *Only Yesterday: The Carpenters Story*. BBC-TV, 2007.

Naglin, Nancy. "The Carpenters Go Country?" *Country Music*, August 1978.

"A New Resting Place for Karen Carpenter?" *Entertainment Tonight/ETonline.com*. http://www.etonline.com/music/2004/02/33452/ (accessed 2004).

"Nixon Thanks Carpenters for Fight Against Cancer." *Associated Press*, August 1972.

Nixon, Richard M. *The Presidential Transcripts*. New York: Dell, 1974.

Nolan, Tom. "The Carpenters: An Appraisal." *A&M Compendium*, July 1975.

————. "Up from Downey." *Rolling Stone*, July 4, 1974.

O'Brien, Lucy. *She Bop: The Definitive History of Women in Rock, Pop and Soul.* New York: Penguin Books, 1996.

O'Dair, Barbara. *Trouble Girls: The* Rolling Stone *Book of Women in Rock.* New York: Random House, 1997.

O'Neill, Cherry Boone. *Starving for Attention.* New York: Continuum, 1982.

Oppenheimer, Peer J. "The Carpenters: Our Whole Life Is Caught Between Two Cultures." *Family Weekly,* May 7, 1972.

Parade, James. "Carpenters: *Christmas Portrait.*" *Record Mirror,* 1978.

Paytress, Mark. "The Carpenters." *Record Collector,* January, 1990.

Petition for Dissolution of Marriage: Karen Carpenter Burris (Petitioner) and Thomas J. Burris (Respondent). County of Los Angeles. Filed November 9, 1982.

Pfenninger, Leslie J. *From Brass to Gold, Volume I: Discography of A&M Records and Affiliates in the United States.* Westport, CT: Greenwood Press, 2001.

———. *From Brass to Gold, Volume II: Discography of A&M Records and Affiliates Around the World.* Westport, CT: Greenwood Press, 2001.

Pinckney, Judy. "Friends Bid Farewell to Karen Carpenter." *Southeast News,* February 7, 1983.

Pleasants, Henry. "The Carpenters: Nice Guys Don't Always Finish Last." *Stereo Review,* February 1972.

Pogoda, Gordon. Interview with John Bettis. *SongTalk,* 1994.

Pool, Bob. "Fans Love Carpenters but Not carpenters." *Los Angeles Times,* February 26, 2008.

Pooler, Frank. "The Choral Sound of the Carpenters." *Choral Journal,* April 1973.

President Richard Nixon's Daily Diary. April 29, 1973.

———. April 30, 1973.

———. August 25, 1972.

———. May 1, 1973.

Ragogna, Mike. "The 40th Anniversary of Carpenters: Interview with Richard Carpenter." *Huffington Post,* May 11, 2009. http://www.huffington post.com/mike-ragogna/emhuffpost-exclusiveem-th_b_201408.html.

Ramone, Phil, and Charles L. Granata. *Making Records: The Scenes Behind the Music.* New York: Hyperion, 2007.

Ramone, Phil. CompuServe Chat Transcript. October 18, 1996.

Rees, Dafydd and Luke Crampton. *Rock Movers and Shakers: An A–Z of People Who Made Rock Happen.* Oxford UK: ABC-CLIO, 1991.

Reitwiesner, William Addams, and Robert Battle. "Ancestry of Richard and Karen Carpenter." www.wargs.com/other/carpenter.html (accessed 2008).

"Remembering Karen Carpenter." *Southeast News,* June 24, 1983.

"Richard Carpenter Has Seen 'Every Single Minute of Filming' of 'The Karen Carpenter Story.'" *San Jose Mercury News*, March 6, 1988.

"Riviera–Las Vegas." *Variety*, September 3, 1975.

"The Rockers Are Rolling in It." *Forbes*, April 15, 1973.

Rosenfeld, Megan. "The Carpenters: 'Young America at Its Very Best.'" *Washington Post*, May 6, 1973.

"Sahara–Tahoe." *Variety*, August 21, 1974.

Schmidt, Randy L. *Yesterday Once More: Memories of the Carpenters and Their Music*. Cranberry Township, PA: Tiny Ripple Books, 2000.

Sedaka, Neil. *Laughter in the Rain: My Own Story*. New York: Putnam, 1982.

Seligmann, Jean A. "A Deadly Feast and Famine." *Newsweek*, March 7, 1983.

―――. "Starvation by Intention." *Reader's Digest*, January 1975.

Short, Don. "The Carpenters: 'Too Shocking to Be Untrue.'" *Sunday Mirror*, November 21, 1976.

―――. "I Need to Be Loved." *Woman*, April 16, 1977.

Simmons, Gene. *Kiss and Make-up*. New York: Crown, 2001.

Sinor, Brad, "Theatrics Overshadow Carpenters' Music." *Oklahoma Daily*, October 26, 1976.

Small, Linda. "Carpenters Are Building an Empire." *Free-Lance Star*, April 1, 1972.

Smith, C.P. "Karen Carpenter: Her Serene Voice Sold 60 Million LPs." *Orange County Register*, February 5, 1983.

Smith, Tierney. "Album Review: Karen Carpenter." *Goldmine*, January 31, 1997.

Smucker, Tom. "The Carpenters: Forbidden Fruit." *Village Voice*, June 2, 1975.

Southall, Brian. *The A–Z of Record Labels*. London: Sanctuary, 2000.

―――. *Yesterday Once More: The Karen Carpenter Story*. BBC Radio, 2004.

St. John, Michael. "The Carpenters: Million Dollar Misfits Set the Record Straight." *Super Rock*, June 1977.

Strong, Martin C. *The Great Rock Discography*. Edinburgh, Scotland: Canongate, 2002.

Summons: Karen Carpenter Burris (Petitioner) and Thomas J. Burris (Respondent). County of Los Angeles. Filed November 24, 1982.

Superstar: The Karen Carpenter Story. London: Wallflowers Press, 2008.

Tatham, Dick. *Carpenters: Sweet Sound of Success*. London: Phoebus, 1976.

"Television Reviews: *The Karen Carpenter Story*." *Variety*, January 18, 1989.

Thegze, Chuck. "Carpenters Have Transformed the Laughter into Bravos." *Los Angeles Times*, August 6, 1972.

"Therapist: Anorexia Not Karen Carpenter's Killer." *USA Today*, February 4, 1993.

Theroux, Gary. "The Carpenters Story." *L.A. Music & Art Review*, December 1978.

Tobler, John. "It Happens in the Middle of the Road: Confessions of a Carpenters Fan." Unknown Publication, 1974.

———. *The Complete Guide to the Music of the Carpenters*. London: Omnibus Press, 1998.

Vaiuso, Teresa. *Yesterday Once More: The Karen Carpenter Story*. BBC Radio, 2004.

Van Valkenburg, Carol. "Carpenters Perform for Middle Missoula." *The Missoulian*, May 19. 1973.

Wallace, Evelyn, and Rosina Sullivan. Carpenters Fan Club Newsletters. 1971–1989.

Wallace, Evelyn. "Carpenters—Superstars." 1975.

"Welcome to A&M Records, Former Home of the Charlie Chaplin Movie Lot." A&M Records Map and History. Revised June 20, 1991.

Whitburn, Joel. *Top Adult Contemporary Singles 1961–2001*. Menomonee Falls, WI: Record Research, Inc., 2002.

Whitty, Stephen. "Yesterday, Once More." *San Jose Mercury News*, October 18, 1990.

Wild, David. *And the Grammy Goes To . . . : The Official Story of Music's Most Coveted Award*. Brockport, NY: State Street Press, 2007.

Windeler, Robert. "Karen and Richard Carpenter Aren't at the Top of the World: They Need to Be in Love." *People*, August 2, 1976.

Wyatt, Justin. "Cinematic/Sexual Transgression: An Interview with Todd Haynes." *Film Quarterly* 46, no. 3. (1993).

SUGGESTED READING

THE FOLLOWING books and articles represent some of the best sources for readers interested in learning more about Karen Carpenter and her music. Certain selections are out of print but still in circulation and available at your local library or online. The fan club newsletters are no longer available in hard copy but may be found archived on various Web sites, including www.karencarpenter.com/newsletter_index.html and www.whizzo.ca/carpenter/newsletters.html.

Carpenter, Richard. "A Brother Remembers." *People*, November 21, 1983.

_____. "Karen Was Wasting Away. . . . I Had A Drug Problem. . . . And We Couldn't Help Each Other." *TV Guide*, December 31, 1988.

Coleman, Ray. "Carpenters: Good, Clean, All-American Aggro!" *Melody Maker*, November 8, 1975.

_____. *The Carpenters: The Untold Story*. New York: HarperCollins, 1994.

Grein, Paul. "The Carpenters: Yesterday Once More: A Critical Reassessment of Their Work." *Goldmine*, March 8, 1991.

Hoerburger, Rob. "Karen Carpenter's Second Life." *New York Times Magazine*, October 6, 1996.

Levin, Eric. "A Sweet Surface Hid a Troubled Soul in the Late Karen Carpenter, a Victim of Anorexia Nervosa." *People*, February 21, 1983.

Mackay, Kathy. "A Carpenter Ties the Knot and Finally That Song's for Karen." *People*, September 15, 1980.

Nolan, Tom. "Up from Downey." *Rolling Stone*, July 4, 1974.

Schmidt, Randy L. *Yesterday Once More: Memories of the Carpenters and Their Music*. Cranberry Township, PA: Tiny Ripple Books, 2000.

Tobler, John. *The Complete Guide to the Music of the Carpenters*. London: Omnibus Press, 1998.

Wallace, Evelyn, and Rosina Sullivan. Carpenters Fan Club Newsletters. 1971–1989.

Windeler, Robert. "Karen and Richard Carpenter Aren't at the Top of the World: They Need to Be in Love." *People*, August 2, 1976.

INDEX